The Butterflies of Oregon

II

The Butterflies of Oregon

by
Ernst J. Dornfeld

Publishers for Northwest writers
PO Box 92
Forest Grove,
Oregon 97116
(503) 357-7192

Timber Press

Dornfeld, Ernst John, 1911-
  Butterflies of Oregon.

  Includes index.
  1. Butterflies—Oregon. 2. Insects—Oregon.
I. Title.
QL551.07D67 595.78'909795 80-51936
ISBN 0-917304-58-6
Copyright 1980 by Timber Press
Printed in The United States Of America

Timber Press
P.O. Box 92
Forest Grove, Oregon 97116

To
SUE

Foreword

Few groups of animals have the universal appeal that butterflies do. This interest occurs in the youngest child and in the seasoned scientist. Butterflies may be enjoyed in backyards or mountain meadows, in grade school classrooms or well equipped university laboratories. Some species are among the most beautiful animals in the world. The final transformation of a caterpillar into a graceful butterfly never ceases to fascinate the fortunate observer. It seems particularly appropriate to me that this book should appear shortly after the State of Oregon designated *Papilio oregonensis* Edwards as the official state insect. It is an attractive and graceful name bearer.

Dr. Ernst J. Dornfeld, the author of this book, began studying the butterflies of Oregon when he first arrived at Oregon State University as an instructor in Zoology in 1938, shortly after he completed his graduate studies in Wisconsin. He retired in 1976 as Chairman of the Department of Zoology having spent his entire formal career as a scientist-educator. Thousands of students benefited from his varied classes in Zoology, including his specialty, which is cell biology. Even as this foreword is being written, Dr. Dornfeld together with one of his colleagues in Zoology, is offering his first "official" course in entomology — a seminar on Lepidoptera genetics. He was the first to receive the Carter Award for Distinguished Teaching and received appropriate recognition for his research as well, culminating with the Distinguished Professor Award given him by the Oregon State University Alumni Association in 1978. Throughout this productive career in the biological sciences, he developed and maintained a consuming interest in butterflies. This book is a logical extension of his scientific and educational capabilities — a sharing of his boundless enthusiasms and of extensive knowledge acquired during the past forty-one years.

The Butterflies of Oregon is the first such comprehensive publication for this state and surely it will be the definitive study for some years to come. As in all areas of science, new information will continue to be added. But it will be made easier because Dr. Dornfeld has clearly pointed out the gaps in our knowledge. Just as he was readying the manuscript of this book for the publisher, a subspecies of butterfly not previously known to occur in the state, was being collected in a remote area of southeastern Oregon by two independent groups simultaneously. There are discoveries that yet remain.

The book is addressed to a well defined audience — those interested in exploring the fascinating world of butterflies at any level. The text is written in a precise but very readable style. It contains many personal observations integrated with information from appropriate scientific literature. The high quality photographs, most-

Foreword continued

ly taken by Dr. Dornfeld, show every species of butterfly known to occur in Oregon. Some books are purchased, shelved and occasionally consulted. Others quickly acquire the scars of constant use. I think that this book will need a sturdy binding.

    John D. Lattin
    Systematic Entomology Laboratory
    Department of Entomology
    Oregon State University
    Corvallis, OR 97331

Table of Contents

Forward VII
Preface and Acknowledgements XI

INTRODUCTION
Historical Background 1
    Oregon Type Localities
Oregon's Physiography and Butterfly Distribution 5
    Coast Ranges; Klamath Mountains; Willamette Valley; Western Cascades; High Cascades;
    Columbia Plateau; High Lava Plains; Basin and Range; Owyhee Upland; Blue Mountains
Biology of Butterflies 17
    Eggs and Egg-laying; Larvae; Pupae; Adults; Significance of Color and
    Pattern; Abnormalities; Migration
Endangered and Extinct Butterflies 25
Evolution, Classification, and Nomenclature 27
    Origin of Butterflies; Taxonomic Categories; Variation Within Populations; Nomenclature
Collecting, Rearing, and Photographing Butterflies 31
    Collecting Techniques; Genitalial Preparations; Rearing; Photography

SYSTEMATIC ACCOUNT
Family Papilionidae (Swallowtails and Parnassians) 39
Family Pieridae (Whites and Sulfurs) 44
Family Satyridae (Woodnymphs, Ringlets, and Arctics) 52
Family Danaidae (Monarch) 57
Family Nymphalidae (Admirals, Painted Ladies, Tortoise-shells, Anglewings,
    Crescents, Checkerspots, and Fritillaries) 59
Family Riodinidae (Metalmarks) 83
Family Lycaenidae (Hairstreaks, Coppers, and Blues) 85
Family Hesperiidae (Skippers) 107

APPENDICES
Color Plates 121
Plates (Black-and-White) 129
Distribution Maps 227
Checklist 261
Glossary 265
Index 269

Preface and Acknowledgements

When the idea of this book took form more than thirty years ago it was clear that a great deal of exploration and data gathering had to be done before it could be written. Existing information based on specimens in collections and on published records was insufficient for a complete account of Oregon's butterflies and their distributions. Thus many years went into the long but absorbing task of systematically searching the State for specimens and data, and its success owes to the generous and enthusiastic help of many fellow lepidopterists. Among these I gratefully name Ray J. Albright, Alton L. Alderman, the late James H. Baker, David L. Bauer, Charles R. Crowe, Thomas C. Emmel, Kenneth M. Fender, Kenneth Goeden, Paul C. Hammond, Stanley G. Jewett, Ralph W. Macy, the late Arthur H. Moeck, William N. Neill, the late C. William Nelson, E. J. Newcomer, John and Vikki Neyhart, Edwin and Stephen Perkins, Robert M. Pyle, Oakley Shields, Jon H. Shepard, and Mark J. Smith. C. Don MacNeill, William W. McGuire, and Jonathan Pelham kindly provided good specimens to illustrate certain rare Skippers.

Special thanks go to my frequent companions in the field, John Hinchliff and David V. McCorkle, the former for his inestimable aid in compiling data and in co-authoring a preliminary checklist, and the latter for sharing his adroit knowledge of life histories and immature stages; both have also provided from their personal collections many fine specimens for study and illustration. To my colleague Paul Roberts I am indebted for valuable discussions on genetic and evolutionary topics and for many helpful suggestions on expository problems. For constant encouragement and support of this project I owe special thanks to John D. Lattin; besides making freely available to me the resources of the Systematic Entomology Laboratory of Oregon State University he has read the entire manuscript and contributed the forward.

No one has more patiently and encouragingly shared with me the long and pleasant experiences that have culminated in this book than my wife, Sue. Together we have swung nets in the Coast Ranges and the Cascades, the Siskiyous and the Warners, the Ochocos and the Wallowas, in the desert and on Steens Mountain. To her I affectionately dedicate this book.

In planning the plates it was considered most useful to show all species and subspecies of Oregon's butterflies in natural size, usually both males and females as well as upper and under surfaces. Black-and-white rather than color photographs were decided upon in deference to an otherwise prohibitive cost of the published volume. Nevertheless, a few color plates have been included to serve a synoptic purpose; from these a clue can be obtained as to the identity or close relationship of a specimen at hand; by

Preface and Acknowledgements continued

further reference to the black-and-white plates, the distributional maps, and the text a positive identification can be reached.

The literature references have been added to help the interested student in finding sources of more detailed information. Most often these are papers in scientific journals that can be found in large technical or university libraries; particularly pertinent are the Journal of the Lepidopterists' Society and the Journal of Research on the Lepidoptera. Readers should also be aware of Robert M. Pyle's useful pocket guide entitled "Watching Washington Butterflies", put out by the Seattle Audubon Society in 1974. Outdoor color photographs of representative butterflies are attractively presented in "Butterflies Afield in the Pacific Northwest" by W. A. Neill and D. J. Hepburn (Pacific Search Books, Seattle, 1976).

E. J. D.

Introduction

Historical Background

With few exceptions, the butterflies known to occur in Oregon are also found in one or more of our neighboring States, over large parts of the West, or even across the continent. It is not surprising, therefore, that most of our species and wider ranging subspecies were first discovered outside of Oregon, in regions that received earlier exploration by naturalists. Until late in the 19th century the sites of discovery were often inexactly recorded. In later years "type localities" were indicated with care, but descriptions lacked information on distributional ranges, data that could be acquired only after a long period of systematic collecting.

A few of our butterflies are of European origin and their names and first descriptions date back to Linnaeus (1758). Certain others are identical with varieties found in eastern North America and hence were known before those of the West. The great majority, however, are strictly Western species or subspecies and their descriptions, with only two exceptions, first appeared in 1852. The publication dates for newly described Oregon butterflies, grouped by 25-year periods, are graphically shown in the chart below.

The great burst of discovery in the quarter century that began in 1850 was largely due to the opening and development of California. The French naturalist Pierre Lorquin, drawn to San Francisco by the goldrush of 1849, was the first noted collector of California's butterflies. The specimens he gathered between 1850 and 1862 were sent to Paris where they were described and named by Jean Baptiste Boisduval. Thirty-five of these butterflies named by Boisduval also occur in Oregon.

The foremost student of Western butterflies during the 19th century was, however, William Henry Edwards of Coalburgh, West Virginia, who described more North American butterflies than any other author. He published 256 papers plus the monumental "Butterflies of North America" which appeared in parts from 1868 to 1897. The names of 47 Oregon butterflies bear his authorship. Edwards obtained his specimens through various West Coast collectors, notably Dr. H. H. Behr and Henry Edwards (no relative) of San Francisco.

By the end of the 19th century two thirds of the names that now apply to species and subspecies of Oregon butterflies had been published. The first one to be based on a specimen actually collected in Oregon was *Lycaena rubidus,* described by Behr in 1866; its type locality, given as "interior of Oregon", was probably southern Klamath or Lake County and it may have been collected by William M. Gabb, a paleontologist employed by the State Geological Survey of California. While engaged in exploring northern California and southeastern Oregon for fossils in 1864, Gabb collected butterflies for his friend Dr. Behr who later became curator of entomology at the California Academy of Sciences. It was also Gabb who collected *Coenonympha tullia ampelos* (t.l., Lake Co.) and probably *Lycaena cupreus* (t.l., "Ore-

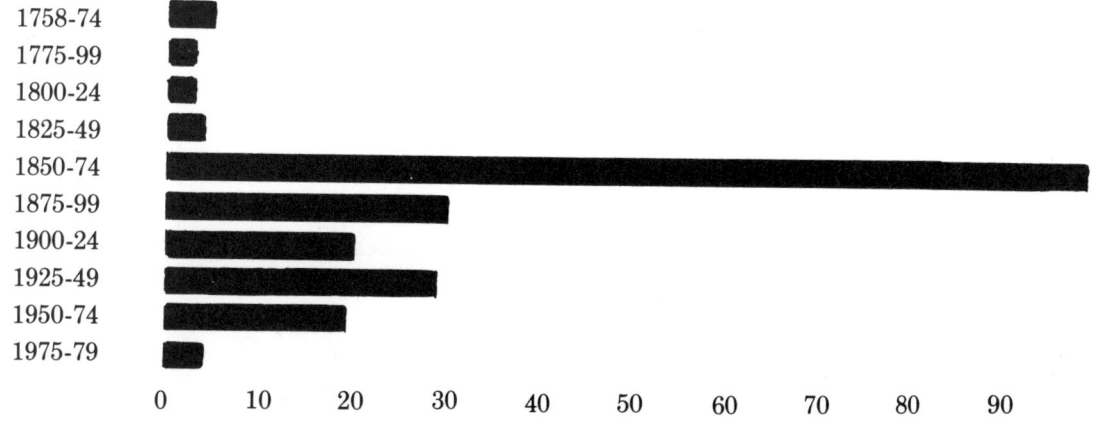

Fig. 1 Number of newly described species or subspecies

gon"), both described by W. H. Edwards. In 1870 William Edwards published the descriptions of *Chlosyne palla sterope* and *Polygonia oreas silenus,* the former collected by W. J. Harford in "Oregon" and the latter by G. W. Dunn in Portland; both type specimens reached the author through Henry Edwards of San Francisco. Henry Edwards was a professional actor and an avid collector, a friend of Behr, and later a trustee of the California Academy. It was he who around 1875 discovered the Oregon Swallowtail near The Dalles. The Hippolyta Fritillary, found by G. M. Dodge near Oceanside in Tillamook County, was described by William Edwards in 1879. In the years 1889 to 1892 William Greenwood Wright of San Bernardino visited Oregon and collected around Portland, Pendleton, and Mt. Hood. Wright's descriptions of *Anthocharis sara flora* (t.l., Portland) and *Euphydryas editha colonia* (t.l., Mt. Hood) appeared in his privately published book (1905), "Butterflies of the West Coast".

Until well into the twentieth century, essentially through the early 1920's, Oregon collecting that resulted in published data was mostly the work of itinerants. There were, of course, some local collectors. In the 1870's Orson Bennett Johnson of Portland, later appointed professor of natural science at the University of Washington, collected natural history specimens in Oregon, including butterflies; these were originally kept in the capitol building at Salem but in 1882 were removed to Seattle. Skinner named the Hairstreak *Mitoura johnsoni* after him in 1904. The first published list of Oregon butterflies appears to be that of Burton L. Cunningham, 1895, a "List of butterflies taken in the vicinity of Ft. Klamath, Ore." (Entom. News 6: 251); it includes 63 names. Mrs. Agnes M. Veazie of Portland, for whom the Checkerspot *Euphydryas anicia veazieae* was named, was an active and enthusiastic collector from about 1915 through the 1930's; articles by her appeared in the Oregonian.

An important book for students of West Coast butterflies appeared in 1927 with the publication of John Adams Comstock's "Butterflies of California". Useful also in Oregon, this book stimulated a new generation of Oregon collectors. Through their lively and enthusiastic efforts many parts of Oregon were systematically explored. Progress was made in assembling distributional data and new geographic races were discovered. Ralph W. Macy, later professor of biology at Reed College and Portland State University, described *Icaricia icarioides fenderi,* named after Kenneth M. Fender who in 1931 published a list of the "Butterflies of Yamhill Co., Ore." (Pan-Pacific Entomologist 7: 179-187). W. F. Lawrence of Medford, exploring the southern Cascades and the Siskiyous, discovered the types of *Speyeria callippe elaine, S. atlantis dodgei,* and *Euphydryas editha lawrencei. Lycaeides argyrognomon ricei* was named after Harold E. Rice of Eugene. James H. Baker concentrated on the butterflies of eastern Oregon, especially of the Elkhorn Mountains in Baker County. Ray Albright of Dayton collected extensively in the Cascades and the Steens Mountain region. Most notable and productive has been the State-wide collecting of Stanley E. Jewett, extending over forty years and still proceeding apace. His extensive material, generously consigned to the Systematic Entomology Laboratory of Oregon State University, forms the major part of that collection's holdings in Lepidoptera. At an earlier time the University received the collection of the late Charles W. Herr of Woodburn (previously of Priest River, Idaho) and more recently that of C. William Nelson of Portland.

After 1950 much of the information on eastern Oregon has come through the efforts of Dr. Alton L. Alderman (for Umatilla and Union Counties), Charles R. Crowe (for northern Harney County), and David L. Bauer (for Morrow County). Rich amounts of distributional data resulted from the energetic Oregon collecting of E. J. Newcomer, well known Washington entomologist; on his many trips south from Yakima he explored the Cascades, the Ochocos, and the Warners. The Columbia Gorge was searched by Edwin M. and Stephen F. Perkins. My own net, since the late 1940's, has been busy mostly in the Coast Range and the Siskiyous, the central and southern Cascades, the Ochocos, the Wallowas, the Warners, and the Steens Mountain area. John Hinchliff of Portland has likewise explored much of Oregon, as has David McCorkle of Monmouth who has also given close attention to immature stages and life histories. Most recently the Alvord Desert and the Pueblo Mountains of southeastern Oregon have yielded new records to Stanley Jewett and Mark J. Smith.

Addendum
Butterflies described from Oregon Type Localities

1. *Lycaena rubidus rubidus* (Behr), 1866 — "Interior of Oregon"
2. *Polygonia oreas silenus* (Edwards), 1870 — Portland
3. *Chlosyne palla sterope* (Edwards), 1870 — "Oregon"
4. *Lycaena cupreus cupreus* (Edwards), 1870 — "Oregon"
5. *Coenonympha tullia ampelos* Edwards, 1871 — Lake Co.
6. *Papilio oregonius* Edwards, 1876 — The Dalles, Wasco Co.
7. *Speyeria zerene hippolyta* (Edwards), 1879 — Oceanside, Tillamook Co.
8. *Anthocharis sara flora* Wright, 1905 — Portland
9. *Euphydryas editha colonia* (Wright), 1905 — Mt. Hood
10. *Euphydryas editha edithana* (Strand), 1914 — Klamath Co.
11. *Philotes battoides oregonensis* Barnes & McDunnough, 1917 — Crater Lake

12. *Chlosyne hoffmanni segregata* Barnes & McDunnough, 1918 — Crater Lake
13. *Euphydryas editha lawrencei* Gunder, 1931 — Mt. Thielsen, Douglas Co.
14. *Speyeria atlantis dodgei* (Gunder), 1931 — Diamond Lake, Douglas Co.
15. *Icaricia icarioides fenderi* (Macy), 1931 — near McMinnville, Yamhill Co.
16. *Lycaeides argyrognomon ricei* (Cross), 1937 — Cultus Lake, Deschutes Co.
17. *Habrodais grunus herri* Field, 1938 — McKenzie Pass
18. *Euphydryas anicia bakeri* Stallings & Turner, 1945 — Cave Cr. near Durkee, Baker Co.
19. *Speyeria callippe elaine* dos Passos & Grey, 1945 — Butte Falls, Jackson Co.
20. *Euphydryas anicia veazieae* Fender & Jewett, 1953 — Jackass Mts., Harney Co.
21. *Euphydryas anicia macyi* Fender & Jewett, 1953 — Wildhorse Cr., Alvord Basin, Harney Co.
22. *Speyeria zerene gloriosa* Moeck, 1957 — Illinois R. Valley, Josephine Co.
23. *Euphydryas editha remingtoni* Burdick, 1959 — Mt. Thielsen, Douglas Co.
24. *Boloria epithore chermocki* Perkins & Perkins, 1966 — Dolph, Yamhill Co.
25. *Coenonympha tullia eunomia* Dornfeld, 1967 — Wilhoit, Clackamas Co.
26. *Chlosyne acastus dorothyi* Bauer, 1975 — Burnt R. Cn., Baker Co.
27. *Chlosyne leanira oregonensis* Bauer, 1975 — Jackson Co.
28. *Lycaena rubidus perkinsorum* Johnson & Balogh, 1977 — The Dalles, Wasco Co.

Oregon Physiography and Butterfly Distribution

A brief inspection of the distribution maps for Oregon's butterflies reveals a number of general facts and patterns. About a quarter of our somewhat over two hundred species and subspecies occur throughout much of the State, though they may inhabit mountainous versus low-lying areas or forested versus open regions. Some twenty percent are found only in western Oregon or parts such as the Pacific shore lands, the coastal mountains, the Willamette Valley, the west slope of the Cascades, or the Siskiyous. About fifty-five percent are indigenous to eastern Oregon or certain of its regions such as the eastern slope of the Cascades, the Columbia Plateau, the Blue Mountains, or the Great Basin.

The reasons for these distributional patterns lie in the past movements or confinements of butterfly populations as caused by geological changes over long periods of time and by genetic mutations that in a multitude of ways have adapted them to specific climatic conditions and ecological environments. The patterns of distribution also reflect the ability or inability of butterflies to move great distances or to cross hostile barriers. Butterflies that are capable of migrating (which are very few) or which can tolerate some degree of environmental diversity and whose foodplants are widely available usually have a broad distribution. Those whose flight ranges are slight, whose adaptive abilities are narrowly restricted with respect to climate and vegetation, tend to form colonies of limited distribution.

Oregon's diverse geology and ecology can be appreciated by a brief consideration of its physiographic provinces (fig. 2). The distribution of our butterflies as shown on the county outline maps can be interpreted in terms of these provinces.

(1) Coast Ranges. Situated between the sea and the Willamette Valley and extending southward to the Coquille River, the Coastal Mountains are relatively low and rounded. Mary's Peak west of Corvallis, the highest point, reaches an altitude of 4097 feet. Geologically these mountains are formed mostly of Tertiary basalt and Oligocene or Eocene shales and sandstones. The largely reddish-brown, heavy, and deep soil is rich in humus. With mild and rainy winters this is a humid region, the annual precipitation on the western slope averaging nearly 80 inches, some 50 on the eastern slope; the summers are dry. The mountains, where not denuded by logging, are densely covered with coniferous woods dominated by Douglas fir and with good stands of Sitka spruce, hemlock, and red cedar. In the deep, narrow valleys alder and bigleaf maple are abundant. The herbaceous vegetation is rich in ferns and mosses.

The valley floors, sunny hillsides, and mountain meadows are well populated with butterflies, particularly the forest edges and clearings along the eastern front. Characteristic are such species as *Anthocharis sara flora, Coenonympha tullia eunomia, Polygonia oreas silenus, Euphydryas editha taylori, Speyeria cybele pugetensis, S. zerene bremnerii, S. hydaspe rhodope, Callophrys dumetorum,* and *Everes comyntas.* Swallowtails and *Parnassius clodius* abound. The McDonald Forest, Oregon State University's arboretum north of Corvallis, is a classic site for Coast Range butterflies (fig. 3).

The Coastal Mountains extend virtually to the shore of the Pacific, leaving only a very narrow coastal strip along which are salt spray meadows, marshy bays, and south of Florence extensive sand dunes. Cool and wet, this region does not harbor any abundance of butterflies, but the rare Hippolyta Fritillary is endemic to it. It is also the only known Oregon location for *Incisalia polios.* Generally neglected by collectors, the coastal strip ought be more thoroughly explored.

(2) Klamath Mountains. Better known by Oregonians as the *Siskiyous*, the rugged Klamath Mountains of southwestern Oregon are continuous with the coastal ranges to the north and southward extend into California. Except for some level areas around Medford and in the Applegate Valley they merge with the southern Cascades on the east. The Siskiyous are the oldest mountains in Oregon, a maze

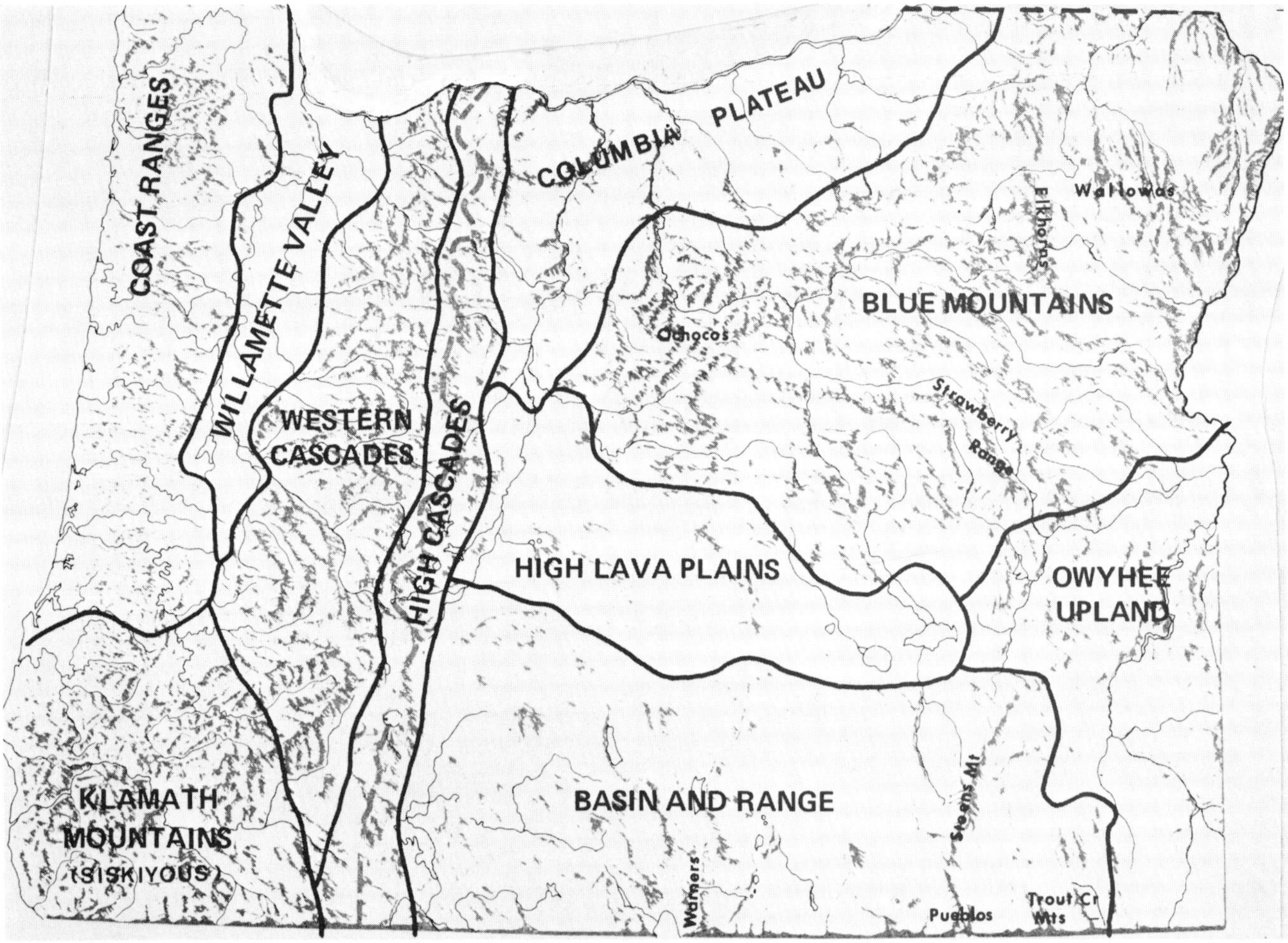

Fig. 2: Physiographic and geological provinces of Oregon (after Franklin & Dyrness, 1973).

Fig. 3: In the McDonald Forest, Benton Co. Rich in Coast Range butterflies.

of ridges and small, narrow valleys. The deeply folded rock strata are of metamorphosed volcanic and sedimentary origin; serpentine and granitic areas are extensive. Average elevations range from two thousand feet near the coast to four thousand inland; the highest peak, Mt. Ashland, reaches 7480 feet (fig. 4). Soils in the western region are deep and moist silty clay loams, but in the eastern part they are dry, shallow, and gravelly. The mean annual precipitation, west to east, ranges from about 80 to 24 inches; there is a long dry season with high summer temperatures. The rather sparse forests support a mixture of conifers that includes Jeffrey and knobcone pine, indicators of serpentine soil, as well as Douglas fir and incense cedar. In the dense layer of shrubs one finds huckleberry oak, tan oak, box-leaved garrya, and California laurel. Oak and madrone grow on the slopes of the Umpqua and Rogue Valleys together with buckbrush and manzanita.

The plants and animals of the Siskiyous are related to those of northwestern California. Among the resident butterflies one will find *Papilio indra, Parnassius phoebus sternitzkii* (at high elevations), *Coenonympha tullia eryngii, Phyciodes orseis, Chlosyne leanira, Euphydryas editha baroni, Speyeria zerene gloriosa, S. callippe elaine, S. egleis oweni, Lycaena gorgon* and *xanthoides, Philotes battoides interme-*

dia and *enoptes enoptes, Ochlodes agricola, Hesperia columbia* and *lindseyi,* and *Thorybes diversus.* Good places for seeing these and many others are the gullies and slopes along the old Siskiyou Pass road, the summit of Mt. Ashland, the Eight-dollar Mt. road along the Illinois River, and the high road leading west from the bridge to the Kalmiopsis Wilderness. The Wilderness itself has hardly been explored.

(3) Willamette Valley. A heavily settled urban and agricultural province, the Willamette Valley extends for some 125 miles from the Columbia River south to Cottage Grove and is nineteen to thirty-one miles wide, bordered on the west by the foothills of the Coast Range and on the east by those of the Cascades. The flat valley floor, with scattered groups of low hills, is an alluvial plain that slopes gently upward from near sea level at Portland to 423 feet at Eugene. Underlain by thick nonmarine sedimentary deposit of Pleistocene origin, the soil is sandy loam to silty clay. The average yearly precipitation of about forty inches occurs mainly in the mild winter; the summers are dry and warm. Stands of white oak and Douglas fir as well as ash, alder, and willow form scattered islands of woodland, whereas the valley is otherwise dominated by cultivated fields and grassland.

The butterflies of the Willamette Valley are mainly those that enter it from the adjacent foothills of the coastal mountains and the Cascades. *Coenonympha tullia eunomia* is endemic to the region, *Atlides halesus,* though scarce, is associated with the oak mistletoe, and *Atalopedes campestris* has recently spread into the valley from the south.

(4) Western Cascades. The western slope of the Cascades, which rises from the Willamette Valley and merges with the Klamath Mountains south of Roseburg, is geologically older than the high region of the volcanic peaks. Formed from Oligocene and Miocene volcanic flows, the upper levels of this slope have been deeply dissected by past glacial drifts and high rainfall into rugged ridges and deep valleys; below, the slope is more gentle. The moist westerly winds from the Pacific are intercepted by the western Cascades to produce a high winter precipitation which ranges from an annual average of forty to eighty or a hundred inches, depending upon elevation. Below 4000 feet the climate is similar to that of the Coast Range. The dense forest covering is dominated by Douglas fir with admixture of red cedar and hemlock.

At lower levels the butterflies of the Western Cascades do not differ much from those of the near Coast Ranges, but above three thousand feet there are gradual additions from the High Cascades. Favorite spots for the lepidopterist lie along the transcascadian highways, such as the South Santiam (US 20) with places like Cascadia (850 ft.), Tombstone Prairie

Fig. 4: Summit of Mt. Ashland (7480 ft.) in the Siskiyous. Here fly *Parnassius phoebus sternitzkii, Euchloe ausonides, Agriades aquilo podarce.*

Fig. 5: Tombstone Prairie (4100 ft.) in the Cascades of Linn County. Rich in species of the high western slope.

(4100 ft., fig. 5), and Lost Prairie (3322 ft.). Here one may expect to see, among numerous other species, *Chlosyne hoffmanni segregata, Euphydryas chalcedona colon* and *editha colonia, Speyeria atlantis dodgei, Mitoura johnsoni* (rare), *Lycaena nivalis, Lycaeides argyrognomon ricei,* and *Hesperia comma oregonia. Papilio rutulus* and *eurymedon,* as well as *Parnassius clodius* are everywhere numerous.

(5) **High Cascades.** Lying generally above 5000 feet and from fourteen to twenty-two airmiles wide, the long stretch of the High Cascades separates eastern from western Oregon. Along its crest rise the great snow-capped volcanic peaks, from Mt. Hood in the north to Mt. McLoughlin in the south. The volcanic rock of this region is younger than that of the Western Cascades, dating from the late Pliocene and Pleistocene and even the recent epoch, the eruption of Mt. Mazama to form Crater Lake having occurred only 6,600 years ago. Soils of the northern sector are largely derived from glacial deposits, whereas in the central and southern regions much of the bedrock is covered with pumice, cinders, and volcanic ash. The winter snowfall is considerable, reaching a depth of thirty-six feet at Crater Lake. The Canadian life zone, lying between 5000 and 6000 feet, broad and gently sloping, has a cover of subalpine forest — western white and lodgepole pine, noble and grand fir, Douglas fir, mountain hemlock, and Engelmann spruce. The undergrowth is of low density and there are many grassy and brushy meadows. Numerous streams and many lakes lie in the area. In the Hudsonian life zone, which lies between 6000 feet and treeline (7500 to 9800 ft.), the forests are composed of mountain hemlock and white-bark pine, with almost no herbaceous undergrowth. Here are also small flowered meadows, barren fields and ridges of lava, and gravely slopes strewn with boulders. Above treeline an Arctic-Alpine life zone exists on only a few isolated peaks, almost devoid of soil and without erect trees. East of the summit, the slope down to about 4500 or 4000 feet is largely an open forest of ponderosa pine with scant undergrowth; also present are many fine flowered meadows, lakes, and streams, as well as expanses of buckbrush and manzanita.

Excellent locations for butterflies are numerous in the Canadian life zone of the High Cascades. Such are the slopes of Mt. Hood, Jefferson Park on Mt. Jefferson, Hoodoo Bowl at the summit of the Santiam Pass, Three-Creeks Meadow south of Sisters (fig. 6), Diamond Lake, and the Sand Creek area on Highway 232. Among the butterflies in the High Cascades there are *Colias interior, Chlosyne palla whitneyi, Euphydryas editha remingtoni* and *lawrencei, Speyeria zerene conchyliatus,* the "Sand Creek" form of *S. egleis, S. callippe semivirida, S. mormonia erinna, Lycaena mariposa* and *shasta, Satyrium fuliginosum* and *behrii, Icaricia lupini, Agriades aquilo podarce, Philotes battoides oregonensis,* and *Thorybes mexicana nevada.*

(6) Columbia Plateau. Rising from the Columbia River between the Cascades and the Blue Mountains, the Columbia Plateau slopes upward from an altitude of a few hundred feet at the river to three thousand feet at its southern and western borders. This huge expanse, which also extends over most of southeastern Washington, is underlain by Miocene basalt to a depth of two to five thousand feet. In the extensive wheat-growing region of northern Oregon and the Washington palouse, characterized by smoothly rolling hills, this basalt is deeply covered by Pleistocene silt. Sagebrush and bunchgrass flourish in the rocky canyons cut into the plateau by the Deschutes, the John Day, and the Umatilla Rivers. The climate of the region is semi-arid; hot and dry summers alternate with very cold winters; the annual precipitation is twelve inches.

Butterflies of this province are best looked for along the Columbia River, in the canyons of its tributaries (fig. 7), and in the hilly and partially wooded terrain toward the Cascades and the Blue Mountains (fig. 8). The sage-lined canyons are the home of the Oregon Swallowtail. The Viceroy, the Pasco Crescent, and the Large White Skipper *(Heliopetes ericetorum)* may be found along the upper Columbia. In Wasco County north of Warm Springs there are good sites for *Phyciodes pallida barnesi, Chlosyne palla sterope, Apodemia mormo, Philotes enoptes columbiae,* and *Thorybes pylades.*

(7) High Lava Plains. Stretching some 130 miles from west to east across central Oregon, roughly between Bend and Burns, this region is a plateau of about 4000 feet base elevation, interrupted at several points by recent cinder cones and lava buttes, notably the Paulina Mountains with Newberry Crater (Paulina and East Lakes). Most of this area is covered with porous pumice soil. Silted basins of extinct lakes lie in the south, and the shallow Harney and Malheur Lakes are at the east end. The scanty average rainfall of twelve inches on the west end drops to seven inches eastward. East of Bend a savanna belt of junipers separates the open ponderosa forest near the Cascades from the shrub-steppe of sage and rabbitbrush to the east. Southward the High Lava Plains grade into the Basin and Range province.

Butterflies along the western end of the High Lava Plains are those generally encountered on the east

Fig. 6: Three-Creeks Meadow (6300 ft.) south of Sisters in Deschutes County. A richly flowered subalpine meadow of the Canadian life zone, well populated with *Speyeria mormonia erinna* and *callippe semivirida, Satyrium fuliginosum,* and *Thorybes mexicana nevada.*

Fig. 7: Deschutes River Canyon near Sherar Bridge, Wasco/Sherman Counties. In the spring one may see *Papilio oregonius* and *indra, Phyciodes pallida barnesi, Chlosyne palla sterope, Philotes enoptes columbiae;* in late summer *Apodemia mormo.*

Fig. 8: A flowered and sparsely wooded slope near Simnasho, Wasco County. A good site for a wide variety of butterflies in May and early June.

Fig. 9: Aspens at Pate Lake on Steens Mountain, 7400 ft. alt. Flowers attract *Speyeria zerene gunderi, S. callippe harmonia,* and *S. mormonia artonis.*

slope of the Cascades. Around Burns and south to Malheur Lake one will see species characteristic of the sage-land, such as *Pieris beckerii, Euchloe hyantis lotta, Cercyonis sthenele paulus, Lycaena rubidus,* and *Pholisora libya lena,* all of which are also common in the adjoining Basin province.

(8) Basin and Range, and (9) Owyhee Upland. These two physiographic provinces have much in common and together represent the northern end of the Great Basin, the vast area between the Rockies and the Sierras that includes most of Nevada, western Utah, and the deserts of southern California. The arid flats of Oregon's Basin and Range province are meagerly watered by intermittent streams and shallow saline lakes, and are enclosed by fault-block mountains. The Owyhee Upland, geologically less faulted, is drained by the Owyhee River. The average annual precipitation ranges from seven to twelve inches; the summers are hot and the winters cold. The basin floor lies at an average elevation of 4500 feet. The major fault-blocks include the Winter Ridge bordering Summer Lake, the Abert Rim edging the Warner Mountains, and Steens Mountain which rises to an almost 10,000 foot summit and is cut by deep glacial gorges headed by classical cirque basins.

On the pumice soil north and east of Klamath Falls, at the west end of the Basin and Range province, much of the terrain is mountainous and covered by open ponderosa forests. The Warner Mountains east of Lakeview are similarly, though more thinly, forested. The vast expanses of the basin, however, are overgrown with sage and rabbitbrush; greasewood, shadscale, and saltbush thrive on the alkaline soil of the poorly drained ancient lakebeds and deserts. Some of the streamsides support willow thickets. On Steens Mountain groves of aspen dot the slopes between 6400 and 7900 feet of altitude (fig. 9); above this level lush and richly flowered grassland is watered by the melting snow fields, and at the summit, with its dramatic view of the Alvord Desert a mile below (fig. 10), there is a small alpine meadow.

In this vast and varied region there are many sites to fascinate the lepidopterist. On Bly Mountain east of Klamath Falls a rich variety of species can be found in the forest clearings and streamside meadows just across the highway pass: *Euphydryas chalcedona macglashanii* and *editha edithana, Speyeria zerene conchyliatus, S. coronis* and *hydaspe purpurascens, Mitoura spinetorum* and *nelsoni, Chlosyne palla palla, Papilio multicaudata,* and many others. Skookum Meadow on Walker Mountain east of Chemult swarms with *Euphydryas editha remingtoni* and is also good for the Sand Creek race of *Speyeria egleis, Lycaena editha* and *cupreus,* and *Icaricia shasta.*

Fig. 10: Wildhorse Lake and Gorge as seen from alpine meadow at summit of Steens Mountain (9600 ft. alt.). Alvord Basin (4000 ft.) in left distance.

Fig 11: The sage-covered summit of Drake Peak (8000 ft.) in the Warner Mountains. *Neominois ridingsii* flies here.

Fig. 12: Beside Crump Lake north of Adel in the Warner Valley (4400 ft. alt.). Good site for *Colias alexandra, Coenonympha sthenele paulus, Papilio multicaudatus,* many Coppers and Blues.

Moving eastward into Lake County, *Satyrium tetra* can be found around Summer Lake. Chandler Wayside is a good place to explore before entering Warner Canyon near Lakeview where one can find *Tharsalea arota* and a variety of Hairstreaks. The Camas Creek road leading south from the highway at the Warner summit is rich in Fritillaries, including *S. egleis oweni,* and on the bald top of Drake Peak north of the highway *Neominois ridingsii* flies in the sagebrush (fig. 11). Descending into the Warner Valley and up the road to Crump Lake (fig. 12), the rabbitbrush is alive with *Colias alexandra,* various Coppers and Fritillaries, and *Cercyonis sthenele paulus.*

The butterfly riches in Harney County may be explored by starting near Frenchglen, where the road from Burns parallels the Blitzen River. At various points the flowering brush and the thistles along the roadside are often loaded with *Lycaena rubidus* and *heteronea,* various Blues, and *Colias alexandra;* flying low in the grass are *Coenonympha tullia ampelos, Cercyonis sthenele paulus,* and *Philotes battoides glaucon.* From Frenchglen the road east, after crossing the Blitzen River, leads up Steens Mountain, best explored after mid-July. In the tall grass beside the Blitzen one will find *Cercyonis alope ariane; Papilio multicaudata* is also about. On Steens Mountain the flowered slopes and meadows around and above Fish Lake teem with butterflies, notably *Speyeria zerene gunderi, S. callippe harmonia,* and *S. mormonia artonis;* also abundant are *Satyrium fuliginosum, Lycaena heteronea* and *editha, Cercyonis oetus,* and *Polites sabuleti;* at higher elevations there are pockets of *Icaricia shasta* and *Lycaena cupreus;* the alpine meadow at the summit is alive with *Philotes battoides glaucon.* Returning to Frenchglen, the road south to Fields and edging the Catlow Valley brings one to the precipitous east face of the Steens and into the Alvord Basin. Hot and dried out in the summer, the Alvord region should be visited in May or early June. Here, near the mouth of Wildhorse Canyon, fly *Euphydryas anicia macyi, Chlosyne acastus,* the Glaucon Blue, and later, *Brephidium exilis.* Near the dunes of the Alvord Desert (fig. 13) the Skippers *Hesperia uncas* and *Pholisora libya lena* may be seen, and also the scarce *Chlosyne leanira alma.* South of the Alvord Basin *Neominois ridingsii* has been found high in the Pueblo Mountains, and at lower elevations here and in the Trout Creek Mountains *Limenitis weidemeyerii* flies among the willows by the streamsides.

Most of the butterflies characteristic of Harney County will also be found in Malheur County, though the latter has been very poorly explored. The Idaho border in the northeast and the canyon of the

14 The Butterflies of Oregon

Owyhee River ought to get some concentrated attention.

(10) Blue Mountains. Bordered on the north by the Columbia Plateau, on the south by the High Lava Plains and the Owyhee Uplands, and on the east by the Snake River, the Blue Mountains province is made up of several ranges separated by faulted valleys and synclinal basins. On the western end the Ochocos arise just east of Prineville, the Strawberry Mountains lie southeast of John Day, the Elkhorns west of Baker, and the Wallowas across the La Grande and Baker Valleys. Major rivers draining these mountains include the Crooked River in the south, the Powder River in the east, and in the north the John Day, the Grande Ronde, and the Imnaha. The Blue Mountain province is geologically complex. While largely covered by Miocene basalt, there are extensive outcroppings of Paleozoic and Mesozoic rocks. Limestone and granite are prominent in the high Wallowas. Noted Tertiary beds of vertebrate fossils are situated along the lower John Day. Pleistocene glaciation is conspicuous in the Wallowas, leaving many cirques and lakes, among them the remarkable terminal moraine at Wallowa Lake. The spectacular Snake River Canyon along the Idaho border, eroded with the rising of the mountains, reaches a mile in depth near Hat Point (Hells Canyon).

The slopes on the western side of the province are generally moderate. The Ochocos rise from valley elevations of around 2700 feet to a maximum altitude of 6900 feet; Strawberry Mountain reaches 9000 feet compared with John Day at 3100. The rugged Wallowa Mountains show the greatest relief and the highest altitudes; while the surrounding land lies between 3000 and 4000 feet, the high peaks have summits between 9500 and 9850 feet; the lush alpine meadows of the lake basin lie between 7200 and 7800 feet.

Precipitation in the Blue Mountains province varies from fifteen to forty inches, the higher figure mainly as snow at the high altitudes. The hot and dry summers are broken with occasional thunderstorms and the winters are cold. The coniferous forests (dominantly ponderosa and lodgepole pine, grand fir, Engelmann spruce, and in the Wallowas also Douglas fir) are moderately dense below to open above, and expansive meadows are common at high altitudes. Of particular interest is that floral and faunal elements of the Rocky Mountains region penetrate the Blue Mountains province, especially at upper levels and along the Idaho border. This is reflected also in the kinds of butterflies.

The Ochocos, easily accessible from Prineville, are rich in numbers and varieties of butterflies. The Viewpoint Road off Marks Creek Guard Station near

Fig. 13: Sage flat and desert in the Alvord Basin (alt. 4000 ft.), a mile below the precipitous east face of Steens Mountain. Area for *Hesperia uncas, Pholisora libya lena,* and *Chlosyne leanira alma.*

Fig. 14: Forest meadow beside Viewpoint Road in the Ochocos (4700 ft. alt.). Eight species of *Speyeria* can be found along this road.

the summit of Highway 26 (fig. 14) is a paradise for Fritillaries, with eight species of *Speyeria* to be found *(cybele leto, coronis, zerene picta, callippe semivirida, egleis macdunnoughi, atlantis dodgei, hydaspe purpurascens,* and *mormonia erinna)*. Also congregated here are *Colias occidentalis* and many Hairstreaks, Blues, and Coppers (including *Lycaena editha, nivalis,* and *cupreus)*. On Big Summit Prairie one can see *Erebia epipsodea, Euphydryas chalcedona wallacensis* and *editha edithana,* and the rare *Boloria selene.*

In the central Blue Mountains area many excellent sites include the Strawberry Mountains, Dixie Butte in Grant County, Pine Creek in the Elkhorns west of Baker, Anthony Lake, the Morgan Lake road south of La Grande, and the east border of Umatilla County. One may expect to find *Papilio indra* and *multicaudata* among the Swallowtails, *Parnassius phoebus* as well as *clodius, Colias interior, Euphydryas chalcedona wallacensis. S. zerene garretti* among the Fritillaries, numerous Blues and Coppers, and possibly the scarce Skippers *Polites mystic* and *Hesperia nevada.*

The Wallowa Mountains, with the great range of altitude afforded, are particularly inviting. The Hurricane Creek and Lostine River roads are very productive, as is the Sheep Creek road east of Joseph. But most enticing are the trails leading to Aneroid Lake (fig. 15), Ice Lake, and the hanging valley of the high lakes basin from where the alpine slopes of the great peaks can be reached. At low and moderate elevations there are Fritillaries galore, *Parnassius phoebus* and *clodius,* swarms of Blues, and at higher elevations *Colias pelidne skinneri, Erebia epipsodea,* and *Euphydryas anicia howlandi. Lycaena phlaeas arctodon* has been found at 9500 feet on the Matterhorn.

The foregoing account of Oregon's physiographic provinces has of necessity been brief and incomplete. Nothing has been said about the flowering plants, a subject which the student of butterfly life histories cannot neglect, and for which botanical handbooks are needed. Such works are listed below together with references for deepening and enriching one's understanding of Oregon's geology and ecology. Finally, though, there is no substitute for the pleasure and excitement of real experience in the field. So load your camera, gird your binoculars, shoulder your net, perhaps also pack a plant press, and start exploring.

Maps are important. The official Oregon Highway Map is good as a general guide, as are State road maps available at service stations. For back country,

Fig. 15: The Aneroid Lake trail in the Wallowas, a three-mile hike from 5000 to 7400 feet of altitude. Along here fly *Erebia epipsodea* and *Colias pelidne*.

forest roads, trails, and detailed topography large scale regional maps are needed. Most useful here are the quadrangle maps of the U.S. Geological Survey, often stocked by large bookstores, and the National Forest Maps to be had at ranger stations; also excellent are those of the Bureau of Land Management issued by the Department of the Interior.

References:

(1) Baldwin, Ewart M. 1976. Geology of Oregon. Kendall/Hunt, Dubuque, Iowa. xi, 147 pp.

(2) Ferguson, Denzel & Nancy. 1978. Oregon's Great Basin Country. Gail Graphics, Burns, Ore. 178 pp.

(3) Franklin, Jerry F. & C. T. Dyrness. 1973. Natural Vegetation of Oregon and Washington. USDA Fst. Service Gen. Tech. Rept. PNW-8. US Gov't. Printing Office, Washington, D.C. vii, 417 pp.

(4) Hitchcock, C. Leo & Arthur Cronquist. 1973. Flora of the Pacific Northwest. Univ. Wash. Press, Seattle. xix, 730 pp.

(5) Lowe, Don & Roberta. 1969. 100 Oregon Hiking Trails. Touchstone Press, Portland, Ore. 240 pp.

(6) McKee, Bates. 1972. Cascadia. The Geologic Evolution of the Pacific Northwest. McGraw-Hill, N.Y. xv, 394 pp.

(7) Peck, Morton Eaton. 1961. A Manual of the Higher Plants of Oregon. Binfords & Mort, Portland, Ore. 936 pp.

(8) Rickett, Harold William. 1969-73. Wild Flowers of the United States. Vol. 5, The Northwestern States, 1971, 666 pp. (in 2 parts) for west of the Cascades. Vol. 6, The Rocky Mountain Region, 1973, 784 pp. (in 3 parts) for east of the Cascades.

Biology of Butterflies

Butterflies are holometabolous insects, which simply means that in their life cycle they pass from egg to adult through the intermediate stages of larva and pupa, stages very different from each other and from the adult. More primitive insects such as grasshoppers, dragonflies, and true bugs lack the pupal stage, the immature form being a nymph which gradually acquires adult characteristics; these insects are hemimetabolous. The difference is also expressed in distinguishing between a pattern of complete and incomplete metamorphosis. In the former (butterflies) growth in size is restricted to the larval stage which is maintained by a juvenile hormone secreted by the corpora allata in the head region. This growth is accompanied by several molts in which the larval skin, incapable of distention, is shed. Molting is triggered by a second hormone, ecdysone, produced by glands in the thorax. It induces pupation when the juvenile hormone is no longer present and also promotes formation of adult tissues within the pupal case. The emerging adult butterfly, or imago, has tiny folded and compressed wings, wrinkled sacs, which in a short while expand through pressure of blood forced into the veins. At some period in the life cycle growth or development may be temporarily arrested, a condition known as diapause, which is hormonally controlled and carries the insect through an unfavorable season. This may affect the larva or pupa, more rarely the egg.

Eggs and Egg-laying

A female butterfly is capable of laying several hundred eggs and usually does so over a protracted period of time following a single mating. This is made possible by storage of the sperm-carrying seminal fluid in a sac, the bursa copulatrix, from which small amounts of sperm pass to the oviduct as the mature eggs are released. Their entrance into the shell-encased egg is through the micropyle, a cluster of tiny channels at one end. Since the size of a butterfly population remains roughly constant, it is obvious that only very few of the eggs reach the adult stage, the vast majority perishing along the way. This huge attrition results from defective development, bacterial and viral diseases of the larvae, parasitism, predation, and environmental inclemencies. The high number is an adjustment to these hazards reached by natural selection.

Eggs are almost always laid on or deposited near the larval foodplant. This is in itself remarkable, since the adult butterfly feeds on the nectar of quite unrelated species. Observations and experiments have shown that cues for this "instinctive" behavior (a term that hides a great deal of ignorance) are based on sight, smell, and even touch. The female recognizes the appropriate plant species by the size and shape of its leaf ("search image") and by its distinctive scent. Young, tender, and nutritious leaves are chosen over older and coarser ones. Experimentally, in the absence of plants, butterflies will lay eggs on paper impregnated with plant extracts, from which they select that of the natural foodplant.

In most butterflies the eggs are laid singly, often one per plant, and cemented to the leaf underside, its edge, its petiole, or onto a flower bud. Other species deposit small batches or chains of five to ten eggs.

Fig. 16: Eggs of Butterflies, magnified. Left to right: *Atalopedes campestris*, *Vanessa annabella* (empty shell), *Pieris rapae*.

Still others produce large clusters of fifty to a hundred; in the case of the Mourning Cloak the mass forms a flat band wrapped around a twig. A few do not attach their eggs at all but broadcast them near the appropriate foodplant, to which the newly hatched larvae later migrate *(Parnassius, Speyeria)*.

Butterfly eggs are small, mostly less than a millimeter in width, but they vary greatly in shape and surface ornamentation. Some are almost round, others flattened or turban-shaped, still others tall and spindle-like (fig. 16). Their surfaces may be smooth or elaborately sculptured with longitudinal ribs and cross-ridges, raised networks, pits, or knob-like tops. They may be white, yellow, brown, or green, and often blend cryptically into the background. As hatching approaches, which is usually in five to ten days, the color generally changes and becomes darker. In many species the newly emerged larvae eat their egg shell and even fail to survive if deprived of it; this first meal is particularly important when immediately followed by diapause.

Larvae

In the life history of a butterfly the business of eating and growing belongs to the larva, or caterpillar, and its structure is adapted to the purpose. In the process of feeding its weight increases ten thousandfold or more.

The larval head, a hard capsule formed from the fusion of six embryonic segments, bears on each side a group of six small simple eyes, or ocelli, not very efficient for acute vision, and a short three-jointed antenna which serves the sense of smell. Most important, though, are the mouthparts (fig. 17), of which the pair of powerful jaws, or mandibles, are the busiest part; from their sides a pair of palpi guide food to the mouth assisted by an upper lip, or labrum. A small projection from the lower lip, or labium, is the spinneret through which modified salivary glands emit silk. The silk is drawn out as a thread by side to side movements of the caterpillar's head and hardens on exposure to the air.

The long body trunk (fig. 18), is made up of a series of segments like the folds of an accordion. The first three of these constitute the thorax and from each extends a pair of stiff, five-jointed legs ending in a single claw. The remaining ten segments belong to the abdomen; five of these are furnished with fleshy, nonjointed prolegs (false legs, not present in the adults) the ends of which are padded and supplied with a ring of tiny hooks (the crochet) for firm grasp in crawling; the last of these prolegs, located on the terminal segment (the others are on segments three to six) are used as claspers. The turgidity of the caterpillar's soft body is maintained by the pressure of its body fluid acting against the body wall muscles; a dead caterpillar is quite limp. A pair of slit-like oval-rimmed openings on the sides of the thoracic and all but the last two abdominal segments are the spiracles, or breathing pores, that lead into the tubular tracheae whose fine ultimate branches deliver oxygen to the individual cells of the internal organs. The larval skin is unable to adjust to the rapid growth of the caterpillar and therefore, under the hormonal control already mentioned, is periodically shed and reformed. The larval stages between the four or five sheddings, or molts, are known as instars and are commonly accompanied by changes in color and markings. Molting is preceded by a day or so of quiescence during which the larvae do not feed.

Aside from the generalized larval features so far recounted there are extensive differences in form, surface specializations, color, and markings which vary with families, genera, and species and which have important roles in providing protection from natural enemies. Whether the larval life is solitary or gregarious usually follows from the pattern of egg laying. Communal larvae frequently live within silken tents or nests and some solitary larvae hide in silk-tied rolled-

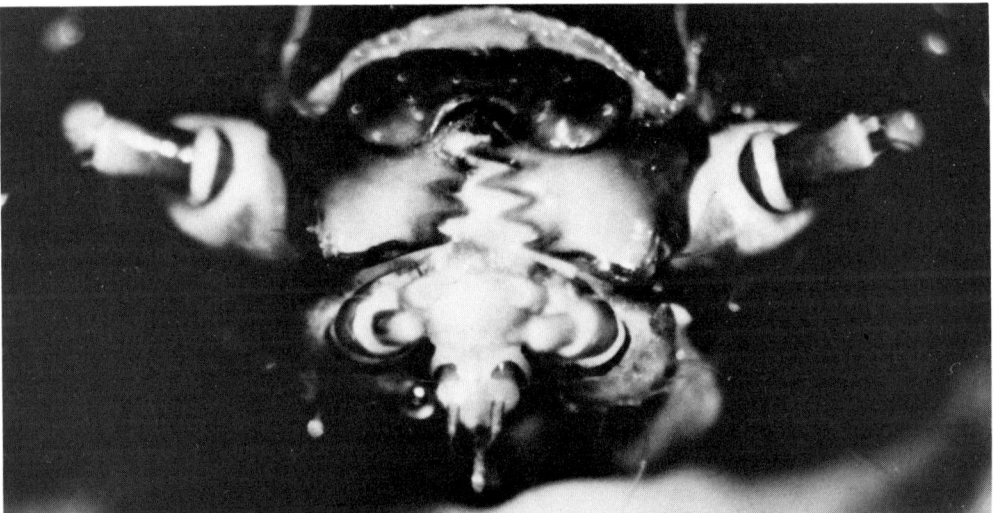

Fig. 17: Larval Mouthparts of the Checkerspot *Euphydryas editha taylori*. Note the tooth-edged pair of mandibles (jaws) with an antenna to each side, the broad labrum above the mandibles, and a pair of palpi below which enclose the labium with the downward projecting spinneret.

up leaves. Larvae may be cylindrical in form, flattened and slug-like, spindle-shaped, or variously crooked and humped. In a great many caterpillars the skin is ornamented with tubercles from which arise spines or bristles (setae) that may be branched or tufted, long or short and furry. Besides giving protection by their unpleasant texture many of these setae connect to sensory organs receptive to touch and to sound vibrations. Swallowtail and Parnassian larvae are provided with a forked, acrid-smelling yellow scent gland, an osmeterium, that on disturbance

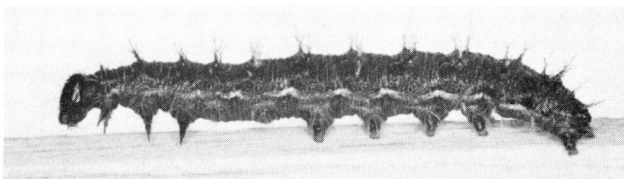

Fig. 18: Above: Larva of *Vanessa cardui* showing the thoracic legs, the abdominal prolegs, and the spiny integument. Below: Larva of *Papilio rutulus* resting on a rolled leaf and showing the false "eyespots" on the thorax.

is everted from a pouch behind the head; this is usually coupled with an alarm response in which the head is suddenly jerked upward. Horns and prominently colored "eyespots" are presumed to act as warning signals, giving second thoughts to would-be predators. Most common, however, and quite effective are cryptic colors, patterns, and postures that conceal or camouflage the larva against its background; the blending can be so remarkable that only a practised eye can find the insect. For details the species accounts should be consulted.

On the subject of feeding habits the specificity in the choice of foodplants has been mentioned in discussing egg-laying. Fully two thirds of the Eurasian and North American species are "specialists", i.e., limit their food choices to one genus or one order of plants, often to but one or a few closely related species. An enquiry into this relationship, its biochemical and physiological implications, and its evolutionary origin ("coevolution") has been the object of much recent research. An important aspect of the phenomenon consists in the development by plants of secondary chemical substances as defenses against insect attacks, to which in turn certain insects by genetic mutation have developed toleration (detoxication mechanisms) and, in effect, turned repellants into attractants. Larval species or species groups differ in respect to the various kinds of attractants to which they respond. As an example the larvae of Pieridae are attracted to mustard oil, originally developed in cruciferous plants to ward off insect predators.

The duration of larval life varies greatly, depending especially on the intervention of diapause. It is also shortened or lengthened by nutritive quality of the foodplant, and thus, indirectly, by the growth season, and by inherited growth rate. Larval life may last from a few weeks to several months, or even to the greater part of a year.

A heavy toll of larvae is taken by bacterial and virus diseases, wasp and fly parasites, predation by mice, moles, toads, birds, and spiders, and by inclemencies of the weather which also affect the foodplant resources; the destructive effects of pesticides are also, of course, obvious.

Pupae (Chrysalids)

At the end of larval life the caterpillar moves from its feeding site to a location suitable for pupation. This may be a twig, a shelter beneath loose bark, the underside of a rock, or even debris on the ground. If the chrysalis is to be suspended a small pad of silk is made into which the tip of the abdomen is inserted and finally attached by the cremaster, a set of minute hooks on the terminal end of the pupa. In Papilionidae and Pieridae an additional silken sling around the thorax enables the pupa to be fixed in an upright position, otherwise it becomes suspended head down (fig. 19). The larval skin splits at the head end and is gradually forced posteriorly and off by vigorous wriggling. After several hours the pupal case hardens and becomes immobile except for the possibility of slight movement of the abdominal segments; it is moisture tight and thus protected against dessication.

Chrysalids of butterflies are bare except in the case of Skippers where they are enclosed in a loosely woven cocoon. In form and color they are almost always well concealed from predators. Some are oval-shaped, others angular and furnished with projections, knobs, and bulges. Some are smooth, others

 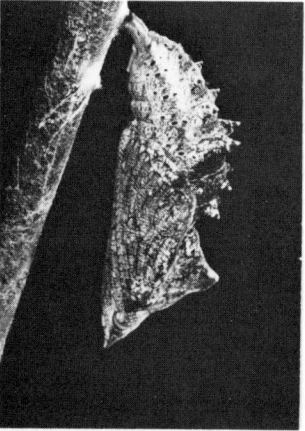

Fig. 19: Chrysalids of the Oregon Swallowtail (left) and the California Tortoiseshell (right).

finely bristled or spined. Green or brown are the usual colors, and mottling, spotting, or striping are common; sometimes silver or golden marks are present as in the beautiful chrysalis of the Monarch. With time the color may change, particularly in the final period when the chrysalis becomes dark and the features of the adult butterfly can be seen through the translucent pupal skin. The shapes of the compressed wings, antennae, proboscis, and compound eyes are, in fact, discernible almost from the start.

Internally, the transformation from larval to adult structures is a process of immense complexity and fine-tuned coordination. A vast reorganization takes place in which the tissues and organs of the caterpillar are either destroyed or remodelled and made into or replaced by those of the butterfly. This involves enzymatic dissolution of larval structures and the differentiation of imaginal tissues. The embryonic rudiments of the adult tissues, the imaginal buds or discs, have as a matter of fact been unnoticeably concealed already in the body of the larva. In eight to ten days, unless protracted by diapause, the adult butterfly will emerge from the chrysalis, after which no further growth takes place.

Adults

The life span of the adult butterfly is normally a week or two, but in hibernating species it may be extended to eight months. Equipped with refined sense organs, with great wings that enable agile movement, deriving energy from sugar-laden nectar, and primarily preoccupied with reproduction, the adult butterfly is in many ways a new creature.

The butterfly's body shows a clear division into head, thorax, and abdomen (fig. 20). On the head, the huge hemispherical compound eyes are composed of several thousand closely set units, the ommatidia, whose individual lenses, the hexagonally shaped facets, can be seen at the surface (fig. 21). These eyes produce a mosaic image that is clear at close range but blurred at more than a few feet of distance; movement, however, is detected with great sensitivity. The ability of butterflies to distinguish colors is well established. The range of their color vision is the broadest of any animal group, extending from red to blue and into the ultraviolet; in not all species, however, is the range this complete.

Fig. 21: Compound Eye, magnified, of *Cercyonis pegala boopis*. Note the numerous closely set ommatidial facets on the surface.

The antennae are sensory organs equipped with olfactory receptors. In butterflies their long shafts end in a swelling or club which is lacking in moths; in Skippers a short pointed projection, the apiculus, extends beyond the club. Under a magnifying lens it can be seen that the antennae are made up of many short segments and are partially covered with scales. The antennae also serve to impart a sense of balance and direction; the flight of butterflies becomes disoriented if they are damaged.

The mouthparts of the adult butterfly, adapted for the uptake of liquid foods, are vastly unlike those of the caterpillar. In the place of biting jaws a greatly elongated pair of maxillary galeae are united to form a tube-like proboscis ("tongue") which sucks up nectar and when not in use coils up like a watch spring (fig. 22). Flanking the base of the proboscis two furry labial palpi extend forward along the face. Their thickly set bristly hairs lead to sensory receptors of taste and touch.

Fig. 20: Body of a male Tiger Swallowtail. Note the head with antennae, compound eyes, and coiled proboscis; the thorax with three pairs of jointed legs; and the abdomen with its terminal clasper.

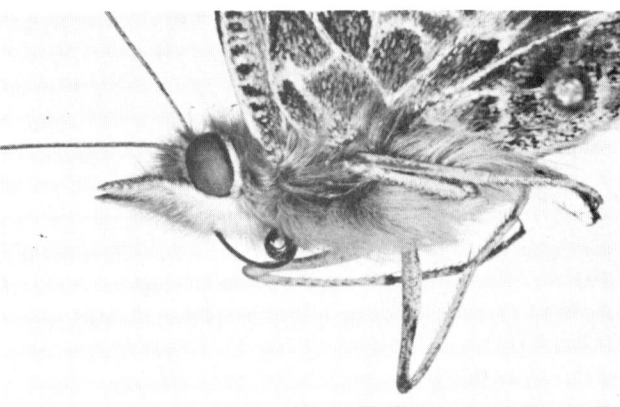

Fig. 22: Head and Thorax of the Painted Lady. Note the compound eye, the labial palpi, the partially coiled proboscis, and four functional legs on the thorax (the forelegs are aborted).

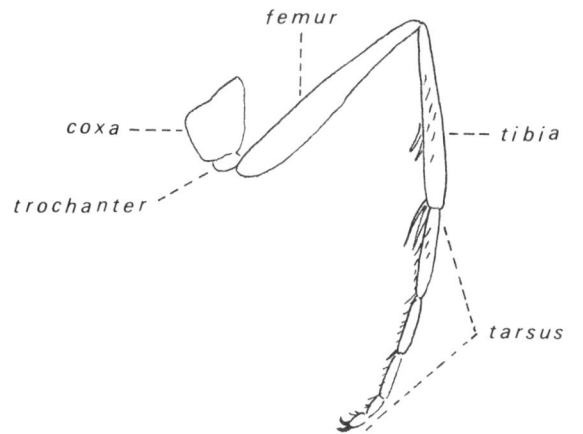

Fig. 23: Diagram of a Butterfly Leg showing its parts.

The three segments behind the head constitute the pro-, meso-, and metathorax and each carries a pair of jointed legs. The parts of a typical leg, beginning at the body, are the coxa and trochanter, both short, the femur and tibia, both long, and the five-jointed tarsus which ends in a pair of claws (fig. 23). The tibia is provided with one or two pairs of terminal spurs; additional spines and hair tufts may also be present. The tarsi of the third pair of legs have sensory setae (bristles) receptive to taste; their stimulation leads to uncoiling of the proboscis. In some families of butterflies (Nymphalidae, Satyridae, Danaidae, and male Riodinidae) the prothoracic legs are not fully developed but remain rudimentary and are useless for walking.

The wings of butterflies are carried on the second and third thoracic segments. They develop as sac-like outgrowths of the integument whose thin walls collapse to form a double-membraned sheet. The upper and lower membranes are firmly fused at the veins which impart stiff support and also serve as conduits for tracheae, nerves, and blood vessels. The disposition of these veins, as between families and genera of butterflies, varies in detail and is important in classification. The terminology applied to them, to the intervein spaces, and to the wing margins and angles is shown in the illustration (fig. 24). Also shown are terms that designate general wing areas; these are useful in pattern descriptions.

The colors and patterns of butterflies, which rate them as the most beautiful of insects, are produced by the microscopic scales that cover the wings and from which the order name, Lepidoptera = scaled wings, is derived. Just as the wings themselves developed from outpocketings of the thoracic integument, so the individual scales are formed from sac-like projections of single cells in the embryonic wing's membranous surface. Before their collapse into rigid plates these sacs capture pigment from the pupal body fluid. This is a remarkable example of efficiency in the utilization of metabolic waste products. The yellow, white, orange, and red pigments of the Pieridae are pterins, breakdown products of uric acid; the brown and black melanins come from the oxidation of tyrosin, an amino acid of protein origin; certain yellowish pigments of Woodnymphs and Skippers, flavones, are derived from foodplants of the larvae. A microscopic examination of the wing will show that any one scale contains just a single pigment. The

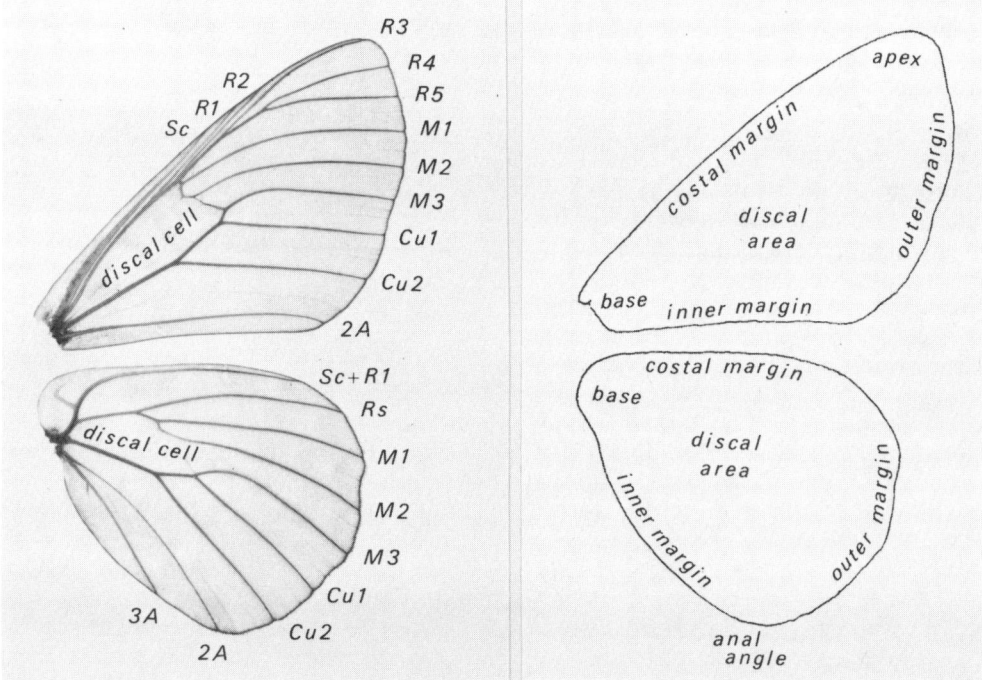

Fig. 24: Wings of the Chalcedona Checkerspot showing the venation and regional areas. The vein names are abbreviated as follows: Sc, subcostal; R, radial; Rs, radial sector; M, median; Cu, cubital; A, anal. The intervein spaces are named after their anteriorly bordering veins; thus, space M_3 lies between veins M_3 and Cu_1. The discal area may also be referred to as the median region.

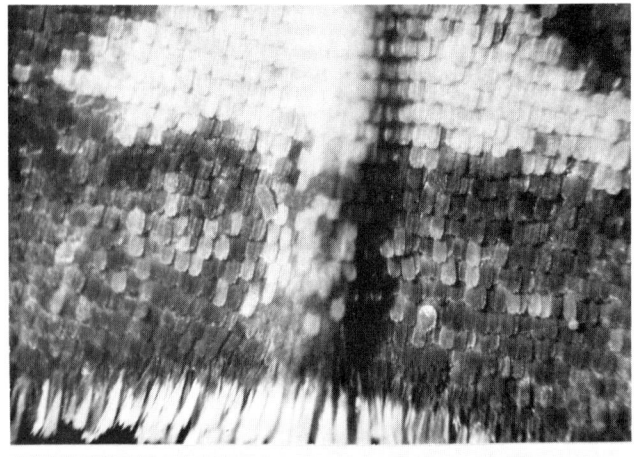

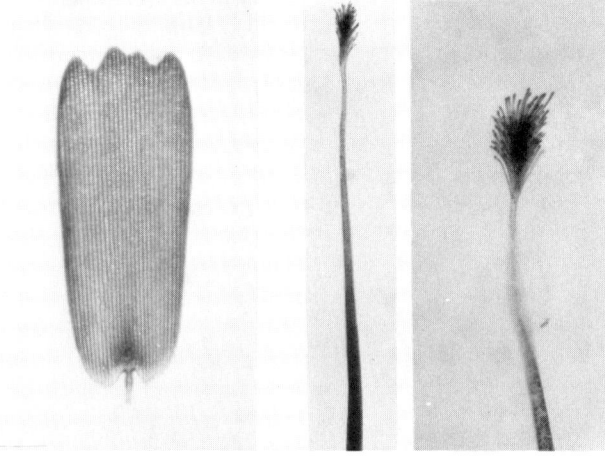

Fig. 25: Top: Scale pattern on the wing of a Hydaspe Fritillary. Bottom left: An individual scale, greatly magnified, from the wing of a Painted Lady. Bottom right: Androconial scales from the sex-patch of a Large Woodnymph; note the plumed tip.

complex pattern of different colors (fig. 25) results from sets of scales having matured at different times and captured the pigment in circulation at the moment. The timing of these coincidental events is ultimately a gene controlled process. Apart from color, wing scales vary considerably in size and shape and in their sculptured fine structure. Certain of them are so elaborately outfitted with closely set parallel ridges, internal meshworks, and minute air chambers that they produce colors by physical interference and diffraction of light rather than by pigmentation. Such scales are responsible for iridescent and metallic colors such as silver, gold, and glossy blues. Finally, there are scales that have little to do with color at all but which serve to disseminate pheromones, perfumes, as it were, that attract the opposite sex. In butterflies these scales, known as androconia, are limited to males and in certain groups (Satyridae, Danaidae, Theclinae, Hesperiidae) are restricted to patches on the wings called scent-pads, sex brands, or stigmata. The bases of these androconial scales connect with glandular cells and their tips are often finely plumed.

The butterfly's abdomen, which is free of appendages, has ten segments. The first seven of these have on their sides pairs of spiracles, or breathing pores, which lead to the interior tracheae. The last two abdominal segments are modified to form the external genitalia. Males can usually be identified by the terminal pair of claspers, or valves, whereas in females these are absent and the tip of the abdomen is pointed.

Differences in the chitinous parts of the genitalia are often important in distinguishing closely related species that are otherwise hard to tell apart. Among Oregon butterflies an examination of these structures is necessary in the genera *Euphydryas, Lycaeides, Philotes, Hesperia,* and *Erynnis*. Male genitalia are more often used than those of the female as the latter are more difficult to dissect and study. The essential features of the male genitalia are shown in Figure 26. A dorsal roof-like plate, the tegumen, articulates on the sides with a U-shaped vinculum to form a ring; extending posteriorly from the top of the tegumen is the terminal uncus which may be variously shaped, forked, or provided with lateral projections known as falces; extending posteriorly from the lower sides of the vinculum are the two valves, or claspers, also variously shaped, toothed or serrated, and often provided with spine-like processes; passing posteriorly through the vincular ring is the aedeagus, or penis.

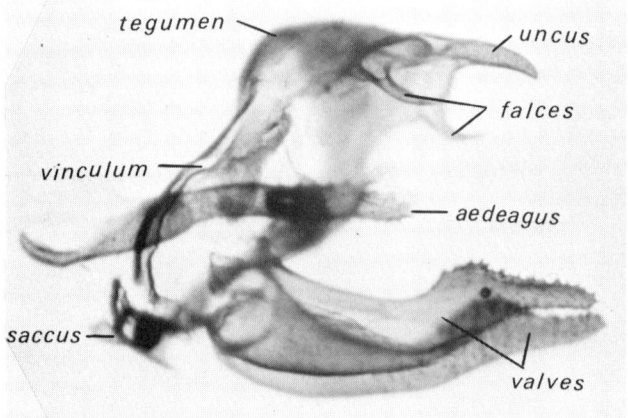

Fig. 26: Genital capsule of the male Woodnymph, *Erebia epipsodea.*

Significance of Color and Pattern

Returning to the subject of color and pattern, something further has to be said concerning their functions. To our human eyes butterflies represent natural beauty of extraordinary degree, matched by few other animals, but we can hardly assume that their evolution proceeded to please our aesthetic sense or that insects are gifted with artistic perception. Careful observations and experiments illuminate their meaning.

The eyes of butterflies, as already mentioned, can distinguish colors and shapes as well as detect movements. These abilities are employed in mate recognition, as can be shown by experiments with artificial decoys. The role of vision in the courtship of butterflies has been reviewed by James Scott (1972, 1975). Pheromones play a secondary role and come into play at close range.

Colors are also concerned with thermoregulation. Butterflies are extraordinarily dependent on the heat of the sun for energizing the muscles of flight. It is a common observation that butterflies are not active during cool periods of the day or under cloud cover. Basking in the sun often precedes flight and is a behavior that serves to warm the body. Colias butterflies are unable to fly at body temperatures below 30 degrees C. (86°F.), as shown by Watt (1969). Dark wing colors aid the warming process by absorbing heat, and such colors are particularly common in butterflies that inhabit forested regions, high altitudes, and cool northern climates. Conversely, light colors deflect excess heat and are more often seen in deserts and on hot prairies. These generalizations, however, have many exceptions as other functions of color take on greater importance.

Most dramatic are the roles of colors and patterns in providing protection against predators. In most species of butterflies the upper and under sides of the wings are very different. The bright upper side is conspicuous in flight, but the usually less vivid underside is exposed in the resting position as the wings are folded together over the back. This underside very often affords concealment by its resemblance to the background. Among woodland butterflies one may take note of the bark-like underside in the species of *Polygonia, Oeneis,* and *Nymphalis.* The ventrally green *Callophrys* Hairstreaks can hardly be seen when they perch on green leaves or blades of grass. Many Blues and Coppers are effectively camouflaged against the flowers on which they feed. In each of these instances it is not unusual to see a pursuing bird lose sight of an alighted butterfly.

Checkered and mottled wings disrupt outlines and imitate the dappled light and shade of the surroundings, an effect further enhanced by an erratic flying habit. Bright colors or "eyespots" near the rear angle of the hindwing (some Hairstreaks and Blues) deflect attention from the vulnerable parts of the body, and a butterfly attacked on such a wing area gets away unharmed. The display of the large "eyespots" on *Cercyonis* Woodnymphs and Buckeyes have the effect of startling would-be predators.

Most remarkable, however, is the phenomenon of mimicry, in which harmless species have evolved to resemble quite unrelated noxious ones, their so-called models. Their colors and patterns serve as warnings to predators that have previously experienced the ill effects of dining on the poisonous models. The mimic relationship of the Viceroy to the Monarch is the best known North American example and is discussed in the account of *Danaus plexippus.* Mimicry is most extensively developed in the tropics where there are many species of the poisonous families Danaidae and Acraeidae.

Abnormalities

Colors and patterns are sometimes bizarrely disturbed by faulty development. This is not a common happening and is more often seen in reared specimens than in the field as such individuals are disadvantaged in nature. Many of these "freaks", or aberrations, are environmentally caused, as by exposure to extremes of temperature or by some injury to the larva or pupa. Others, however, are of genetic origin and can be traced to chromosomal mishaps or unfortunate mutations.

Of these abnormalities the most spectacular is bilateral gynandromorphism. Individuals so affected have male characteristics on one side of the body and female on the other (fig. 27). They are reproductively sterile. This situation is caused in early development by a misdistribution of the sex-determining chromosomes. In most insects, as in man, males have an X and a Y chromosome, females two X's. In Lepidoptera this is reversed, with females being XY and males XX (the nomenclature is sometimes changed to ZW and ZZ to indicate the reversal). Bilaterality is established in the early cell divisions of the embryo, and when in a male egg (XX) a mishappen chromosome distribution delivers only one X to one of its two daughter cells, the progeny of that cell will develop female tissue (the Y chromosome need not be present). If this accident happens in later stages of development only patches of the butterfly will show female characteristics rather than an entire half, resulting in a sex mosaic.

Fig 27: Aberrations. Upper left: Bilateral gynandromorph of *Celastrina argiolus echo,* with male features on the left side, female on the right. Upper right: Albino mutant of *Incisalia fotis mossii.* Lower left: Scale-deficient mutant of *Anthocharis sara flora.* Lower right: Melanic *Euphydryas editha taylori.* Compare these aberrations with the normal butterflies shown on the plates.

Genic mutations may produce anomalies of structure affecting various parts of the body or processes that disurb normal pigment production. Illustrated is one in which the formation of normal wing cuticle is affected, resulting in faulty development of scale sockets and the loss of scales. Another shown is albinism in which pigment formation is suppressed. Rather less rare is melanism in which a superabundance of black scales is produced; excess melanin formation can also be environmentally induced by exposure of late larvae and pupae to low temperatures. The reader interested in pursuing this subject, as well as Lepidoptera genetics in general, will find it well covered in the large monograph by Robinson (1971).

Not to be confused with aberrations are hybrids which look odd because they combine to various degrees the characteristics of the two parental species. In nature they are not infrequently found in the genera *Limenitis, Vanessa,* and *Colias* and have been produced by hand pairing in Swallowtails and some other butterflies. Hybrids usually have reduced fertility or are completely sterile.

Migration

Butterfly migrations always excite attention and are indeed remarkable phenomena. Such mass movements over long distances are limited to relatively few species of which the Monarch is the most famous. Among Oregon butterflies they are also seen in the Painted Lady and the California Tortoiseshell and details are given in the discussions of these species. The reasons for butterfly migrations are not well understood but among the hypotheses advanced are overcrowding, lack or insufficiency of food, and climatic factors. Breeding occurs along the migrational pathway and establishes temporary colonies. Return flights occur in the Monarch but not in the Painted Lady or the California Tortoiseshell. At the start of migration the butterflies have large fat body reserves which are depleted at the end of the journey. Nothing certain is known regarding the navigational means whereby the direction of flight is governed, but it has been conjectured that orientation is provided by polarized light of the sun. The discussion of butterfly migrations by Shields (1974) summarizes the main facts and proposed explanations.

References

(1) Bernard, Gary D. 1979. Red-absorbing visual pigment of butterflies. Science 203: 1125-1127.

(2) Ehrlich, Paul R. 1958. The integumental anatomy of the Monarch butterfly *Danaus plexippus* L. (Lepidoptera: Danaiidae). Univ. Kansas Sci. Bull. 38: 1315-1349.

(3) Ehrlich, Paul R. 1958. The comparative morphology, phylogeny and higher classification of the butterflies (Lepidoptera: Papilionoidea). Univ. Kansas Sci. Bull. 39: 305-370.

(4) Ehrlich, Paul R. & Peter H. Raven. 1965. Butterflies and plants: a study in coevolution. Evolution 18: 586-608.

(5) McFarland, Noel. 1972. Notes on describing, measuring, preserving and photographing the eggs of Lepidoptera. J. Res. Lepid. 10: 203-214.

(6) Rausher, Mark D. 1978. Search image for leaf shape in a butterfly. Science 200: 1071-1073.

(7) Robinson, Roy. 1971. Lepidoptera Genetics. Pergamon Press, N.Y. 687 pp.

(8) Scott, James A. 1972. Mating of butterflies. J. Res. Lepid. 11: 99-127.

(9) Scott, James A. 1973. Lifespan of butterflies. J. Res. Lepid. 12: 225-230.

(10) Scott, James A. 1975. Mate-locating behavior of Western North American butterflies. J. Res. Lepid. 14: 1-40.

(11) Shields, Oakley. 1974. Toward a theory of butterfly migration. J. Res. Lepid. 13: 217-238.

(12) Shields, Oakley, John F. Emmel & Dennis E. Breedlove. 1969. Butterfly larval foodplants records and a procedure for reporting foodplants. J. Res. Lepid. 8: 21-36.

(13) Slansky, Frank, Jr. 1976. Phagism relationships among butterflies. J. N.Y. Entom. Soc. 84: 91-105.

(14) Tietz, H. M. 1972. An index to the described life histories, early stages, and hosts of the macrolepidoptera of the continental United States and Canada. Allyn Museum of Entomology, Sarasota, Fla. 1041 pp.

(15) Watt, Ward B. 1969. Adaptive significance of pigment polymorphisms in *Colias* butterflies. II. Thermoregulation and photoperiodically controlled melanin variation in *Colias eurytheme*. Proc. Nat. Acad. Sci. 63: 767-774.

Endangered and Extinct Butterflies

The availability of appropriate larval foodplants is critical for the survival of butterflies and their populations decline when these foodplants become scarce. In the case of species or varieties with small populations that occupy a narrow range, a sufficient deterioration of the food supply may easily cause extinction. Population declines and extinctions have, of course, always been natural consequences of climatic and ecological changes, but human activities have greatly hastened these processes. Natural habitats are destroyed by land clearing, road and dam construction, industrialization, and urbanization. The extensive use of herbicides, the conversion of wild acreage to agricultural purposes, the draining of marshlands, overgrazing, deforestation — these all alter the native ecology. Their destructive effects on plant and animal life are now well recognized and have given rise to the Endangered Species Act.

Habitat destruction has already caused the total extinction of several kinds of butterflies, most of these in the San Francisco Bay region. The Sthenele Satyr (*Cercyonis sthenele sthenele*) disappeared in the 1880's, the Xerces Blue (*Glaucopsyche xerces*) in 1943. Also gone are the Pheres Blue (*Plebejus icarioides pheres*), Strohbeen's Parnassian (*Parnassius clodius strohbeeni*), and the Atossa Fritillary (*Speyeria adiaste atossa*). Many more butterflies are on the Endangered Species List. Here in Oregon we should be concerned about the Hippolyta Fritillary (*Speyeria zerene hippolyta*) and the Silver-bordered Meadow Fritillary (*Boloria selene tollandensis*). Certain other rare and local species remain for the time protected by the remoteness of their habitats.

Intensive collecting of butterflies in populations that are rare, very local, weak, depleted, or environmentally stressed should be avoided. There is, however, no evidence that healthy populations are damaged by moderate collecting. In order to acquire a series of specimens it is advisable to collect at different times and from different populations. Especial care should be exercised not to disturb the habitats.

In 1971, under the leadership of Robert M. Pyle, a movement was initiated to promote butterfly conservation. Organized as the Xerces Society (named after the extinct California Blue), its program was patterned after that of the British Nature Conservancy. The society's journal, Atala, and its newsletter, Wings, plus various Educational Leaflets keep the membership informed on the status of rare, endangered, and threatened species. The society also sponsors various conservation measures, including projects for the acquisition of threatened habitats. Its interests have recently been expanded to include other terrestrial arthropods. Membership applications may be directed to the society's treasurer, Roger Pasquier, 1260 21st Street NW, Washington, D.C. 20036.

Evolution, Classification and Nomenclature

Among the orders of insects that of the Lepidoptera, which includes the moths and butterflies, is after the Coleoptera, or beetles, the largest. There are some 120,000 described species in the world of which about 11,000 occur in the United States and Canada; most of them are tropical. Furthermore, the great majority of the Lepidoptera are moths and there are doubtless many more of them to be discovered. Butterflies, on a world-wide basis, make up around thirteen percent of the total, in North America somewhat over six percent or roughly seven hundred species. They represent two lepidopterous superfamilies, the Papilionoidea, or true butterflies, and the Hesperioidea, or Skippers, and are often referred to as the Rhopalocera, a word that means clubhorned and points to their swollen-tipped antennae.

Origins

The fossil record of Lepidoptera is scanty. Insects of primitive orders have been preserved in Silurian deposits (Paleozoic), a period estimated to go back 425 Million years, but the earliest Lepidoptera come from Cretaceous amber (Mesozoic), about 100 million years ago. The best butterfly fossils have been found in the ancient lake beds at Florissant, Colorado and date from the lower Oligocene (Tertiary) which is some thirty-five million years in the past; these already represent recognizable modern families, which points to an earlier origin. In general, Lepidoptera are assumed to have evolved along with the flowering plants on which they feed, and this also would account for their huge variety in the tropics where the diversity of flowering plants is highest.

So far as North American butterflies are concerned, particularly those of the Northwest, most of their closest relatives are today found in Europe and northern Asia. The evidence from zoogeography together with what is known of past land movements and climates indicates that many of our butterfly genera came from northern Asia during warm Tertiary times by way of the Bering Straits bridge and that such migrations continued during Pleistocene interglacial periods. The genera *Anthocharis, Euchloe, Speyeria, Habrodais,* and *Celestrina* are among these. During the interglacials eastern and western species on the North American Continent also became shifted about, of which today we have many cases, including some remnants of once more widely distributed species that are now isolated in the Western mountains, of which *Boloria selene* is a striking example. A few genera and species of our area migrated north from centers of dispersal in Central and South America, such as the genera *Phyciodes, Satyrium,* and *Neophasia*. The Red Admiral and the Cabbage butterfly are examples of species introduced from Europe by the hand of man, the latter as recently as the 1860's.

Taxonomic Categories

The butterflies we see today, as well as their present distributions, represent, as it were, a snapshot in time. In their classification we recognize various degrees of similarities, inherited likenesses that reflect ancestral relationships. Thus, a number of species that share certain common features are combined in a genus and genera with structural similarities are united into families. Categories such as superfamilies, subfamilies, and subgenera are also employed. A diagram of their natural relationships would resemble the branchings of a tree; listing them in a linear sequence, as in a checklist, does not adequately convey this information.

The category of *species* is rather special and is incompletely defined by the English word "kind" though it correctly implies application to a collection of individuals. The notion that all individuals of the same species look alike is also unsatisfactory and, in fact, false. Among sexually reproducing animals a species represents a population or a group of populations the individuals of which are actually or potentially capable of interbreeding and producing fertile offspring and are reproductively isolated from other such groups. Variability is not excluded as long as the ability to interbreed is not disturbed. In genetic language the members of a species share a common gene pool. However, once the spectrum of variability is known, appearance can after all become a reasonable guide to identification, a comforting fact for the museum worker.

As mentioned elsewhere most butterflies do not move great distances and their populations are of a more or less localized nature. In the long haul, however, displacements do occur along with changes in the landscape and ecology. Populations may eventually become sufficiently removed from one another that exchanges of individuals become impossible. Populations distant from one another are described as allopatric. In these circumstances accumulations of new mutations are no longer exchanged between the separated populations and they give rise to visibly distinct geographic races, or subspecies. Sometimes tenuous links remain or connections are reestablished, in which case individuals of intermediate appearance are seen and the continued interfertility of the populations is demonstrated. If such phenotypically changing populations remain more or less contiguous, the limits of the geographic subspecies will not be well defined and changes in appearance will be gradual over a considerable geographic range, constituting a cline. Species in which a series of geographic races, or subspecies, can be recognized are said to be polytypic. Species that migrate frequently and over long distances fail to form them and remain monotypic.

When mutations accumulate that create a barrier to cross-fertility between populations, such reproductive isolation prevents all actual and potential hereditary exchange. This marks the beginning of a new species. Such mutations can be a number of small ones whose combined action confers hybrid sterility, chromosomal alterations that prevent the formation of viable germ cells, structural changes of the genitalia that preclude successful mating, discrepancies in the flight period (allochrony) so that adults do not meet, or even behavioral changes which fail to evoke an attentive response.

Variation Within Populations

Besides the variations that we see in polytypic species, that is, between geographic races, there are those that occur within single populations. Most striking, perhaps, are the differences, apart from genitalia, that commonly distinguish males from females. Such sexual dimorphism may express itself in wing shape, color, pattern, or any combination of these. Note, for instance, the conspicuous differences between males and females of *Colias, Anthocharis sara flora, Speyeria cybele pugetensis, Plebejus saepiolus,* and *Celestrina argiolus,* to select just a few. Superimposed on these sexual differences may be additional variations expressed only in one sex, such as in the females of *Colias* where white individuals appear with high frequency as well as yellow or orange ones like the males; also in the females there may be great variation in the amount of black markings, notably in *Colias occidentalis*. These polymorphisms, in which even the scarcest alternative form appears in more than one percent of the population, are determined by simple or multiple gene differences. Subtle quantitative variations are the most common. In populations of certain *Speyeria* species the spots of the ventral hindwing may be silvered, partially silvered, or unsilvered; in *Cercyonis* Woodnymphs the number and size of the underside "eyespots" show small differences; size variations of individuals are common within populations of *Plebejus acmon*. In short, variation is a characteristic of sexually reproducing populations.

The phenomenon of seasonal polyphenism appears in some species that produce more than one annual brood. In the spring generation of *Pieris napi marginalis* the veins on the underside of the hindwing are strongly outlined by black scales, whereas in the summer form these scales are lacking; in the yellow Woodnymphs of the genus *Coenonympha* the spring forms are darker beneath than those of the summer. Since these regularly recurring differences take place in the same populations and affect all individuals they are not attributable to genetic differences but are environmentally caused and have been traced to the effect of changing daylength on pupal development, of photoperiod rather than temperature as long thought.

Nomenclature

Human tribes have given names to animals and plants in almost all ages and cultures and with remarkable discrimination. The vocabularies of all languages have been enriched by them. The English word "butterfly" is known to have been used by the Saxon scribe Aelfric about 1000 A.D.; it is believed to refer to the butter-yellow color of the Common Sulfur. The French speak of "papillons" (derived from the Latin "papilio"), the Germans of "Schmetterlinge" or "Tagfalter". The butterfly we call a Mourning Cloak is known in Britain as the Camberwell Beauty; the Cabbage Butterfly and the Small White are, respectively, American and English names for the same species; so are the terms Spring Azure and Holly Blue. Many species are known even in the same region by different names. All of this illustrates a basic difficulty with vernacular or "common" names: they are not uniform and not internationally useful. Yet as native terms they are desirable and easily understood. In the case of mammals and birds they have been widely accepted but for butterflies they are in general use (at least in America, less so in Britain) mainly for common species or familiar groups, e.g., the Monarch, the Painted Lady, the Tiger Swallowtail, the Viceroy, Blues, Hairstreaks, Skippers. English-language names are available or have been devised for almost all of our butterflies and there is no reason why their acceptance and popular use should not be encouraged.

For scientific purposes names need greater precision, universality, and informative content. This has been achieved by the development of the International Code of Zoological Nomenclature which has its roots in the binomial system invented by the great Swedish naturalist Linnaeus (Carl von Linné). The tenth edition of his Systema Naturae (1758) has been adopted as the foundation for all subsequent naming practice, and the earliest names still in use come from this monumental work. Numerous additions and refinements to the system are spelled out in periodic revisions of the Code (see Blackwelder, 1967, for a thorough discussion). Taxonomic practice also observes rules for scientific description, the designation of "type specimens", and much more. The whole procedure has become a legalistically punctilious art, much savored by its practitioners. (This indiscretion may cost me some friends.)

Scientific names are Latin, the universal language of learning in Linnaeus' day, presumably still understood everywhere, and as a dead language offensive to no one. Among the formalized conventions category names above the level of species are capitalized. Family names end in -idae, superfamilies in -oidea, subfamily names in -inae. A species name is combined with and preceded by that of its genus (the binomial principle), and a subgenus name may be intercalated in parentheses. If a subspecies is to be indicated it follows the name of the species, making a trinomial. It is further customary (on first reference) to append the name of the author who described and named the species or subspecies, together with the date. An author's name in parentheses implies an original association with another genus. The use of the author's name and date avoids possible confusion with an identical name given at a later date to the same taxon by someone else or applied at some time to a closely related one; it also helps to locate the original description in the literature. The rule of priority requires the use of the oldest name for a taxonomic unit, later ones becoming synonyms. In the case of a polytypic species the species name is repeated to designate one of the geographic races (the "nominotypic" subspecies). Etymologically names may be descriptive, indicate a habitat or geographic affiliation, celebrate a mythological figure, honor or memorialize someone, or be composed in some more enigmatic way. The names of genera, species, and subspecies are always italicized. Some of the above points are illustrated in the following examples:

Lycaena (Chalceria) rubidus rubidus (Behr), 1866
Colias pelidne skinneri Barnes, 1897
Speyeria cybele pugetensis Chermock & Frechin, 1947

One may think that scientific names, because of their intended universality, have a quality of permanence, but this is unfortunately not true. Taxonomic revisions result in all kinds of changes, such as the discovery of older names which must replace synonyms, the reassignment of species names to subspecific status or vice versa, new name associations resulting from the splitting of a genus into two or more (including the elevation of a subgenus name to genus rank), etc. Disconcerting perhaps, but taxonomy is no more static than other scientific practices and all is in the interest of refined perceptions, the incorporation of new data, and the sanctity of the Code.

Many are troubled by the pronunciation of scientific names. In English-speaking countries the names are pretended to be English and are pronounced accordingly (which often takes some doing), but on the European Continent classical Latin pronunciation is employed. Blackwelder (1967) devotes eight pages to the problem!

Something should finally be said about the rule that requires the descriptions of newly named species or subspecies to be supplemented with the designation of type specimens. These serve as points of reference when the exact application of the name is in doubt, and such specimens are deposited in major museums for safekeeping. A single specimen is selected as the holotype; one of the opposite sex is called an allotype; additional specimens which help to demonstrate the range of variability are known as paratypes; all of which were used by the author in devising his description. A neotype is a specimen which replaces a lost holotype; a topotype is any specimen from the original type locality.

References:
(1) Blackwelder, Richard E. 1967. Taxonomy. A text and Reference Work. Wiley, N.Y. xiv, 698 pp.
(2) Ford, E. B. 1965. Ecological Genetics. 2nd ed. Methuen, London. xv, 335 pp.
(3) Hovanitz, William. 1958. Distribution of butterflies in the New World. *In* Zoogeography. Am. Assoc. Adv. Sci., Publ. No. 51: 321-368.
(4) Mayr, Ernst. 1963. Animal Species and Evolution. Harvard Univ. Press, Cambridge. xiv, 797 pp.
(5) Robinson, Roy. 1971. Lepidoptera Genetics. Pergamon Press, N.Y. ix, 687 pp.
(6) Shapiro, Arthur M. 1976. Seasonal polyphenism. Evolutionary Biology 9: 259-333.
(7) Shields, Oakely. 1976. Fossil butterflies and the evolution of Lepidoptera. J. Res. Lepid. 15: 132-146.

Collecting, Rearing and Photographing Butterflies

Learning to know our butterflies should include firsthand experience in the field, whether this be collecting, photographing, or simply close observation. For many building a collection has been the introduction to a life-long interest in biology, for others, unfortunately, only a temporary exercise in acquisitiveness. With ever more widespread recognition of the need for protecting and preserving nature, other ways of studying butterflies have gained in popularity. Among them are close observations and analyses of habits and behavior, detailed and complete explorations of life histories, attention to the characteristics of populations, and enquiry into the effects of environmental disturbance. As a substitute for specimens, as well as an excellent means for recording behavior and habitat, photography is highly recommended.

Fig. 28: A maestro at work. Good form with a net.

Collecting Techniques

A good net can be made or purchased. It should be of light weight and be provided with a handle of wood or aluminum tubing about three feet long; nets with sectional handles can be bought but add weight and offer no great advantage. The rim of the net should be of heavy gauge wire or preferably spring-steel banding and should be demountable so that the net bag can be changed; a diameter of about 15 inches is best. The bag, of fine-meshed, light-weight white nylon and twice as long as the rim diameter, should be reinforced at the rim by a muslin sleeve; its bottom should not come to a point but be bluntly rounded. In using a net it is rather fruitless to swing wildly after a butterfly in full flight; best wait for it to settle, approach cautiously, and with an easy motion sideswipe it into the net while using one hand to hold the net open (fig. 28). If the net is clapped down over a specimen (this may bend the frame if done carelessly), the butterfly should be allowed to fly into the raised end of the bag and the lifted net then closed by flipping the rim.

If the butterfly is not to be taken alive it should be dispatched quickly and humanely. Taking care that the wings are folded over the back, it may be stunned with a quick pinch of the thorax. Small specimens are easily damaged by such handling and the method too often leaves the butterfly alive and injured. Quick transfer to a killing jar, charged with a rapidly acting lethal chemical, is better. The jar should be wide-mouthed, not unnecessarily large, and provided with a bakelite or plastic screw-cap (a metal one corrodes). I prefer two sizes, one that is 3¼ inches deep and has a cap 1½ inches in diameter, another 4¼ inches deep with a 2¼ inch cap (fig. 29).

The standard and most effective killing agent is potassium cyanide, a deadly poison to be handled with great care and kept out of the reach of small children. Cyanide jars can be purchased but are easily made. The older method is to mix the granular cyanide with dry sawdust placed in the bottom of the jar and to cover this with a layer of plaster of paris; when the plaster has thoroughly dried it is kept free of later absorbed moisture by a snugly fitted disc of blotting paper. Jars so made are heavy and cannot be recharged. A better way is to place the cyanide into a hollowed cork fitted to the jar cap. The original cap liner should first be removed and replaced by one of firm cardboard cut to shape and solidly attached with airplane ("Duco") cement. A good quality cork, one-half to three-quarters inch thick and in diameter just less than that of the jar opening, should be drilled with a large hole that will contain the cyanide; the two surfaces of the cork should be ground smooth with sandpaper. One surface should then be covered with a patch of fine-meshed bolting silk firmly stretched over the hole and attached with cement; a quarter-inch of overlap should be slitted and bound to the side of the cork with cloth adhesive tape. The cork is then turned over and the hole packed with cyanide. Finally the jar lid, its lining thickly smeared with fresh cement, is inverted over the cork which is then firmly centered and left to dry. The finished jar should be clearly labelled "Poison/Cyanide" and the date added; annual replacement of the cork will keep the jar well charged.

Safer in the hands of children are jars charged with ethyl acetate. This is a volatile fluid which must be replaced every few hours from a stock bottle carried in the field. It can be poured onto cotton or felt attached to the jar lid.

The open killing jar is inserted into the net and over the specimen, then carefully removed and capped. A well-charged jar acts in seconds, but specimens should be left for fifteen or twenty minutes to guard against recovery. Butterflies whose wings have flipped downward should have these carefully turned back before they stiffen, as the upperside scales are easily rubbed off. The accumulation of too many specimens in one jar also damages them. Butterflies should always be handled with forceps.

At convenient intervals during collecting, the specimens should be "papered". This protects them prior to mounting and affords a means of indefinite storing. They are placed individually or in twos into small envelopes or paper "triangles" (fig. 30). I prefer 2½ x 3½ inch drug envelopes with broadside flaps (left unsealed); these lend themselves to systematic filing. "Triangles" can be folded (as shown in the illustration) from pads of five-inch square paper or other convenient size. The essential field data, or a code number that refers to a notebook entry, should be written on each envelope or triangle. Specimens without data are of no value. The minimum information includes place of capture, altitude, date, and the initials of the collector. Additional useful information includes habitat, plant on which found (especially for egg-laying females), weather, etc. If carefully boxed, papered specimens will keep indefinitely and can be mounted at any future time.

If not mounted while fresh (usually within twenty-four hours), papered specimens must first be "relaxed". This is accomplished by placing the envelopes

Fig. 29: Killing jars charged with cyanide.

into an airtight box (a plastic food-storage box, perhaps 7 x 5 x 3 inches, is fine), the bottom of which contains a layer of wetted sand (fig. 30). The envelopes should be elevated above the sand on a galvanized screen and left for three to four days. A common mistake is to attempt mounting too soon. One may guard against mold by adding some naphthalene flakes to the sand.

Mounting is done on spreading boards, which can be bought or made (fig. 31). They consist essentially of two narrow and parallel panels of soft, fine-grained wood about fifteen inches long, separated by a gap to accommodate the body of the insect. These are mounted on end-pieces to give them proper height and rigidity, and the bottom of the gap is lined with a strip of cork to hold the pin supporting the butterfly. The panels should be cut so that the top sides, away from the gap, angle upward about five degrees; this forestalls drooping of the wings if they later absorb any moisture. Also, if one of the panels is attached to the endpieces by movable brackets, the width of the gap can be adjusted to fit various body sizes.

Mounting is begun by inserting an "insect pin" perpendicularly through the center of the butterfly's thorax, consistently leaving one-fourth of its length projecting above the body. Insect pins must be purchased. They are about 1½ inches in length, rust-proof, of black japanned finish or stainless steel, and come in various thicknesses; sizes 1 and 3 are best suited for butterflies (reserve size 1 for small ones). The pin bearing the butterfly should be pushed straight down into the cork of the spreading board until the bases of the wings are at panel level. The wings are then maneuvered into position and held down until dry with strips of strong paper, an art that wants care and practice. The positioning is accomplished by inserting the point of an insect pin behind a strong vein and in step-wise moves advancing the wings until the inner margins of the two forewings form a straight line at right angles to the body axis and the hindwings are brought up as shown in the figures. The paper strips (best cut from architect's tracing linen, which does not tear and is very smooth) should be held in place with glass-headed steel pins; these are 1¼ inches long, very sharp and strong, and easy on the fingers. It is best to use two strips on each side so that the wings are firmly set and protectively covered. One should practice on medium-sized or large butterflies. After the wings have been set, insect pins are used to hold the antennae in place and to support the abdomen. Specimens mounted upside-down to show the underside should have the legs pressed against the body by placing a strip across the thorax; a small hole in the center of such a strip allows it to pass over the head of the pin. Data labels should be pinned beside the specimens. Butterflies mounted fresh may take a week to dry; papered ones that have been relaxed are usually dry in a couple of days; a good test of dryness is the rigidity of the abdomen.

After the specimens are dry the labels should be transferred to the specimen pin. They should be small in size, of high quality heavy paper, written with indelible black ink and a fine pen-point, or printed with diamond-point type (fig. 32). Dates are best indicated in the form "4 Aug 76", not 4/8/76 which can be read April 8.

Mounted specimens are stored in boxes or cabinet drawers (fig. 33). The least expensive boxes are made of cardboard and have hinged or removable lids; they are ordinarily 13" x 9" or 12" x 10¼" and have an

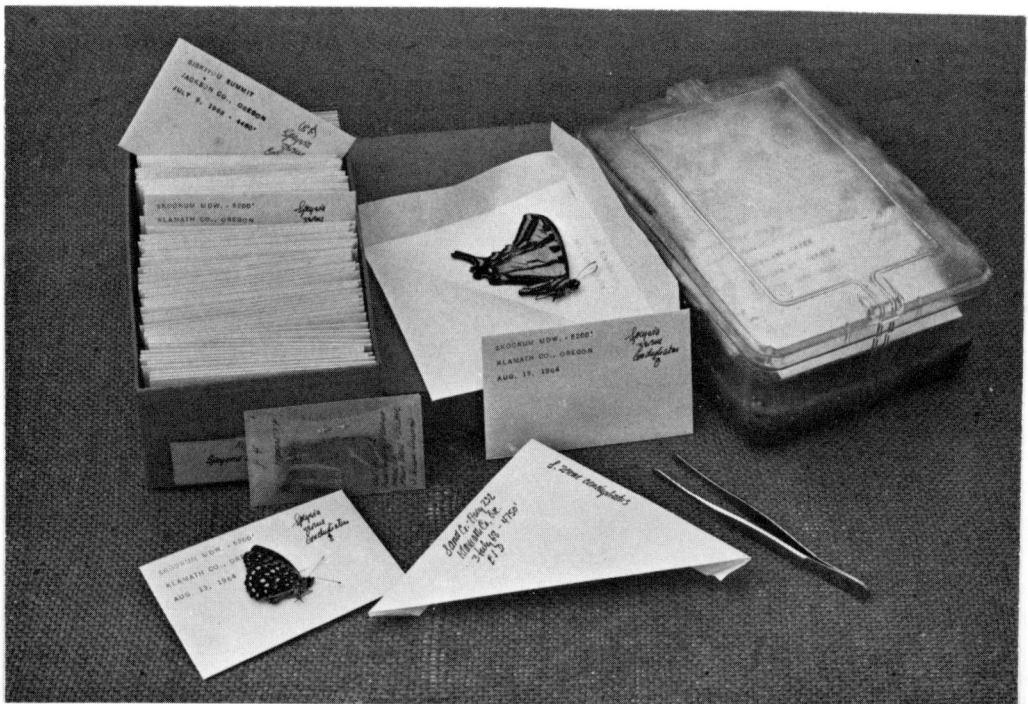

Fig. 30: Papered specimens and relaxing box.

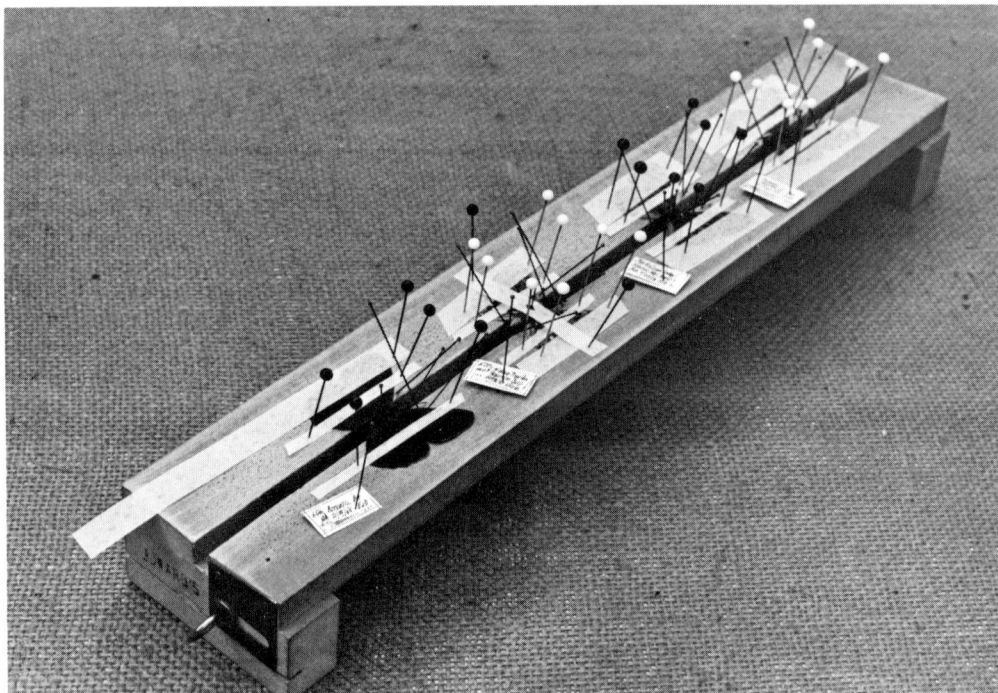

Fig. 31: Spreading board.

inside depth of 2 inches; the bottoms are lined with cork or polyethylene foam for pinning. Wooden boxes of similar dimensions are sturdier and give better protection, as the lids are fitted against a wooden liner and, if well built, all corners are tightly joined. Glass-topped cabinet drawers, 19" x 17" x 2½" (California Academy size), are the most elaborate and expensive form of storage, standardly used by museums; their large size allows the supplementary use of inserted "unit trays", small cardboard boxes for easy shifting of specimens. Collections should be protected against Dermestes, small beetles whose larvae are very destructive to museum specimens. Tightly fitted boxes help to keep them out, but they may be introduced with infected specimens. Their presence can be recognized by brown dust underneath a mounted butterfly, in which case the specimen should be destroyed or a drop of lighter fluid applied to the body to kill the intruder. Museum collections are periodically fumigated and cabinet drawers fitted with packets of repellent.

For display purposes butterflies can be put up in Riker Mounts, shallow cardboard boxes filled with absorbent cotton and fitted with glass lids. In preparing specimens for these, they are best spread on a flat sheet of cork, upside-down and with the legs pressed against the body, after which the specimen pin is removed from the body. Since the colors of butterflies fade on prolonged exposure to light, Riker Mounts should be stored in the dark when not being exhibited.

Genitalial Preparations

As discussed elsewhere, differences in the structure of the male genitalia may be important in separating certain otherwise very similar species. When these differences are not externally apparent after simply brushing away the adjacent scales and terminal fragments of the body wall, the chitinous genital capsule must be removed. This is not difficult but requires the aid of a binocular dissecting microscope. The abdomen or its posterior portion is broken off and soaked for a few moments in 95% alcohol. It is then transferred to a vial of 10% potassium hydroxide and left overnight; this treatment digests the soft tissues. After rinsing in water the abdomen is next placed into a dissecting dish (Syracuse watch glass), covered with water, and set under the microscope. The genital capsule is pressed out of the softened abdominal wall with the help of a dissecting needle and a fine-pointed (watchmaker's) forceps. After picking away any resid-

Fig. 32: Specimen labels and genitalial vial (lower right).

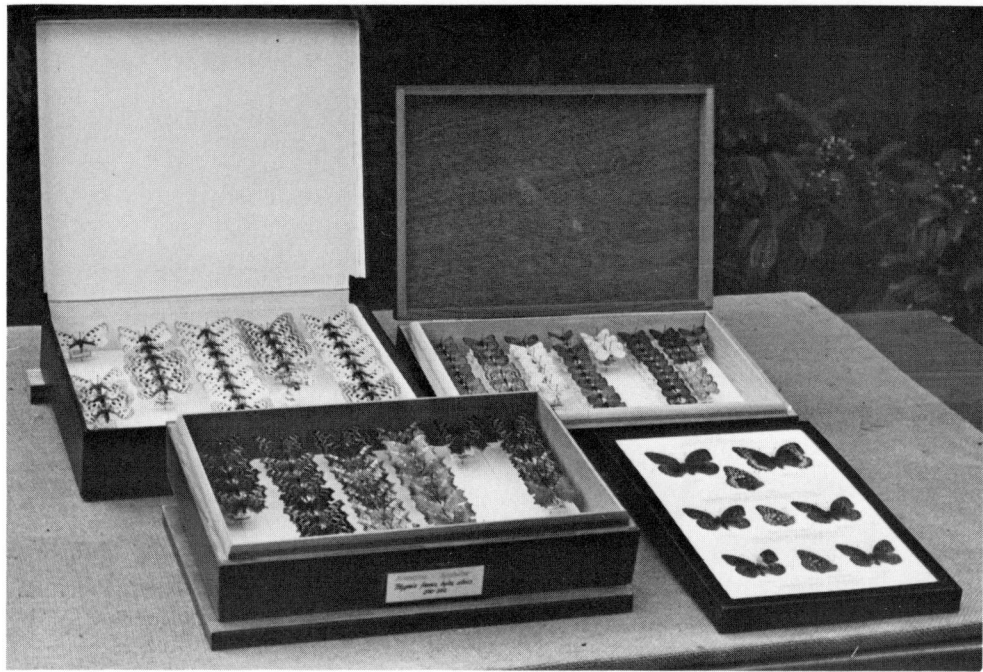

Fig. 33: Storage boxes. Riker Mount at lower right.

ual soft tissue, hairs, and scales, it is ready for study. The genital capsule is best stored in a tiny stoppered vial ("genitalial vial") containing a drop of glycerine, from which it can be removed at any later time for further examination (fig. 32). The vial can be mounted on an insect pin passed through the stopper, cross-labelled to the mounted butterfly, and pinned beside it.

Rearing

Most species of butterflies can be easily reared from collected eggs or larvae, or from eggs laid in captivity by gravid and mated females. What is needed is only an ample supply of the larval foodplant and an enclosure to prevent escape. A breeding cage with sides of fine-meshed wire screen and a door or removable top can be easily made (fig. 34). More simply, large muslin-covered jars can be used. Sprigs of the foodplant should be fresh, regularly replenished, and set in wet sand rather than water into which the larvae may drop and be drowned. When the time for pupation nears, twigs or small sticks should be provided for suspension of the chrysalids.

Fig. 34: Breeding cage.

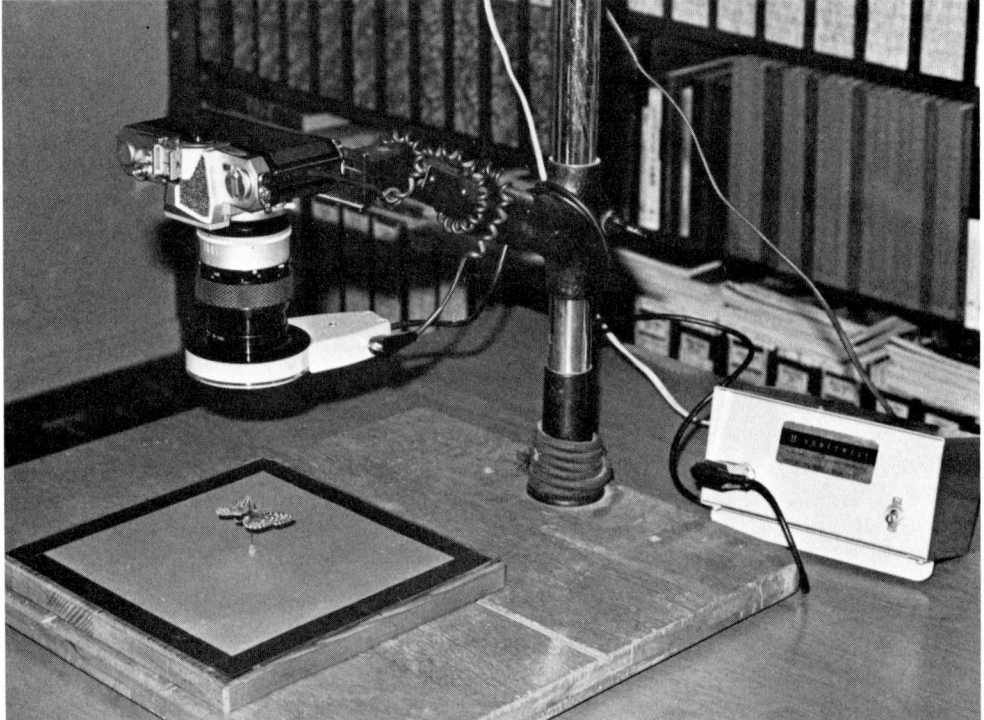

Fig. 35: Photographic set-up using a macro lens and an electronic flash ring-light.

To prevent harming young larvae they should be handled with care, preferably moved with a small camel's-hair brush. Many field-collected larvae are parasitized and one will find wasps rather than butterflies hatching from their chrysalids. Hibernating larvae or pupae should be protected against dessication by temporary housing in small boxes lined with moss or paper tissue that is occasionally dampened.

Photography

Photographing butterflies in the field calls for patience as well as quick and skilled action at the right moment. A large and heavy camera is unsuited to the purpose and a tripod is of limited usefulness. A good hand-held 35 mm. camera that allows through-the-lens focussing and metering is ideal; it should be equipped with extension tubes and a 200 mm. telephoto lens, or better, an equivalent zoom lens. With such a system even a small butterfly can fill the camera field without getting too close. Since depth of focus is important and the camera is hand-held, a film of high sensitivity and good resolving quality is needed, thus permitting the use of a small diaphragm aperture at fast shutter speed, such as f 16 x 125th second. This requirement is well met by Kodak Ektachrome 400 or by Tri-X for black-and-white pictures.

For the photography of mounted specimens a more convenient optical system is a standard 50 mm. lens used with extension tubes, bellows, or close-up lenses, or better, a high resolution macro lens with or without an extension ring. The camera should be mounted on a copy stand furnished with a means of even illumination. The black-and-white photographs on the plates were made with a Nikkor 55 mm. auto-micro lens, an electronic flash front-mounted ring-light (Honeywell Prox-O-Lite 7), a diaphragm stop of f 22, and a shutter speed of 1/60th second, using Panatomic-X film; shadowing was reduced to a minimum by pinning the specimen over a silver background (which comes out white in printing) (fig. 35).

Sources of Entomological Supplies and Equipment:
   (1) BioQuip Products, P.O. Box 61, Santa Monica, California 90406
   (2) Carolina Biological Supply Co., Powell Laboratories Division, Gladstone, Oregon 97027
   (3) Ward's Natural Science Establishment, Inc., P.O. Box 1749, Monterey, California 93940.

Systematic Account

Family PAPILIONIDAE

The family Papilionidae is world-wide in distribution and contains some six hundred species, most of which are tropical; twenty-seven have been recorded in North America north of Mexico. Included in this family are the large and showy Swallowtails (many of which are not tailed!), the giant "Bird-wings" of the tropics, the mainly mountain-inhabiting Parnassians, and a unique tailless and possibly primitive member of the family, *Baronia brevicornis,* known only from Mexico. While most Swallowtails inhabit tropical climates, *Papilio machaon* is able to live in the subarctic; Parnassians may be found in the far North and at high elevations elsewhere.

Certain structural features characterize the Papilionidae. The forelegs are fully developed and bear a spur (epiphysis) on the tibial segment. The cervical sclerites are joined beneath the neck. The hind wing (except in *Baronia*) possesses only one anal vein (emanating from the wing base and not the discal cell). The larvae of the genus *Papilio* are provided on the prothorax with an osmeterium, an eversible forked organ that emits a pungent odor and is presumably defensive in function. The pupae of the Swallowtails are roughly angled, resemble brown or gray bark, and are attached by a caudal silken button and a silken girdle slung around the midsection. In Parnassians the pupae are enclosed in a silken cocoon and found among debris on the surface of the ground; after mating, the adult females possesses a rigid pouch (sphragis) below the tip of the abdomen, a waxy structure secreted by the male.

The seven species of Swallowtails found in Oregon can be considered as falling into three groups: *Papilio oregonius, zelicaon,* and *indra* are members of the *machaon* group (named after the first named member, a European butterfly); *Papilio rutulus, multicaudata,* and *eurymedon* belong to the *glaucus* group (the Eastern Tiger Swallowtail); *Battus philenor* represents a genus whose larvae feed on Aristolochiaceae and whose closest relatives are tropical. There are two species of *Parnassius: clodius* and *phoebus.*

References:

(1) Ehrlich, Paul R. 1958. The comparative morphology, phylogeny and higher classification of the butterflies (Lepidoptera: Papilionoidea). Univ. Kansas Sci. Bull. 39 (8): 305-370.

(2) Munroe, Eugene. 1961. The classification of the Papilionidae (Lepidoptera). Canad. Entomologist, Suppl. 17, 51 pp.

(3) Slansky Jr., Frank. 1972. Latitudinal gradients in species diversity of the New World swallowtail butterflies. J. Res. Lepid. 11: 201-217.

Papilio oregonius Edwards, 1876
The Oregon Swallowtail

Plate 1, fig. 1. Map 1.

This strikingly beautiful Swallowtail, recently declared the State Insect, fittingly heads the list of Oregon butterflies. A true native of the Northwest, it was first described from a specimen collected about 1875 near The Dalles by Henry Edwards, an eminent actor of the San Francisco stage, friend of John Muir, enthusiastic lepidopterist, as well as trustee and vice president of the San Francisco Academy of Sciences. He loaned this specimen to William H. Edwards of Coalburgh, West Virginia, the foremost student of American butterflies (no relative), for description and naming. On June 6, 1977 the United States Postal Service brought this splendid butterfly to the attention of all Americans through issuance of a postage stamp, one of a set of four showing for the first time selected American butterflies in color.

The Oregon Swallowtail is at home in the lower sage-brush canyons of the Columbia River and its tributaries, including the Snake River drainage. Its range extends northward into Washington and British Columbia. The larvae feed on tarragon sage (*Artemesia dracunculus*), a most unusual foodplant for butterflies and particularly for Swallowtails of the *machaon* group, which normally live on Umbelliferae. The adults are attracted to thistles, but being wary and strong fliers are not easily captured. There are two broods, the first flying from end of April to June, and the second from July to end of September.

The spherical eggs of *oregonius*, laid on the foliage of the foodplant, are pearly white in color, pitted on the surface, and hatch in six days. The larvae pass through five instars. In the first three they are black, except for a yellow saddle-like patch across the sixth and seventh segments, and roughened with several rows of tubercles. In the fourth and fifth instars the tubercles disappear and the body color changes to pale green, or bluish green, with each segment crossed by a black stripe followed by diagonal black dashes that are separated by yellow spots. The first thoracic segment has a fold that conceals the eversible osmeteria which are protruded when the larva is disturbed. The total larval period lasts thirty to thirty-five days. The pupa, attached by a silken girdle and terminal button to the stem of the plant, and with protuberances on the head and thorax, is at first light green, later turning mottled grayish brown. It hatches in ten to fifteen days, except in the second generation, where overwintering extends the pupal life to eight or nine months.

This species is often confused with *Papilio zelicaon*. The two may be separated by the following characters:

P. oregonius	*P. zelicaon*
Thorax largely yellow beneath	Thorax largely black beneath
Side of abdomen yellow with narrow black stripe	Side of abdomen black with narrow yellow stripe
FW below with large flash of yellow in basal half of cell	FW below black in basal half of cell
FW below with strong yellow scaling inward of marginal yellow band	FW below with slight or no yellow scaling inward of marginal yellow band
HW above with marginal yellow spots large and tending to join	HW above with marginal yellow spots usually smaller and well separated
FW tending to be angled outward toward apex	FW not angled outward toward apex
Larvae feed on tarragon sage	Larvae feed on various Umbelliferae

References:

(1) Brown, F. Martin. 1975. The types of the papilionid butterflies named by William Henry Edwards. Trans. Am. Entom. Soc. 101: 1-31.

(2) Newcomer, E. J. 1964. Life histories of *Papilio indra* and *P. oregonius*. J. Res. Lepid. 3: 49-54.

(3) Perkins, Stephen F., Edwin M. Perkins & F. Stuart Shininger. 1968. Illustrated life history and notes on *Papilio oregonius*. J. Lepid. Soc. 22: 53-65.

Papilio zelicaon Lucas, 1852
Zelicaon Swallowtail

Plate 1, fig. 2. Map 2.

Among the Western members of the *"machaon"* group, the Zelicaon Swallowtail is the commonest and most widespread, ranging from British Columbia and Alberta to California, Arizona, and New Mexico. It occurs throughout Oregon, but is generally not very abundant. In the Willamette Valley it is the first Swallowtail to appear in the spring, and since it breeds continuously it may be found from March to September. This butterfly has the habit of congregating on hilltops, where it is most readily found. The significance of this "hilltopping" has been debated, but the careful observations and experiments of Shields and Scott argue persuasively in favor of a territorial behavior associated with courtship and mating. At such sites a patrolling flight pattern and aggressiveness towards other males are easily observed.

The differences between *P. zelicaon* and the very similar *P. oregonius* have been given in the discussion of *oregonius*. The larvae of *zelicaon* feed on various Umbelliferae. When fully grown, they are green, with orange-spotted black stripes crossing each segment.

References:

(1) Guppy, Richard. 1953. *Papilio zelicaon* and hilltops. Lepid. News 7: 43-44.

(2) Guppy, Richard. 1969. Further observations on "hilltopping" in *Papilio zelicaon*. J. Res. Lepid. 8: 105-117.

(3) Shields, Oakley. 1967. Hilltopping. An ecological study of summit congregation behavior of butterflies on a southern California hill. J. Res. Lepid. 6: 69-178.

(4) Scott, James A. 1968. Hilltopping as a mating mechanism to aid the survival of low density species. J. Res. Lepid. 7: 191-204.

Papilio indra indra Reakirt, 1866
Indra Swallowtail

Plate 1, fig. 3. Map 3.

The Indra Swallowtail, the third member of the *"machaon"* group in Oregon, is easily recognized by its short or absent tails, the reduced yellow coloration on both fore and hindwings, and the satin sheen of the black scaling on the underside. Like *P. oregonius*, its restricted distribution and relative rarity make it a prized catch. On the wing from April to June or July, it may be sought in the ravines of the Deschutes and Metolius Rivers, in similar habitats of the Blue Mountains and Wallowas, along the Snake River and its tributaries, in the canyons of Steens Mt., and in the Siskiyous of southwestern Oregon.

The males have a rapid and erratic flight but frequently settle and congregate at the sides of streams, springs, and puddles, particularly in draws and mountain canyons between two and seven thousand feet altitude. Females tend to remain on the higher ridges and are hard to find. The black larvae, decorated with pink transverse bands, feed on umbelliferous plants, especially *Lomatium*.

References:

(1) Newcomer, E. J. 1964. Life histories of *Papilio indra* and *P. oregonius*. J. Res. Lepid. 3: 49-54.

(2) Emmel, John F. & Thomas C. Emmel. 1968. The population biology and life history of *Papilio indra martini*. J. Lepid. Soc. 22: 46-52. (*P. i. martini* is a subspecies of the southern California deserts.)

Papilio rutulus rutulus Lucas, 1852
Western Tiger Swallowtail

Plate 2, fig. 1. Map 4.

Common throughout Oregon and generally abundant, the Western Tiger Swallowtail closely resembles its Eastern counterpart, *Papilio glaucus*. Unlike the latter, however, which has two female forms, one of which is dark (melanic), the female of *P. rutulus* is always yellow like the male. A leisurely flyer, it is on the wing from early spring to late fall and a common sight in town gardens, in the countryside, and in the mountains. It ranges from British Columbia to California, and eastward to the far edge of the Rocky Mountains. Lincoln Brower has studied in close detail the morphological and ecological relationships of *Papilio rutulus* to other members of the *"glaucus* group": *glaucus, multicaudatus,* and *eurymedon*.

The green larva, which possesses eye-like spots on the swollen third thoracic segment, is usually concealed in the rolled-up leaf of its foodplant, which may be maple, aspen, alder, poplar, cottonwood, or willow. The dark brown chrysalis is covered with irregular granulations.

References:

(1) Brower, Lincoln P. 1958. Larval foodplant specificity in butterflies of the *Papilio glaucus* group. Lepid. News 12: 103-114.

(2) Brower, Lincoln P. 1959. Speciation in butterflies of the *Papilio glaucus* group. i. Morphological relationships and hybridization. Evolution 13: 40-63. — ii. Ecological relationships and interspecific sexual behavior. Evolution 13: 212-228.

Papilio multicaudata Kirby, 1884
Two-tailed Tiger Swallowtail

Plate 2, fig. 3. Map 5.

This lordly Swallowtail, formerly known as *Papilio daunus,* is Oregon's largest butterfly. Though superficially similar to *Papilio rutulus,* it is readily distinguished by its double tails, the generally larger size, and the narrower black bands. A soaring and powerful flyer, it easily evades capture. Ranging from British Columbia to Mexico and eastward to the high plains beyond the Rockies, in Oregon this Swallowtail is found east of the Cascades and in the Siskiyous. Double-brooded, it flies from May to August, frequenting sunny canyons and the banks of streams, often in company with *P. rutulus.*

The apple-green larva, somewhat resembling that of *rutulus,* possesses thoracic "eyespots" that are club-shaped; behind these are yellow and black transverse bands and dorsal rows of small blue points. The foodplants are chokecherry and serviceberry, but the larva has also been found on willow and ash. The dark green chrysalis is stout and mottled. A good account of the life history has been given by Pronin.

References:
(1) Pronin, George F. 1955. Notes on the life-history and methods of rearing the giant Tiger Swallowtail, *Papilio multicaudatus.* Lepid. News 9: 137-140.
(2) See under *P. rutulus.*

Papilio eurymedon Lucas, 1852
White Tiger Swallowtail

Plate 2, fig. 2. Map 6.

Papilio eurymedon, the White, or Pale Tiger Swallowtail, generally resembles *Papilio rutulus,* but has a whitish instead of yellow ground color and broader black bands; in females the ground color tends often to be creamish. *Eurymedon* is almost as common as *rutulus* and occurs in mountainous wooded country throughout the State, its total range extending from British Columbia to southern California and eastward to the Rockies. Also double-brooded, it flies from May to August, usually in company with *rutulus.*

The soft-green larva is much like that of *P. rutulus* but has smaller "eyespots" and a purple head. Unlike *rutulus* it feeds on Rhamnaceae (*Ceanothus,* cascara, buckthorn) and certain Rosaceae (ocean-spray, hawthorn). The chrysalis is wood-brown in color and shaped like that of *rutulus.*

References:
See under *Papilio rutulus.*

Battus philenor hirsuta (Skinner), 1908
Pipevine Swallowtail

Plate 2, fig. 4. Map 7.

Until recently there has been no record of the Pipevine Swallowtail in Oregon. This splendid butterfly, blackish-blue and iridescent, is well known in the East and across the central and southern Midwest to Arizona. The subspecies *hirsuta,* which is smaller than the eastern race and has a hairy body, is established in the San Francisco Bay and Sacramento Valley regions of central California. Both forms are closely associated with *Aristolochia* (pipevine), the principal larval foodplant. The Oregon record is a unique report, given to me by Robert M. Pyle, of a fresh *philenor* caught on the radiator of a car driving southward into the coastal town of North Bend in Coos County. If the species is a resident of this region, which appears likely but should be verified, there is probably some cultivated *Aristolochia* in the area, or its larvae feed on the closely related wild ginger (*Asarum*) which grows profusely in the nearby forested habitat.

On the underside the outer half of the hindwings sparkles with iridescent blue-green scaling that encloses a row of seven large reddish orange spots; a series of creamy white spots lies along the margin. In the male a fold along the inner edge of the hindwings contains androconial scales. Females are dorsally not as glossy as males. There is evidence that this Swallowtail is distasteful and avoided by predators; among eastern butterflies this affords protection to several mimicking species.

The rough-surfaced, spherical egg of the Pipevine Swallowtail is russet in color. The larva is bluish black and ornamented with fleshly orange tubercles. The green or brown pupa is wide at the middle and strongly sculptured.

Parnassius clodius Menetries, 1855
The Clodius Parnassian

Plate 3, figs. 1, 4. Map 8.

This handsome Parnassian, in one or another of its many named subspecies, ranges from central California to Alaska and eastward to western Montana and Wyoming. A mountain butterfly, like all Parnassians, it is abundant in the Coast Range, the Cascades, the Siskiyous, and the Blue Mountains, flying along roadsides and in forest openings from May to late summer. Its leisurely manner of flight and frequent settling makes it easy to observe. The populations in western Oregon and the Cascades may be referred to the subspecies *P. c. claudianus* Stichel, 1907, which also extends into western Washington. Those of northeastern Oregon are close to *P. c. altaurus* Dyar, 1903, which occurs in Idaho; in this race the hindwing spots and submarginal dark markings tend to be reduced. One should note, however, that individual variability within Parnassian populations is considerable.

In the male Parnassian the abdomen is thickly covered with yellowish hair, while in the female the body is dorsally naked and shiny black. Females that have mated are adorned with a sphragis, a waxy pouch below the end of the body that is secreted during copulation by the male, and whose color and shape are species specific; in *clodius* it is large and white.

The eggs of Parnassians are strewn on the ground near the larval foodplant, which in the case of *clodius* is bleeding heart (*Dicentra*). The mature larvae are flattened and somewhat slug-shaped, covered with velvety black down and decorated with yellow spots on each segment. Before reaching maturity the young larvae hibernate and complete their growth the following spring. Unlike other butterflies (except Skippers), the pupae, smooth and brownish in color, are encased in a loose cocoon and are found among debris on the ground.

Parnassius clodius and the next species, *Parnassius phoebus*, are often confused. The distinctions are as follows;

P. clodius	*P. phoebus*
Antennae wholly black	Antennae with alternate white and black rings
Spots in discal cell of FW no darker than other dark markings	Spots in discal cell of FW much darker than other dark markings
Middle dark spot in discal cell of FW bar-shaped and extending fully across cell	Middle dark spot in discal cell of FW roundish and not extending to bottom of cell
Sphragis of female large and white	Sphragis of female small and dark brown

Parnassius phoebus Fabricius, 1793
The Phoebus Parnassian

Plate 3, figs. 2, 3, 5. Map 9.

Parnassius phoebus, divided into many subspecies, occurs in both Eurasia (the Alps, the Urals, and across Siberia) and North America (from Alaska to California and eastward through the Rockies). The North American populations were at one time covered under the name *P. smintheus,* a term properly reserved for a subspecies of *phoebus* found in the Canadian Rockies. Two geographic races of *phoebus* occur in Oregon, and both can be distinguished from *Parnassius clodius* by the features tabulated under *clodius.*

Parnassius phoebus xanthus Ehrmann, 1918 (The Creamish Parnassian) inhabits the Blue Mountains and Wallowas of northeastern Oregon, where it flies together with *P. clodius.* Apart from the distinguishing features already mentioned, it is smaller than *clodius,* has a creamish ground color, less amount of translucent wing area, and the females are more strongly patterned. Northward this race grades into the Canadian subspecies *smintheus* Doubleday, 1847.

Parnassius phoebus sternitzkyi McDunnough, 1936 (Sternitzky's Parnassian) is geographically remote and well isolated from *xanthus,* flying at high altitudes in the Siskyou Mountains of southwestern Oregon and in northern California. It is larger in size, whitish in ground color, and has a broader marginal clear zone. Unlike *xanthus,* also, the tips of the veins are not strongly blackened and the forewing margins lack the prominent white identations between the vein tips (most noticeable in males). Because of its restricted range this is a relatively little known Parnassian.

The larvae of *P. phoebus* feed on stonecrop (*Sedum*). Not unlike those of *clodius,* the mature larvae are also velvety black and yellow-spotted in color, hibernate in an early instar, and complete their life cycle the following summer.

Reference:

(1) Ferris, Clifford D. 1976. A proposed revision of non-Arctic *Parnassius phoebus* Fabricius in North America (Papilionidae). J. Res. Lepid. 15: 1-22.

Family PIERIDAE

World-wide in distribution, the Pieridae comprise some thousand species of small to medium sized butterflies, of which about fifty occur in the United States and Canada. Most are white, yellow, or orange in ground color, simply patterned, and often black margined. The sexes are usually dissimilar, and seasonal diphenism is also common. Closely related to the Papilionidae, the forelegs are fully developed but lack tibial spurs. The first median vein of the forewings arises from the third radial vein instead of the discal cell, and the hindwings possess two anal veins. Unlike other butterflies, the wing pigments are derived from uric acid wastes of the body, leucopterin accounting for the white color, xanthopterin for yellow, and a mixture of xanthopterin and erythropterin for orange. The green patterns on the underside of some pierids are due to intimate mixtures of black and yellow scales.

While most butterflies of this family fly in sunny fields, clearings, meadows, or desert flats, some, such as the Pine White and the Margined White, are forest dwellers. Certain southern pierids, notably members of the genera *Phoebus* and *Ascia,* are migratory and annually appear in dense flights. Though butterflies are seldom of agricultural importance, the Cabbage Butterfly is a notorious exception. Alfalfa fields may be infested by *Colias eurytheme,* and *Neophasia menapia* is occasionally damaging to stands of fir and pine.

The eggs of pierids are elongate and ribbed. The larvae are green and slender, often longitudinally striped, but otherwise not markedly ornamented. The Whites, Orange-tips, and Marbles feed on various crucifers and the Sulfurs on legumes. The pupae possess a conical forward projection, and like those of Swallowtails, are suspended by a silken girdle and a caudal cremaster.

Neophasia menapia tau (Scudder), 1861
Pine White

Plate 4, fig. 1. Map 10.

A common butterfly in coniferous forests throughout Oregon, the Pine White becomes abundant in late summer, flying from July to October. The Pacific Coast subspecies is somewhat smaller than its counterpart in the Rocky Mountain states (*N. menapia menapia*). It is a primitive pierid, closely related to certain genera of the American tropics. The males are pure white in ground color, but the females have a creamish cast and a heavier black pattern on the hindwings which are also attractively tinged along the margins and anal veins with orange or red, particularly on the underside.

While delicate appearing in flight, these butterflies often swarm amidst the higher branches of pine and fir trees, which, in fact, their larvae may on occasion defoliate. Severe outbreaks are on record for different regions of the Northwest, in which the destruction of ponderosa pine reached levels up to twenty-five percent of the stand.

The flask-shaped eggs, laid in rows along pine needles, are emerald green, fluted along the sides, and decorated with a circle of bead-like knobs at the upper end. The dark green and cylindrical larvae have a white band on each side and on the back, and possess two short anal tails. They feed on the needles of Douglas fir, ponderosa pine, and lodge-pole pine. When mature they may be seen dangling by silken threads as they drop to the base of the trees to pupate. The slender chrysalids are dark green and marked with white stripes.

Pieris (Pontia) beckerii Edwards, 1871
Becker's White

Plate 4, fig. 2, 3. Map 11.

Becker's White is a common and widespread pierid of the central and eastern Oregon plains and semi-arid brushlands, and is only rarely found, probably as a stray, west of the Cascades. In its total range it extends from southern British Columbia to California and eastward to the western slopes of the Rockies. Being double-brooded, it flies from April to September.

In addition to the marginal and submarginal rows of black spots, which in the female are heavier and extend to the hindwings, a distinctive bold and quadrate spot with white center lies at the end of the forewing discal cell. Beneath, the veins of the hindwing, covered by yellow scales, are heavily bordered with green, a pattern partially interrupted at the middle of the wing by a white band. An early spring brood of Becker's White (form "pseudochloridice") is smaller in size; the underside vein borders appear broader and more solidly green.

In the open, Becker's White has a rapid and irregular flight pattern, making it difficult to capture. Great numbers may, however, congregate along roadsides on wild mustard and other crucifers, the larval foodplants, when they are easily taken.

The eggs, laid on crucifers, are spindle-shaped and longitudinally ridged. The greenish-white larva is segmentally marked with transverse orange bands and is stippled with gray dots and black bristles. The smooth, gray pupa has whitish wing-cases.

References:

(1) Hovanitz, William. 1962. The distribution of the species of the genus *Pieris* in North America. J. Res. Lepid. 1: 73-83.

(2) Chang, Vincent C. S. 1963. Quantitative analysis of certain wing and genitalia characters of *Pieris* in western North America. J. Res. Lepid. 2: 97-125.

(3) Brown, F. Martin. 1973. The types of the pierid butterflies named by William Henry Edwards. Trans. Am. Ent. Soc. 99: 29-118. (Brown treats Becker's White as a subspecies of the Asiatic *Pontia chloridice*.)

(4) McHenry, Paddy. 1962. The generic, specific and lower category names of the nearctic butterflies. Part 1 — The genus *Pieris*. J. Res. Lepid. 1: 63-71.

Pieris (Pontia) sisymbrii sisymbrii Boisduval, 1852
California White

Plate 4, fig. 4. Map 12.

Pieris sisymbrii ranges from the Pacific states to the eastern slope of the Rockies. In Oregon it is usually found on dry open ground and rocky slopes east of the Cascades and in the Siskiyous. Seldom numerous, it exists in isolated populations and is probably two-brooded, flying from April to June and again in July and August.

A small pierid, with spotting pattern similar to that of other members of the *Pontia* group, the veins on the upperside of the forewing are narrowly outlined in black. Beneath, the veins of the hindwing have well defined greenish-brown borders; near the middle of the wing these borders diverge slightly to produce markings like the prongs of arrows. The female butterflies are dimorphic, their ground color being either white (like the males) or yellowish (form "flava").

The eggs of the California White are yellow, conically elongated, and ribbed. The larvae, which feed on rock cress *(Streptanthus)* and other crucifers, are light yellow and have transverse black stripes on each segment. The dark brown chrysalids have a granular surface.

References:

See under *Pieris beckerii*.

Pieris (Pontia) protodice
Boisduval & LeConte, 1829
Checkered White

Plate 4, fig. 5. Map 13.

The Checkered White (*P. protodice*) and the Western White (*P. occidentalis*) are very similar butterflies and have sometimes been regarded as forms of a single species. However, a careful study by Chang, including statistical analysis of wing pattern, venation, genitalia, as well as geographic distribution, provides evidence in favor of their separation. While the females of these two butterflies are almost identical in appearance, the males are not difficult to distinguish. In those of *protodice* the black markings on the forewings are less extensive and do not, as in *occidentalis*, make up an extended marginal and submarginal row; on the underside the black spot at the inner margin of the forewing is large and squarish, whereas in *occidentalis* it is small (this character also differentiates females); the hindwing underside is immaculate.

Pieris protodice is a common butterfly over most of the United States east of the Rockies, but becomes scarce in the West except in southern California and Arizona. In Oregon its distribution overlaps that of the very abundant *P. occidentalis,* but colonies are rare and very local. Like *occidentalis* it flies in open fields and along roadsides. Specimens on record were taken July to September. Spring specimens from overwintering chrysalids (form "vernalis") are smaller and the male hindwings are not immaculate below but have veins bordered by dark scales.

References:

(1) Shapiro, A. M. 1968. Photoperiodic induction of vernal phenotype in *Pieris protodice* Boisduval and LeConte (Lepidoptera: Pieridae). Wasmann J. Biol. 26: 137-149.

(2) Shapiro, Arthur M. 1976. The biological status of nearctic taxa in the *Pieris protodice-occidentalis* group (Pieridae). J. Lepid. Soc. 30: 289-300.

(3) See under *Pieris beckerii*.

Pieris (Pontia) occidentalis
Reakirt, 1866
Western White

Plate 5, figs. 1, 2. Map 14.

The Western White ranges from central California to Alaska and eastward to the Rockies. It occurs throughout Oregon but is most abundant east of the Cascades, where it flies in great numbers in open spaces, along roadsides, and in forest clearings. As it breeds continuously it may be found from April to September.

The black wing pattern is heavier in females than in males and extends over the lower wings. Underneath, the hindwing veins have yellowish-green borders, which are more strongly developed in females. For differences between *Pieris occidentalis* and *protodice* see under the latter.

Early spring specimens, hatching from overwintering chrysalids, especially in colder climates and higher altitudes, are small (form "calyce") and the veins of the hindwing underside have more intense, sharply defined, and darker green borders.

The yellow, spindle-shaped eggs are longitudinally ridges. The larvae, which feed on a variety of mustards and other crucifers, are dull green, ringed with light and dark bands. The bluish-gray chrysalis is speckled with black.

References:

(1) Shapiro, A. M. 1973. Photoperiodic control of seasonal polyphenism in *Pieris occidentalis* Reakirt. Wasmann J. Biol. 31: 291-299.

(2) See under *Pieris beckerii* and *Pieris protodice*.

Pieris (Artogeia) napi marginalis
Scudder, 1861
Margined White

Plate 5, figs. 3, 4. Map 15.

Pieris napi is a highly variable species of circumpolar distribution that ranges across Europe, Asia, and North America. The Pacific Northwest subspecies *marginalis* inhabits damp woods in the Coast Range and along the western slope of the Cascades. Populations of *Pieris napi* in the mountains of northeastern Oregon are closer to the Rocky Mountain race *macdunnoughi* Remington, 1954, but need further study.

The Margined White is adapted to cool temperatures and is one of the first butterflies to appear in the spring. It derives its name from the appearance of the first generation which hatches from overwintering chrysalids. On the underside the veins of the wings are broadly bordered with black scales; the hindwings and forewing apices are yellowish in ground color. Females may be either white or creamish yellow above; in addition to black vein borders a wide black band extends along the inner margin of the forewings, usually ending in a submarginal black spot with another spot above it. Butterflies of the second generation (form "pallida") appear in June or July and are quite unlike the first, almost completely lacking the dark vein borders. While the males are almost pure white above, the forewings of the females possess the dark spots and inner marginal stripe of the spring form.

The larvae of the Margined White feed on woodland crucifers such as *Dentaria, Cardamine,* and

Arabis. The life history and details of the immature stages have not been recorded. In view of the sharp seasonal diphenism of this butterfly, a careful study of the development and life history would be an interesting undertaking.

Pieris (Artogeia) rapae (Linnaeus), 1758
Cabbage Butterfly

Plate 5, fig. 5. Map 16.

Common and a garden pest over nearly all of North America, the Cabbage Butterfly is not a native insect but was introduced from Europe into Quebec about 1860, from where it spread rapidly over the continent. It is most abundant in cultivated areas, where its damage to garden crucifers (cabbage, cauliflower, broccoli, mustard greens, etc.) may reach destructive proportions.

White or creamish-white in ground color, the tips of the forewings have a triangular black patch, beneath which the males have one black spot and the females two. Early spring specimens (the Cabbage Butterfly is multibrooded and flies from March to October) may lack the black spots and most of the apical patch. On the underside, the apex of the forewings and the entire hindwing are yellowish, and except for some light dusting of black scales over the inner half of the hindwing, the veins do not have colored borders.

The yellow eggs, usually laid on the underside of the leaves, are pear-shaped and longitudinally ribbed. The green larvae, closely matching the host plant in color, are finely dotted with black and have a yellow line along the back and a broken line on each side. The chrysalids may be green, gray, or brown and are speckled with black.

References:

(1) Hovanitz, William & Vincent C. S. Chang. 1963. Selection of allyl isothiocyanate by larvae of *Pieris rapae* and the inheritance of this trait. J. Res. Lepid. 1: 169-182.

(2) Kolyer, John M. 1969. Effects of environmental factors on the markings of *Pieris rapae* (Pieridae). J. Lepid. Soc. 23: 77-94.

Colias eurytheme eurytheme
Boisduval, 1852
Alfalfa Butterfly; Orange Sulfur

Plate 6, figs. 1, 2. Map 17.

A common butterfly from coast to coast and from southern Canada to Mexico, *Colias eurytheme* is abundant throughout Oregon. It is especially numerous in cultivated areas, as the larvae feed on alfalfa, clover, and vetches. Multibrooded, this Sulfur flies from April to November.

Spring and late fall specimens (form "ariadne") may be somewhat smaller than those of the summer broods (form "amphidusa") and their orange color is restricted to a central flush on otherwise more yellow wings. On the underside, the lower wings of *eurytheme* (and also of *philodice*) have a distinct row of submarginal dark spots. Besides the marked sexual difference in the black marginal borders (characteristic of almost all *Colias* species), some of the females are white (form "alba") instead of orange. Genetic studies have shown this white color to be determined by an autosomal dominant gene whose expression is suppressed in the male. The frequency of white females is higher in early broods than later ones, and increases generally in the northern range of the species.

The eggs of *eurytheme* are white and spindle-shaped, bearing the usual type of pierid longitudinal ridges. The larvae are dark green and covered with minute white hairs; a white-bordered red line runs along the back and each side. The green chrysalis is marked with black spots and yellow lateral dashes.

References:

(1) Hovanitz, William. 1950. The biology of *Colias* butterflies. I. The distribution of the North American species. Wasmann J. Biol. 8: 49-75.

(2) Hovanitz, William. 1950. The biology of *Colias* butterflies. II. Parallel geographical variation of dimorphic color phases in North American species. Wasmann J. Biol. 8: 197-219.

(3) McHenry, Paddy. 1963. The generic, specific and lower category names of the nearctic butterflies. Part 2 — The genus *Colias*. J. Res. Lepid. 1: 209-221.

(4) Remington, Charles L. 1954. The genetics of *Colias* (Lepidoptera). Advances in Genetics 6: 403-450.

(5) Watt, Ward B. 1969. Adaptive significance of pigment polymorphisms in *Colias* butterflies. II. Thermoregulation and photoperiodically controlled melanin variation in *Colias eurytheme*. Proc. Nat. Acad. Sci. 63: 767-774.

Colias philodice eriphyle
Edwards, 1876
Common Yellow Sulfur

Plate 6, fig. 3. Map 18.

Whether the Common Yellow Sulfur is a Western subspecies of the common Eastern *Colias philodice* or a color variant of *Colias eurytheme* has been much disputed. Both *eurytheme* and *philodice* possess the same wing patterns, including the submarginal row of dark spots on the lower surface of the hindwings; the females of both include white forms which are essentially indistinguishable. In Oregon their ranges are identical, though continentally the yellow form extends farther northward (into Alaska) and is uncommon in the Southwest. Interbreeding is known to occur (studied on Eastern populations), but such hybrids are of lowered fertility and are not common. Since conspecificity requires free exchange of genes (uninhibited natural interbreeding) between the individuals within a population, it would seem that *eurytheme* and *philodice*, though closely related, should be considered as separate species.

The early stages of the Common Yellow Sulfur are similar in appearance to those of *Colias eurytheme*, and the larvae utilize the same food plants.

References:

(1) Ae, Shigeru A. 1959. A study of hybrids in *Colias* (Lepidoptera, Pieridae). Evolution 13: 64-88.

(2) Hovanitz, William. 1949. Interspecific matings between *Colias eurytheme* and *Colias philodice* in wild populations. Evolution 3: 170-173.

(3) See under *Colias eurytheme*.

Colias occidentalis occidentalis Scudder, 1862
Western Sulfur

Plate 6, figs. 4, 5. Map 19.

Colias occidentalis is a butterfly of the Pacific Northwest, ranging from northern California to British Columbia. In Oregon it is principally at home at middle altitudes in the mountains, particularly in the northern Cascades, the Ochocos (where it seems to be most numerous), the Blue Mountains, and the Wallowas. Its flight pattern, compared to other Sulfurs with which it is usually found, tends to be fast and erratic.

The males superficially resemble *C. philodice eriphyle* but are of somewhat larger average size, the forewings a bit more rounded at the apex; the black margins are relatively narrower, the wings strongly pink-edged (most noticeable below), and the black spot at end of the discal cell is smaller. On the underside the row of submarginal spots is absent, and the lower wings are evenly dusted with black scales. Occasional males have an orange cast.

The females of *occidentalis* are extremely variable. The black marginal pattern, compared to that of *philodice*, ranges from less than full expression to complete absence; in most specimens it is reduced to an outer remnant and is poorly defined. The wing color in the female may be yellow, white, rarely light orange, and may show various degrees of intergradation.

The larvae feed on legumes, but the early stages have not been studied in detail.

References:

See under *Colias eurytheme*.

Colias alexandra edwardsii Edwards, 1870
Edward's Sulfur

Plate 7, figs. 1, 2. Map 20.

Colias alexandra is a wide ranging Sulfur of western North America, found throughout the Rocky Mountain area, eastward into the high plains of southern Canada and the northern United States, and westward through the Great Basin to the edge of the Cascades and Sierras. The populations found in Oregon were formerly known as *C. a. emilia* Edwards. F. Martin Brown has recently shown that they do not differ, and are not geographically isolated, from the Nevadan *C. a. edwardsii*, which name has priority. William Edwards named this butterfly in honor of the California lepidopterist Henry Edwards. In Oregon, Edward's Sulfur is widely distributed east of the Cascades and is particularly abundant in the open and semi-arid southeastern sector, often congregating on the rabbitbrush along roadsides near wet areas.

This is the largest Sulfur to be found in Oregon. The outer margin of the forewing is characteristically straight and accentuates the apical angle. The black marginal band of the male varies in width but is often rather narrow in relation to the total wing size. The forewing discal spot is small and the fringes of the wings are yellow (occasionally with trace of pink). In females the dark marginal band is poorly defined, variable in amount and sometimes absent. In both sexes occasional specimens are lightly flushed with orange. The yellow color of some females may be so light as to appear almost white. On the underside, the hindwings of both sexes are pale to medium yellow, or of grayish-green cast due to heavy and diffuse dusting with black scales; the light spot at the end of the discal cell is often reduced to a small white speck.

Edward's Sulfur has been taken from April to September but is commonest in middle and late summer. The early fliers come from caterpillars which overwinter in the third instar and pupate in the spring. The yellowish green larvae, marked with white bands and orange dashes, feed on various legumes, but the details of the life history have not been studied.

References:
   (1) Brown, F. Martin. 1973. The types of the pierid butterflies named by William Henry Edwards. Trans. Am. Entom. Soc. 99: 29-118.
   (2) Ellis, Scott L. 1974. Field observations on *Colias alexandra* Edwards (Pieridae). J. Lepid. Soc. 28: 114-125.
   (3) See under *Colias eurytheme.*

Colias interior interior Scudder, 1862
Pink-edged Sulfur

Plate 7, fig. 3. Map 21.

Colias interior is a northern species, distributed across southern Canada from the Gulf of St. Lawrence to British Columbia. In the United States it may be found in New England and upper New York; southward in the Appalachians; in northern Michigan, Wisconsin, and Minnesota; and from western Montana to the Cascades of the Northwest. In Oregon it is restricted to localized populations in the Cascades, Blue Mountains, and Wallowas. Not given to large open spaces, it should be sought in the pine forests near the larval foodplants, various species of *Vaccinium* (blueberry, huckleberry).

The male of *Colias interior* somewhat resembles *C. occidentalis,* but the black marginal band of the forewing is broadened at the apex and strongly arched inward, the inner edge of the band being also more jagged; the black discal spot is small and often suppressed; the orange discal spot on the hindwing is bright and conspicuous. On the underside the wings are evenly yellow, but sometimes lightly dusted with black scales. The female is usually yellow like the male, but occasional white forms occur; the black marginal band is characteristically restricted to the apex of the forewing, extending only slightly along the lateral margin. The wing fringes of *C. interior* are pink, as in *occidentalis.*

Captures of this species have been recorded from early June to mid-August. It is single-brooded and hibernation takes place in the larval stage. Feeding on *Vaccinium,* the mature larva is dark yellowish-green, with a darker dorsal and bluish-green lateral stripe; its surface is covered with small, downy papillae.

References:
   See under *Colias eurytheme.*

Colias pelidne skinneri Barnes, 1897
Skinner's Sulfur

Plate 7, fig. 4. Map 22.

In the East, *Colias pelidne* is an Arctic butterfly found in Labrador, on Baffin Island, and along the eastern shore of Hudson Bay. In the West, this sulfur occurs at higher altitudes in the northern Rockies.

Our subspecies, *C. p. skinneri,* was discovered in Yellowstone Park. It is one of the rarest of Oregon butterflies and is known only from higher elevations in the Wallowa Mountains. Unless settled at wet places to sip moisture, Skinner's Sulfur is a difficult capture as it is a rapid and erratic flyer over the rough terrain of bolder-strewn mountain slopes. It may be sought at elevations of 6000 feet and above during July and August.

Somewhat resembling *C. interior,* the male of this butterfly can be immediately recognized by examining the underside of the forewing, where a dark cloud of black scales occupies the discal area; the yellow of the hindwing is diffusely dusted with black scales, and the discal spot is mainly dark pink with the pearly center much reduced. On the upperside the black discal spot of the forewing is very small, and a cloud of black scales extends over the anal area of the hindwing. Females may be yellow or white; the black marginal border is jagged along its inner edge and extends along the entire lateral margin and partially onto the hindwings. The fringe scales are pink, as in *C. interior.*

The larvae of Skinner's Sulfur, like those of *C. interior,* feed on *Vaccinium,* but the details of the early stages are undescribed.

References:
   See under *Colias eurytheme.*

Nathalis iole Boisduval, 1836
Dwarf Yellow

Plate 7, fig. 5. Map 23.

This is the smallest butterfly of the family Pieridae. A common species in the Southeast and the Mississippi Valley, and also known in southern California and the northern Great Plains, it has only rarely been reported from the Northwest. A record from Asotin County, Washington, at the junction of the Grand Ronde and Snake Rivers, places a specimen within five miles of the Oregon border. Unfortunately this corner of Oregon has been little explored and should be searched for further examples. The Dwarf Yellow flies in late summer in dry, open, grassy areas, close to the ground. It is easily overlooked.

There is no possibility of mistaking the identity of this tiny yellow butterfly. The forewing bears a large brownish-black apical patch and a broad dark bar along its inner margin. Females have dark markings also on the hindwings, which are frequently orange. The undersurface has a yellowish-green cast.

The larvae of *Nathalis iole* feed on various marigolds and chickweed. They are green, marked along the back with a broad purple stripe, and have yellow and black stripes along the sides. The green pupae differ from those of other pierids in lacking the projection that extends forward from the head.

Anthocharis sara Lucas, 1852
Sara Orange Tip

Plate 8, figs. 1, 2. Map 24.

A wide ranging Western butterfly, the Sara Orange Tip occurs in the Rocky Mountains from Wyoming to New Mexico, and extends westward to the coast from Alaska to southern California. Eight or nine partially intergrading subspecies have been recognized, of which at least two can be identified in Oregon.

The largest of the subspecies is *A. sara flora* Wright, 1905. It inhabits the Willamette Valley and the adjoining slopes of the Coast Range and Cascades. Appearing in March, it is one of the first butterflies of the season and may be found to mid July, generally in abundance. The large size and intense color dimorphism, with white males versus yellow females, are striking, as is the bold red-orange apical patch of the males.

East of the Cascades the Sara Orange Tip is smaller in average size, and while similar to the Rocky Mountain subspecies *julia* Edwards, this race is usually known as *A. sara stella* Edwards, 1879. The females are yellow, as in *flora,* but in some specimens the yellow color of the forewings grades into white toward the inner border. The eastern and western populations are not sharply separated, the change from *flora* to *stella* being a clinal one with evident intergradation. The taxonomy of *sara* populations needs much more study.

The spindle-shaped and ridged egg of the Sara Orange Tip is yellow. The mature green larva, dorsally tinged with yellow, has a whitish lateral line and transverse rows of black papillae. The chrysalis, with its elongated beak-like palpal case, is brown and marked with a dark lateral stripe. The larvae feed on *Arabis, Sisymbrium,* and other members of the mustard family.

Reference:

(1) Dornfeld, Ernst J. 1970. A field-captured scale-deficient mutant of *Anthocaris sara*. J. Res. Lepid. 9: 25-28.

Anthocharis (Falcapica) lanceolata lanceolata Lucas, 1852
Lanceolate Marble

Plate 8, fig. 3. Map 25.

A scarce mountain-dwelling butterfly, the Lanceolate Marble is known in Oregon only from the Siskiyous and adjacent southern Cascades, where it may be sought in wooded canyons during the spring months. In California it occupies similar habitats in the Sierras and the San Bernardino Mountains. It is easily recognized by the outwardly bent (falcate) apex of the forewings and the net-like brown mottling on the underside of the hindwings. An erratic flyer, it skillfully evades netting.

The larva feeds on *Arabis* and other crucifers. Green in color, it bears a broad white lateral stripe and is dorsally peppered with minute black and white specks. The palpal case of the brown pupa is strongly recurved at its forward end.

Euchloe hyantis (Edwards), 1871
Pearly Marble

Plate 8, fig. 4. Map 26.

Formerly regarded as a form of *Euchloe creusa, E. hyantis* is now recognized as a separate species through the work of Paul Opler in his comprehensive revision of the North American *Euchloe. Hyantis* is found from British Columbia to southern California and eastward to Idaho, Utah, and Arizona, as well as in western Colorado and New Mexico. It can be distinguished from *E. ausonides* by its smaller size, the pure white upperside of the wings, and on the hindwing underside the distinctive pearly luster and the usually broader green marbling.

Two subspecies occur in Oregon. The nominotypic *E. h. hyantis* (Edwards), principally at home in the northern California coastal ranges, is found in the forests of the Siskiyous. In this race the black patch on the middle of the forewings is small, as in *E. ausonides*.

The subspecies *E. h. lotta* (Beutenmuller), 1898, is widely distributed over open areas east of the Cascades, favoring the sage flats and the rocky landscapes that are broken by low hills and dry streambeds. In this race the forewing black patch is robust and squarish. Populations tend to be local, but at these sites the butterflies are often very numerous. Appearing early in the spring, they fly from April to June.

The larvae of *Euchloe hyantis* feed on *Arabus, Caulanthus, Streptanthus,* and other crucifers. They are apple green in color, stippled with black points and laterally striped with a wide white line. The elongated eggs are lemon yellow and the pupae brownish.

Reference:
(1) Opler, Paul A. 1966-74. Studies on the nearctic *Euchloe*. J. Res. Lepid. 5: 39-50, 185-195; 7: 65-86; 8: 153-169; 13: 1-20.

Euchloe ausonides ausonides (Lucas), 1852
Creamy Marble

Plate 8, fig. 5. Map 27.

Like *Euchloe hyantis, E. ausonides* has a wide distribution which extends from the Canadian and American Rockies westward to Alaska and California; it also occurs in southern Manitoba and Ontario. In Oregon it is found in the Siskiyous and is widely distributed east of the Cascades. Unlike *hyantis,* however, it is generally associated with moister habitats and favors forested parts. It is often found among the jack pine, in clearings and canyons, and on nearby rocky meadows. Appearing early, it is on the wing from April to July. The Creamy Marble tends to fly low and in a zig-zag pattern. I have found it abundant on the wet summit meadows of Mt. Ashland.

The vernacular name of *E. ausonides* derives from the dull creamy white color of the wings, which is particularly noticeable in females. The species differs from *hyantis lotta* also in the larger size, the narrower black discal spot of the forewings, and the usually thinner cords of green marbling.

The larval foodplants include *Arabis, Brassica, Sisymbrium,* and other crucifers. The elongated and ribbed egg varies in color from blue green to light orange. The dark green caterpillar possesses yellow lateral stripes. The "beaked" chrysalis is brown except for the creamish dorsal portion of the thorax and abdomen.

Reference:
See under *Euchloe hyantis.*

Family SATYRIDAE

The family Satyridae, which includes the Wood-nymphs, Ringlets, Alpines, and Arctics, is worldwide in distribution. It is well represented in temperate and arctic regions, but finds its greatest diversity in the tropics. Its members are found at all elevations, but many genera and species have very restricted habitats. The Oregon satyrids belong to northern genera with close affinities to butterflies of Europe and Asia.

Almost all satyrids are small to medium in size and grayish or brown in color, their wings usually adorned with eyespots (ocelli). The veins of the forewings are characteristically swollen at the base, except in the genera *Lethe* and *Oeneis*. The antennal club is only slightly thickened and the forelegs are greatly reduced and brush-like. Most species have a low, weak, and bouncing flight through grasses and shrubs.

The eggs of satyrids are usually dome-shaped, often flattened on top, and have a raised, net-like surface. The smooth and spindle-shaped larvae have a notched posterior end and are green or light brown, marked with longitudinal stripes. They feed on grasses and sedges and generally overwinter before pupating. The unornamented pupae are green or brown, suspended from a cremaster, or drop to the ground and are found under rocks and debris.

Coenonympha tullia (Mueller), 1764
Tullia Ringlet

Plate 9, figs. 1-6. Maps 28-30.

The Tullia Ringlet is found in northern latitudes and mountainous areas of Europe, Asia, and North America. It is a complex and variable species which has been divided into numerous intergrading geographic races that differ in shades of ground color, markings of the ventral wing surface, and degrees of ocellation. In North America *tullia* ranges from California to Alaska, eastward through the Great Basin and the Rockies, and across the northern Great Plains and Canada to New Brunswick and Newfoundland. For a long time the many North American populations have been grouped into some five separate species, but this is an arbitrary practice and biologically unwarranted. *Coenonympha haydenii,* of Montana and Wyoming, is, however, unrelated to the *tullia* complex.

The Ringlets of Oregon consist of three subspecies of *C. tullia*. Each of these is double brooded, the second generation (late summer) differing somewhat in appearance from the first which is derived from overwintering larvae. They are common in grassy meadows.

C. tullia eunomia Dornfeld, 1967, inhabits the Willamette Valley and adjacent foothills of the Coast Range and Cascades. It is the darkest in color, especially below, and is completely devoid of ocellations. Tawny above, the under surface is darkly ferruginous except for an apical and peripheral zone which has a grayish-green cast; the extra-discal ventral light bands are minimally developed. The second generation is lighter above and below, the underside being tannish brown and without greenish margins; the vertical light bands are more fully developed.

C. tullia ampelos Edwards, 1871, is widely distributed east of the Cascades. (The name *ampelos* has for many years been misapplied to the Willamette Valley populations.) This subspecies is lighter than *eunomia* on both upper and undersides, the mid-wing yellow bands of the lower surface are more extensive, and small ocelli are present in most (though not all) individuals, appearing ventrally near the apex of the forewing and along the hindwing margin. In the paler second generation the wings are almost straw yellow, which is especially striking on the lower surface whose forewing apices show little if any darkening.

C. tullia eryngii Henry Edwards, 1876, is limited to southwestern Oregon, the region of the Siskiyous and adjacent southern Cascades, extending into northern California. Unlike the tawny colored previous subspecies, *eryngii* is essentially creamish white. Eyespots and light vertical bands are much as in *ampelos,* and it appears that intergrading with *ampelos* occurs where these races meet. Second generation specimens of the late summer show less dark scaling on the underside of the hindwings.

The life history of various *Coenonympha* "species" has been studied long ago by William H. Edwards. The broad eggs are rounded at their base and provided with a button-like knob on their flattened top. The slender larvae, green or brown and longitudinally striped, resemble the grasses on which they feed. The chrysalids hang from a cremaster and are translucent green or brown.

References:

(1) Brown, F. Martin. 1964. W. H. Edwards' life histories of North American *Coenonympha*. J. Res. Lepid. 3: 121-128.

(2) Davenport, Demorest. 1941. The butterflies of the satyrid genus *Coenonympha*. Bull. Mus. Comp. Zool. 87: 215-349, 10 pls.

(3) Dornfeld, Ernst J. 1967. On the yellow forms of *Coenonympha tullia* (Satyridae) in Oregon. J. Lepid. Soc. 21: 1-7.

Neominois ridingsii stretchii (Edwards), 1870
Stretch's Satyr

Plate 10, fig. 1. Map 31.

The rarest of all Oregon satyrids, Stretch's Satyr has until June, 1979 been known from only one location in the State, the sage-covered 8000-foot summit of Drake Peak in the Warner Mountains of Lake County, where it was discovered in 1963 by E. J. Newcomer. It has now also been found atop the Pueblo Mountains in southeastern Harney County by Mark Smith. South of the Oregon border Stretch's Satyr is known from high elevations in the Great Basin area. The nominate subspecies, *E. ridingsii ridingsii,* is widespread in the Rockies and differs from *stretchii* in being somewhat smaller and darker.

Stretch's Satyr has a characteristic low and erratic flight and must usually be flushed out of the grass. It alights rapidly, bending over on its side, perhaps an adaptation to the wind. Since it is also protectively colored, a sharp eye is required to locate its resting position in the dry grass below the sagebrush. It should be sought in late June to August. This light brown satyrid is easily distinguished from all others by the bold pattern of large creamish spots.

The eggs of Stretch's Satyr are chalky white and barrel-shaped, broader at the base. The reddish-buff larva, with pale green sides and a mid-dorsal black stripe, is covered with minute tubercles and short, whitish hairs. It feeds on grasses. Pupation takes place under the ground, the chrysalis colored red-brown but with green abdominal segments and wing-cases.

Reference:

(1) Burdick, W. N. 1942. The rediscovery of *Eumenis stretchii* Edw. (Lepidoptera, Rhopalocera). Canad. Entom. 74: 204-205.

Cercyonis pegala (Fabricius), 1775.
Large Woodnymph

Plate 10, figs. 2, 3; plate 11, figs. 1, 2. Maps 32, 33.

The North American genus *Cercyonis* (incorrectly equated with the Eurasian *Minois)* contains four species, all single-brooded; three are found in Oregon. The largest in size, *Cercyonis pegala,* extends through most of the United States and southern Canada, from the Atlantic to the Pacific, and is quite variable.

The subspecies *C. pegala boopis* (Behr), 1864, is widespread and common throughout the State, flying in meadows and open woods from late June to September. Its total range includes the southern and central Rockies, thence westward to the Pacific Coast from central California to British Columbia. The males are dark brown, the females somewhat lighter and near the color of milk chocolate. The forewings possess two black eyespots with white, dot-like centers; these are much larger in the female and encircled by a yellow rim, both ocelli, moreover, lying in a yellowish-brown field of variable extent. The males possess a patch of sex-scales which appears as a dark diagonal flush beneath the discal cell. On the underside the eyespots of the forewings are more pronounced and rimmed with yellow in both sexes; a variable number of eyespots may appear on the hindwings, from none to six, arranged in two groups of three each. The inner half of each wing is ventrally traversed by a dark longitudinal band with an irregular margin; the under surface is, moreover, mottled with fine bark-like striations.

The female of the Large Woodnymph lays 200 to 300 eggs that are deposited singly on grass stems. The newly hatched larvae go into diapause and resume feeding and growth late in the following spring. They mature in two and a half to three months after six instars; they are grass green in color and marked with lengthwise stripes. The chrysalids are suspended from blades of grass and hatch in about twenty days. The adult butterfly lives five to ten days.

In the Great Basin area of southeastern Oregon, and extending into Nevada and Utah, one finds the very localized *C. pegala ariane* (Boisduval), 1852. This subspecies is distinguished by strongly developed hindwing eyespots, both dorsally and ventrally, a more conspicuous striated pattern of the lower wing surface, and decidedly greater development of the yellow flush around the dorsal forewing ocelli which in females may extend over the outer half of the hindwings as well. Females in which the yellow is extraordinarily extensive have been known as the form "stephensi"; however, the amount of yellow is a matter of gradation. *Ariane* inhabits grassy marshes at the borders of the Warner Lakes in Lake County and of the Blitzen River in Harney County.

A variety of *pegala* even lighter than *ariane* has recently been discovered in the swampy alkaline region of the Sheldon Antelope Range in Humboldt County, Nevada, and has been described in 1972 as *C. pegala blanca* by Emmel and Mattoon. Since the type locality is only ten miles south of the Oregon border, on the road from Adel to Denio, *blanca* may also occur in Oregon.

References:

(1) Brown, F. Martin. 1964. The types of satyrid butterflies described by William Henry Edwards. Trans. Am. Entom. Soc. 90: 323-413.

(2) Brown, F. Martin. 1965. Comments on the genus *Cercyonis* Scudder, with figures of types (Satyridae). J. Res. Lepid. 4: 131-148.

(3) Emmel, Thomas C. 1969. Taxonomy, distribution and biology of the genus *Cercyonis* (Satyridae). I. Characteristics of the genus. J. Lepid. Soc. 23: 165-175.

(4) Emmel, Thomas C. & Sterling O. Mattoon. 1972. *Cercyonis pegala blanca,* a "missing type" in the evolution of the genus *Cercyonis* (Satyridae). J. Lepid. Soc. 26: 140-149.

(5) Newcomer, E. J. 1965. Type locality of *Cercyonis stephensi* revisited. J. Lepid. Soc. 19: 161-164.

Cercyonis sthenele (Boisduval), 1852
Small Woodnymph

Plate 10, fig. 4; plate 11, figs. 3, 5. Map 34.

The Woodnymphs of this species group are all Western. The form that was first described and named, *C. s. sthenele,* existed in and was limited to the San Francisco Bay area but became a victim of urbanization and has been extinct for almost a hundred years. A few specimens remain in some major museums.

Unlike the highly local and vanished *sthenele,* the subspecies *silvestris* (Edwards), 1861, is common in southern California and extends northward west of the Sierras, becoming scarce and of very spotty occurrence in the Northwest. Our specimens are decidedly darker than those at the southern end of the range. They are distinctly smaller than *Cercyonis alope boopis* and have relatively broader wings, but in color and pattern they resemble the larger species. I have long been puzzled by these Woodnymphs, but Thomas Emmel, who has studied the genus extensively, assures me that they are *silvestris*. They are adapted to wooded habitats and in the late summer may be found in the Siskiyous and in isolated spots in the Cascades. Because of frequent confusion with *alope,* many of the reported locality records are unreliable, and we do not at present know the real extent of *silvestris* distribution in Oregon.

More easily recognized is the subspecies *C. s. paulus* (Edwards), 1879, which is common on the semi-arid plateaus of southeastern Oregon, but also found in dry and open habitats of the northeastern counties, more sparingly on the east slope of the Cascades, and even in parts of the Siskiyous. It is abundant in the Great Basin area of northeastern California and Nevada. In many Oregon locations *paulus* is sympatric with *Cercyonis oetus,* but the two usually fly at different times. Compared with *oetus, paulus* has a lighter brown color; the forewing ocelli are better developed and nearly equal in size; the dark vertical band crossing the hindwings on the ventral side does not have sharply toothed or zigzagged margins, but has a somewhat squared-off outer border at the discal level; a broad frosting of white scales lies outside this band; and the hindwing ocelli are usually more pronounced and distinctly brown-rimmed.

The immature stages of *C. s. silvestris* and *paulus* resemble those of *pegala boopis* except for a larval life of five instars instead of six.

References:
See under *Cercyonis pegala.*

Cercyonis oetus oetus
(Boisduval), 1869
Least Woodnymph

Plate 11, figs. 4, 6. Map 35.
Similar in size and general appearance to *C. sthenele, Cercyonis oetus* is a wider ranging species, common over most of the mountain regions of the western United States and adjacent Canada. The Pacific subspecies, *C. o. oetus,* extends from the central Sierras of California northward through the Cascades and from there eastward to the mountains of northern Nevada and western Idaho. In part of its range it overlaps *C. sthenele paulus.* In middle and late summer this butterfly is exceedingly abundant in the ponderosa belt of central Oregon and is a familiar sight along roadsides as it gathers in considerable numbers on *Eriogonum* and composites.

The Least Woodnymph is generally darker brown than *C. s. paulus,* and from the distance looks almost black. The posterior ocellus of the forewing is usually smaller than the anterior and tends to be offset toward the wing margin; it is frequently absent dorsally in the male. The most distinctive characteristic is the mesial dark band on the underside of the hindwing; its outer margin runs a strongly jagged course, with an acute indentation at the end of the discal cell, and its inner margin is deeply lobulated. The general underside color varies from very dark brown to grayish, caused by dusting with white scales. The darker specimens are characteristic of the Cascades, and in these the pattern of the mesial band is sometimes considerably obscured.

The life cycle resembles that of the Small Woodnymph.

References:
See under *Cercyonis pegala.*

Oeneis nevadensis
(Felder & Felder), 1866
Great Arctic

Plate 12, figs. 1, 2. Map 36.
Members of the genus *Oeneis* are mainly satyrids of the Far North or of high altitudes, many species living in arctic and subarctic regions or at increasing elevations to the south. Some are adapted to forest habitats, others to prairies and steppes, and still others to arctic tundra or alpine summits.

Oregon's only known *Oeneis,* the Great Arctic, is a forest dweller and, paradoxically, may be found at relatively low elevations. It is common throughout the Cascades and Siskiyous, but rare and local in the Coast Range. It also occurs in the Sierras of northern California, the Cascades of Washington, and on Vancouver Island.

This tawny-orange butterfly is our largest woodnymph. The male has either one or two eyespots on the forewing as well as an extensive androconial patch which darkens the entire discal area. The eyespots of the female may be two or three in number. The under surface, particularly of the hindwings, is bark-like in its mottling, making an effective concealing pattern when the butterfly alights on fallen tree trunks and dead limbs. Its jerky flight through the sun and shade of forest glades and its habit of rapid settling are tantalizing to the observer or collector. The males display a perching and patrolling habit, a territorial behavior associated with mating. A special expression of this is the "hilltopping" described by Guppy for Great Arctics on Vancouver Island (see also *Papilio zelicaon*).

A remarkable fact is that *Oeneis nevadensis* flies, June to August, only in even-numbered years; out-of-phase exceptions are very rare. This is partially explained by its two-year life cycle, but it is difficult to understand why a staggering of populations has not developed. This ought to be an interesting problem for a population biologist. Moreover, the details of the immature stages need to be fully worked out. The larvae feed on grasses and pupation occurs on the ground, the chrysalids being found under debris and at the roots of grasses.

It seems strange that no *Oeneis* has yet been found in the Blue Mountains or Wallowas of northeastern Oregon. One might expect the Rocky Mountain species, *O. chryxus* (Doubleday), to show up. It is lighter and more golden orange than *nevadensis,* somewhat smaller, and an inner dark zone of the forewing sends a beak-like projection toward the outer wing margin.

References:

(1) Guppy, Richard. 1962. Collecting *Oeneis nevadensis* (Satyrinae) and other genera on Vancouver Island, with a theory to account for hilltopping. J. Lepid. Soc. 16: 64-66.

(2) Masters, John H. & John T. Sorensen. 1969. Field observations on forest *Oeneis* (Satyridae). J. Lepid. Soc. 23: 155-161.

(3) Masters, John H. 1974. Biennialism in *Oeneis macounii* (Satyridae). J. Lepid. Soc. 28: 237-242.

Erebia epipsodea hopfingeri Ehrlich, 1954
Common Alpine

Plate 12, figs. 3, 4. Map 37.

Like *Oeneis,* the genus *Erebia* is largely arctic and alpine. Circumpolar in distribution, it is well represented in the European Alps and in the Far North of our continent. All members are medium-sized or small dark brown butterflies, some nearly black. *Erebia epipsodea* is the commonest and most widespread North American species, and the only one known from Oregon. It occurs throughout the Rockies, from New Mexico to British Columbia, extends northwestward to the Yukon and Alaska, and eastward to the plains of Alberta, Saskatchewan, and Manitoba. The subspecies of Oregon, Washington, and Idaho is *hopfingeri.* In our State it may be found from late May to July in moist meadows and on grassy mountain slopes of the Ochocos, Blue Mountains, and Wallowas.

The males are dark brown and the females somewhat lighter, markedly so on the under surface. A submarginal row of white-pupilled ocelli on both fore and hind wings is embedded in a flush of orange-red color. The dark mesial band of the ventral hindwings is more conspicuous in the female.

The low, gentle, and zigzag flight habit of the Common Alpine resembles that of the Large Woodnymph. Its activity is strongly dependent on solar radiation and the butterfly may be observed to bask with its wings spread open as it absorbs the warmth of the sun. It has been shown to be an extensive wanderer, with much interchange of individuals between neighboring populations.

The subconical eggs are laid singly on grass, the food-plant of the larvae. After the second or third molt the larvae hibernate and remain inactive until the following spring, when they resume feeding. When full-grown they pupate in a tent made by loosely tying several blades of grass together with silk. The thickened thorax gives to the brown chrysalis a somewhat egg-shaped appearance.

References:

(1) Brussard, Peter F. 1971. Field techniques for investigations of population structure in a "ubiquitous" butterfly. J. Lepid. Soc. 25: 22-28.

(2) Brussard, Peter F. & Paul R. Ehrlich. 1970. The population structure of *Erebia epipsodea* (Lepidoptera: Satyrinae). Ecology 51: 119-129.

(3) Brussard, Peter F. & Paul R. Ehrlich. 1970. Adult behavior and population structure in *Erebia epipsodea* (Lepidoptera: Satyrinae). Ecology 51: 880-885.

(4) Ehrlich, Paul R. 1955. The distribution and subspeciation of *Erebia epipsodea* Butler (Lepidoptera: Satyridae). Univ. Kansas Sci. Bull. 37 (I): 175-194.

Family DANAIDAE

The Danaidae, except for the genus *Danaus* to which the familiar Monarch belongs, are mainly tropical and most varied in Asia. They are medium-sized to large butterflies and their structural characteristics include naked (scaleless) antennae and atrophied and clawless forelegs. The males possess a patch of scent scales (androconia) on the hindwings and a pencil of eversible hairs on the last abdominal segment which the butterfly rubs over the scent scales for transfer to the female.

The larvae are brightly colored, hairless, and provided with fleshy filaments which project from the mesothorax and sometimes other body segments. The pupae are short, smooth, and barrel-shaped, usually ornamented with metallic colors; they hang freely suspended by a silken cord, or cremaster. The stout, flat-topped, conical eggs are sculptured with ribs and crosslines.

The Danaidae are of particular interest because of their generally poisonous effects on predators, which rapidly learn to avoid them. The poison is acquired by the larvae through feeding on noxious plants of the milkweed and nightshade families. The poisonous danaids, in turn, serve as "models" for many non-related sympatric butterflies which closely resemble them, this mimicry affording effective protection for the harmless species. This remarkable relationship has been the subject of numerous careful observations and recent experimental confirmation.

References:

(1) Brower, Lincoln P. 1969. Ecological chemistry. Scientific American 220 (2): 22-29.

(2) Pliske, T. E. & T. Eisner. 1969. Sex pheromone of the Queen butterfly: biology. Science 164: 1170-1172.

(3) Wickler, Wolfgang. 1969. Mimicry in plants and animals. World University Library, McGraw-Hill, N. Y. 255 pp. (Paperback).

Danaus plexippus (Linnaeus), 1758
Monarch

Plate 13, figs. 1, 2. Map 38.

Of all North American butterflies the Monarch is surely the most widely known, as it ranges over the entire continent, its life history has become a schoolroom classic, its spectacular migrations have awed the observer, and its relation to the Viceroy has become a standard example of model and mimic.

While the Monarch has been recorded from all parts of Oregon, it is an abundant summer butterfly only where there is an ample supply of milkweed, the larval foodplant. It is therefore more numerous in southern and eastern Oregon than in the Willamette Valley. In its summer breeding populations a continuous succession of generations is produced, the life cycle being only three weeks in length.

In the fall Monarchs gather for the great southward migrations, overwintering in southern California and Mexico (or Florida and Texas for eastern populations). Flights begin in Canada, and as the western Monarchs arrive in California they establish transient or overwintering roosting sites. The most famous such site is at Pacific Grove, California, where great swarms of thousands roost in the Monterey Pines. A great tourist attraction, the butterflies of Pacific Grove enjoy legal protection. In their fall migration Monarchs may fly from fifteen to forty miles a day; even an instance of eighty miles is known. The longest recorded flight (traced by wing tagging and recapture) is 2400 miles, from Alberta to Mexico.

The progeny of the fall migrants and a few of the original migrants move north in the spring, laying eggs on the way. The northward flight is not massed and overnight roosts are not established. Most of the butterflies fly only part of the way and form local summer colonies.

In feeding on poisonous species of milkweeds the larvae acquire from the latex and transmit to the body tissues of the adult butterfly toxins known as cardenolides (heart poisons) which are distasteful and noxious to vertebrate predators. Birds quickly learn to avoid the Monarch and, by reason of close resemblance, also avoid the unrelated and quite harmless Viceroy (*Limenitis archippus*). This model-mimic relationship has been thoroughly explored and experimentally verified by the Browers. For such mimicry to be effective the two butterflies must, of course, occupy the same area, which in Oregon is true only for the northeastern part of the State. Both species are far more abundant in the Midwest and the East.

The Monarch egg, a delicate pale green cone with a ribbed and cross-lined surface, is laid on the underside of milkweed leaves. The greenish larva, striped across the back with black and yellow bands, possesses two fleshy black "tentacles" on each end. The beautiful bullet-shaped chrysalis, which hangs from the underside of the leaf by a silken cremaster, is pale green and studded with rows of metallic golden dots. In the male butterfly one may note the patch of scent scales (sex-brand) on the second cubital vein of the hindwing. The wing veins have heavier black outlines in the female.

References:

(1) Brower, Jan Van Zandt. 1958. Experimental studies of mimicry in some North American butterflies. I. The Monarch, *Danaus plexippus*, and Viceroy, *Limenitis archippus*. Evolution 12: 32-47.

(2) Ehrlich, Paul R. 1958. The integumental anatomy of the Monarch butterfly *Danaus plexippus* L. (Lepidoptera: Danaidae). Univ. Kansas Sci. Bull. 38: 1315-1349.

(3) Munger, Francis. 1973. An improved method for rearing the monarch butterfly. J. Res. Lepid. 12: 163-168.

(4) Reichstein, T., J. von Euw, J. A. Parsons & Miriam Rothschild. 1968. Heart poisons in the Monarch butterfly. Science 161: 861-866.

(5) Urquhart, F. A. 1960. The Monarch butterfly. Univ. Toronto Press, Toronto. 361 pp.

(6) Urquhart, F. A., P. Beard & R. Brownlee. 1965. A population study of a hibernal roosting colony of the Monarch butterfly (*D. plexippus*) in northern California. J. Res. Lepid. 4: 221-226.

(7) Urquhart, F. A., N. R. Urquhart & F. Munger. 1968. A study of a continuously breeding population of *Danaus plexippus* in southern California compared to a migratory population and its significance in the study of insect movement. J. Res. Lepid. 7: 169-181.

(8) Urquhart, Fred A. 1976. Found at last: the Monarch's winter home. Nat. Geographic 150: 161-173 (August, 1976).

Family NYMPHALIDAE

This largest and cosmopolitan family, the Nymphalidae, consists of butterflies that are mainly medium to large in size. In outward appearance they represent a tremendous diversity. Most species have wings of orange-brown ground color strongly and variously patterned with black; others, however, are basically blue, red, black, or multicolored.

All adult nymphalids have their forelegs reduced to hairy stumps, hence are known as "brush-footed butterflies". Their scaly antennae are moderately long and end in a pronounced club. The palpi are robust and hairy. The cell of the hindwing is open (not closed by a tubular vein).

The larvae are quite varied, but generally dark in color and spiny. They feed on a wide variety of plants. The pupae tend to be ornamented with conspicuous projections, giving them an angular appearance. They are usually suspended from the tip of the abdomen by a silken cremaster.

The arrangement of the Nymphalidae into subfamilies or tribes is unsettled, depending on the inclusiveness with which the group is viewed, some systematists including here the Satyridae, Danaidae, and Libytheidae (all of which have reduced forelegs). The narrower concept, here adopted, still encompasses a huge assemblage. Several subfamilies are essentially tropical. Following the arrangement of dos Passos, the Oregon species of nymphalids fall into five groups: (1) the Limenitinae (*Limenitis* and *Adelpha*), (2) the Vanessinae (*Vanessa* and *Junonia*), (3) the Nymphalinae (*Nymphalis* and *Polygonia)*, (4) the Melitaeinae (*Phyciodes, Chlosyne,* and *Euphydryas*), and (5) the Argynninae (*Boloria* and *Speyeria*).

Limenitis archippus (Cramer), 1776
Viceroy

Plate 13, figs. 3, 4. Map 39.

The Viceroy, so named because of its well known mimic relationship to the Monarch (see discussion under *Danaus plexippus),* is common throughout the eastern and central United States and Canada, extending westward to the Rockies and to some areas beyond them. In the Pacific Northwest it occurs in eastern Washington and northeastern parts of Oregon, specifically in the upper Columbia and Snake River drainages. Here it flies from June to September and may be seen along water courses near willows and poplars.

But for its smaller size and the postmedian black line on the hindwing, the Viceroy's resemblance to the Monarch is remarkable. In a recently described population from northern Nevada (*L. a. lahontani* Herlan, 1970) the postmedian line is incomplete or even absent; some Oregon specimens approach this condition, and it may be found to be regular in southeastern Oregon where little collecting has been done.

Hybrids have been found between all sympatric species of the genus *Limenitis (Basilarchia* in older literature), which suggests close interspecific relationship. Such a hybrid between the red-colored Viceroy and the blue Lorquin's Admiral was taken at Hermiston by Judy Fisler and is shown in our plate. These hybrids, however, are rare and most likely of reduced fertility, which can be investigated by experimental mating (see Platt, 1969).

The larva of the Viceroy, a night feeder on willows and poplars, is a grotesque-looking affair, greyish white on the thorax and mid-abdomen, a patch of brown in between and posteriorly, a pair of plume-like horns extending forward from the thorax, and further ornamentation with nodules and dark spots. The approximate resemblance to a bird dropping is probably protective. The half-grown larva passes the winter in a hibernaculum, a rolled up leaf attached by silk to a twig of the foodplant. Growth continues the next spring until pupation. The brown and white chrysalis has a prominent hump, like a saddle horn, and large wing cases.

References:

(1) Brower, Jane Van Zandt. 1958. Experimental studies of mimicry in some North American butterflies. I. The Monarch, *Danaus plexippus,* and Viceroy, *Limenitis archippus.* Evolution 12: 32-47.

(2) Herlan, Peter J. 1970. A new subspecies of *Limenitis archippus* (Nymphalidae). J. Res. Lepid. 9: 217-222.

(3) Perkins, Edwin M. & Edward V. Gage. 1970. On the occurrence of *Limenitis archippus* x *L. lorquini* hybrids (Nymphalidae). J. Res. Lepid. 9: 223-226.

(4) Platt, Austin P. 1969. A simple technique for hand-pairing *Limenitis* butterflies (Nymphalidae). J. Lepid. Soc. 23: 109-112.

Limenitis weidemeyerii latifascia Perkins & Perkins, 1967
Weidemeyer's Admiral

Plate 14, fig. 1. Map 40.

Weidemeyer's Admiral is essentially a Rocky Mountain butterfly and has been unknown in Oregon until it was taken in 1964 by Charles Remington, flying among willows in Malheur County, forty miles west of Jordan Valley. There are now additional records from southeastern Oregon.

This *Limenitis* looks very much like *L. arthemis arthemis,* the Banded Purple of Canada and the northern tier of states east of the Rockies. In *arthemis,* however, the ground color of the underside is rusty red rather than blue with heavy basal dusting of white. Oregon specimens of *weidemeyerii* belong to the subspecies *latifascia,* recently described as the Great Basin form; as the name implies, this race shows the widest development of the white band. In the Mono Basin of the California Sierras, *L. weidemeyerii* hybridizes with *L. lorquini;* some Oregon specimens also show traces of this cross.

Weidemeyer's Admiral flies from late June to August, frequenting streamsides, riverbeds, and sage-flats, always in the vicinity of willows, aspens, or poplars, on which the larvae feed. These larvae are greyish, mottled with grey and white patches; they resemble those of the Viceroy and, like the latter, spend the winter in a hibernaculum.

Reference:

(1) Perkins, Stephen F. & Edwin M. Perkins. 1967. Revision of the *Limenitis weidemeyerii* complex, with description of a new subspecies (Nymphalidae). J. Lepid. Soc. 21: 213-234.

Limenitis lorquini burrisonii
Maynard, 1891
Lorquin's Admiral

Plate 14, fig. 2. Map 41.

Common throughout Oregon, Lorquin's Admiral is easily recognized by its white bands and the orange patches at the apex of the forewings. Pierre Lorquin, who discovered this butterfly around 1850, was a French prospector in the California gold rush and the first important explorer of West Coast butterflies. The range of Lorquin's Admiral extends from southern California to British Columbia, eastward across the Great Basin, and northward to Wyoming, Montana, and Alberta. Our subspecies, *burrisonii,* is the northern variety; the California and Great Basin subspecies (including also some populations in southernmost Oregon) is *L. l. lorquini* (Boisduval), 1852, in which the orange apex is broader.

Lorquin's Admiral flies from May to October, is double brooded in climatically favorable locations, and may be commonly found along water courses, roadsides and clearings in the woods, as well as in city parks and gardens. It moves with quick beats of the wing and also glides. From perches on twigs and leaves of trees it darts out to pursue passing butterflies, dragonflies, or even birds, evidently an aggressive territorialism or undiscerning mating behavior.

The round and pale green egg of Lorquin's Admiral is laid singly at the tip of a willow, poplar, or apple leaf. Immature larvae of the late summer pass the winter in a hibernaculum; when full-grown the larvae are olive brown, have a white patch on the abdomen, and are provided with two plume-like horns that project over the head. As in other members of the genus, the chrysalis has a pronounced dorsal hump behind the thorax and large, dark olive-purple wing cases.

Reference:

(1) Perkins, Edwin M. & Stephen F. Perkins. 1966. A review of the *Limenitis lorquini* complex (Nymphalidae). J. Lepid. Soc. 20: 172-176.

Adelpha bredowii californica
(Butler), 1865
California Sister

Plate 14, fig. 3. Map 42.

Representing an otherwise neotropical genus, *Adelpha* (formerly *Heterochroa) bredowii* extends northward from Central America, one subspecies, *eulalia,* occurring in the southwestern states, the other, *californica,* in California and western Oregon. It may be found as far north as Portland and is abundant in the Siskiyous. The California Sister has been taken from May to October but is most numerous in middle and late summer.

This species commonly flies with Lorquin's Admiral which it superficially resembles. The apical orange patch is, however, much larger and sharply defined, and the under surface is marked with light blue stripes and connected marginal lunules. It is also more sedate in flight, though given, like Lorquin's Admiral, to a perching habit.

The larva, which feeds on oak, is well camouflaged by its mottled dark green color, which is ventrally lighter and brownish; it is ornamented with six pairs of long green tubercles. In the brown pupa two horn-like projections extend forward from the head.

Reference:

(1) Macy, Ralph W. 1958. On the occurrence of *Adelpha bredowii* (Nymphalidae) in Oregon. J. Lepid. Soc. (Lepid. News) 12: 199-200.

Vanessa atalanta rubria
(Fruhstorfer), 1909
Red Admiral

Plate 15, fig. 1. Map 43.

One of the most widespread and best known butterflies, the Red Admiral is common throughout the temperate zone of the Northern Hemisphere. First described in Europe by Linnaeus in 1758, the North American form, which differs only slightly, is now known as the subspecies *rubria*. Occurring everywhere in Oregon, the Red Admiral may be seen in city yards and parks, along roadsides, in shrubby fields, or in woodlands.

Being multibrooded, this butterfly is on the wing from April to November, or for that matter even on warm days in the winter, since fall-hatching adults can overwinter in protected hiding places. In flight it is fast and characteristically jerky in its movements; it also displays a territorial behavior in the late afternoon habit of patrolling along roads and walks, perching at times before darting off again.

The eggs, laid singly on leaves of nettles and hops, the larval foodplants, are pale green, barrel-shaped, and bear nine longitudinal ribs. The solitary caterpillars live in nests that are constructed by rolling up a leaf with silk. They are usually black with rows of yellow spots, but may be mottled white, light green, or brownish; they are further ornamented with ranks of branching spines. Pupation may occur in the larval nests. The chrysalids are brown or gray, decorated with gold-flecked tubercles, and suspended by a cremaster.

Hybrids between the Red Admiral and the Western Lady (*Vanessa annabella*) have been found in southern California.

References:

(1) Dimock, Thomas E. 1973. Three natural hybrids of *Vanessa atalanta rubria* x *Cynthia annabella* (Nymphalidae). J. Lepid. Soc. 27: 274-278.

(2) Field, William D. 1971. Butterflies of the genus *Vanessa* and of the resurrected genera *Bassaris* and *Cynthia* (Lepidoptera: Nymphalidae). Smithsonian Contrib. Zoology, No. 84, 105 pp.

Vanessa (Cynthia) virginiensis (Drury), 1773
Virginia Lady

Plate 15, fig. 3. Map 44.

The Virginia Lady, the Painted Lady, and the Western Lady have recently (Field, 1971) been separated from the genus *Vanessa* and assigned to *Cynthia*. Since natural hybrids are known between the Red Admiral and the Western Lady, the relationship between *Cynthia* and *Vanessa* is very close and the justification of the separation may be argued. *Vanessa virginiensis* (once known as *hunteri,* so named in 1775 by Fabricius after John Hunter, the famous 18th century British naturalist and surgeon) is found from the Atlantic to the Pacific and from southern Canada to the northern coast of South America. While commoner in the eastern and midwestern states, it shows up sparingly most anywhere in Oregon. Being double brooded and able to survive the winter in the adult stage, the Virginia Lady has been taken from May to end of October. It may be easily distinguished from the other two members of the *Cynthia* group by the two large and only eyespots on the underside of the hindwing.

The larvae construct net-like nests by loosely tying together the tops of their foodplants, nettles and various composites (*Gnaphalium, Antennaria, Anaphalis, Artemesia, Senecio*). They are lilac colored and have velvety black saddle-like patches across each segment that bear small orange spots and branched black bristles; larger white spots lie along the sides of the abdomen. The pendulous brown chrysalids are provided with orange-tipped tubercles.

Reference:
See under *Vanessa atalanta rubria*.

Vanessa (Cynthia) cardui (Linnaeus), 1758
Painted Lady

Plate 15, fig. 4. Map 45.

The Painted Lady has the distinction of being the most widely distributed butterfly in the world, appearing throughout Eurasia, Africa, North America, and northern South America; it is absent from Australia and New Zealand. Nevertheless, in most temperate climates it is a transient, unable to survive cold winters, and its reappearance depends on vast northward migrations from southern and warmer permanent habitats. Since these migrations are not annual, the populations fluctuate from year to year. In some years the Painted Ladies may be exceedingly abundant everywhere in Oregon, in others they are scarce or even absent. When present, the butterflies produce a series of broods and may be found from April to November. In mild winters late hatches may survive till the next spring. In our region the northward flights arise from southern California and Mexico, and large recent migrations took place in 1958, 1966, and 1973. Few records of major return movements have been reported (Emmel & Wobus, 1966; Williams, 1970). Despite numerous observations and hypotheses, the reasons for these migrations and the factors guiding their direction remain obscure. My most memorable experience took place when a symposium on animal migration was held at Oregon State University in May of 1966, fortuitously coinciding with a great northward flight of Painted Ladies. The participants needed only to step out of the lecture hall to behold this spectacular event!

The Painted Lady averages larger in size than either *V. virginiensis* or *annabella*. It can be recognized by the row of five black postmedium spots on the upperside of the hindwing and five small eyespots on the under surface. Also, the diagonal light bar near the apex of the forewing is white rather than orange.

The delicate lilac caterpillar has yellow transverse lines between the segments, a yellow lateral stripe, scattered small black spots, and rows of light colored branched bristles. It builds nests like the larva of *virginiensis* and likewise feeds on nettles and composites, especially thistles, as well as mallows and lupines. The dark brown pupa, provided with golden-tipped tubercles, resembles that of the Virginia Lady.

References:

(1) Abbott, Charles H. 1962. A migration problem — *Vanessa cardui* (Nymphalidae), the Painted Lady butterfly. J. Lepid. Soc. 16: 229-233.

(2) Emmel, Thomas C. & Reinhard A. Wobus. 1966. A southward migration of *Vanessa cardui* in late

summer and fall, 1965. J. Lepid. Soc. 20: 123-124.

(3) Shields, Oakley. 1974. Toward a theory of butterfly migration. J. Res. Lepid. 13: 217-238.

(4) Tilden, J. W. 1962. General characteristics of the movements of *Vanessa cardui* (L.). J. Res. Lepid. 1: 43-49.

(5) Williams, C. B. 1970. The migration of the Painted Lady butterfly, *Vanessa cardui* (Nymphalidae), with special reference to North America. J. Lepid. Soc. 24: 157-175.

Vanessa (Cynthia) annabella (Field), 1971
Western Lady

Plate 15, fig. 5. Map 46.

Long known as *Vanessa carye,* William Field found that this name was given by Hübner (1812) to a South American species, and he renamed the Western Lady *annabella*. A common butterfly from the Rockies to the Pacific Coast and from southern British Columbia to Mexico and Central America, the Western Lady may be found at all altitudes and in all life zones. Like the Virginia Lady and the Painted Lady it produces multiple broods and may be seen from April to November, overwintering adults sometimes flying on warm days before spring.

Unlike *cardui,* the postmedian spots on the upper surface of the hindwings have blue centers, and on the underside the eyespots are more completely filled with dark scales. The diagonal light bar near the apex of the forewing above is orange instead of white.

The nest-building larvae vary in color from tan to black, possess yellow or orange segmental crosslines, a scattering of fine white hairs, and rows of spinecarrying tubercles. They feed on nettles and plants of the mallow family. The pendulous brown chrysalids are ornamented with white-pointed tubercles.

The occurrence of hybridization with *Vanessa atalanta* has been mentioned in the discussion of the Red Admiral. Various aberrant forms of the Western Lady occasionally show up, in one of which the postmedian spots are white. Breeding experiments are needed to determine whether these have a genetic basis.

References:

(1) Dimock, Thomas E. 1978. Notes on the life cycle and natural history of *Vanessa annabella* (Nymphalidae). J. Lepid. Soc. 32: 88-96.

(2) See under *Vanessa atalanta rubria*.

Junonia coenia coenia (Hübner), 1822
Buckeye

Plate 15, fig. 2. Map 47.

The strikingly patterned Buckeye cannot be mistaken for any other kind of Oregon butterfly. Some specimens are lighter or darker than others and variation is common in the size of the eyespots, these differences being largely conditioned by season and climate.

Often listed as *Precis coenia,* this generic assignment has recently been found in error (Tilden, 1973). *Junonia* and *Precis* are mainly tropical genera, but *J. coenia* is widely distributed in North America, being found from the northeastern states southward to the American tropics and across the central states to the Southwest and California. In Oregon it is of regular occurrence in the southern counties, but in warm years migrates sparingly and temporarily to the latitude of central Oregon. In its permanent habitat the Buckeye produces two generations and is able to hibernate in the adult stage. It may be taken from June to August or thereafter, but is commonest in late summer (second brood).

Frequenting unkempt fields, gravel roads, and stream beds, the Buckeye is a wary insect, at one moment basking spread-winged in the sun, at another darting off in rapid and erratic flight, and then quickly settling again. Males can be seen to occupy a perch from which they patrol a "territory", take after passing females, or pugnaciously attack other males, dragonflies, grasshoppers, or even birds.

The dark green, flattened, and ribbed eggs are laid on the larval foodplants which include plantain, monkeyflower, stonecrop, and verbena. The caterpillars are dark olive gray, longitudinally striped or spotted with yellow or orange, and adorned with branching spines of which a pair projects from the head. The wood-brown, mottled chrysalis is strongly arched on the back and concave below.

References:

(1) Scott, James A. 1975. Variability of courtship of the Buckeye Butterfly, *Precis coenia* (Nymphalidae). J. Res. Lepid. 14: 142-147.

(2) Tilden, J. W. 1970. Comments on the nearctic members of the genus *Precis* Hübner. J. Res. Lepid. 9: 101-108.

(3) Tilden, J. W. 1973. *Junonia* and *Precis*. A correction. J. Res. Lepid. 12: 216.

Nymphalis vau-album watsoni
(Hall), 1924
Watson's Tortoise-Shell

Plate 16, fig. 1. Map 48

Very rare in Oregon, this butterfly has up to now been reported only from Mill Creek Canyon, three miles south of Kooskooskie, Washington, just below the State border in Umatilla County, where specimens were taken on March 2, 1968 by Edward McMackin. Called Compton's Tortoise-Shell (*N. v. j-album*) in the eastern United States, our subspecies occurs in the Northwest and is known from Alaska, British Columbia, Alberta, Montana, Wyoming, Idaho, and adjacent eastern Washington. It is generally scarce except for unusual occasions when numbers of these butterflies may gather at mud puddles or decaying fruit. Despite being uncommon, *Nymphalis vau-album* has an extensive world distribution, ranging from eastern Europe across temperate Asia to China and Japan, and in America across southern Canada and the northern United States.

This Tortoise-Shell, which is larger than but somewhat resembles *Nymphalis californica,* derives its name (*vau-album*) from a tiny, silvery-white V-shaped speck at the center of the ventral hindwing. Its yellowish-brown and black mottling, and especially the bark-like underside, is adaptively protective, its habitat being wooded river courses and sunspangled canyons. Hibernating adults appear in the early spring, with the next brood flying in late summer.

The larvae, which live gregariously on willows and poplars, are light green marked with yellowish flecks and stripes, and bear bristly black spines.

Nymhalis californica
(Boisduval), 1852
California Tortoise-Shell

Plate 16, fig. 2. Map 49.

The California Tortoise-Shell is a well-known Western butterfly whose abundance is subject to great fluctuation, some years being relatively scarce, in others exceedingly numerous. Its range extends from British Columbia to southern California and east to the Rockies. Found wherever *Ceanothus* grows, it is at home in all mountainous areas of Oregon, and has been taken from March to November, the earliest captures being those of hibernating adults. In its protectively colored, bark-like underside the California Tortoise-Shell resembles other members of the genus *Nymphalis*. Individuals vary greatly in the darkness or lightness of this underside.

The California Tortoise-Shell is noted for occasional vast migratory movements and population "explosions", when startled travelers encounter swarming clouds of these butterflies on mountain highways, sometimes clogging radiator grills, slickening the pavement, and slowing traffic. These events invariably attract public attention, bring on news reports, and prompt telephone enquiries. Such mass movements and staggering population increases are unpredictable and sporadic. In Oregon they happened in 1952, 1959, and 1971, with most intense activity in the Cascades, lasting several weeks during July and August. Unlike other migrating butterflies, the California Tortoise-Shell is a permanent Oregon resident, which makes these mass movements a special problem. Powell has suggested that emigrations follow high population increases in localized areas, leading to new colonizations that breed to produce secondary "explosions". Shapiro has adduced evidence that migrations are upslope in the spring and downslope in the fall; he hypothesizes that the availability of nutritionally suitable *Ceanothus* foliage is involved rather than population density, such that upslope migrations follow June deterioration of the foodplant in the lowlands, with reversal of migration in the fall.

The California Tortoise-Shell produces two to three broods per year, the generation time being about eight weeks. The larvae are velvety black and finely speckled with white dots; yellow patches lie in front of the spine bases above, blue ones on the sides. Feeding on *Ceanothus,* high populations of the caterpillars virtually defoliate the plants. The ashy-gray chrysalids have a bluish sheen, but the abdominal region is yellowish-brown; a pair of black processes extend from the head end, and two angular projections arise from the brown-mottled thorax.

References:

(1) Fender, Kenneth M. & James H. Baker. 1953. Notes on the migration of *Nymphalis californica*. J. Lepid. Soc. (Lepid. News) 7: 15.

(2) Newcomer, E. J. 1959. Large numbers of *Nymphalis californica* in the Pacific Northwest in 1959. J. Lepid. Soc. 13: 64.

(3) Powell, Jerry A. 1972. Population expansions and mass movements of *Nymphalis californica* (Nymphalidae). J. Lepid. Soc. 26: 226-228.

(4) Shapiro, Arthur M. 1974. Movements of *Nymphalis californica* (Nymphalidae) in 1972. J. Lepid. Soc. 28: 75-78.

(5) Shapiro, Arthur M. 1975. Why do California Tortoiseshells migrate? J. Res. Lepid. 14: 93-97.

(6) Whittaker, R. H. 1953. Notes on a migration of *Nymphalis californica*. J. Lepid. Soc. (Lepid. News) 7: 9-10.

Nymphalis milberti furcillata
(Say), 1825
Milbert's Tortoise-Shell

Plate 16, fig. 3. Map 50.

Smaller than our other species of *Nymphalis*, Milbert's Tortoise-Shell is easily recognized by the broad orange-and-yellow band along the outer half of the fore- and hindwings. In the Western subspecies, *furcillata*, the yellow inner part of this band is wider than in the Eastern nominotypic variety. *Nymphalis milberti* is found from Newfoundland south to West Virginia, and westward to the Pacific Coast. Widespread throughout Oregon, this attractive butterfly may be seen in fields and along roadsides near woods and water courses, but is most abundant on moist mountain slopes and high meadows in the Cascades, the Blue Mountains and Wallowas, and on Steens Mountain. Flying from April to October, Milbert's Tortoise-Shell produces several broods through the year and is capable of adult hibernation.

The colony-forming larvae, which feed on nettle (*Urtica*), are black above, orange and greenish yellow on the sides, finely stippled with white dots, and furnished with bristly spines. The chrysalids vary from off-white to blackish, have paler colored wing-cases, and are provided with short, spiny projections.

Nymphalis antiopa antiopa
(Linnaeus), 1758
Mourning Cloak

Plate 16, fig. 4. Map 51.

While seldom seen in large numbers, the Mourning Cloak is nevertheless one of our most familiar butterflies, occurring everywhere in Oregon. In fact, its vast range includes the entire temperate zone of the Northern Hemisphere, Europe, Asia, and North America. In Great Britain it is rare, essentially a migrant from the continent, and is known as the Camberwell Beauty, named after the 18th century village from where its first capture, in 1748, was recorded; Camberwell is now engulfed in London.

The Mourning Cloak inhabits sunny glades, open woodlands, canyons, and even city yards. It is especially partial to streamsides, where it sails about trees and shrubs, and when settled with folded wings on a fallen log or tree trunk is well camouflaged by its bark-like underside. Long-lived and hardy, the first of these dark maroon Beauties emerge from adult hibernation in the early spring. Two or three broods later they may be seen till late fall.

The female Mourning Cloak lays its barrel-shaped and top-flattened eggs in a cluster around twigs of elm, willow, or poplar. The newly hatched larvae lead a gregarious life, sometimes in such numbers as to reach pest proportions. The velvety mature caterpillars are purplish-black, peppered with tiny white dots; red spots lie in a row along the back, and the abdominal false legs (prolegs), too, are red; branched black spines are aligned in rows along the back and sides. When ready to pupate, the caterpillars move down the tree trunk or drop to the ground, the gray and thornbedecked chrysalids hidden away under bark or fallen leaves.

Polygonia satyrus neomarsyas
dos Passos, 1969
Satyr Anglewing

Plate 17, fig. 1. Map 52.

The Anglewings (genus *Polygonia*) obtain their name from the ragged appearance of their outer wing margins. They are woodland butterflies, beautifully adapted against predation by their colors and patterns, the mottled orange and black of the wing uppersides like the colors of fallen leaves, and the undersides deceptively like bark. Further protection is afforded by their fast and erratic flight, and their manner of quick settling, with folded wings and often head down, on the trunk of a tree or a fallen log. They are also known as Comma Butterflies, since all possess near the center of the ventral hindwing a small silver fleck in the shape of a comma, a C, or a V. Circumpolar in distribution, the Anglewings are familiar butterflies in the northern parts of both the Old and the New World. The various species are rather similar in appearance and require some practice in their identification. Our Northwest Anglewings are most readily distinguished by the color and pattern of the wing undersides, taking also into account that males and females may differ; in some Eastern species there is, in addition to this sexual dimorphism, a seasonal variability. Late hatching adults are capable of overwintering by hiding in crevices, under debris, or in other protected places; they will take wing on any warm day early in the year.

The Satyr Anglewing (*P. satyrus*) is widespread in the Western states and extends eastward along the northern states and adjacent Canadian provinces as far as Newfoundland, New England, and New York. *P. s. neomarsyas* (the former name *marsyas* is unusable, since Edwards in 1870 thereby mistakenly described a specimen of the European *Polygonia c-album*!) ranges over most of Oregon, though it is apparently scarce along the east slope of the Cascades. Flying along trails through the woods and in sunny openings near streams, it is especially at home in the glades and canyons of mountainous country, though apt to appear also in wooded parks and yards. On warm days in the later winter or early spring these Anglewings are likely to be worn specimens that have survived the winter; a second, more abundant brood appears in the summer and early fall.

The Satyr Anglewing can be readily told by the brown color of the underside. In the male there is a pronounced pattern of fine vertical striations; in the female this is less conspicuous, so that the undersurface is more concolorously light brown, somewhat washed-out in appearance. The silver fleck is C-shaped, thicker than in other species, and with slightly hooked ends; in females the C-mark is thinner. Like all Anglewings it is a wary butterfly and easily eludes the net. Territorial in behavior, it is also pugnacious, aggressively taking after passers-by of its own and other kinds.

The larval foodplant is nettle. The female butterfly lays its green and vertically ribbed eggs in groups of three or four on the underside of the leaves. The caterpillars live in a tent-like nest made by loosely tying together a number of leaves with silken threads. When fully grown they are black, with a greenish stripe along the back, and armed with rows of light colored spines. The pendulous brown pupa is rather angulate, with thorn-like projections over its body.

References:

(1) Brown, F. Martin. 1967. The types of the nymphalid butterflies described by William Henry Edwards. Part III. Nymphalinae, Limenitidinae, Apaturinae and Charaxinae. Trans. Am. Entom. Soc. 93: 319-393.

(2) dos Passos, Cyril F. 1969. A name for *Polygonia satyrus marsyas* Auctorum (Lepidoptera: Nymphalidae). Trans. Am. Entom. Soc. 95: 153-159.

Polygonia faunus rusticus (Edwards), 1874
Faun Anglewing

Plate 17, fig. 2. Map 53.

In the East, *Polygonia faunus* may be found from southern Canada to northern Georgia and westward to Minnesota and Iowa. It shows up again in western Montana and Wyoming and throughout the Pacific Northwest as the subspecies *rusticus*. In Oregon this butterfly is common in the Coast Range, the Cascades, the Blue Mountains, and the Wallowas, being especially at home in sunny clearings of the forested mountain country. Like other Anglewings, the adults are capable of surviving the winter and may be found flying in the early spring; in the late summer and early fall, however, the butterflies of the following generation are more abundant. Territorial and aggressive, the Faun Anglewing resembles other species of the genus in its behavior.

The dark border on the upper surface of the hindwings is very broad and fully encloses the row of rather small yellow spots. On the underside the wings are gray, contrastingly mottled in the male, and with two submarginal rows of greenish spots; in the female, however, the gray underside tends to be concolorous and washed-out-looking, the submarginal spots reduced to an inner row of small black specks, and the silvery C-mark quite slight.

The larval foodplants of the Faun Anglewing include willow, alder, currant, azalea, and rhododendron. The eggs are attached singly to the upper surface of the leaves. The fully grown larvae are reddish or yellow-brown, with a white saddle near the center of the back and a broken band of dull orange along each side; rows of whitish spines complete their apparel. The brownish-yellow and glossy chrysalids are ornamented with several metallic spots.

Polygonia zephyrus (Edwards), 1870
Zephyr Anglewing

Plate 17, fig. 3. Map 54.

The Zephyr Anglewing is a butterfly of the mountanous West. It ranges through the Rockies from Alaska and British Columbia to Manitoba, thence south to New Mexico; also along the Sierras of California and the Cascades of the Northwest. Though absent from the Coast Range, this is the commonest Anglewing in all other mountainous regions of Oregon, flying mostly at altitudes above three thousand feet.

It can be told from other species by its lighter overall color, the narrower dark outer margin, and the large submarginal yellow spots which are much elongated inwardly and sometimes almost confluent; the bottom black spot near the lower margin of the forewing is single, not double as in our other species. On the underside the wings are a cool soft gray, or grayish-brown, and are marked with subdued fine striations; the tiny black spots which form a submarginal row are often ringed with yellow. There are no striking differences between males and females.

The larvae feed on currant and gooseberry (*Ribes*), azalea, and rhododendron. Fullgrown, they are black, with a dorsal pattern resembling a row of backward pointing arrowheads; the lateral spines are black, the dorsal ones reddish-buff on the thorax and white on the abdomen. The salmon-and-olive mottled chrysalids have two short protuberances on the head and a prominently humped thorax; the back is decorated with silver specks.

Polygonia oreas silenus (Edwards), 1870
Silenus Anglewing

Plate 17, fig. 4. Map 55.

A scarce butterfly, the Silenus Anglewing is hardly ever seen in numbers, a few solitary specimens being the usual year's find. It is a native of the Northwest, occurring from Oregon to British Columbia. It should be sought along wet spots in the heavy coniferous forests of the Coast Range, the Siskiyous, and the western slope of the Cascades. In eastern Oregon it is also found in the Blue Mountains and the Wallowas. Overwintering adults in the Coast Range may show up in March, while a later generation flies through September.

Patterned much like *Polygonia satyrus* on the upper surface, the outer wing margins are somewhat more deeply incised and the hindwing tail is more robust; the submarginal yellow spots are well developed, sometimes approaching the condition in *zephyrus*. The most distinctive characteristic, however, is the very dark underside, brownish-black, or nearly black in some fresh specimens, with closely set fine striations as in *zephyrus*. The silver mark is sharply right-angled and has pointed ends. In females the dark color of the underside is less intense, the silver mark thinner, and the hindwing more rounded.

The details of the early stages have not been recorded, but the larvae, like those of *zephyrus*, feed on currant, gooseberry, azalea, and rhododendrons.

Phyciodes tharos pascoensis Wright, 1905
Pasco Crescent

Plate 18, fig. 1. Map 56.

Familiar butterflies of fields and roadsides, the Crescents belong to a genus, *Phyciodes*, which is restricted to the New World and whose representatives, though mostly tropical, may be found from the Arctic shores of Canada to southern Argentina. They owe their name to the presence on the underside of the hindwing of a conspicuous and often pearly-white crescentic spot, an enlarged lunule of a row that extends along the outer margin.

Phyciodes tharos, the most abundant member of the genus in the Eastern and Midwestern United States, where it is known as the Pearl Crescent, ranges over most of North America, from central Canada to southern Mexico, but does not occur west of the Sierra Nevada and the Cascades. It is readily distinguished from other Crescents by the bold black border (especially marked in males) and the relatively large unbroken orange of the central area; on the underside the prominent brown patch at the outer angle of the hindwing is also characteristic. Our subspecies, *P. t. pascoensis* (central and eastern Washington, northeastern Oregon, Idaho, and Utah) differs from the nominotypic Eastern variety mainly in lacking spring and fall seasonal forms that are more darkly colored beneath than those of the summer generation, an effect regulated during development by differences in photoperiod. The Pasco Crescent resembles the summer form of *P. tharos tharos*. Oregon records are from fields and roadsides of the upper Columbia and Snake River basins, and extend from June to September. This butterfly often displays an aggressive behavior, pugnaciously attacking other and larger species.

The eggs of *Phyciodes tharos* are deposited on leaves of asters and related composites, often in clusters of over a hundred and even two or three layers deep. These hatch into sizeable colonies of larvae which, when mature, are black, marked with a yellow stripe on each side, dots along the back, and covered with brownish spines. The gray to brown chrysalids are mottled with darker spots and lines and abdominally decorated with short tubercles.

References:
(1) Forbes, W. T. M. 1944. The genus *Phyciodes* (Lepidoptera, Nymphalinae). Entomologica Americana 24: 139-208.
(2) Oliver, Charles G. 1976. Photoperiodic regulation of seasonal polyphenism in *Phyciodes tharos* (Nymphalidae). J. Lepid. Soc. 30: 260-263.
(3) Vawter, A. T. & Peter F. Brussard. 1975. Genetic stability of populations of *Phyciodes tharos* (Nymphalidae: Melitaeinae). J. Lepid. Soc. 29: 15-23.

Phyciodes campestris campestris (Behr), 1863
Field Crescent

Plate 18, figs. 2, 3. Maps 57, 58.

A wide ranging and the most abundant Western species, *Phyciodes campestris* inhabits most of the region west of the Great Plains, from the Arctic North to Mexico. Our subspecies represents its Pacific component, stretching from Alaska to southern California and eastward to Wyoming and central Nevada. Flying from May to September, it is abundant almost everywhere in Oregon except along the coast, frequenting streamsides, flowered prairies, and especially the aster-covered mountain meadows.

In both sexes the Field Crescent is heavily marked with black, leaving the orange regions broken into patches and interrupted bands. The contrast between light and dark markings is more prominent in the female. On the underside the male hindwings are usually of a diffuse orange yellow color; with the network of darker lines much subdued; in the female the reticulate pattern is more pronounced and the row of submarginal crescents better defined.

As in *Phyciodes tharos*, the eggs are laid in clusters on the leaves of asters. The mature black and spiny larvae have a brown under surface and light colored bands along the sides. The soft brown chrysalids are marked with a network of darker lines and speckles.

At higher altitudes occasional specimens are more brightly and completely orange, with a tendency for the dark pattern to be strongly reduced. In males the dark brown markings of the hindwing under surface may be completely suppressed. In the alpine regions of the central and northern California Sierras such individuals characterize whole populations and are regarded as a separate subspecies, *P. c. montana* (Behr), 1863. In Oregon, however, they appear only

Phyciodes orseis orseis Edwards, 1871
Orseis Crescent

Plate 18, fig. 4. Map 59.

One of the rarest of North American butterflies, the Orseis Crescent is restricted in its distribution to the Coast Ranges of northern California and southwestern Oregon. It may be sought in the Siskiyous of Jackson County, principally along small streams in the canyons of the Applegate River tributaries. It flies together with *P. campestris* and *mylitta,* but unlike these species it is single-brooded and on the wing during the month of May and not much later.

The Orseis Crescent may be easily confused with *P. campestris,* which it strongly resembles on the upper surface. It is, however, very dark and averages larger in size. The shape of the wings is less rounded: the forewing has a straighter costal margin and a more produced apex; the hindwing has an outer margin that is more vertical in its upper portion and angled inward near the middle. On the underside both sexes have the hindwings contrastingly and sharply patterned, like *mylitta* rather than *campestris*. In its behavior *orseis* also resembles *mylitta*: the males perch on shrubs and patrol a flyway throughout the day, darting at passing objects in search of females.

The early stages of the Orseis Crescent have recently been carefully studied by James Scott. Clusters of barrel-shaped and ribbed eggs are deposited on the leaves of thistles, the larval foodplants (as in *mylitta*). The fully grown caterpillars are maroon black with white stripes and rows of dark brown or black spines. The mottled brown chrysalids, dorsally adorned with abdominal tubercles, are much like those of *mylitta*. The period of development, from egg to adult, averages 51 days for males, 58 for females; the pupal duration is correspondingly 10 to 13 days.

References:

(1) Brown, F. Martin. 1966. The types of nymphalid butterflies described by William Henry Edwards — Part II, Melitaeinae. Trans. Am. Entom. Soc. 92: 357-468.

(2) Scott, James A. 1973. Early stages and biology of *Phyciodes orseis* (Nymphalidae). J. Res. Lepid. 12: 236-242.

(3) Scott, James. 1975. Early stages of *Phyciodes pallida, P. orseis,* and *P. mylitta* (Nymphalidae). J. Res. Lepid. 14: 84.

Phyciodes mylitta mylitta (Edwards), 1861
Mylitta Crescent

Plate 18, fig. 5. Map 60.

Like *Phyciodes campestris,* the Mylitta Crescent is a common and widespread Western butterfly, found from British Columbia to Baja California and eastward to the Rockies. Adapted to a wider range of habitats than *campestris,* it occurs everywhere in Oregon and at all altitudes, from sea level to timberline. It inhabits city lots, dry and wet meadows, forest glades, roadsides, the coastal plain, and mountain highlands. One of the first butterflies to fly in the spring, it is multibrooded and may be seen from March to October; in late summer it can be very abundant.

Averaging somewhat smaller in size than other Crescents, *mylitta* has a pattern of thin black lines whereby the area of orange-yellow ground color is correspondingly increased. The network of lines, spots, and bands on the underside of the hindwings is cleanly developed in both males and females. Spring and summer specimens, however, differ in that the former have more extensive brown patches with bands and spots that tend to be silvery white, whereas in the latter the brown areas are reduced and the bands and spots are yellow; these differences are especially noticeable in males.

The whitish eggs are flattened on the top and bottom. The larvae feed on thistles and when fully grown are velvety black, with faint yellow streaks along the back and sides; the spines are black, except for the bottom rows which are yellow. The wood-brown to ash-gray chrysalids have a golden sheen and bear three dorsal rows of tubercles.

References:

See under *Phyciodes tharos pascoensis* and *P. orseis orseis*.

Phyciodes pallida barnesi Skinner, 1897
Barnes' Crescent

Plate 18, fig. 6. Map 61.

The largest butterfly of the genus *Phyciodes,* Barnes' Crescent lives in the dry plateau land of the upper Columbia and Snake River basins, from British Columbia to northcentral Oregon, and from here extends into similar terrain of Idaho, eastern Nevada, Utah, Wyoming, and Montana. Despite this relatively wide distribution it is not common, the colonies being widely separated. In Oregon it should be sought in the lower Deschutes River basin of Wasco and northern Jefferson Counties, especially in the area of Warm Springs and Sherar Falls. Its habitat is in the streambeds and on the hillsides of dry gullies. Unlike the Mylitta Crescent it has but one brood and flies from April to June.

Barnes' Crescent is roughly similar to *P. mylitta*, with which it may fly, but is decidedly larger. At the middle of the inner margin the forewings have a bold and squarish black spot; the central black markings of the hindwings tend to be suppressed, exposing a large area of bright yellow-brown ground color. On the underside the hindwings are creamish rather than fulvous, with the row of submarginal lunules prominent and pale, and the brown patch of the outer angle only vaguely expressed. On both upper and under surfaces females are more strongly and contrastingly patterned, with portions of the light bands on the dorsal forewings often being cream colored. Large specimens may at first sight be mistaken for some kind of Checkerspot (*Chlosyne*)! The males of Barnes' Crescent are aggressive in behavior, like those of *P. orseis* and *mylitta*.

As in *Phyciodes mylitta*, the mature and spiny larvae are dull black, but mottled with orange rather than lined with yellow. They feed on thistles.

Chlosyne (Charidryas) acastus (Edwards), 1874
Acastus Checkerspot

Plate 19, fig. 1. Map 62.

The genus *Chlosyne* is a large and varied assembly of North and South American butterflies that can be divided into a number of subgenera made up of closely related species groups. Thus in Oregon the species *acastus, palla,* and *hoffmanni* belong to the subgenus *Charidryas,* and *leanira* to *Thessalia*. In older literature these and others were included in the genus *Melitaea* which is now restricted to the Old World.

The Acastus Checkerspot is essentially a butterfly of the arid land overgrown with sage and rabbitbrush. It is a single-brooded species that flies in May and June. The populations in the Alvord Basin, off the eastern escarpment of Steens Mountain, belong to the nominotypic subspecies *C. a. acastus*. The bands of orange spots on the upper surface are separated by thick black lines. In the females, which are often surprisingly large, portions of the bands are almost yellow. The under surface is very light, the band-forming patches being glossy white to creamish and sharply rimmed by thin black lines; those of the submarginal row enclose small, light orange-brown spots, each with a tiny white center.

Populations from the canyons of the Burnt and Snake Rivers in Baker County have been named *C. acastus dorothyi* by David Bauer (*in* Howe, 1975). In these the black markings of the upperside are bolder.

The immature stages of the Acastus Checkerspot have not been fully described. The spiny larvae feed on rabbitbrush and resemble those of *Chlosyne palla,* being black and decorated with rows of crescentic orange spots and specks of white.

Reference:
(1) Bauer, David L. 1975. Tribe Melitaeinae (p. 157). *In* W. H. Howe, The Butterflies of North America. Doubleday, New York. 633 pp.

Chlosyne (Charidryas) palla (Boisduval), 1852
Northern Checkerspot

Plate 19, figs. 2-5. Maps 63-65.

Distributed in a great arc around the northern Great Basin, the species *Chlosyne palla* is found in the Rocky Mountains and westward to the Pacific States. Over this large area a number of subspecies can be distinguished, of which three occur in Oregon. Of these, *C. palla palla* (Boisduval) is the most widespread. It inhabits the southern mountains and the northern coastal ranges of California, and in Oregon the Siskiyous, southern Cascades and Warners, as well as all mountain regions of eastern Oregon, southeastern Washington, and adjacent Idaho. Flying from May to August, the Northern Checkerspot frequents canyons of the foothills, forest openings, and particularly tends to congregate at streambeds, damp ground, and puddles.

The upper surface of the male has bands of deep orange to red-brown spots interrupted by moderately heavy black lines; below, the bands of the hindwings are cream colored to pale yellow, the submarginal one encloses large rich orange-brown spots with tiny white centers, and the outer wing margin is edged with a red-brown stripe. The females of this subspecies are of two kinds (dimorphic). Some resemble the males in that they are mostly orange-brown above though with admixture of lighter, yellowish spots. Others are very dark (melanic), the black pattern being so much broadened as to reduce or partially obliterate the orange spots; these females are known as the form "eremita" (Greek for dark or black).

The larvae of the Northern Checkerspot feed on various kinds of paintbrush *(Castilleja)* and possibly some species of composites. Full-grown they are dull black with dorsal and lateral orange spots and white patches, and bear five rows of branching black spines. The brown to gray or black pupae have light brown spots and streaks and three rows of small glossy tubercles.

On the eastern slope of the central Cascades, and also at high altitudes in the Sierra Nevada, *C. palla palla* is replaced by *C. palla whitneyi* (Behr), 1863. Whitney's Checkerspot flies in June and July. It differs from *C. p. palla* mainly in lacking the "eremita" type of dark females, both sexes being orange-brown. In some individuals the black pattern consists of thinner lines, causing the orange to cover more wing surface. The larvae feed on rabbitbrush.

Our third subspecies is *C. palla sterope* (Edwards), 1870. It is confined to the semiarid Palouse region of the upper Columbia Plateau, which includes the lowlands of eastern Washington and northcentral Oregon. The type locality is Tygh Valley in Wasco County. The Palouse Checkerspot can be found from May to August in the sage-covered hills and canyons.

Chlosyne (Charidryas) hoffmanni segregata (Barnes & McDunnough), 1918
Hoffmann's Checkerspot

Plate 19, fig. 6. Map 66.

Adapted to higher elevations, Hoffmann's Checkerspot occurs in subalpine meadows and canyons of the Sierra Nevada, northward along the crest of the Oregon Cascades, then along the eastern slope of the Washington Cascades to the Canadian border; it is also present in the higher coastal ranges of northwestern California and southwestern Oregon. Our subspecies, *segregata,* was first discovered at Crater Lake. It may be seen from late May to August but is never abundant; in many places it flies with the commoner *C. palla.*

Roughly resembling the Northern Checkerspot, the outline of the spread wings is more squarish. On the upper surface the black at the base of the hindwings extends farther outward and impinges sharply on the inner band of light spots which are distinctly paler and more prominent than the orange ones of the outer rows; the lower spots are somewhat reduced in size. The orange spots near the forewing apex often tend to run together. On the underside the wings are very much like *palla palla.*

The males are dorsally orange-brown, like those of *palla palla,* with the inner row of spots more yellowish; ventrally, however, the wings are pale, reminding one of *Chlosyne acastus:* the bands are dull white, the submarginal one enclosing a row of small orange spots. All of the females are of the dark "eremita" form, black, and with spots that are cream colored; ventrally they are like the males, but the bands may be yellowish instead of white. The early stages of *sterope* have not been fully described, but the larvae are known to feed on rabbitbrush (*Chrysothamnus viscidiflorus*).

The early stages of Hoffmann's Checkerspot are known only from Newcomer's account for the closely similar Washington subspecies, *C. hoffmanni manchada* (Bauer). The eggs are deposited in clusters on the leaves of asters. The mature larvae are dorsally black, speckled with white, but brown beneath the cream colored irregular line that runs along the sides; the bristles are black above this line and brown below it. The pupae are white to brown in color and bear irregular brown to blackish markings.

Reference:
(1) Newcomer, E. J. 1967. Early stages of *Chlosyne hoffmanni manchada* (Nymphalidae). J. Lepid. Soc. 21: 71-73.

Chlosyne (Thessalia) leanira (Felder & Felder), 1860
Leanira Checkerspot

Plate 19, fig. 7; plate 48, fig. 5. Map 67.

This elegant species can be recognized immediately by the unique color and pattern of the underside. Its range extends from southern Oregon through the California coastal ranges and central Sierran foothills to northern Baja California, then westward through the deserts of the southern Great Basin as far as Colorado and Arizona.

We have two subspecies. *C. leanira oregonensis,* recently named by David Bauer (*in* Howe, 1975), occurs in Josephine, Jackson, and southern Douglas Counties. Its isolated colonies lie in hidden canyons and on hillsides beside small streams in the Siskiyous and Cascadian foothills. From here they extend into adjacent northern California. On the upperside the wings are black, patterned with rows of small yellow spots; the apical region of the forewing has a flush of red which is more extensive in the female. Below, the forewing is broadly washed with rusty red; on the hindwing the handsome broad yellow bands are interrupted by a submarginal black one which encloses six yellow dots, and by an irregular black mesh at the base. It flies in June and July.

The subspecies *C. leanira alma* (Strecker), 1878, has very recently been found in the Alvord Basin and Trout Mountains of southeastern Harney County, flying in late May. This is a desert race previously known from Nevada and other regions of the Great Basin. While the underside bears the unmistakable *leanira* color and pattern, the upperside is extensively, and in females almost wholly, orange red, with the wing veins and margins outlined in black, plus some black patches in the basal area; the bands of yellow spots, so conspicuous in *oregonensis,* are greatly reduced or obsolescent.

The larvae of *Chlosyne leanira* feed on various species of paintbrush (*Castilleja*) and on bird's beak (*Cordylanthus pilosus*). They are black, marked with orange spots and stripes; black spines are arranged in seven rows along the body. The white chrysalids have their under surface and sides streaked with black lines.

Reference:
(1) Bauer, David L. 1975. Tribe Melitaeinae (p. 166). *In* W. H. Howe, The Butterflies of North America. Doubleday, New York. 633 pp.

Genus *Euphydryas*

The attractive Checkerspots of the genus *Euphydryas* occur in the northern regions of both the Old and the New World. Many of them, including the three found in Oregon, are highly polytypic in that they tend to form numerous geographic races, or subspecies. In order to relate these races to their respective species it is often necessary to examine the male genitalia which remain fairly constant. Color and pattern of the wings will usually suffice to distinguish the species within the confines of any one locality, but these criteria become frustrating and less dependable when specimens from different, especially distant, regions are compared. The three Oregon species may be separated by the following characteristics of the male genitalia:

E. chalcedona: Upper prong of valval clasp projecting at a right angle to the lower and very short.

E. anicia: Upper prong of valval clasp long and curved downward, approximately parallel to the lower.

E. editha: Upper prong of valval clasp long and projecting upward at an angle of more than 90 degrees to the lower.

Except for the desert populations of southern California and Arizona, *Euphydryas* Checkerspots are single-brooded and fly in the spring or early summer (depending on altitude). The half-grown larvae soon go into protracted diapause and complete their development and pupation early in the following year. The butterflies are intensely colonial and remain confined to very restricted areas within which, however, they may be quite abundant. The isolation of the colonies in regions of differing ecology and the lack of vagility contribute to promoting the formation of the many geographic races.

The characteristics of the *Euphydryas* populations have been intensively studied by Paul Ehrlich and his associates. Their papers should be consulted for detailed analysis of factors controlling colony sizes, flight movements, foodplant dependencies, genetic control of variabilities, gene flow between populations, etc.

Higgins has recently subdivided the genus *Euphydryas,* grouping the closely related species of the North American West under the name *Occidryas.*

chalcedona *anicia* *editha*

References:

(1) Brussard, P. F. & P. R. Ehrlich. 1970. Contrasting population biology of two species of butterfly. Nature 227: 91-92.

(2) Brussard, P. F., P. R. Ehrlich & M. C. Singer. 1974. Adult movements and population structure in *Euphydryas editha.* Evolution 28: 408-415.

(3) Ehrlich, Paul R. 1961. Intrinsic barriers to dispersal in checkerspot butterfly. Science 134: 108-109.

(4) Ehrlich, Paul R. & Larry G. Mason. 1966. The population biology of the butterfly *Euphydryas editha.* iii. Selection and the phenetics of the Jasper Ridge colony. Evolution 20: 165-173.

(5) Ehrlich, Paul R. et al. 1975. Checkerspot butterflies: a historical perspective. Science 188: 221-228.

(6) Higgins, L. G. 1978. A revision of the genus *Euphydryas* Scudder (Lepidoptera: Nymphalidae). Entomologist's Gazette 29: 109-115.

Euphydryas (Occidryas) chalcedona
(Doubleday), 1847
Chalcedon Checkerspot

Plate 20, figs. 1-7. Maps 68-71.

The Checkerspots of the *Euphydryas chalcedona* complex are inhabitants of the Pacific coast states and certain immediately neighboring areas to the east. The Oregon members of this group include our largest Checkerspots. They are predominantly dark on the upper wing surface, the jet black ground color contrasting strongly with the rows of creamish white spots and the red marginal bands and discal patches.

The nominotypic subspecies *E. c. chalcedona* (Doubleday), 1847, essentially a butterfly of the Californian Coast Ranges, extends into the southern parts of Jackson, Josephine, and Curry Counties, where it grades into *E. c. colon*. It differs from the latter in a more extensive development of the cream spots, especially in the possession of a central third row on the hind wings. An avid visitor of flowers and easily netted, it may be abundant during May and June along roadsides, small streams, and in clearings, sometimes flying with the usually scarcer *E. editha baroni* distinguished by its row of bold reddish spots and more rounded wing shape. The spiny black larvae, marked with white stripes or speckles and rows of orange spots, feed mainly on penstemons, monkey-flowers, and paintbrush.

A closely similar subspecies of the Californian Sierras extends into southern Klamath and Lake Counties. This is *E. chalcedona macglashanii* (Rivers), 1888 (Macglashan's Checkerspot). In the month of June it is quite abundant at Chandler Wayside north of Lakeview and in the draws and meadows of Bly Mountain east of Klamath Falls. On the average, this butterfly slightly exceeds *E. c. chalcedona* in size and white spotting. However, the Bly Mountain population is strongly mixed with *colon*-like specimens, presenting a population complex that needs more detailed study. On the western fringe of its Oregon distribution (Jackson County), Macglashan's Checkerspots forms a cline with *E. c. chalcedona*. The larvae feed on penstemons. Within the population areas of *E. c. macglashanii* one also finds occasional specimens of *E. editha edithana*, which can be readily distinguished by its smaller size and submarginal row of bold red spots.

Most of Oregon is inhabited by the subspecies *colon* and the closely related *wallacensis*. The Colon Checkerspot, *E. c. colon* (Edwards), 1881, is widely distributed west of the Cascadian divide, often in substantial colonies along roadsides and in flowered clearings and canyons of the forested hills. Depending upon altitude, it flies from May to July. In certain regions of the northern Cascades, notably on Monument Peak in Linn County, it flies with the much less numerous and very reddish *E. editha colonia*; in Benton and Polk Counties it is sympatric with *E. editha taylori* which, however, is on the wing several weeks earlier. Large and very dark, the yellow spots of the outer row are much reduced in the Colon Checkerspot, and the middle row on the hindwing is practically absent, leaving a wide band of jet black. On the underside of the forewing the discal area is strikingly brick red, due to the relative reduction of the macular pattern. The bristly black larvae build small webs among the leaves of the foodplant, *Symphoricarpus* (snowberry). Within the curled and fallen leaves they pass the winter in diapause.

East of the Cascades *colon* is replaced by the very similar but smaller *E. c. wallacensis* Gunder, 1928, named after the place of its discovery, Wallace, Idaho. The marginal red spots of Gunder's Checkerspot are more pronounced than those of *colon*, and in many individuals the rows of yellow spots are more completely developed, sometimes including on the hindwings the middle row characteristic of *chalcedona* and *macglashanii*. This butterfly is found throughout eastern Oregon and Washington, Idaho, and in western Montana. Within their respective ranges in northeastern Oregon, *wallacensis* is sympatric with *E. anicia bakeri*, *E. a. veazieae*, and *E. a. howlandi*; in southern Klamath and Lake Counties and in the Ochocos it flies with *E. editha edithana*, and along the east slope of the Cascades with *E. e. remingtoni*.

David Bauer has advanced reasons for separating the southern *chalcedona* and the northern *colon* groups of races into two species. Since these rest mainly on primary foodplant and minor larval differences, I prefer to keep the complex together until interracial sterility can be demonstrated by breeding tests.

References:

(1) Bauer, David. 1975. Genus *Euphydryas* Scudder. *In* W. H. Howe, The Butterflies of North America, Doubleday, N. Y., pp. 174-195.

Euphydryas (Occidryas) anicia
(Doubleday), 1847
Anicia Checkerspot

Plate 21, figs. 1-7. Maps 72-75.

Unlike the *chalcedona* and *editha* Checkerspots, the *anicia* species complex is strongly represented in the Rocky Mountain states, from where it extends northwestward as far as the Yukon Valley and the Washington Cascades and in the south to the eastern foothills of the Sierra Nevada. In Oregon this species is restricted to the eastern Blue Mountain and Great Basin counties.

Three of our four subspecies are rather similar and best distinguished in series. Superficially they are intermediate in appearance between the dominantly dark *chalcedona* and the dominantly reddish *editha*. On the ventral surface the white (rather than creamish) maculations are prominently rimmed with black — a characteristic less conspicuous in either *chalcedona* or *editha*. (These distinctions do not hold, incidentally, for Rocky Mountain subspecies.) The male genitalia, as previously described, are diagnostic.

The subspecies *E. a. veazieae* Fender & Jewett, 1953 (Veazie's Checkerspot) is the darkest of the three and superficially may resemble *E. chalcedona wallacensis* but for bolder white maculations and a usually prominent middle row of red spots on the upper side of the hindwings (sometimes white). First found in the Jackass Mountains west of Frenchglen, its range covers much of the sagebrush country of eastern Oregon and southern Washington. The bristly black larvae, which feed on Penstemon, are dorsally marked with rows of small white spots and adorned with tubercles, of which the middle ones have orange bases.

E. a. bakeri Stallings & Turner, 1945, is the lightest of this group, due to broader development of the red spots on both fore and hind wings, often giving to the butterfly an overall orange color. It is very local and should be sought in its type locality, Cave Creek, near Durkee in Baker County. It was discovered by James H. Baker, after whom it is named (Baker's Checkerspot). Its immature stages have not been described.

E. a. macyi Fender & Jewett, 1953 (Macy's Checkerspot) resembles *bakeri* but is somewhat less red and of larger average size. The distinction is best seen in series. It flies during June in the Alvord Basin off the east escarpment of Steens Mountain (type locality, Wildhorse Creek) in Harney County. It also occurs in the nearby Trout Creek Mountains. Its early stages are also unknown.

A fourth subspecies of *anicia*, known in Oregon only from the Wallowa Mountains, is *E. a. howlandi* Stallings & Turner, 1947 (Howland's Checkerspot). Quite unlike the previous three, this butterfly is dominantly deep red above and easily mistaken for an *editha* unless the genitalia are examined. The light spots are relatively reduced and more cream colored than white. It is also smaller than the others. Distinctly northern and montane, *howlandi's* distribution extends from the mountains of western Montana and northern Idaho westward along the U.S.-Canadian border to the east slope of the Washington Cascades. The Wallowa population appears to be isolated. The larva resembles that of *E. a. veazieae* and feeds on Penstemon.

References:
(1) Fender, Kenneth M. & Stanley G. Jewett. 1953. Two new races of *Euphydryas anicia* Doubleday & Hewitson (Lepidoptera: Nymphalidae). Wasmann J. Biol. 11: 115-119.
(2) Stallings, D. B. & J. R. Turner. 1945. Two new races of butterflies. J. Kansas Ent. Soc. 18: 82-83.

Euphydryas (Occidryas) editha
(Boisduval), 1852
Editha Checkerspot

Plate 22, figs. 1-6. Maps 76-81.

The *editha* Checkerspots, like those of the *chalcedona* complex, are most extensively represented in the western coast states, from British Columbia to the Mexican border; a few races occur in the northern Rockies. The male genitalia easily separate *editha* from other species. While the wing pattern varies considerably between subspecies, the red maculations tend to be prominent and often give to these Checkerspots a dominantly reddish color. The web-building black larvae are striped or speckled with white and bear orange or black tubercles armed with black bristles. They feed primarily on plaintain or certain Scrophulariaceae, especially *Collinsia* and *Castilleja;* the foodplant and oviposition preferences have been well discussed by Michael Singer. Of the six named subspecies occurring in Oregon, four were originally described from localities within the state.

The darkest Oregon subspecies of *editha* is Taylor's Checkerspot, *E. e. taylori* (Edwards), 1888. Its rows of cream and deep red spots are well separated by heavy black lines or bands, and the wings are proportionally broader and rounder than those of the other races. Its spotty colonies extend southward from Vancouver Island to the Willamette Valley. Taylor's Checkerspot is one of the first butterflies to appear in the spring and during April and May fairly swarms on the meadows beside Oak Creek in the McDonald Forest north of Corvallis. It is, however, very local and not reported outside of Lane, Benton, and Polk Counties. The larvae feed on plantain. They are black, with white speckles forming a mid-dorsal and lateral line; the tubercles behind the thorax have orange bases, and all are tufted with black bristles.

A geographic race of the northern California coastal ranges extends across the Oregon border into Josephine and Jackson Counties. This is Baron's Checkerspot, *E. edith baroni* (Edwards), 1879. Larger than *taylori* and of more angular wing shape, the red spotbands in this butterfly are wider and the yellow spots of the outermost row tend to be reduced and partially reddened. The larva, much like that of *taylori* in appearance, feeds on *Pedicularis* (Scrophulariaceae).

Smaller but otherwise much like *baroni* in pattern and coloration is the Edithana Checkerspot, *E. e. edithana* (Strand), 1914. It ranges northward from the Modoc Plateau of northeastern California and adjacent Nevada into the mountains of central Oregon east of the Cascades. A vigorous colony occurs on Big Summit Prairie in the Ochocos. Part of the type material came from Klamath County. The early stages have not been recorded.

Distributed along the Cascadian crest, all the way from central Washington southward through Oregon, is the large and splendidly red Colonia Checkerspot, *E. e. colonia* (Wright), 1905. It was first described from Mt. Hood. In this butterfly the central red band of the forewing is greatly widened, and on the hindwing the submarginal yellow spots are frequently edged or completely replaced by red scales; this is particularly common in females. *Colonia* should be sought in forest openings and along outcroppings of rock, usually at higher elevations. It is ordinarily not found in any great numbers, but a fine colony exists on Monument Peak (Linn Co.) where it flies in early July with the much more abundant *E. c. colon*.

Also very red, but smaller than *colonia,* is *E. e. remingtoni* Burdick, 1959. In this subspecies the submarginal red spot-bands rarely show any trace of yellow at all. Remington's Checkerspot is found at elevations from 4000 to 6000 feet in the central Oregon pumice country on the east slope of the Cascades, from Klamath to Deschutes County, where it forms populous colonies in forest openings and mountain meadows. In late June and July, when the mosquitoes are at their worst, Remington's Checkerspot fairly swarms on Skookum Meadow below the summit of Walker Rim. The larvae feed on paintbrush.

A high altitude population of very dwarfed *editha* Checkerspots occurs on the slopes of Mt. Thielsen near timberline (around 7500 ft.). This is *E. e. lawrencei* Gunder, 1931 (Lawrence's Checkerspot). It seems to differ in no respect from *remingtoni* except size and may be a climatically induced modification of the latter. It may be significant that in certain years such dwarf forms occur at lower elevations, e.g. near Gilchrist and at Davis Lake (about 4400 ft.), usual territories for typical *remingtoni*.

References:
(1) Burdick, William N. 1958. A new race of *Euphydryas* from the Cascade Range of Oregon (Nymphalidae). J. Lepid. Soc. (Lepid. News) 12: 165-170.

(2) Singer, Michael C. 1971. Evolution of food-plant preference in the butterfly *Euphydryas editha*. Evolution 25: 383-389.

(3) Tilden, J. W. 1958. Notes on the life history of *Euphydryas editha bayensis*. J. Lepid. Soc. (Lepid. News) 12: 33-35.

(4) See under Genus *Euphydryas*.

Boloria selene tollandensis (Barnes & Benjamin), 1925
Silver-bordered Meadow Fritillary

Plate 23, fig. 1. Map 82.

While Oregon can claim only two kinds of Meadow Fritillaries, there are many other species in colder climates, at high altitudes in the Rockies and in northern regions across the continent. The genus *Boloria* is, in fact, circumpolar and occurs also in the Old World. Its present distribution in North America seems to be related to the history of glaciation.

Boloria selene, present in both Eurasia and North America, is easily recognized by the silver markings of the under surface. It is a common butterfly in wet meadows and bogs of the upper Midwest and the East, including Canada. Colonies also occur in marshes at high altitudes in the Rocky Mountains. In the Pacific Northwest, however, this species, which appears to have been widespread at one time, is now found in only a few widely separated small colonies. It may be on the verge of extinction. The colony at Moxee Bog in Yakima County, Washington, has recently been protected through land purchase by the Nature Conservancy Society. Only a single colony is known in Oregon, which occupies about ten acres of marshy ravine adjoining Big Summit Prairie in the Ochoco Mountains of Crook County. The Meadow Fritillaries of these relict populations closely resemble and are tentatively assigned to the Coloradan subspecies *tollandensis*.

B. selene is usually double-brooded or more, depending on location. The larvae feed on violets, usually at night, and those of the last generation spend the winter in hibernation. Cylindrical in shape and olive-brown in color with greenish mottling, they bear several rows of barbed spines of which the prothoracic ones are four times as long as the others. The yellow-brown chrysalids, with lustrous spots of darker color, are pendent and bear two rows of dorsal cone-shaped tubercles.

References:
(1) Albright, Ray. 1960. A record of *Boloria selene* in Oregon. J. Lepid. Soc. 14: 158.

(2) Newcomer, E. J. & Wesley H. Rogers. 1963. Notes on *Boloria selene* (Nymphalidae) in the Pacific Northwest. J. Lepid. Soc. 17: 171-172.

(3) Kohler, Steve. 1977. Revision of North American *Boloria selene* (Nymphalidae) with description of a new subspecies. J. Lepid. Soc. 31: 243-268.

Boloria epithore (Edwards), 1864
Western Meadow Fritillary

Plate 23, figs. 2, 3. Maps 83, 84.

Unlike *Boloria selene,* the species *epithore* is limited to the American Far West, where it is very abundant. Its range extends from British Columbia to California and northeastward through Idaho to the western fringes of Alberta and Wyoming. For a long time it was thought to be monotypic, i.e., without distinguishable geographic races, but recent restudy has revealed the existence of four subspecies, of which two occur in Oregon.

B. epithore chermocki Perkins & Perkins, 1966, is common throughout western Oregon, from the coast to the eastern slope of the Cascades. It extends northward through Washington as far as southwestern British Columbia, and southward into northern California. Appearing as a spring butterfly in May and flying until August, Chermock's Meadow Fritillary may be seen in moist forest clearings as well as on wet meadows of mountains and valleys. After melting of the snow it is numerous on the 4000-foot summit of Mary's Peak in the Coast Range. Easily separated from *B. selene* by the absence of silver markings on the underside, the orange-brown and somewhat mottled ventral hindwing is crossed by a band of yellowish patches, outside of which runs a row of brown spots. The larvae, like those of *selene,* feed on the leaves of violets and hibernate before completing growth and pupation in the following spring. The type locality for *B. e. chermocki* is Dolph in Yamhill County.

The populations of *epithore* occurring in the northeastern corner of Oregon belong to the Rocky Mountain subspecies *B. e. borealis* Perkins, 1973. This differs from *chermocki* in only subtle details: a somewhat duller orange color above, the forewing margins dusted with black scales, and a more extensive black basal area; ventrally the hindwings are more brown than orange-brown, and the light patch against its anterior margin is yellowish rather than whitish as found in *chermocki*. *Borealis* extends northward into central British Columbia. There is no information concerning its early stages.

References:

(1) Perkins, Edwin M. & Stephen F. Perkins. 1966. A new race and discussion of the *Boloria epithore* complex (Nymphalidae). J. Lepid. Soc. 20: 103-117.

(2) Perkins, Edwin M. & W. Craig Meyer. 1973. Revision of the *Boloria epithore* complex, with description of two new subspecies (Nymphalidae). Bull. Allyn Museum 11: 1-23.

Genus *Speyeria*

The orange-brown Fritillaries of the genus *Speyeria* must be counted amongst the most beautiful of our butterflies. Medium to large in size, they are easily recognized by the bold silvery or sometimes cream-colored spots that ornament the underside of the hindwings. During the summer months these Fritillaries may be abundant in forest clearings, by roadsides, along streambanks, in canyons, and especially on flower-strewn slopes and meadows in the mountains. Though capable of strong flight as well as gentle wafting, they frequently settle and as avid nectar feeders are particularly attracted to thistles, wild asters and sunflowers, penstemons, mint, dogbane, and rabbit-brush. Conspicuous and not overly wary, they are easily netted.

The dark, mottled, and sharply spined larvae, on the other hand, are seldom seen. Well hidden and mainly nocturnal, they feed on various kinds of violets. When newly hatched they spend the winter in hibernation, completing their development in the following year. Detailed knowledge of the immature stages has until recently been hindered by difficulties in rearing, but with this problem now resolved, life history studies are proceeding with success. For Fritillaries of the Northwest such studies are being ably pursued by David V. McCorkle.

The strictly North American *Speyeria,* long included in the Old World genus *Argynnis,* differ from their Eurasian relatives in genitalic structure. All but three species are extremely variable, the Western ones in particular fragmenting into numerous geographic races which are often clinally conjoined. This, added to parallel variation between species, makes the identification of Fritillaries often very difficult and frustrating. In McDunnough's 1938 checklist they appeared (as *Argynnis*) under 81 names grouped into 39 species. By 1946 one hundred and nine names had been proposed! In 1947 dos Passos and Grey completely revised this group of butterflies in accordance with newer concepts of speciation and systematics, reducing the number of species to thirteen, under which they arranged 96 subspecies. Since that time additional subspecies have been described and a few previous names declared synonyms. Some recent opinion would also recognize a few more than thirteen species, which simply illustrates the difficulty of passing judgment in classifying Fritillaries.

Of the thirteen species of North American *Speyeria* (as listed by dos Passos, 1964), eight may be found in Oregon, including a large number of subspecies. The beginner is likely to find the separation of these butterflies troublesome. It is helpful to concentrate attention initially on specimens that are found in the same local area, since in this situation each species is ordinarily represented by only one subspecies.

By and large it will be found that the different species and subspecies differ one from another in one or more of the following characters: overall size; sexual dimorphism; dorsally by the general ground color, coarseness and intensity of the black markings, degree of dark basal suffusion, prominence of the marginal band, thickness of the veins; ventrally by the general color of the discal region, size and shape of the spots and whether or not they are silvered, color and width of the submarginal band between the two outer rows of spots. While the characters may vary somewhat even within subspecies, their fluctuations are usually within recognizable limits as will be apparent after some experience. Females are generally paler in ground color than the corresponding males; they also have more rounded wing outlines, and the silver or cream spots tend to show on the upper surface as light areas. In some species, especially *callippe* and *coronis,* the principal flight period of females follows that of the males by two or more weeks.

There is great need for genetic studies on Fritillaries, as well as experiments designed to reveal the effects of climate and other environmental factors. Such work would lead to better understanding of the variability encountered in the field, of the possible existence and degree of hybridization in nature, and of inter-and intraspecific relations generally.

References:
(1) dos Passos, C. F. & L. P. Grey. 1947. Systematic catalogue of *Speyeria* (Lepidoptera, Nymphalidae) with designations of types and fixations of type localities. Am. Mus. Novitates, No. 1370: 1-30.
(2) Mattoon, S. O., R. D. Davis & O. D. Spencer. 1971. Rearing techniques for species of *Speyeria* (Nymphalidae). J. Lepid. Soc. 25: 247-256.
(3) Moeck, Arthur H. 1957. Geographic variability in *Speyeria*. Milwaukee Entom. Society. Special Paper, 48 pp.
(4) Shields, Oakely. 1963. A trip into California and Oregon for *Speyeria*. J. Lepid. Soc. 17: 111-116.

Speyeria cybele (Fabricius), 1775
Great Spangled Fritillary and Relatives

Plate 23, figs. 4-6. Maps 85, 86.

The species complex *Speyeria cybele,* which includes the well known Great Spangled Fritillary (*S. c. cybele*) of the East and Midwest, extends from the Atlantic to the Pacific. Most of its members are large butterflies, and all possess silver spots and a broad yellow submarginal band on the underside of the hindwing. The western races show a sexual dimorphism in which the ground color of the female becomes yellow.

The most startling and spectacular expression of this dimorphism occurs in the Puget Sound Fritillary, *S. c. pugetensis* Chermock & Frechin, 1947. From late June to early September this magnificent butterfly may be found, rather locally, in draws and canyons of the Coast Range and at lower elevations on the west slope of the Cascades, occasionally also in the Willamette Valley. It ranges northward through western Washington to British Columbia. Strongly attracted to thistles, the males often visit the purple flowerheads in considerable numbers; the females, however, remain hidden in the forest and only rarely venture into the open. For every fifty males one may be lucky to see one female.

For many years confused with *S. c. leto,* the coastal *pugetensis* is more melanic, so that the dark and light portions of the wings stand in greater contrast. In males the shaded inner half of the wings is wider and sharply demarcated from the light outer half; ventrally the hindwing discal area is rich cinnamon brown. In females the ventral disc is dark purple-brown. In both sexes the silver spots are relatively small and of irregular shape.

The Leto Fritillary, *S. c. leto* (Behr), 1862, replaces *pugetensis* east of the Cascades and occupies similar habitats in the wooded canyons of the mountainous terrain. Its total range extends from the Californian Sierras and northern Nevada to British Columbia and east across Idaho to western Wyoming, Montana, and Alberta. As already pointed out, it is much like *pugetensis* in general appearance but less melanic. The basal shading of the male wings is less wide and grades into the light outer portion; the underside of the hindwing disc is bright reddish brown, and chocolate brown in females; within the disc the silver spots are larger.

Concerning the immature stages, David McCorkle informs me that in both subspecies egg-laying occurs in middle or late summer. The first instar larvae hibernate near the leaves of violets, resuming development the next spring. The full-grown larvae are uniformly black; some of the tubercles, all of which bear prominent spines, have orange bases; the dorsally angular head capsule is mostly black, but orange behind.

References:
(1) Chermock, F. H. & D. P. Frechin. 1947. A new *Speyeria* from Washington. Pan-Pacific Entom. 23: 111-112.

Speyeria coronis (Behr), 1864
Coronis Fritillary

Plate 24, figs. 1-4. Map 87.

The several forms of this Western species range from the Rockies to the Pacific States. Our Northwest subspecies, *S. c. simaetha* dos Passos & Grey, 1945 and *S. c. snyderi* (Skinner), 1897, are medium-sized to large Fritillaries. They are somewhat squarish in wing outline, with the apices of the forewings tending to protrude outward. The color of the upper side ranges from yellowish orange to orange brown. Below, the silver spots are large and accentuated by rims of black scales; the disc varies from shades of olivaceous buff to light brown.

Widespread from the summit of the Cascades eastward, and in the Siskiyous, the two subspecies intergrade in Oregon. Typical *simaetha*, described from the northern Cascades of Washington, is smaller than *snyderi* and possesses a smaller submarginal light band between the two outer rows of silver spots. As Oregon populations of *coronis* extend southward and eastward they take on more of the characteristics of the Great Basin subspecies *snyderi* — larger size and broader band. Since most populations are of intermediate or mixed character, they are best described by the clinal terminology *S. coronis* cl. *simaetha-snyderi*.

These large and boldly silvered Fritillaries often congregate on hillsides and meadows overgrown with rabbit-brush and sage. In forest openings they are strongly attracted to the flowers of mint and thistle along the borders of mountain streams. The males of *coronis* generally appear two weeks in advance of the females, and may be on the wing in early June, before arrival of other species.

Successfully reared by David McCorkle, the mature larvae of *coronis* are variegated brown and black, a light stripe running along the back. The head capsule is rounded. The conical tubercles, those along the sides having light colored bases, bear coarse black spines.

Speyeria zerene (Boisduval), 1852
Zerene Fritillary

Plates 25-27. Maps 88-94.

If one were to select an Oregon butterfly to illustrate the principles of geographic variability and subspeciation, none would serve this purpose better than the Zerene Fritillary. The range of this species extends from the Rockies to the Pacific Coast, and in Oregon alone eight subspecies can be distinguished which are clinally interconnected. In one form or another this butterfly occurs in most of the mountainous areas of the state (except the western slope of the Cascades) and at scattered points along the immediate coast.

The Fritillaries of the *zerene* species-complex are medium to large in size. The upperside ground color varies from deep orange to pale yellow. The underside of the hindwings shows great variability, depending on geographic location: the ground color of the inner discal area ranges from maroon through various shades of reddish brown and tan; the broad band outside of the disc runs from lavender to tan or yellow; the well-defined light spots are usually, but not always, silvered and are "shadowed" within the band by masses of dark scales. The distinguishing features of the several subspecies are best appreciated when specimens are seen in series.

The *zerene* populations of the southern Cascades represent the subspecies *S. z. conchyliatus* (Comstock), 1925, the Royal Fritillary. Large in size, this butterfly is deep orange-brown above. Its name, an allusion to the royal purple derived by the ancient Phoenicians from marine shells, refers to the purplish cast of the dark brown disc and the lavender-colored band. Not infrequently, however, the hindwing underside may approach a dull brick color, thus resembling somewhat the nominotypic Sierran subspecies with which *conchyliatus* intergrades. Unsilvered specimens may be easily confused with *Speyeria hydaspe*, but in the latter the discal spots are larger and less conspicuously "shadowed" in the submarginal band. In northern Klamath and Deschutes Counties the butterflies assignable to this subspecies tend to be smaller in size but are otherwise indistinguishable.

Westward off the range of *conchyliatus* in southern Oregon, in the river valleys of the Siskiyou Mountains (the Illinois and Applegate Valleys), *zerene* is represented by *S. z. gloriosa* Moeck, 1957. The large size, beauty, and restricted habitat of this subspecies make it a real prize for collectors. In the males of *gloriosa* the ventral hindwing disc is reddish brown, the band ochre. The gloriously colored females, however, have a disc that is deep chocolate, and a broad buff band overlaid with a violet cast. *Gloriosa* may be thought of as intermediate between *conchyliatus* to the east and *bremnerii* to the north. Its peak flight period is in the month of July.

Continuing westward to the immediate coast of southern Oregon, we come upon a Zerene Fritillary in the unlikely habitat of the weather-beaten Pacific shoreland, where gales and spray blow over the grassy cliffs and coastal meadows. This is Behrens' Fritillary, *S. z. behrensii* (Edwards), 1869, heretofore unreported from Oregon but known from the coastal counties of northern California. The colony on Cape Blanco in Curry County lies within the boundaries of a state park. One would hope that its habitat will receive protection; the campground has fortunately been designed to minimize destruction of the surrounding vegetation. Behrens' Fritillary is slightly smaller than southern Oregon *conchyliatus*, somewhat paler above, but with the basal portion of the wings heavily shaded with dark scales. In both sexes the discal region of the ventral hindwings is rusty red-brown, the brown scales strongly invading the deep yellow band between the outer rows of well silvered spots.

Moving northward along the coast, beyond the sand dunes that end above Florence, the very rare Hippolyta Fritillary, *S. z. hippolyta* (Edwards), 1879, occupies sites similar to those of Behrens' Fritillary. Not unlike *behrensii* in general appearance, it is, however, smaller and more yellowish orange above; the submarginal band of the ventral hindwing is strikingly yellow and not so strongly invaded by the reddish brown scales of the disc. Like *behrensii*, the Hippolyta Fritillary is a late flyer, appearing in August and September. Construction projects, road-building, and over-grazing have conspired to destroy many of the former habitats of this rare Fritillary and it is threatened with extinction. A movement led by David McCorkle is resulting in measures to conserve and protect some of its remaining territory.

Circling back to the inland and into the mountains of the northern Oregon Coast Range, a large version of *hippolyta* can be found along the forest roads and in the moist ravines of the eastern slope. This is Bremner's Fritillary, *S. zerene bremnerii* (Edwards), 1872, whose range extends into western Washington and British Columbia. Unlike its coastal relative it flies early, late June to July, in the company of *Speyeria hydaspe* and *cybele pugetensis*. It is, however, scarce and some years cannot be found at all. Bremner's Fritillary can be easily identified by its yellowish-orange upperside, a hindwing ventral disc that is red-brown with strong admixture of yellow, and a broad bright yellow band. Occasional specimens are deficient in silvering.

Except for stray specimens, *zerene* does not occur on the west slope of the central and northern Oregon Cascades. On the east slope, however, and more especially in the Ochocos, the Blue Mountains, and the Wallowas, it is represented by the cline *picta-garretti*. *S. z. picta* (McDunnough), 1924, the Painted Fritillary, is characteristic of central Oregon, i.e., the Cascadian slope above the range of *conchyliatus*, and the Ochocos. Somewhat resembling *bremnerii*, the ventral hindwing disc of this butterfly has a reddish cast and the slightly narrower band is yellowish tan. Eastward of this region the *zerene* populations, while still containing many individuals close to *picta*, blend toward the subspecies of the northern Rockies, *S. z. garretti* (Gunder), 1932, Garrett's Fritillary. A bit paler above, the hindwing underside is relatively drab, the disc being dull orange brown and the band of a yellowish tan shade. The spots are invariably silvered in both *picta* and *garretti*.

Finally, in the Great Basin region of southeastern Oregon we find the lightest colored of all Fritillaries, the startlingly pale Gunder's Fritillary, *S. zerene gunderi* (Comstock), 1925, known for some time under the synonym *S. z. cynna* dos Passos & Grey, 1945. The pale buff of its disc hardly makes any contrast with the almost yellow band. Unlike the other subspecies, which inhabit forested areas, *gunderi* flies over the open expanses of sage and rabbit-brush, blending perfectly into this background. In company with *Speyeria callippe* and *mormonia artonis* it fairly swarms on the brushy slopes and meadows of Steens Mountain.

The larvae of *Speyeria zerene* resemble those of *S. coronis* in general appearance. George Hardy has recorded the life history of *S. z. bremnerii*. A comparative study of the immature stages and life histories of the eight Oregon subspecies would be interesting in view of their diversity and adaptation to different climatic and ecological environments.

References:

(1) Grey, L. P. & A. H. Moeck. 1962. Notes on overlapping subspecies. I. An example in *Speyeria zerene* (Nymphalidae). J. Lepid. Soc. 16: 81-97.

(2) Hardy, George A. 1958. Notes on the life histories of three species of Lepidoptera from southern Vancouver Island, British Columbia. Proc. Entom. Soc. Brit. Col. 55: 27-30.

(3) McCorkle, David V. 1975. Silverspot salvation summaries. I. *Speyeria zerene hippolyta* in Oregon. Atala (Journal of the Xerces Society) 3: 9-10.

Speyeria callippe (Boisduval), 1852
Callippe Fritillary

Plates 28, 29. Maps 95-97.

The Fritillaries of the *callipe* species-complex, which extends from the Rockies to the Pacific States, are medium to large in size. The several geographic forms have certain common features by which they are ordinarily separable from those of other species. On the upper side the ground color of the wings varies from reddish to yellowish brown and worn specimens are frequently very pale; the pattern of dark markings is sharply defined and the positions of the silver spots beneath are conspicuously indicated by light areas. On the under side the disc of the hind wings is commonly powdered with green scales, but this feature is variable as in certain races and individual specimens the disc is brown. The usually silvered spots are characteristically narrowed and elongated.

The populations of *callippe* extending from the east slope of the Cascades across central and most of eastern Oregon are loosely assigned to the subspecies *S. c. semivirida* (McDunnough), 1924. Near the Cascades most of these butterflies have a ventral disc that is olivaceous green mottled with brown (hence "*semivirida*") and a yellowish submarginal band. This coloration, however, is far from uniform, as some individuals are more pervasively green or brownish. This mixture of phenotype becomes greater east of the Cascadian slope and is not consistent with the concept of a clinal change; variation in size is also common. Appropriate breeding experiments may clarify the genetic aspect of this commixture. As in *Speyeria coronis*, the flight of the males precedes that of the females by a couple of weeks. Unanticipated huge swarms of the butterflies have occasionally been noted in the Paulina Lakes district of Deschutes County, a region ordinarily not good for collecting.

In the Great Basin region of southeastern Oregon, especially on Steens Mountain, the *callippe* populations lack the variability of disc color associated with *semivirida* and are more consistently bright green below, with a somewhat paler yellowish-green band. These may be considered as the subspecies *S. c. harmonia* dos Passos & Grey, 1945, which is common in Utah and western Nevada. On Steens Mountain they fly in the company of *S. zerene cynna* and *mormonia artonis*.

The Siskiyou Mountains and the Rogue River country of southwestern Oregon harbor the very restricted though locally common subspecies *S. callippe elaine* dos Passos & Grey, 1945. Somewhat more squarish in wing outline, Elaine's Fritillary is heavily patterned above, deeply shadowed at the base, and the veins are prominently thicked by black scaling. On the underside the disc is entirely brown and the submarginal band varies from tan to yellow. In many specimens the spots are partially or wholly unsilvered. Across the California border this race grades into the somewhat larger *S. c. rupestris* (Behr). Fresh specimens of *elaine* are best taken in May and June. In the gulleys and canyons around Siskiyou Pass they are strongly attracted to the flowers of mint, and to dogbane along roadsides.

The immature stages and life histories of our Callippe Fritillaries have not been documented.

References:

(1) dos Passos, C. F. & L. P. Grey. 1945. A new species and some new subspecies of *Speyeria* (Lepidoptera, Nymphalidae). Am. Mus. Novitates, No. 1297: 1-17.

(2) Hovanitz, William. 1943. Geographical variation and racial structure of *Argynnis callippe* in California. Am. Naturalist 77: 400-425.

Speyeria egleis (Behr), 1863
Egleis Fritillary

Plate 30; plate 31, figs. 1, 2. Maps 98-101.

The Fritillaries of the *egleis* complex comprise an assemblage which is not easy to characterize when one includes the populations over the entire range which extends from the Rockies to Oregon and California. Limiting ourselves to Oregon, however, the resemblance between our four subspecies is sufficient to distinguish these from other Fritillaries. They are mostly small or medium in size; the nearly always well-silvered spots are usually roundish rather than elongate as in *callippe,* but as in the latter their positions are strongly reflected on the upper side as light blotches; the veins of the male forewings are noticeably thickened.

In the Siskiyous, the southern Cascades, and the Warner Mountains *egleis* is represented by Owen's Fritillary, *S. egleis oweni* (Edwards), 1892, whose type locality is Mt. Shasta. It is not very large, orange-brown above, the hindwing ventral disc is dull reddish brown, and the submarginal band uniformly tan. Compared with other species that fly with it, *egleis oweni* is not very abundant.

Northward, in the pumice country that owes its origin to the eruption of Mt. Mazama (Crater Lake), we find a unique, small-sized *egleis* whose well-defined territory in Klamath and southern Deschutes County entitles it to separate subspecific status but is as yet unnamed. Informally known as the "Sand Creek type" (following Arthur Moeck, 1957, who called attention to it), this butterfly is consistently small in size and is darker in the ventral disc than *oweni*. It is abundant in mid-summer and flies with *S. mormonia erinna* with which it is often confused.

It may be distinguished by the thickened veins of the male forewings, the darker color of the hindwing underside, and the more rounded shape of the silver spots. I have seen great numbers of these small "Sand Creek" *egleis* congregated on the yellow rabbit-brush near Chemult.

In the northeastern corner of Oregon a small Fritillary is very sparingly found which is close to *egleis oweni* but blends towards *S. e. linda* (dos Passos & Grey), 1942. Definitive populations of Linda's Fritillary are centered in the Sawtooth Mountains of central Idaho. In these butterflies the hindwing underside has a greenish disc. Oregon specimens vary from reddish-brown to greenish.

Our largest and most heavily patterned *egleis, S. e. macdunnoughi* (Gunder), 1932, occurs in the Ochocos, the Blue Mountains, and the Wallowas. The fulvous upperside is deeply shadowed at the base; the outer wing margins are thickly black-bordered; the yellow blotches above the silver spots are strikingly prominent; the swollen veins of the male forewings are edged with black scales. On the underside the generally well-silvered spots contrast strongly with the ground color of the disc which ranges from brown to deep olive-green; the yellowish-brown submarginal band is sometimes heavily invaded by dark scales from the disc. In the Ochoco Mountains McDunnough's Fritillary is usually to be found at elevations higher than for other species and is seldom abundant. Originally known from southern Montana, it also occurs in western Wyoming, the mountains of Idaho, and restricted parts of northern Utah. With few exceptions, the Rocky Mountain populations are more uniformly brown-disced.

Nothing has been recorded regarding the immature stages of *egleis* Fritillaries in Oregon.

References:

(1) Moeck, Arthur H. 1957. Geographic variability in *Speyeria*. Milwaukee Entom. Society. Special Paper, 48 pp.

(2) Tilden, J. W. 1963. The *Argynnis* populations of the Sand Creek area, Klamath Co., Oregon. Part I. The effect of the formation of Mt. Mazama on the area and its possible influence on the butterfly faunas of the Sand Creek Basin. J. Res. Lepid. 1: 109-113.

Speyeria atlantis (Edwards), 1862
Atlantis Fritillary

Plate 31, figs. 3, 4. Map 102.

The Atlantis Fritillary, like *Speyeria cybele,* is represented in both eastern and western North America, but is absent from the western Great Plains. The nominotypic subspecies occurs from the Great Lakes to the northern Atlantic coast. *Atlantis* appears again in the Rocky Mountains, from British Columbia south to Arizona and New Mexico, and extends westward to the Cascades and Sierras. While a total of some twenty subspecies have been recognized, only one occurs in Oregon. This is Dodge's Fritillary, *S. atlantis dodgei* (Gunder), 1931. First found at Diamond Lake, it is at home in the Cascades, the Ochocos, the Blue Mountains, and the Wallowas.

Dodge's Fritillary is deep fulvous above, with heavy black markings and a moderate dark basal suffusion; the veins of the forewings, outlined in black, are prominently thickened in both males and females, and the ventral spots show through as light areas. On the underside the disc of the hindwings is rusty orange to chocolate brown and the spots are creamish instead of silver, in this respect resembling *Speyeria hydaspe;* unlike *hydaspe,* however, the spots of the marginal row are very large, and there is much creamish coloration in the submarginal band and on the underside of the forewings.

Dodgei is strongly confined to the mountainous fir and pine forests and may be seen in canyons, along creeks, and in small clearings and meadows. It is abundant in the Ochocos, where it is strongly attracted to mint, together with other Fritillaries.

The newly hatched larvae of *atlantis* spend the winter in hibernation and resume development and pupation the following spring. The blackish and velvety mature caterpillars are ornamented with rows of branching spines that arise from tubercles with orange colored sides.

Speyeria mormonia (Boisduval), 1869
Mormon Fritillary

Plate 33. Maps 105-106.

The species *mormonia* is a small-sized Fritillary whose distribution ranges from the Rocky Mountain states and provinces westward to the Cascades and Sierras. It is a native of mountain meadows and the grassy banks of highland streams; only in Alaska does it descend to sea level. Thin-veined and light orange-brown in ground color, this butterfly is not easily confused with other species, except, perhaps, the small forms of *egleis* as noted earlier.

The dominant subspecies in Oregon is *S. mormonia erinna* (Edwards), 1883. It occurs in great numbers on the meadows of the high Cascades and on the broad eastern slope, in the Ochocos, the Blue Mountains, and the Wallowas. The ventral disc of the Erinna Fritillary is characteristically reddish-brown mottled with yellow, but a varying amount of greenish overscaling is not uncommon. The band is yellow and often partially invaded by the red-brown scales of the disc. The somewhat elongated spots are brightly silvered but occasional unsilvered specimens may be found. Populations with dominantly green discs, such as occur in Washington (*S. m. washingtonia*) and in the Rockies (*S. m. eurynome*) do not appear in Oregon.

On the high meadows of Steens Mountain in Harney County *erinna* is replaced by *S. mormonia artonis* (Edwards), 1881. The underside of this butterfly is strangely pale and washed-out looking, almost concolorously yellow. Except for rare specimens the faint hindwing spots are totally lacking in silver. In July and August the Artonis Fritillary fairly swarms on the moist, grassy meadows above Fish Lake, at altitudes between 7000 and 10,000 feet. It is also found in the Ruby and Jarbridge Mountains of northern Nevada.

The larvae of *Speyeria mormonia* are paler than those of other species, being gray-brown to tan-brown and showing a light mid-dorsal stripe. The spines are uniformly short and have pale bases.

Speyeria hydaspe (Boisduval), 1869
Hydaspe Fritillary

Plate 32. Maps 103, 104.

Adapted to moist environments in the forested mountains, Hydaspe Fritillaries are widespread at suitable elevations in the Rockies from British Columbia to central New Mexico, occur commonly in the Cascades and Sierras, and are abundant in the Coast Ranges of the Pacific Northwest. Over this large range various subspecies have been recognized, most of which are clinally intergrading. Medium to large in size, all of these butterflies are characterized by a heavy dorsal wing pattern on a usually dark orange-brown ground color; on the underside the disc and band are of some shade of brown, often with a lavender cast, and the spots are cream colored.

The subspecies *S. hydaspe purpurascens* (H. Edwards), 1877, is our most widespread Fritillary, common in the Siskiyous and Cascades as well as the mountain ranges to the northeast. The purplish cast of the ventral disc and submarginal band varies in intensity; in southern populations it is more pronounced than in those farther north. In some individuals, especially females, the marginal row of spots may show traces of silvering. Some specimens of *atlantis dodgei* and of unsilvered *zerene conchyliatus* may be confused with *hydaspe purpurascens;* the distinctions have been discussed before.

The Hydaspe Fritillaries of the northern Oregon Coast Range differ perceptively from those of southern, central and eastern Oregon, especially when seen in a series. The wings are dorsally more melanic, the basal portions being widely suffused with black scales, much the way *cybele pugetensis* differs from *c. leto*. The ventral disc and band vary in color from orange to chestnut-brown, or from lilac-brown to maroon. These coastal populations represent a clinal change from *purpurascens* toward *S. h. rhodope* (Edwards), 1874. Definitive *rhodope,* distinguished by a deep chocolate color of the disc and band and silvered spots in the marginal row, occurs in coastal Washington and British Columbia; it is the darkest form of *hydaspe.*

Hydaspe Fritillaries fly from June to September, depending upon altitude. The larvae are very dark, almost black, and without a distinct mid-dorsal stripe. The bases of the branching spines are black on the dorsum, yellow-orange to orange-brown on the sides.

Family RIODINIDAE

The butterflies of the family Riodinidae are found mainly in the American Tropics. Though this is a large family, only a few genera occur in the United States, and, indeed, only one species in Oregon. They are small to medium in size, possess elongated antennae and reduced forelegs in the males of which the first segment, or coxa, is greatly extended beyond its articulation with the second, or trochanter. In many tropical species the wings are brightly and diversely colored and sometimes tailed. On the underside the wings often bear irridescent metallic flecks on account of which these butterflies are known as Metalmarks. When at rest they tend to hold their wings open and spread flat, like geometric moths, often preferring shade and alighting on the underside of leaves (but not Oregon's *Apodemia mormo*). Males are usually smaller than females and have more pointed forewings.

The eggs of Riodinidae are dorso-ventrally flattened, or turban-shaped, and have a reticulated surface. The stout and large-headed larvae are adorned with tufts of bristles which arise from raised spots known as verrucae. The plump and ventrally flattened pupae have a protruding prothorax and down-turned head, are covered with fine hairs, and anchored to their substrate (debris or plant base) with a silken girdle and posterior cremaster.

Apodemia mormo mormonia (Boisduval), 1868
Mormon Metalmark

Plate 34, fig. 1. Map 107.

Our only butterfly of the family Riodinidae, the Mormon Metalmark is not often seen. Though numerous enough where it occurs, its colonies are very local, associated with the hot canyons along the tributaries of the upper Columbia. A late flyer, August and September is the time when it may be sought along the Wasco County roads near Sherar's Bridge, settling on wild clematis and rabbit-brush, with its wings characteristically held at an open angle like a skipper. Other records of this Metalmark come from well separated points in southern Oregon, and it is likely that its distribution is wider than now known; the larval foodplant, *Eriogonum,* has an extensive range.

Our subspecies of *Apodemia mormo* is very dark above, the several rows of white spots contrasting strongly against the black ground color; a rusty brown flush appears on the middle and upper margin of the forewing. The hindwings are ventrally ashen gray except for the irregularly-shaped white spots. Other geographic races occur southward to Baja California and westward across the Great Basin and the southwestern deserts to the Rockies.

The turban-shaped eggs of the Mormon Metalmark have a pitted surface. The purplish and tufted larvae spend the winter in hibernation before pupating the following spring. The chrysalids are mottled brown, short and ventrally flattened, with head bent below the forward-extended thorax.

Reference:

(1) Opler, Paul & Jerry A. Powell. 1961. Taxonomic and distributional studies on the western components of the *Apodemia mormo* complex (Riodinidae). J. Lepid. Soc. 15: 145-171.

Family LYCAENIDAE

A large family of small butterflies, the Lycaenidae are found throughout the world, in all climates and at all altitudes. Though occurring almost everywhere, they are especially abundant in the high meadows of mountainous country. Despite their diminutive size many are of exquisite beauty, veritable jewels of the insect world. In anatomical characteristics the radial vein of the forewings has only three or four branches and the hindwings lack a humeral vein; the facial region between the eyes is flattened; the forelegs of the males are reduced and without tarsal claws or pad. The eggs of lycaenids are small, flat, and elaborately sculptured; the slug-shaped larvae are covered with short, fine hairs; the pupae are compact and suspended by a silken girdle and a posterior cremaster.

Within our region the Lycaenidae fall into three well represented subfamilies. The Theclinae, whose hindwings often bear hair-like tails and patterns of vertical thin lines on the under surface, are known as Hairstreaks. In the tropics these butterflies often show brilliant metallic colors, but ours are mostly gray or brown above except for the iridescently blue *Atlides halesus*. In all except *Habrodais grunus* the radial vein of the forewing has only three branches. Usually fast and jerky in flight, they perch with wings folded over the back. The males are generally distinguishable by possession of androconial scales encased in a small patch on the forewings. Our genera include *Habrodais, Harkenclenus, Satyrium, Strymon, Incisalia, Mitoura, Callophrys,* and *Atlides.*

The Lycaeninae, or Coppers, are restricted to temperate climates, and are mainly found in the northern hemisphere. Usually tailless, they are copper-colored or dull grayish brown above, but one is blue! Stout-bodied and with well developed thoracic musculature, the Lycaeninae are strong flyers. The forewing radial vein is four-branched, and the underside of both wings bears a pattern of black spots. The male wings do not show androconial patches, but the sexes can usually be told apart by differences in color and pattern. Our genera include *Tharsalea* and *Lycaena,* the latter recently divided by Miller & Brown into *Chalceria, Gaeides, Epidemia,* and *Lycaena.*

The Plebejinae, mainy confined to the tropical, temperate, and arctic zones of the northern hemisphere, are the small and attractive Blues. Those in our area are tailless except for the genus *Everes,* and most are sexually dimorphic, the males being blue or lavender above and the females usually brownish. The grayish undersides are speckled with black dots, and along the margin of the hindwings there may be orange lunules and scales of iridescent blue or silver. Delicate bodied, these butterflies have a weak flight, and they often congregate in large numbers at wet spots. Some are among the first butterflies to appear in the spring. Our genera include *Brephidium, Lycaeides, Plebejus, Everes, Philotes, Glaucopsyche,* and *Celastrina.*

Of special interest is that some species of lycaenids, particularly among the Blues, are symbiotically associated with ants which herd the larvae in order to feed on the exudates of their "honey-dew" glands. In the European Large Blue, *Maculinea arion,* the ants even convey the larvae into their nests, where they become carnivorous and subsist on the ants' brood, a predation the adult ants tolerate as long as the prized honey-dew is available! After pupation the newly hatched butterfly emerges from the ant nest.

Many lycaenids are also remarkable in that their pupae have been found to emit sound. The chirping, buzzing, or clicking noises are produced by integumental stridulating organs, rasps and files between the abdominal body segments which are rubbed together by rapid dorsoventral movements of the abdomen. The function of the pupal sound may be defensive or, since the pupae also possess exudate glands, the sound may attract ants.

References:
(1) dos Passos, Cyril F. 1970. A revised synonymic catalogue with taxonomic notes on some nearctic Lycaenidae. J. Lepid. Soc. 24: 26-38.
(2) Downey, John C. 1966. Sound production in pupae of Lycaenidae. J. Lepid. Soc. 20: 129-155.
(3) Downey, John C. & Arthur C. Allyn. 1973. Butterfly ultrastructure. 1. Sound production and associated abdominal structures in pupae of Lycaenidae and Riodinidae. Bull. Allyn Museum, No. 14, 47 pp.
(4) Downey, John C. & Arthur C. Allyn. 1978. Sounds produced in pupae of Lycaenidae. Bull. Allyn Museum, No. 48, 14 pp.
(5) Hoegh-Guldberg, Ove. 1972. Pupal sound production of some Lycaenidae. J. Res. Lepid. 10: 127-147.
(6) Malicky, Hans. 1970. New aspects on the association between lycaenid larvae (Lycaenidae) and ants (Formicidae, Hymenoptera). J. Lepid. Soc. 24: 190-202.
(7) Miller, Lee D. & F. M. Brown. 1979. Studies in the Lycaeninae (Lycaenidae). 4. The higher classification of the American Coppers. Bull. Allyn Museum, No. 51, 30 pp.

Habrodais grunus (Boisduval), 1852
Chinquapin Hairstreak

Plate 34, fig. 2. Map 108.

A stubby-tailed Hairstreak of dull brownish-yellow color, *Habrodais grunus* should be looked for in the late summer, always in close association with its Oregon foodplant, *Castanopsis* (Chinquapin), a small tree or shrub easily recognized by its reddish bark, olive-green leathery leaves, and clusters of spiny burs. Chinquapin grows in the Cascades, the Siskiyous, and the foothills of the Coast Range. Usually active at dusk, the Hairstreaks perch on its leaves, dart rapidly from one spot to another, and being well camouflaged in color are easily lost sight of.

Males of the Chinquapin Hairstreak are darker above than the females in which the golden yellow of the disc extends farther out toward the brown border. Underneath the wings of both sexes are dull yellow and inconspicuously marked near the middle by a vertical row of short and dark dashes; a series of tiny silvery crescents edged with black scales runs along the outer margin of the hindwings.

Cascadian populations should be referred to the subspecies *H. g. herri* Field, 1938. Specimens from the Siskiyous and the Coastal Mountains are somewhat smaller and more grayish-yellow beneath; they represent the subspecies *H. g. lorquini* Field, 1938. The range of *Habrodais grunus* extends from the Columbia River to southern California where the larva is associated with Canyon Oak, *Quercus chrysolepis*.

The slug-shaped bluish-green larvae, which hatch in the spring from overwintering eggs, are covered with fine olive-brown points and short white hairs. The pupae, also pale bluish-green, are formed on the foodplant.

Reference:

(1) Field, W. D. 1938. Variation in *Habrodais grunus* (Boisduval) (Lepid.: Lycaenidae). Bull. So. Calif. Acad. Sci. 37: 23-29.

Harkenclenus titus immaculosus (Comstock), 1913
Coral Hairstreak

Plate 34, fig. 3. Map 109.

The Coral Hairstreak, *Harkenclenus titus* (widely known in the older literature as *Strymon titus*) occurs throughout most of the United States and southern Canada, and is fairly common in the East and the Midwest. However, the Western subspecies, *H. t. immaculosus,* found from British Columbia to northern California and east to the Rockies, is a scarce butterfly and is known in Oregon only from scattered points east of the Cascades. Its appearance, in mid-summer and usually by the flowered streamside of a sunny canyon, is always a surprise.

This tailless Hairstreak is grayish brown above and usually has some spots of orange along the lower margin of the hindwings, in females also orange flushes on the outer portion of the forewings. The males possess a prominent, light-colored scent pad of androconial scales. On the underside a row of coral spots extends along the outer border of the hindwings and the disc of both wings is crossed by a vertical row of small black points.

The Coral Hairstreak is single brooded. Its overwintering eggs hatch into green and pink, slug-shaped larvae which feed on species of *Prunus* (chokecherry and wild plum), also, reportedly, on oak and *Eupatorium*. An association of the larvae with ants has been observed.

Satyrium fuliginosum (Edwards), 1861
Sooty Hairstreak

Plate 34, fig. 4. Map 110.

This solidly grayish brown and drab little butterfly with rounded wings and no tails can be easily mistaken for a female Blue, the more so since it flies in habitats where Blues are common and whose larvae, like those of the latter, feed on lupines. The Sooty Hairstreak, found at higher elevations from northern California to British Columbia and east to the central Rockies, may be looked for from the summit of the Cascades eastward and in the Siskiyous. The records of Oregon captures extend from May to August, but the peak period is July. Well populated colonies occur on various high meadows of the Cascadian east slope, on the sagebrush plateaus of central Oregon, and on Steens Mountain.

The variability in this butterfly is considerable. In the Cascades and Siskiyous the upper side is very dark, and the somewhat lighter grayish brown underside is traversed by two, often indistinct, rows of small black dots slightly rimmed by white scales; in some specimens the pattern of dots is almost indiscernible. On the sagebrush slopes of Steens Mountain the butterfly is lighter in color, both above and below; the underside is covered by much white scaling, giving it a gray appearance, and on the hindwings the black dots are reduced to barely perceptible pinpoints enclosed in large spots of white. The latter populations come close to those of western Wyoming which Klots (1930) described as the subspecies *S. f. semiluna*. Specimens from the chaparral of central Wasco County are intermediate in appearance. In the sagebrush environment the coloration of *Satyrium fuliginosum* is so concealing, and its flight so erratic, that a sharp eye is needed to keep the butterfly in sight.

Satyrium behrii behrii (Edwards), 1870
Behr's Hairstreak

Plate 34, fig. 5. Map 111.

Like *Satyrium fuliginosum, S. behrii* (also known as *Callipsyche behrii*) ranges from California to southern British Columbia and eastward to the middle Rockies. It is, however, a much more abundant butterfly and in Oregon may be found wherever bitter-brush grows, *Purshia tridentata,* the larval foodplant. This yellow-flowering rosaceous shrub, adapted to the coarse soil of the pumice and rocky arid lands, is widespread along the east slope of the Cascades, the canyons of the middle Columbia plateau, and the highlands of southeastern Oregon.

Behr's Hairstreak is easy to recognize. Its orange disc is broadly black-bordered along the forewing costa and more narrowly along the sides. The male has a gray scent pad above the discal cell and the dark margins generally extend deeper into the discal area. Underneath, the wings are grayish brown and bear rows of irregularly shaped black flecks that are edged with white; a patch of blue scales lies at the anal angle of the hindwings.

Though recorded in Oregon from May to August, *S. behrii* is most abundant in mid-summer, and can be encountered in great numbers in brushy openings of the Ponderosa forests. The adults are strongly attracted to the profusely blooming *Eriogonum* (false buckwheat).

The light green larvae of Behr's Hairstreak hatch from overwintering eggs and are effectively camouflaged on the leaves of the bitter-brush. They metamorphose into light tan chrysalids freckled with dark brown patches.

Reference:
 (1) Newcomer, E. J. 1973. Notes on life histories and habits of some Western Theclinae. J. Lepid. Soc. 27: 13-15.

Satyrium tetra (Edwards), 1870
Gray Hairstreak

Plate 34, fig. 6. Map 112.

Long known as *Strymon adenostomatis* (H. Edwards), 1877, the Gray Hairstreak, now correctly recognized under the older name *tetra,* is a little known butterfly in Oregon. Its distribution is limited by the presence of the larval foodplant *Cercocarpus betuloides,* mountain mahogany, which grows in the Warner Mountains of southern Lake County and westward to the Siskiyous. South of us the range of *S. tetra* extends to southern California and into the mountains of western Nevada.

In wing shape and pattern this tailed Hairstreak strongly resembles *Satyrium saepium,* but is mousegray in color instead of rusty brown and slightly larger in average size. On the underside a row of small, crescent-shaped black spots extends along the lateral wing margins; a patch of blue scales lies at the anal angle of the hindwings and is flanked on either side by a heavy black dot; an irregular dark line of broken segments edged outwardly by white scales runs vertically across the middle of both wings.

The Gray Hairstreak appears in mid-summer and is usually abundant in its localized colonies, flying about the shrubbery and alighting on the flowers of *Eriogonum*. It is single-brooded. The pale green and slug-shaped larvae, well concealed on the leaves of the hostplant, are ornamented on the sides with diagonal bluish bars covered with short orange hairs.

Satyrium saepium saepium
(Boisduval), 1852
Russet Hairstreak

Plate 34, fig. 7. Map 113.

The rich chestnut brown upperside of this Hairstreak distinguishes it at once from its relatives. Unlike the Gray Hairstreak, which it otherwise resembles in wing shape and the pattern of its underside markings, *S. saepium* is very abundant over a considerable part of Oregon, wherever *Ceanothus* can be found. Thus it is particularly common on the east slope of the Cascades and in the Siskiyous, but may also be seen in the Coast Range and in the Blue Mountains. Records of its capture run from May to September, but its period of abundance is late summer when of a sunny afternoon the *Ceanothus*-covered clearings in the ponderosa belt may almost swarm with these butterflies. Such can at times be seen on the chaparral expanses along the Century Drive near Bend.

Newcomer has given an account of the immature stages of the Russet Hairstreak, the larvae of which are protectively colored to match the undersides of the *Ceanothus* leaves. When full-grown they are light green, ornamented with two whitish stripes along the back and one on each side; they are covered with short golden hairs; the head is brown. The chestnut-brown pupae are finely spotted with dark flecks.

Satyrium saepium ranges from southern California to British Columbia and eastward to the Rocky Mountains. Some variation in the shade of color and the intensity of the pattern occurs, but in Oregon this species is quite uniform.

Reference:
 (1) Newcomer, E. J. 1973. Notes on life histories and habits of some Western Theclinae. J. Lepid. Soc. 27: 13-15.

Satyrium sylvinus sylvinus
(Boisduval), 1852
Sylvan Hairstreak

Plate 35, fig. 1. Map 114

Scattered colonies of the Sylvan Hairstreak occur in both western and eastern Oregon, but this butterfly is generally not found in the Cascades. Very local and always associated with willows, it should be sought along stream bottoms in foothills and canyons and on wet meadows at higher elevations. Though it has been taken from May to August, most records have July dates. In its wider range this species is found from the west slope of the southern Rockies to California and northward to Washington.

Satyrium sylvinus is easily confused with *S. californica*, a far commoner Hairstreak. Both are brown above, with a flush of orange near the tail on the hindwings and in some specimens also along the outer edge of the forewings; in females this orange may be more extensive. They differ, however, on the underside. In *sylvinus* the ground color is pearly gray, sometimes almost whitish, and a single orange spot adjoins the blue patch at the lower angle of the hindwings. Specimens from the arid parts of eastern Oregon tend to be somewhat lighter below than those from the Siskiyous, but intergrades are sufficiently common to make subspecific distinctions questionable.

The Sylvan Hairstreak is single-brooded. The pale green larvae match the color of the willow leaves on which they feed. The greenish brown pupae are densely covered with small dark spots.

Satyrium californica (Edwards), 1862
California Hairstreak

Plate 35, fig. 2. Map 115.

The California Hairstreak, which closely resembles *Satyrium sylvinus* above, can be distinguished by the underside. This is dark grayish brown rather than light gray; instead of a single orange patch near the anal angle of the hindwings, a series of such spots extends upward along the wing margin and often onto the forewing, becoming smaller in size as they progress anteriorly; the vertical rows of black marks are also heavier.

This butterfly is far more common and widespread than *sylvinus,* and may be found during the summer months in the foothills, mountains, and canyons of all parts of the State, particularly from the Siskiyous and Cascades eastward. Like many other Hairstreaks, its flight pattern is rapid and jerky, so that it is hard to follow, but it settles often on flowers along the roadside and is then easy to capture. In some locations, if willows are nearby, both *Satyrium californica* and *sylvinus* may be found. The total range of *S. californica* includes all states west of the Continental Divide as well as southwestern British Columbia.

The larvae of the California Hairstreak feed on ceanothus, oak, and mountain mahogany. They are grayish brown and marked mid-dorsally with a row of large gray blotches; their underside is grayish green. The reddish brown, black-spotted pupae have ivory green wing cases.

Strymon melinus Hübner, 1818
Common Hairstreak

Plate 35, fig. 3. Map 116.

Known throughout the United States, *Strymon melinus* is found from coast to coast and from southern Canada to Central America. In some parts of the country it is quite common, but this is hardly true for Oregon. Though found in every part of the State, its occurrence is erratic and only occasionally does it show up in numbers. There seems to be no preferential habitat. *Melinus* may appear in urban gardens, along streams in woods or lowland meadows, by the roadside, in forest clearings, in the canyons and on the plateaus of central Oregon, by lakesides in the mountains or on high meadows — yet most of the time this Hairstreak is seen not in colonies but singly.

Strymon melinus is easy to recognize. The upperside is dark slate gray; a prominent and well defined orange patch lies near the anal angle on the hindwings and a tail arises from either side of it, the lower one longer than the upper; a series of small blue spots lies in front of the orange patch and one behind it. The underside ground color is steel gray (somewhat variable with respect to being lighter or darker); a vertical row of black dashes traverses the middle of the hindwing and the upper half of the forewing, the dashes being outwardly edged with white and inwardly with or without tiny amounts of orange. There is no distinct scent-pad on the male forewing.

Most Oregon populations of this Hairstreak are best assigned to the subspecies *S. m. setonia* McDunnough, 1927. Individuals that are darker below and with black markings that are a bit heavier come close in their appearance to *S. m. atrofasciata* McDunnough, 1921; these are, however, unusual specimens and do not seem to dominate any Oregon populations.

Strymon melinus is multibrooded and, depending upon local climate, can be found from March to September. The early spring butterflies that hatch from hibernating pupae are usually smaller and darker than those of later generations. The larvae, which vary in color from green to reddish brown, are covered with short light-brown hairs. Unlike the larvae of most Hairstreaks, indeed of most butterflies, they are quite unspecific with regard to choice of foodplants; they are known to feed on many kinds of legumes, on mallows, knotweed, St. John's Wort, labiates, eriogonum, clovers, apple, strawberries, stonecrops, and others; in the East they have been reported at times to be economic pests of beans and hops; since their sites of feeding include flower parts, the larvae can be found in fruit and ripening seeds. The pupae are of light brownish shade, mottled with dark brown spots of various sizes; equipped with stridulating structures, they can produce sound.

Mitoura spinetorum (Hewitson), 1867
Thicket Hairstreak

Plate 35, fig. 4. Map 117.

Usually scarce, this beautiful Hairstreak occurs through much of the West, from the Rocky Mountains to the Pacific Coast, and from southern British Columbia to Baja California, always in association with the larval foodplant, *Arceuthobium,* the dwarf mistletoe parasitic on conifers. Oregon records of *M. spinetorum* are from the forested lands of the Cascades and eastward; one is from the Siskiyous of southwestern Josephine County. Though occasionally seen in numbers, one usually sees but isolated specimens visiting the flowers in a forest clearing or along the wooded roadside.

Singularly steel blue above, the underside of this butterfly is dark chestnut brown, with both wings vertically traversed by a bold white line whose lower portion is angulated in a zigzag fashion. The male forewings possess a distinct scent-pad.

The Thicket Hairstreak has been taken from May to August and produces two broods. The yellowish-olive larvae are well hidden on the similarly colored mistletoe and within the tangled branching of this parasitic plant transform into dark brown pupae heavily mottled with black.

Reference:

(1) Shields, Oakley. 1965. *Callophrys (Mitoura) spinetorum* and *C. (M.) johnsoni:* their known range, habits, variation, and history. J. Res. Lepid. 4: 233-250.

Mitoura johnsoni (Skinner), 1904
Johnson's Hairstreak

Plate 35, fig. 5. Map 118.

Johnson's Hairstreak, which is closely related to *M. spinetorum,* has long been thought to be a very rare butterfly. First described from the area of Seattle and a site in southern British Columbia, it is now known to occur from southern British Columbia to the Cascades and Sierras of northern California. In Oregon it has been found in the coastal mountains and in the forests along the western slope of the Cascades; one certified record comes from near Baker in northeastern Oregon.

Mitoura johnsoni differs from *spinetorum* in one obvious respect. Instead of being steel blue above it is dark chocolate brown. The underside color and pattern is very much like that of *spinetorum* but of somewhat darker shade, and on the hindwings the marginal row of six dark spots is reduced to the bottom three.

Johnson's Hairstreak has been taken from May to July and is probably double brooded. The life history, habits, and ecology of this species have been intensively studied by David McCorkle. Its larva is indistinguishable from that of *spinetorum* and also feeds on the dwarf mistletoe of conifers.

References:

(1) Dornfeld, Ernst J. 1959. *Mitoura johnsoni* in Oregon and California. J. Lepid. Soc. 13: 183.

(2) McCorkle, David V. 1962. Notes on the life history of *Callophrys (Mitoura) johnsoni* Skinner (Lepidoptera, Lycaenidae). Proc. Wash. State Entom. Soc., No. 14, April, 1962.

(3) McCorkle, David V. (1973). An autecological study of *Callophrys johnsoni* Skinner (Lepidoptera, Lycaenidae) with emphasis upon its relationship to the Dwarf Mistletoe of Western Hemlock. In MSS.

(4) Shields, Oakely. 1965. See under *Mitoura spinetorum.*

Mitoura nelsoni nelsoni (Boisduval), 1869
Nelson's Hairstreak

Plate 35, fig. 6. Map 119.

Nelson's Hairstreak is smaller in size than either *M. spinetorum* or *johnsoni.* On the upperside the wings are mahogany brown in color; beneath they are rusty brown; the hindwings, often tinted with lavender, bear patches of blue scales near the outer margin and a short row of black spots; the vertical and irregular white line that crosses both wings is often incompletely expressed, especially in its lower portions.

Oregon flight records of *M. nelsoni* extend from April to August, and in eastern Oregon, at least, there seem to be two broods. Unlike *M. spinetorum* and *johnsoni* this species is often very abundant, especially in the open juniper country of central Oregon. On sunny days it may gather in great numbers on yellow composites and on yarrow (*Achillea millefolium*).

The slug-shaped green larvae, which feed on cedars or junipers, are ornamented with raised lobulations, a series of irregular yellow streaks along the upper sides, and a covering of tiny brown hairs. Overwintering occurs in the pupal stage; the pupae are blunt and dark brown.

This Hairstreak may be found from British Columbia to southern California and eastward into western Idaho and Nevada. Kurt Johnson has recently contended, however, that there are actually several species involved which can be distinguished only by subtle genitalial differences and whose larvae utilize separate foodplants. According to his analysis only the populations feeding on incense cedar are *Mitoura nelsoni;* those associated with junipers are *M. siva;* and a further group which utilizes western red cedar (and possibly junipers) is a new species, *M. barryi.* Further observations, however, are needed, including breeding experiments, before these taxonomic views can be accepted.

Reference:

(1) Johnson, Kurt. 1976. Three new nearctic species of *Callophrys (Mitoura),* with a diagnosis of all nearctic consubgeners (Lepidoptera: Lycaenidae). Bull. Allyn Museum, No. 38: 1-30.

Incisalia polios obscurus
Ferris & Fisher, 1973
Hoary Elfin

Plate 36, fig. 1. Map 120.

The tailless brown Hairstreaks of the genus *Incisalia* are butterflies of the spring. The Hoary Elfin, *I. polios,* has two geographic components, an Eastern one which extends from the North Atlantic Coast across southern Canada and the northern United States to the Great Lakes, and a Western one which ranges across Canada to Alaska, thence southward along the coast to Oregon and in the Rockies south to New Mexico. The Western component represents the subspecies *obscurus.* It is known in Oregon only from isolated coastal localities in Lincoln County where it flits about the kinnikinnick (*Arctostaphylos uva-ursi),* the larval foodplant. It is scarce and should be looked for in April and May.

Both males and females of the Hoary Elfin are evenly dark grayish brown on the upperside, with the males possessing a distinct scent-pad. Underneath, the wings are dark brown, the outer half of the hindwings and a strip along the forewings heavily frosted with white scales. The latter feature distinguishes this species from *I. fotis.* A faint and irregular white line separates the outer and inner portions of the wings.

Though *polios* must at present be considered a rare butterfly in Oregon, it is possible that careful search of the northern coast may turn up additional colonies. Its life history also needs study.

Reference:

(1) Ferris, Clifford D. & Michael S. Fisher. 1973. *Callophrys (Incisalia) polios* (Lycaenidae): Distribution in North America and description of a new subspecies. J. Lepid. Soc. 27: 112-118.

Incisalia fotis mossii (H. Edwards), 1881
Moss's Elfin

Plate 36, fig. 2. Map 121.

Incisalia fotis, a Western species closely related to *I. polios,* has a spotty distribution from the Rockies to the Pacific, and from southern British Columbia to California and Arizona. The race *mossii* is found from Vancouver Island southward along the coast to Oregon and at lower and middle elevations in the mountains of the Northwest. Always quite local and relatively scarce, Moss's Elfin may appear as early as March and is gone by the end of spring. It should be looked for flying in an erratic pattern close to the ground in canyons and along steep slopes and rocky ridges, places where one may expect to find stonecrop (*Sedum),* the larval foodplant. An interesting account of its habitat has been given by Richard Guppy.

In size and shape of wings Moss's Elfin resembles *I. polios.* The males are dorsally dark grayish brown but the brighter colored females reddish brown. In both sexes the underside is rich mahogany brown, with the inner discal region darker than the outer limbal area which is separated from the former by an irregular white line; a series of dark brown patches extends along the hindwing margin and within this is a row of dark spots. A checkered fringe of white and brown scales makes up the outer wing border.

An account of the life history and immature stages of this Elfin has been given by Newcomer, and of the closely related Californian subspecies, *I. fotis bayensis,* by Emmel and Ferris. The light bluish green eggs are deposited on the basal leaves of stonecrop. The larvae, which are first light tan, mature to become green in color, ornamented with dorsal and lateral pink stripes, dark red diagonal dashes on each segment, and a covering of golden brown hairs. The pupae, found under debris on the ground, are blunt and purplish brown.

References:

(1) Emmel, John F. & Clifford D. Ferris. 1972. The biology of *Callophrys (Incisalia) fotis bayensis* (Lycaenidae). J. Lepid. Soc. 26: 237-244.

(2) Guppy, Richard. 1959. Collecting *Incisalia mossii* (Lycaenidae) on Vancouver Island. J. Lepid. Soc. 13: 101-103.

(3) Newcomer, E. J. 1973. Notes on life histories and habits of some Western Theclinae. J. Lepid. Soc. 27: 13-15.

Incisalia augustinus iroides
(Boisduval), 1852
Brown Elfin

Plate 36, fig. 3. Map 122.

Incisalia augustinus is the most wide ranging species of the genus. It is found through most of the East and Midwest except the flatlands of the Gulf states, extends from Newfoundland westward across southern Canada to British Columbia and Alaska, thence southward through the Pacific states and the Rockies to New Mexico and Arizona. Our subspecies, *I. a. iroides,* which occupies most of the Western area, is common in the Cascades and Siskiyous, and is also found in the coastal mountains and more sparingly in eastern Oregon.

A spring butterfly like other Elfins, its most characteristic habitat is the chaparral associated with coniferous forests, particularly the cover of ceanothus and manzanita in the ponderosa belt of the Cascadian east slope. It perches on the shrubbery, darts at passing insects, basks in the sun, and in the late afternoon engages in mating. Low flowering plants such as *Eriogonum* are much visited for nectar. The behavior of *iroides* has been described in interesting detail by Jerry Powell.

The brown Elfin is easily identified. Both sexes are brown above, the basal and marginal regions, especially in males, deeply shaded to give a smoky appearance. Underneath the wings are reddish brown; the inner half of the hindwings bears dark patches; laterally a row of small dark spots extends along both wing.

Unique among *Incisalia,* the larvae of *iroides* are not restricted to a single foodplant but have been found on dodder, buckbrush (*Ceanothus*), apple, salal (*Gaultheria*), manzanita, and madrona. At first yellowish green, these larvae mature to become olive or apple green in color and are ornamented with yellowish bars, a row of white-bordered saddle-like patches along the dorsum, and a covering of brown hairs.

References:

(1) Powell, Jerry A. 1968. A study of area occupation and mating behavior in *Incisalia iroides* (Lepidoptera: Lycaenidae). J. N. Y. Ent. Soc. 76: 45-57.

(2) Powell, Jerry A. 1968. Foodplants of *Callophrys (Incisalia) iroides.* J. Lepid. Soc. 22: 225-226.

Incisalia eryphon eryphon
(Boisduval), 1852
Western Pine Elfin

Plate 36, fig. 4. Map 123.

Our largest and most abundant Elfin, *Incisalia eryphon* is always associated with pine forests and may be found in such habitats throughout the western mountains from central California to British Columbia and eastward to the Rockies; in the north it extends even to upper Manitoba and Michigan. In Oregon the Western Pine Elfin may be seen along the coast and in the Siskiyous but is most numerous in the great ponderosa stands east of the Cascadian summit. At low elevations this butterfly may appear in March or April but at higher altitudes is most abundant in late spring and early summer. Flitting about sunny clearings and along small streams, *eryphon* is much attracted to low-flowering *Eriogonum;* males, from their perches on shrubbery, dart after intruders and passing females.

The males are dorsally dark grayish brown, the females lighter and reddish brown. The fringes along the wing margins are checkered with alternating patches of brown and white scales. Underneath, both sexes are rusty brown with a violet overcast; dark zig-zag bands on the hindwings interlace in the discal area and submarginally they form a row of inward pointing chevrons In coastal specimens the underside is darker, the overcast is more deeply reddish purple, and the bands are heavier, tending to dense fusion in the discal area. These coastal populations have been designated *I. eryphon sheltonensis* by Chermock & Frechin (1948).

The larvae feed on various species of *Pinus;* on Vancouver Island Hardy has also found them on willow catkins. The flattened and chalky white to light green eggs of *eryphon* are deposited at the base of the pine needles. The honey colored, newly hatched larvae mature to be cryptically rich green with two pairs of cream stripes along the sides and a velvety covering of short brown hairs. The overwintering pupae are evenly dark brown.

References:

(1) Chermock, F. H. & D. P. Frechin. 1948. A new race of *Incisalia eryphon* from Washington (Lepidoptera: Lycaenidae). Pan-Pacific Entomologist 24: 212.

(2) Hardy, George A. 1959. On the life history of *Incisalia eryphon* (Lycaenidae) on southern Vancouver Island. J. Lepid. Soc. 13: 70.

(3) Newcomer, E. J. 1973. Notes on life histories and habits of some Western Theclinae. J. Lepid. Soc. 27: 13-15.

Callophrys dumetorum dumetorum (Boisduval), 1852
Bramble Green Hairstreak

Plate 36, fig. 5. Map 124.

The Hairstreaks of the genus *Callophrys* can at once be recognized by the green underside color of the hindwings. Separating the different species and varieties, however, is quite another matter and is often perplexing even to experts. Genitalial features, useful in certain other taxonomically difficult genera, are of no help in *Callophrys*. One is best guided by (a) using fresh, not worn specimens, and (b) having at hand both males and females from the same population. Particular attention should be given to these characters: (1) color of the female upperside, whether gray (like the male) or brownish; (2) the posterior extent of the green color on the forewing underside, whether replaced by grayish-brown nearly up to its center (up to or beyond vein Cu_1) or not so far; (3) underside color of the hindwing fringe-scales, whether almost wholly white or extensively tipped with grayish brown; (4) completeness and shape of the postmedian white line on the ventral hindwing; (5) the shade of the hindwing green color, whether yellowish, bluish, or variable. Unfortunately these characters in single specimens are not always sharp or consistent, but their combination, the average appearance of a population, and attention to the locality will usually lead to a satisfactory determination.

Callophrys dumetorum is our largest and most easily distinguished Green Hairstreak. The males are dorsally grayish, the females brown (but rarely nearly grayish in some Polk County localities). The gray-brown flush of the forewing underside extends upward from the hind margin to nearly the center of the wing. The postmedian white line is extremely variable: it may be completely absent, is most commonly reduced to a few dots, or may be almost fully developed; in shape it buckles outward slightly near the middle. The fringe-scales of the hindwing underside have tips that are mixed white and grayish brown. The shade of green is somewhat variable, usually flat green but may range from yellowish to bluish within the same population.

C. dumetorum ranges from Baja California to northern Washington. It is the characteristic Green Hairstreak of western Oregon but is also found east of the Cascades in Jefferson, Wasco, and Hood River Counties. In the latter region the specimens are of slightly smaller average size and may constitute a separate unnamed subspecies. Gorelick (1968) has introduced the name *C. dumetorum oregonensis* to designate all Oregon and Washington *dumetorum*, a distinction that I believe to be unwarranted; most of our populations appear to be identical to those of California.

This butterfly is single-brooded and flies early in the year. It should be looked for on sunny hillsides on warm days in April and May. Rapid and erratic in flight, it settles frequently, resting on a blade of grass or a green leaf, perfectly camouflaged by the green color of its folded wings. The larvae, also green in color and bearing two light stripes subdorsally, feed on *Eriogonum* or *Lotus*. The brown pupae are formed among the litter on the ground.

References:

(1) Clench, Harry K. 1944. Notes on lycaenid butterflies. a. The genus *Callophrys* in North America. Bull. Mus. Comp. Zool. 94: 217-229.

(2) Clench, Harry K. 1963. *Callophrys* (Lycaenidae) from the Pacific Northwest. J. Res. Lepid. 2: 151-160.

(3) Gorelick, Glenn Alan. 1968. A new subspecies of *Callophrys (Callophrys) dumetorum* from Washington and Oregon. J. Res. Lepid. 7: 99-104.

(4) Tilden, J. W. 1963. An analysis of the North American species of the genus *Callophrys*. J. Res. Lepid. 1: 281-300.

Callophrys sheridanii (Carpenter), 1877
Sheridan's Green Hairstreak

Plate 36, figs. 6, 7. Maps 125, 126.

Callophrys sheridanii is a more eastern species than *dumetorum*. Its stronghold, in fact, lies in the Rocky Mountain area and extends from Arizona and New Mexico to Alberta and British Columbia. Westward it reaches the Cascades of Washington and Oregon, the Sierras of California, and the deserts of southern California and Nevada.

The subspecies *C. s. newcomeri* Clench, 1963 (Newcomer's Green Hairstreak), a Northwestern variety, occurs in central and eastern Oregon. It is the smallest of our Green Hairstreaks. The mouse-gray color of the male is shared by the female, though occasional females have a tinge of brown. The green of the forewing underside extends down to vein Cu_2. The hindwing underside tends to be bluish green, and the tips of the fringe scales are white except at the upper and extreme lower angles. The postmedian white line is thin and commonly broken into a few short segments; it is, however, relatively straight as compared to *dumetorum* and thus appears to lie nearer the center of the wing. An early flier, Newcomer's Hairstreak should be sought in April and May. Its habitat includes the hillsides, canyon slopes, washes, and sagelands east of the Cascades. The larvae feed on *Eriogonum*, but the details of the early stages and life history are in need of study. Ferris has given an account of these for a Wyoming population of *C. s. sheridanii*.

C. s. lemberti Tilden, 1963 (Lembert's Green Hairstreak) is a high altitude variety (sometimes regarded as a separate species), with type locality at Tioga Pass in Yosemite Park. In Oregon it occurs at Crater

Family LYCAENIDAE 93

Lake, on Mt. Thielsen, Mt. Ashland, and on Drake Peak in the Warners — all elevations above 7000 feet. It is somewhat larger than *newcomeri*. Like the latter, the females are gray above, and the green of the forewing underside extends down to Cu_2. The tips of the ventral fringe scales are snow white except for a small patch at the anal angle. The postmedian white line, usually broken, is slightly convex, and the green ground color is lighter than in *newcomeri*. The early stages and life history of *lemberti* are unknown.

References:
(1) Ferris, Clifford D. 1973. Life history of *Callophrys s. sheridanii* (Lycaenidae) and notes on other species. J. Lepid. Soc. 27: 279-283.
(2) See under *C. dumetorum*.

Callophrys affinis washingtonia Clench, 1944
Washington Green Hairstreak

Plate 36, fig. 8. Map 127.
Callophrys affinis is the least known of our Green Hairstreaks. It belongs to the sage country and its distribution extends from western Montana, Wyoming, and Colorado to eastern Washington, Oregon, and central Nevada.

The Northwestern subspecies *washingtonia* occurs in northeastern Oregon, where it overlaps the range of *C. sheridanii newcomeri*. Unfortunately the Oregon records of *affinis washingtonia* are scanty and in need of improvement; observations on the habitat and life history of this butterfly are lacking.

Like *dumetorum*, the females of *C. a. washingtonia* are dorsally brownish. The green of the ventral forewings, however, descends to vein Cu_2 as in *sheridanii*. The ventral hindwings are yellowish green and the postmedian white line is faint or absent; the tips of the fringe scales are light brown or checkered with white. In size this butterfly is larger than *C. s. newcomeri* and approaches *dumetorum*. Oregon specimens have been taken from the beginning of April to early July. The larvae feed on *Eriogonum*.

References:
See under *C. dumetorum*.

Atlides halesus corcorani Clench, 1942
Great Blue Hairstreak

Plate 37, fig. 1. Map 128.
One of the largest and most spectacular of North American Hairstreaks, *Atlides halesus* is mainly native to Mexico and the southern United States, stretching from the Atlantic across to the Pacific. Often straying northward, it is, however, definitely established in Oregon, where breeding populations may be found in Jackson County and the Willamette Valley in association with oak mistletoe (*Phoradendron*), the larval foodplant. There are two broods, one in the early spring (April) and another in late summer (July to October). Specimens of the latter generation are more likely to be found, and then sparingly, seldom more than single specimens attracted to flowers.

The wonderful iridescent blue of this butterfly is bordered by a black margin which is wider in the female. A compound scent patch is present on the male forewing. The hindwing is single-tailed in the male, but two-tailed in the female. The dark gray underside is ornamented with patches of iridescent green at the anal angle of the hindwings; in the male a flash of blue lies below the discal cell of the forewing. The underside of the abdomen is bright orange.

The green larvae, covered with a downy pile of short orange hairs, are slugshaped. The brown, black-mottled pupae are hidden in the recesses of the oak bark or lie in the debris at the base of the trees.

Tharsalea arota arota (Boisduval), 1852
Arota Copper

Plate 37, fig. 2. Map 129.
Tharsalea arota is the only Oregon Copper provided with tails. Our subspecies ranges southward to central and southern California; eastward it extends to the western slope of the Sierras. Other geographic races occur on the eastern side of the Sierras and in the Rocky Mountain states from southern Wyoming to New Mexico.

On the upperside, the wings of the male are solidly copper-brown except for a narrow black border and some orange lunules and black dots near the tail; in the female, however, the coppery ground color is extensively broken by patches of orange, a wider dark border on the forewing, and a pronounced chain of orange lunules along the hindwing outer margin. On the underside the sexes look alike: a pattern of black dots occupies the discal area of both wings; the hindwing ground color is grayish-brown and its discal area is separated from the margin by a vertical stripe of whitish lunules.

The Arota Copper is not a common Oregon butterfly. It occurs in scattered small colonies in our California-bordering counties, although specimens from the latitude of the Willamette Valley are also known. The colonies are generally found in small valley bottoms during July and August, along water courses edged with shrubs and little pockets of clearings. The butterflies do not stray from these colonies and seldom move more than a few hundred feet. Both sexes are strongly attracted to yellow and white flowers, but the males spend the morning hours pursuing mates and passing intruders from perches on shrubs and trees. This territorial behavior is interestingly described by James Scott in his observations on a Colorado colony.

The whitish eggs of *Tharsalea arota,* which are turban-shaped and sculptured with ribs and crossribs, are laid on the branches of gooseberry (*Ribes*), the larval foodplant. They pass the winter in diapause and hatch the following spring. The mature larvae are slug-shaped, green, and covered with minute white granulations; two white lines extend along the back, and a thin yellowish one along each side. The pupa is brown and attached by a silken girdle that passes around the thorax.

References:

(1) Scott, James A. 1974. Population biology and adult behavior of *Lycaena arota* (Lycaenidae). J. Lepid. Soc. 28: 64-72.

(2) Tilden, J. W. 1955. A revision of *Tharsalea* Scud. (s. str.), with description of a new subspecies (Lepid., Lyc.). Bull. So. Calif. Acad. Sci. 54: 67-77.

Lycaena (Chalceria) rubidus (Behr), 1866
Ruddy Copper

Plate 37, figs. 3-5. Map 130.

This showy bright orange Copper is widely distributed through the West, its range extending from the edge of the Great Plains to the Pacific States, and from central California and southern Arizona northward to Washington and Alberta. In Oregon it flies east of the Cascades, in the semi-arid country along the upper Columbia and on the sage-land of the central and eastern plateaus. At times it may be seen in great numbers on the rabbit brush along roadsides and near the borders of meadows and streams.

In contrast to the fiery color of the males, the females are dorsally grayish brown except for residual patches of yellowish orange that vary greatly in amount and are sometimes entirely absent; they are also marked with a bold row of post-median black spots and a few in the disc. The underside in both sexes is very pale: the forewings are creamish, often slightly flushed with salmon-pink, and bear heavy black spots; the hindwings are whitish to cream or olive-buff and may be immaculate or faintly spotted.

Johnson and Balogh, in a recent revision of the taxonomy of *L. rubidus,* strongly influenced by considerations of geological history, recognize three subspecies as occurring in Oregon. The populations in southern Oregon (Harney and Lake Counties) are assigned to *L. r. rubidus* (Behr): in these the females have extensive areas of orange and the hindwing undersides (males and females) are whitish and immaculate. The populations of eastern Oregon (Baker, Grant, and Harney Counties) are assigned to *L. r. duofacies* Johnson & Balogh, 1977; here the females are dominantly darker and the hindwings of both sexes are ventrally creamish and faintly spotted. Along the Columbia Gorge the populations are assigned to *L. r. perkinsorum* Johnson & Balogh, 1977; in these the females are mostly dark and the hindwing undersides of both sexes are olive-buff and marked with a row of small but distinct black postmedian spots as well as white submarginal crescents.

The Ruddy Copper is single-brooded, but the life history is incompletely known. The larvae feed on *Rumex* (dock). Richard Funk, observing a colony of *rubidus* in Arizona, noted that newly laid eggs were carried off by ants, an association with these insects not uncommon in lycaenids.

References:

(1) Funk, Richard S. 1975. Association of ants with ovipositing *Lycaena rubidus* (Lycaenidae). J. Lepid. Soc. 29: 261-262.

(2) Johnson, Kurt & George Balogh. 1977. Studies in the Lycaeninae (Lycaenidae). 2. Taxonomy and evolution of the nearctic *Lycaena rubidus* complex, with a description of a new species. Bull. Allyn Museum, No. 43, 62 pp.

Lycaena (Chalceria) heteronea (Boisduval), 1852
Blue Copper

Plate 37, figs. 6, 7. Map 131.

On meeting a male of *Lycaena heteronea* for the first time, one is startled to find a "Copper" that is bright blue. Its identity as a Copper can be confirmed by a glance at the underside spot pattern and by the appearance of the females which closely resemble those of *Lycaena rubidus.*

Like *L. rubidus,* the Blue Copper has a wide range, which extends from the Rockies (southern British Columbia to Colorado and northern Arizona) westward to the coastal states. In Oregon it may be found from the crest of the Cascades eastward, and at high elevations in the southern Siskiyous. This butterfly tends to favor dry areas and should be sought in high sunny meadows, in forest clearings, and on the sage flats. In mid-summer it is often very numerous and flies in the company of other Coppers, Blues, and Hairstreaks.

In contrast to the shining blue color of the males, the females are dorsally drab grayish-brown and black-spotted; dark specimens may be hard to tell from those of L. *rubidus*. On the underside the ground color of both sexes is silvery white to pale creamish; the forewings bear black spots, but the hindwings vary from being immaculate to heavily spotted. The latter kind dominate the populations along the Cascades and the adjacent eastern slope (including all of Wasco County); they correspond in appearance to the Coloradoan *L. h. gravenotata* Klots, 1930, a subspecific name not properly applicable to our distantly removed Oregon populations. Elsewhere in eastern and southern Oregon the hindwing undersides are unspotted or nearly so and may be regarded as the nominotypic subspecies *L. h. heteronea* (Boisduval), possibly showing a northeasterly cline toward *L. h. klotsi* Field, 1936 (weakly spotted populations of the northern Rockies). The factors that govern the degree of hindwing spotting — genetic, ecological, climatic — and their taxonomic implications, need to be studied.

A matter of possible taxonomic significance concerns the haploid chromosome number of *L. heteronea,* which is 68, a startling departure from the 24 found in all other species of *Lycaena* except *rubidus* which, interestingly, has 38.

The Blue Copper is single-brooded, and the larvae, which feed on *Eriogonum* (wild buckwheat), hatch from overwintering eggs. Detailed life history observations on different populations ought to be pursued.

Reference:
(1) Maeki, K. & C. L. Remington. 1960. Studies of the chromosomes of North American Rhopalocera. 3. Lycaenidae, Danaidae, Satyrinae and Morphinae. J. Lepid. Soc. 14: 127-147.

Lycaena (Gaeides) xanthoides xanthoides
(Boisduval), 1852
Great Copper

Plate 38, fig. 1. Map 132.

Aptly named, the Great Copper vies with *Lycaena gorgon* for size. While fairly common in central California, it is only sparsely found in Oregon, mainly in the Siskiyous of the southwestern counties. Recently, after a gap of forty years, it has been rediscovered in the Willamette Valley, found, in fact, by young Joe Schmitt in an undeveloped field in the middle of Corvallis! Very likely small colonies are hidden in unexpected places elsewhere in western Oregon. In the Siskiyous this butterfly appears during the summer months on grassy hillsides, along watercourses in open gulches, and in forest clearings.

The males are dorsally brownish gray in color; a small row of black spots edged with orange lies along the outer margin of the hindwings. In the females the ground color is interrupted by irregular patches of orange, and the marginal spots of the hindwings lie within a broad band of orange lunules. Underneath, the wings of both sexes are light tannish gray and are strewn with small brown spots; the outer margin, especially of the hindwings, bears a row of orange crescents.

Within the small colonies formed by the Great Copper, the males exhibit perching behavior, and in the warmth of the afternoon both males and females busily visit a variety of flowers. Scott and Opler report that the life span of the adult male averages nine days, that of the female fourteen. The species is single-brooded. Eggs are laid on debris below the larval foodplant, *Rumex* (dock), and hatch the following spring. The larvae are either greenish in color, or dark orange banded with magenta. The pupae, formed in a slight cocoon of loosely woven silk, are pinkish buff, blotched with black.

Reference:
(1) Scott, James A. & Paul A. Opler. 1975. Population biology and adult behavior of *Lycaena xanthoides* (Lycaenidae). J. Lepid. Soc. 29: 63-66.

Lycaena (Gaeides) editha editha
(Mead), 1878
Edith's Copper

Plate 38, fig. 2. Map 133.

Edith's Copper could pass for a small edition of *Lycaena xanthoides,* particularly with respect to color and pattern of the upperside. Below, however, the brown spots are larger and more closely set, the marginal band tends to be darker and on the hindwings is inwardly limited by a more prominent scalloped line of white crescents.

Lycaena editha replaces *xanthoides* east of the Cascades and is very abundant in its montane habitat at middle and high elevations in Klamath and Lake Counties, on Steens Mountain, in the Ochocos, the Blue Mountains, and the Wallowas. It frequents roadsides and sunny openings in the conifer forests as well as fields and meadows. Usually flying in the company of other Coppers and of Blues from mid-June to late August, it is strongly attracted to flowers, especially yarrow.

Edith's Copper is single-brooded, but the details of its life cycle have not been reported. The larvae feed on *Potentilla* (cinquefoil), *Horkelia,* and *Rumex* (dock).

This species extends from the west slope of the middle Rockies to southeastern Washington and southward to the California Sierras, Nevada, and Utah. Our populations belong to the Pacific subspecies.

Lycaena (Gaeides) gorgon (Boisduval), 1852
Gorgon Copper

Plate 38, fig. 3. Map 134.

Our largest Copper, except for *L. xanthoides* which equals it in size, the Gorgon Copper occurs along the California border. During June and to mid-July one may look for it on the lightly wooded and brushy hillsides that border streams and gulches in the Siskiyous. It is a fairly scarce butterfly, but becomes commoner southward, its range extending to Baja California.

On the upperside, the male is solidly reddish-brown, often showing a purplish cast; the female, however, has extensive patches of yellow-brown and on the hindwing a row of orange lunules along the outer margin. Underneath, the ground color in both sexes is grayish white, sometimes approaching creamish in the female; against this light background the pattern of black spots stands out in strong contrast; a row of black-edged red lunules lies along the hindwing outer margin.

The eggs of the Gorgon Copper, creamy white and deeply sculptured, are laid singly or in pairs on the stems of *Eriogonum,* the larval foodplant. The bluish-green mature larvae are camouflaged by a coat of white hairs. The pale, also bluish-green pupae are covered with tiny, trumpet-shaped tubercles, and are attached to the foodplant by a silken girdle.

Lycaena (Epidemia) mariposa mariposa Reakirt, 1866
Mariposa Copper

Plate 38, fig. 4. Map 135.

The Mariposa Copper, closely related to *Lycaena nivalis* and *helloides* and dorsally resembling them, occurs in the conifer forests of the Cascades, the Ochocos, the Blue Mountains, and the Wallowas. Often locally abudant in the late summer at elevations between 3000 and 7000 feet, it flits about in the sun and shadow of small moist openings and glades in the stands of ponderosa and lodgepole pines. In such habitats this species may be found from southern Alaska and British Columbia to northern California, thence eastward to the northern and middle Rockies.

The dark brown males often have a purplish sheen; the outer wing borders are vaguely blackish and an obscure row of dark orange lunules appears near the hindwing lower margins. In the lighter colored female the brown ground color is partly and sometimes extensively replaced by orange, except for the broad and dark outer border of the forewings; the marginal lunules of the hindwings are conspicuously developed and the usual spot pattern of female Coppers is present on both wings. Underneath, in both males and females, the disc of the forewing is yellowish orange, the marginal band gray; the distinctively ashen gray hindwings are finely marked with black points, a postmedian line of curved dashes, and a row of white-capped submarginal chevrons.

Lycaena mariposa is single-brooded and the larva feeds on knotgrass (*Polygonum*). The details of the life history and the immature stages have not been described.

Lycaena (Epidemia) helloides (Boisduval), 1852
Purplish Copper

Plate 39, fig. 1. Map 136.

The distribution of *Lycaena helloides,* the most wide-ranging Copper in America, fans westward from the Great Lakes to the Pacific and extends from southern Canada to the lower border of California. It occurs in all parts of Oregon, at all elevations, and, since it breeds continuously, may be found from May to October at lower altitudes. It inhabits uncultivated fields, forest openings, mountain meadows, roadsides, and is not uncommon in yards and gardens.

The overscaling of the coppery brown males gives them a purplish sheen; the outer wing margins are narrowly dark-bordered, and on the hindwings a prominent row of orange lunules forms a crenulated band; the pattern of black spots is usually well developed on both wings. The females are mainly orange, except for the dark forewing border and a suffusion of dark scales that spreads outward from the wing bases; the spot pattern is bolder than in the males, but the purplish sheen is absent. Underneath, in both sexes, the ground color of the forewings is yellowish orange; the hindwings are evenly orange brown, slightly lilac tinged, and bear tiny black spots and orange marginal lunules.

The larvae of the Purplish Copper feed on various species of *Polygonum* (knotweed), *Rumex* (dock), and *Potentilla* (cinquefoil). When mature they are grass green, marked on the sides of each segment with slanted yellowish dashes below which there extends a bright yellow lateral line. Hibernation occurs in the pupal stage; the pupae are greenish, lightly speckled with brown and black, and adorned with small bristle-bearing tubercles.

Reference:

(1) Ferris, Clifford D. 1977. Taxonomic revision of the species *dorcas* Kirby and *helloides* (Boisduval) in the genus *Epidemia* Scudder (Lycaenidae: Lycaeninae). Bull. Allyn Museum, No. 45, 42 pp.

Lycaena (Epidemia) nivalis
(Boisduval), 1869
Nivalis Copper

Plate 39, figs. 2, 3. Maps 137, 138.

On the upperside the Nivalis Copper closely resembles *Lycaena helloides* except for a reduced amount of spotting in the male; below, however, differences in coloration distinctly separate these species. Moreover, *nivalis* is not as generally distributed, but is restricted to the Western mountains, where it occurs on flowered slopes and meadows, in forest openings and in canyons, often in company with *helloides*. Its range extends from the middle Rockies to the Cascades of the Northwest and down to central California.

Compared to *helloides,* the Nivalis Copper is quite variable and represents a complex of phenotypes and races the nature of which has not been fully clarified. Newcomer has called attention to this matter with respect to the Northwest populations, and a taxonomic revision of the complex is awaited from the hands of F. M. Brown.

In Oregon we find at least two distinct forms. The first of these is indigenous to the Cascades and Steens Mountain; together with the second form it also occurs in the Siskiyous, the Blue Mountains, and the Wallowas. It is the larger in average size and the males are dorsally a bit darker. The underside is strikingly characteristic: the ground color of the forewing is intensely deep yellow as is also the inner half of the two-toned hindwing; the contrasting outer half of the hindwing is rich lilac-pink; the black spots on the forewing are bold, but on the hindwing tiny to absent. Newcomer suggests that this form may be more adapted to areas of higher precipitation than the second.

The second form, a bit smaller and with males of slightly lighter dorsal shade, is characteristic of the Ochoco and Warner Mountains of central Oregon, but is found together with the first in the Siskiyous and the mountains of northeastern Oregon. The underside of its forewings is pale straw-yellow, except for the apices and outer borders that are delicately lilac; the hindwings, not as sharply two-toned as in the Canadian form, are mainly lilac, but may show a weakly defined straw-yellow basal area. The spot pattern is the same.

Somewhat parallel form differences occur in the Rocky Mountains, and it remains to be learned to what extent these are environmentally determined or represent populations sufficiently unlike genetically to be worthy of subspecific or even specific separation (as suggested by areas of overlapping distribution).

The life history of the Nivalis Copper has been worked out by Newcomer. Though the butterfly may be found from late May to end of August, it is single-brooded (unlike *helloides*), and the eggs, which are flattened, pitted, and pale bluish, remain unhatched until the following spring. The larvae, which feed on *Polygonum douglasii,* are pale green when mature, marked dorsally with a claret line flanked by a pair of narrow white lines, and adorned with brownish hairs and small white tubercles. The straw yellow pupae have brown spots and trumpet-shaped hairs.

Reference:

(1) Newcomer, E. J. 1963. The synonymy, variability, and biology of *Lycaena nivalis*. J. Res. Lepid. 2: 271-280.

Lycaena (Lycaena) phlaeas arctodon
Ferris, 1974
Beartooth Copper

Plate 39, figs. 4-6. Map 139.

Thus far only a single specimen of *Lycaena phlaeas* is known from Oregon. This was taken by C. W. Nelson at an altitude of 9500 feet on the east face of the Matterhorn in the Wallowa Mountains. It comes closest in appearance to the subspecies *arctodon* which Ferris has recently described from Beartooth Pass (10,300 ft.) in Carbon Co., Montana, and which is also known from high altitudes (treeline and above) in Wyoming and Idaho. *Lycaena phlaeas* occurs in Europe as well as North America. Whereas the subspecies *americana* Harris is common in the northeastern United States and adjacent Canada, from where it extends to the northern Midwest and into the southern Appalachians, all other American subspecies are arctic-alpine and extremely local. *L. p. hypophlaeas* (Boisduval) occurs on the rocky slopes of the high Sierras around Yosemite.

The upperside of the forewing in the male of *L. p. arctodon* is brassy copper and dusky, marked with black spots and a dark marginal border; the hindwing is wholly dark except for an orange marginal band along whose inner edge there extends a row of small blue spots. The female is similar but less dusky. On the underside the hindwing in both sexes is pale gray in ground color and is distinctly patterned with small black spots.

At Beartooth Pass the larval foodplant of this Copper is *Rumex acetosa* (dock), but more likely it is *Oxyria digyna* (mountain sorrel) in the high Wallowas (where *Rumex* does not appear) as it is for *L. p. hypophlaeas* in the Sierras.

References:

(1) Ferris, Clifford D. 1974. Distribution of arctic-alpine *Lycaena phlaeas* L. (Lycaenidae) in North America with designation of a new subspecies. Bull. Allyn Museum, No. 18, 13 pp.

(2) Shields, Oakley & Johnson C. Montgomery. 1966. The distribution and bionomics of arctic-alpine *Lycaena phlaeas* subspecies in North America. J. Res. Lepid. 5: 231-242.

Lycaena (Lycaena) cupreus cupreus (Edwards), 1870
Lustrous Copper

Plate 39, fig. 7. Map 140.

A jewel among Coppers, the flash and sparkle of this butterfly in the sunlight is not easily forgotten. It is not common, and is usually encountered only in small numbers at elevations of 4500 to 8500 feet in central and eastern Oregon. On the high slopes of Steens Mountain colonies of *Lycaena cupreus* may be found during July and into August, but at lower elevations (east slope of the southern Cascades and in the Ochocos) this Copper is best sought in June. One may come upon it in small meadows, along stretches of open roadside in the forest, or among the rocks higher up. The flight pattern of the Lustrous Copper is fast, erratic, and tantalizing, and for a close look one must wait for it to alight, as it frequently does, on some flower (it is fond of yarrow and pussy-paws), on the roadside gravel, or among the boulders, whence it is quickly off again in a golden glitter.

Our subspecies ranges southward into the high Sierras of California and Nevada; it has also been found in the northern Cascades of Washington. In the southern and central Rockies *L. cupreus* occurs as the subspecies *snowi* (Edwards); in northern British Columbia and the adjacent edge of Alaska as *L. c. henryae* (Cadbury).

Brilliantly reddish-copper above, both fore- and hindwings are black-bordered and patterned with black spots that are larger in the female than in the male; the hindwing of the female is moreover partially suffused with dark scales that spread outwardly from the base. Beneath, the forewings are orange except for a gray marginal band and the black spots; the hindwing is gray in ground color, spotted, and at its margin bears a thin band of bright orange lunules.

The larvae of the Lustrous Copper are known to feed on *Rumex* (dock), but the details of the life history and immature stages remain to be explored.

Brephidium exilis (Boisduval), 1852
Pigmy Blue

Plate 40, fig. 1. Map 141.

This smallest of North American butterflies, mainly neotropical in distribution, occurs commonly from Texas to central and southern California. Occasionally it has been found farther north, from Nebraska to eastern Oregon. The few Oregon records are from the Great Basin area. Since the habitat of this species includes weedy dry land and alkali flats, its distribution in southeastern Oregon is probably wider than now known. Because of its small size the Pigmy Blue can be easily overlooked. In southern California this butterfly is multibrooded and may be seen from April to October, but it is most abundant in late summer and early fall. The Oregon specimens were taken in July and August.

Apart from its small size, *Brephidium exilis* is easily identified. The upperside wing color is brown, with a flush of blue scales spreading outward from the base; a row of black spots extends along the outer margin of the hindwings. Beneath, the ground color is basally grayish white, becoming brownish outwardly; a pattern of short, vertical white dashes extends over both wings; along the hindwing outer margin there is a row of prominent black spots which are edged with metallic golden scales. The fringes of the wing are white.

The larvae of the Pigmy Blue, which hatch from delicately bluish green eggs ornamented with a network of white ridges, feed on *Atriplex* (orache, saltwort) or *Chenopodium* (pigweed) and are attended by ants. When mature these larvae are pale or yellowish green, bear a whitish line along the back and a bright yellow stripe along each side; a covering of minute white hairs borne on closely set brown tubercles gives to the larvae a frosted appearance which conceals them on the similarly colored leaves of the foodplant. The chrysalis is light brownish yellow except for a dusky line along the back and wing cases that are pale yellowish green.

Lycaeides argyrognomon ricei (Cross), 1937
Rice's Blue

Plate 40, fig. 2. Map 142.

Lycaeides argyrognomon is a circumpolar species of which some dozen North American races have been named. These tend to grade into one another and even within populations the individuals show considerable variability. Genitalial measurements are often necessary to distinguish some populations from the species *melissa*. These matters are fully treated in the monograph by Nabokov (1949).

L. argyrognomon may be found from Alaska south to central California, in the Rockies from British Columbia to southern Colorado, and across the northern portion of the Continent to the Atlantic Coast of Canada and New England. In Oregon *argyrognomon* is represented by the subspecies *ricei,* which is indigenous to the Cascades of the Northwest; its type locality is Big Cultus Lake in Deschutes County. Near our southern border there is a clinal gradation into the northern Californian race *L. a. anna* (Edwards), 1861.

The males of Rice's Blue are solidly lilac-blue on the upperside except for a narrow black marginal line and white fringe scales. Beneath they are grayish white in ground color, almost chalky; a row of small black spots runs down the center of the forewings and extends across the disc of the hindwings; a chain of yellowish-orange lunules (aurorae) is aligned along the outer margin of both wings but tends to fade out anteriorly; the lunules are inwardly capped by black scales, and near the lower angle of the hindwings they include traces of iridescent silver. The females are brown above and marked with a submarginal band of yellowish-orange crescents which on the hindwings enclose dark spots; these crescents are often obsolescent, especially on the forewings; the underside resembles that of the males except that the ground color has a creamish tint and the submarginal aurorae tend to be more clearly expressed.

Rice's Blue is fairly common at middle and higher altitudes throughout the Cascades and usually flies in the company of other Blues on the meadows and in forest clearings. The larvae feed on lupines and other legumes (*Lathyrus, Vicia*). Details of the life-cycle and early stages have not been recorded.

Shepard (1964) has mistakenly assigned the *Lycaeides* populations of the eastern Oregon highlands (Ochocos, Blue Mountains, and Wallowas) to *L. argyrognomon atrapraetextus* (Field). The latter subspecies occurs in the Priest River region of northern Idaho and can be recognized by the possession, in males, of a wide black border in addition to its distinctive genitalial characters. These features are not present in the eastern Oregon *Lycaeides* which are, in fact, *L. melissa*.

References:
(1) Nabokov, V. 1949. The nearctic members of the genus *Lycaeides* Hübner (Lycaenidae, Lepidoptera). Bull. Mus. Comp. Zool. 101: 479-541. (The author of this monograph is the late Vladimir Nabokov of literary fame, who was at the time a research fellow at Harvard's Museum of Comparative Zoology and an expert student of lycaenid butterflies.)

(2) Shepard, Jon H. 1964. The genus *Lycaeides* in the Pacific Northwest. J. Res. Lepid. 3: 25-36.

Lycaeides melissa melissa (Edwards), 1873
Melissa Blue

Plate 40, fig. 3. Map 143.

A widespread North American species, *Lycaeides melissa* occurs over most of the western United States, the adjoining Canadian Provinces, and northern Mexico. One subspecies, the scarce Karner Blue (*L. m. samuelis* Nabokov), is found in the region of the Great Lakes and in the Northeast. In portions of their ranges *L. melissa* and *argyrognomon* overlap, and the two species are at times difficult to separate except by the male genitalia, which differ in respect to the relative lengths of the falcial arms, as exemplified.

The nominotypic subspecies, *L. m. melissa,* ranges from the western edge of the Great Plains to the Pacific States. In Oregon it is widely distributed and common in the sage lands, the open ponderosa forests, and the mountain meadows east of the Cascades, including high elevations in the Wallowas and the summit of Steens Mountain.

On the upperside, the lilac-blue males of the Melissa Blue resemble Rice's Blue; so do the brown females, except that the orange submarginal band is always complete and more boldly developed. The underside ground color is in both sexes light gray or fawn-colored, never chalky; the orange aurorae along the margins are partially confluent on the forewings, but on the hindwings sharply defined and fully developed, with their outer edges sparklingly silvered.

L. melissa may produce two or three broods a year, depending on altitude and climate. The eggs are laid on the leaves and stalks of lupines, the larval foodplant, or on nearby twigs and pebbles. A symbiotic relationship between ants and the larvae is known to exist, but detailed studies of this and the life history of the Melissa Blue ought to be pursued.

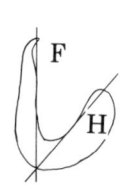
L. argyrognomon ricei
Frog Camp (Cascades)
Lane Co., Ore.
F/H = 1.289

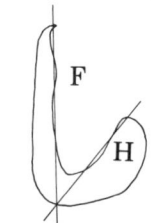
L. melissa melissa
Viewpt. Rd. (Ochocos)
Crook Co., Ore.
F/H = 1.581

References:
See under *L. argyrognomon ricei.*

Plebejus saepiolus saepiolus (Boisduval), 1852
Glossy Blue

Plate 40, fig. 4. Map 144.

This common and widespread species ranges from Alaska and British Columbia to southern California and eastward to the Rockies; also across central and southern Canada to the Great Lakes and Maine. Our subspecies is found from the mountains of central California to British Columbia, across the Great Basin, and in the northern Rockies. Generally associated with grassy and wet slopes and meadows, bogs, and moist glades in the forest, this butterfly is very abundant from the Cascades and Siskiyous eastward across the high plains and mountainous areas of Oregon. Less commonly it also occurs in the coastal mountains. Flight records extend from May through August.

The glossy light blue color of the males is very distinctive and has a somewhat silvery sheen; a dark marginal band narrows to a row of black spots on the hindwing. The underside ground color is silvery gray and is spotted with rows of black dots and marginal crescents; the crescents at the anal angle usually include a trace of orange scales; a bluish flush characterizes the basal area of the hindwings. The females of *P. saepiolus* are reddish brown and remind one of male Mariposa Coppers, with which they sometimes fly; a band of orange spots lies along the outer margin of the hindwings. Underneath, the females are tannish brown but otherwise are marked like the males.

The Glossy Blue flies close to the ground. The males are more active and aggressive than the females, which move more gently and tend to remain secluded. Both sexes do not wander far from patches of clover (*Trifolium*) on which the larvae feed. The details of the immature stages remain to be described.

Reference:
(1) Sharp, Margaret A. & David R. Parks. 1973. Habitat selection and population structure in *Plebejus saepiolus* Boisduval (Lycaenidae). J. Lepid. Soc. 27: 17-22.

Icaricia icarioides (Boisduval), 1852
Boisduval's Blue

Plate 40, figs. 5-8. Map 145.

Boisduval's Blue is a very common but quite variable species whose range includes all of the States and Provinces west of the central Great Plains. Along the Pacific Coast it may be found from Alaska to southern California. Always closely associated with lupines, it is often exceedingly numerous in open habitats where these plants abound. Some dozen geographic races have been named whose centers of distribution lie, respectively, in the southern and northern Rockies, in western Canada, in the Great Basin, in the deserts of the Southwest, in the Sierras, and in the valleys along the Coast. Many of these intergrade with one another, and even within the center of named populations a high degree of individual variability may exist.

In Oregon the distribution of *icarioides* closely resembles that of *Plebejus saepiolus* and *Icaricia acmon;* these species, in fact, commonly fly together. The Cascadian populations and those of the Siskiyous most nearly resemble the nominate race of the Californian Sierras, *I. i. icarioides* (Boisduval). The males are bright blue above, more velvety and less glossy than *P. saepiolus,* but with similar dark margins. The brown females have varying amounts of blue extending outwardly from the wing bases. Underneath, the ground color in both sexes is more or less silvery gray, somewhat darker in females; the black spots on the forewings are decidedly larger than those of the hindwings which are reduced to small points encircled by rings of white; the crescents along the borders are not strongly expressed.

The populations in the semi-arid regions of southeastern Oregon intergrade with the Great Basin subspecies *I. i. ardea* (Edwards), 1871. In this race the spots of the ventral hindwings have mainly lost their black pupils and are completely white; also, the marginal lunules have almost disappeared.

In northeastern Oregon and along the Upper Columbia the trend of variation runs toward *I. i. pembina* (Edwards), 1862, a race of the northern Rockies. Here the black border of the male upperside is somewhat wider; the females are almost wholly brown; the underside ground color is darker, with the hindwing spots and marginal crescents generally well defined.

Finally, at the western edge of the Willamette Valley there are small and rather scarce colonies of a race marked by females that are completely brown above; their underside ground color is decidedly creamish tan and bears a pattern of strong black spots only narrowly ringed with white, reminding one of the brown females of *P. saepiolus*. The males, except for the slightly tannish underside, are more like the Cascadian *I. i. icarioides*. This race was named *fenderi* by Ralph Macy (1931). It is very similar to *I. i. pardalis* (Behr), 1867 of the central California coastal valleys, which, without good reason, has long been listed as a separate species. While *fenderi* occurs at low elevations, *icarioides* from higher altitudes in the Coast Range (e.g., Mary's Peak) cannot be distinguished from the Cascadian populations.

John Downey has, over a period of many years, made a close study of *Icaricia icarioides* and his papers are recommended for informative reading. He has substantiated the restriction of this species to *Lupinus* as its foodplant, many species of which are utilized, though only a single one for any given population of the butterfly. It seems strange that no specimens of *icarioides* have so far been reported from the immediate Oregon coast, where certain lupines are well established. It should also be mentioned that *icarioides* is single-brooded, and that overwintering (diapause) occurs in the second larval instar, with further growth and pupation ensuing the following year.

The larvae of Boisduval's Blue are attended by several species of ants which feed on the exudates of the larval honey-glands located on the tenth body segment and which become functional in the third and fourth instars. This relationship is not obligatory, but, since the ants have been observed to attack potential hymenopterous parasites of the larvae, the butterfly gains protection by this symbiotic relationship ("myrmecophily").

References:
(1) Downey, John C. & Woodson C. Fuller. 1961. Variation in *Plebejus icarioides* (Lycaenidae). I. Foodplant specificity. J. Lepid. Soc. 15: 34-42.
(2) Downey, John C. 1962. Myrmecophily in *Plebejus (Icaricia) icarioides* (Lepid.: Lycaenidae). Ent. News 73: 57-66.
(3) Macy, Ralph W. 1931. A new Oregon butterfly (Lepid. Lycaenidae). Ent. News 42: 1-2.
(4) Tilden, J. W. 1973. Specific entities of the subgenus *Icaricia* Nabokov (Lycaenidae). J. Res. Lepid. 12: 11-20.

Icaricia shasta shasta (Edwards), 1862
Shasta Blue

Plate 41, fig. 1. Map 146.

A delicate and very local butterfly, the Shasta Blue is generally associated with high altitudes, especially in Colorado and California, though in Oregon colonies may be found as low as three thousand feet along the Metolius. The range of this species extends from the western Great Plains across the Rockies to the Cascades and Sierras. In Oregon the Pacific subspecies, *I. s. shasta,* occurs on the east slope of the central Cascades, at higher elevations in the Warner Mountains, and on Steens Mountain. One seldom finds more than a few specimens at any site, except on the high meadows of Steens Mountain where the colonies are usually well populated, even to a height of 9500 feet near the summit. It should be looked for in July and August. The Shasta Blue has a weak flight, close to the ground, usually near small streams in sunny forest openings (Cascades) or near the melting snow fields on the high slopes and meadows of Steens Mountain.

The males are dusky blue-violet above and have dark wing borders that vary greatly in width and on the hindwing enclose a row of black dots. The females are brown, but may show a flush of blue near the wing bases; the dark dots along the margin of the hindwings are partially capped with orange lunules. Underneath, both males and females are grayish brown; the black discal and postmedial spots are white-rimmed; the marginal black spots of the hindwing are mixed with iridescent silver scales and are capped by orange and black lunules from which elongated white chevrons extend inwardly.

The Shasta Blue is single-brooded, but the details of its life history are still unrecorded. The larvae feed on legumes: *Astragalus* (locoweed) and probably species of *Trifolium* (clover). Much remains to be learned about the early stages and the habits of this butterfly.

References:
(1) Ferris, Clifford D. 1976. Revisionary notes on *Plebejus (Icaricia) shasta* (Edwards). Bull. Allyn Museum, No. 36, 16 pp.
(2) Tilden, J. W. 1973. Specific entities of the subgenus *Icaricia* Nabokov (Lycaenidae). J. Res. Lepid. 12: 11-20.

Icaricia acmon (Westwood & Hewitson), 1852
Acmon Blue

Plate 41, fig. 2. Map 147.

Another of our common and locally abundant Blues, the species *Icaricia acmon* occurs throughout the West, from the edge of the Great Plains to the Pacific Coast. It is a quite variable butterfly, as may be expected from its wide range, and is composed of three currently recognized subspecies which intergrade at their borders; there is, moreover, a close affinity to, and in Oregon an actual intergrading with *Icaricia lupini,* so that the latter qualifies only with difficulty as a separate species.

The subspecies *I. a. acmon* (Westwood & Hewitson) occurs throughout California, from where it extends northward into Oregon and Washington as well as into southwest Idaho and western Nevada. In the high plateaus and mountains of eastern Oregon and Washington intergrading occurs with *I. a. lutzi* (dos Passos), 1938, the race of the northern Rocky Mountain area. The males of the subspecies *acmon* are pale blue above (sky blue) and have very narrow black wing borders; in *lutzi* the ground color is slightly darker, approaching purple, and the black wing borders are less narrow; the submarginal band of crescents on the hindwing (which encloses a row of black spots) is pinkish in *acmon,* more orange in *lutzi*. The females of both subspecies are brown, though spring specimens may have much blue overscaling at the wing bases and across the disc (form "cottlei"); the marginal band of the hindwings is orange and usually wider than in males. The underside of both sexes is grayish white and bears the usual pattern of black spots; on the hindwings the submarginal orange aureoles rest on a row of silver-encrusted black dots along the outer border.

Depending on altitude and climate, *acmon* can have several broods, and may be found from April to September. In northwestern Oregon it is relatively scarce, but from the Cascades eastward and in the Siskiyous *acmon* occurs in abundance and may be found flying with other Blues in open areas.

The larvae of *acmon* feed on several species of *Eriogonum* (buckwheat), hatching from eggs laid on the flowers or leaves. In California the larvae of this species are also known to utilize the leguminous genera *Lotus* and *Astragalus*. Overwintering takes place in the young larval stage. The mature larva is dirty yellow, has a narrow green stripe along the back, various markings on the sides, and is covered with downy white hairs. The pupa is brown except for a greenish abdomen. Opler has reported seeing *acmon* larvae attended by ants in Contra Costa County, California.

References:
(1) Goodpasture, Carll. 1973a. A new subspecies of *Plebejus acmon* (Lepidoptera: Lycaenidae). Pan-Pacific Entomologist 49: 149-159.
(2) Goodpasture, Carll. 1973b. Biology and systematics of the *Plebejus (Icaricia) acmon* group (Lepidoptera: Lycaenidae). I. Review of the group. J. Kansas Entom. Soc. 46: 468-485.
(3) Goodpasture, Carll. 1974. Foodplant specificity in the *Plebejus (Icaricia) acmon* group (Lycaenidae). J. Lepid. Soc. 28: 53-63.

(4) Gorelick, Glenn Alan. 1969. Notes on larval host acceptance in a California population of *Plebejus acmon* (Lycaenidae). J. Lepid. Soc. 23: 31-32.

(5) Opler, Paul A. 1968. Myrmecophily reported for *Icaricia acmon* and *Philotes enoptes bayensis* (Lycaenidae, Lepidoptera). Pan-Pacific Entomologist 44: 79-80.

(6) Tilden, J. W. 1973. Specific entities of the subgenus *Icaricia* Nabokov (Lycaenidae). J. Res. Lepid. 12: 11-20.

Icaricia lupini lupini (Boisduval), 1869
Lupine Blue

Plate 41, fig. 3. Map 148.

Oregon populations of *Icaricia lupini* are characteristic of middle altitudes in the Cascades where they may be found, often in profusion, in dry, brushy openings of the ponderosa forests. Excellent colonies occur in the Sand Creek region east of Crater Lake.

Very close to *acmon* in appearance, the males average larger and more constant in size; they are more purplish in ground color and the dark borders of the forewings are broader; the hindwing submarginal band is orange-red rather than pink, and the marginal black dots are not well separated from the black terminal line. Females are difficult to distinguish from *acmon* but are larger in average size.

While *Icaricia acmon* and *lupini* are genitalically distinguishable in California and do not interbreed (see Goodpasture, 1973b; Tilden, 1973), Oregon populations of these two "species" intergrade east of the Cascades, with many individuals showing intermediate genitalial structure as well as wing coloration. A southwestern race of *acmon*, *I. a. texanus* (Goodpasture), 1973, also has genitalia of intermediate morphology.

Icaricia lupini is single-brooded and its larvae are known to feed only on shrub-like species of *Eriogonum*. They do not feed on lupine, as the name of this species mistakenly suggests!

References:
See under *Icaricia acmon*.

Agriades aquilo podarce (Felder & Felder), 1865
Arctic Blue

Plate 41, fig. 4. Map 149.

One of our scarcest Blues, this is a species of the Far North or of high altitudes in the Western mountains. It is present also in the Old World. Our subspecies occurs in the high meadows of the California Sierras and is known from a few restricted sites in Oregon: Crater Lake (Annie Springs), Diamond Lake (foot of Mt. Bailey in Douglas County), and at the summit of Mt. Ashland (Jackson County). In these locations, if one is lucky, the Arctic Blue may be found on the marshy slopes and meadows that are lushly overgrown with deep grass and dense stands of false hellebore. It has been found on the wing from late June to end of July. In contrast to the scarcity of this butterfly in Oregon, the Rocky Mountain subspecies, *A. aquilo rustica* (Edwards), is common and abundant in Colorado at altitudes above 8500 feet.

The male of our race, *A. a. podarce*, is shiny grayish blue above; a dark border extends along the outer margin of the forewing and breaks into a row of black dots on the hindwing; the forewing discal cell ends in a distinct black speck. The female upperside is russet brown and has similar though less obvious marginal markings plus the discal speck. Underneath, the ground color is grayish brown, leaning more toward a deeper brown in the female; against this dark ground the white-circled black spots of the disc stand out prominently on both wings; the lunule-capped rows of black spots along the margins are also well defined and at the hindwing anal angle are associated with weakly developed orange aureolae.

The early stages of this butterfly are poorly known. In the Californian Sierras the larvae have been reported to feed on *Dodecatheon* (shooting star). There is opportunity here for a good life history study.

Everes comyntas comyntas (Godart), 1824
Eastern Tailed Blue

Plate 41, fig. 5. Map 150.

The Blues of the genus *Everes* can be quickly recognized by the hair-like tail that projects from the lower angle of the hindwings. There are two North American species, both of which occur in Oregon, and they are often confused. The species *comyntas*, widespread and common throughout the central and eastern United States, from the Rocky Mountain states to the Atlantic coast, is present in isolated populations west of the Cascades, where it may be found together with *Everes amyntula*.

The two species can be told apart by genitalial differences and, in the case of Oregon populations, by color and pattern of the underside. *Everes comyntas* averages smaller in size than *E. amyntula*. In the male genitalia the distal outlines of the uncus, as seen from above, are as follows:

comyntas

mesial tooth-like projection flanked by high "shoulders"

amyntula

gradual taper to mesial projection and no "shoulders"

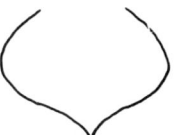

In *comyntas* the ground color of the underside is gray, but in *amyntula* chalky white; the discal and marginal black spot pattern is complete and distinct in *comyntas,* reduced or obsolete in *amyntula;* the orange marginal lunules of the ventral hindwings are well expressed in *comyntas,* suppressed or absent in *amyntula*.

Both species appear early in the spring, produce two or more broods, and fly until fall. In *comyntas* the males of the spring generation tend to be lighter in color than those hatching later; early females have much blue overscaling, but later generations are solidly dark brown. The Tailed Blues fly low to the ground, frequently visit flowers, and are fond of moisture, often gathering in numbers at puddles by the roadside. Look for them in damp meadows and in sunny glades near water.

Females lay their eggs singly on the flower heads of various legumes, particularly clover (*Trifolium*). The greenish, variously marked larvae feed on the flower parts and hibernate within the pods when fully grown in the fall. They are equipped with integumentary honey-glands, but association with ants has not been often observed. The pupae possess stridulating organs between the abdominal segments and can produce sound.

References:

(1) Lawrence, Donald A. & John C. Downey. 1966. Morphology of the immature stages of *Everes comyntas* Godart (Lycaenidae). J. Res. Lepid. 5: 61-96.

(2) See under Family Lycaenidae.

Everes amyntula amyntula (Boisduval), 1852
Western Tailed Blue

Plate 41, fig. 6. Map 151.

Everes amyntula ranges over most of western North America, from the Rockies to the Pacific Coast; in Canada its distribution also extends eastward to the Gaspé Peninsula. In Oregon this species occurs on both sides of the Cascades but has not been reported from the semi-arid regions of the southeastern counties. Like *comyntas,* the Western Tailed Blue prefers moist habitats and is particularly at home in the mountains. June is a good time to look for fresh specimens in the Cascades.

The characteristics which distinguish this species have been discussed under *Everes comyntas.* Seen in series, it is easy to recognize the larger size, the chalky white and sparsely marked underside, and the persistence of blue overscaling in the females. In western Oregon both species are found, but *amyntula* is commoner. The immature stages are similar. The larvae of *amyntula* feed on the legumes *Astragalus* (locoweed), *Lathyrus* (sweet pea), and *Vicia* (vetch).

Philotes (Euphilotes) battoides (Behr), 1867
Battoides Blue

Plate 42, figs. 1-3. Maps 152-154.

The small Blues of the genus *Philotes* have in recent years received a great deal of study, especially by Langston, Shields, and Mattoni. They are taxonomically difficult since many of them look much alike. All of the North American species are Western. The genus has also been subjected to division, with the name *Euphilotes* (Mattoni, 1977) most recently applied to five closely related species that include the two in Oregon (superseding their previous assignment to *Shijimiaeoides* by Shields).

Our *Philotes* (or *Euphilotes*) superficially resemble *Icaricia acmon* and *lupini*. They can be readily distinguished, however, by the wing fringes, which are not solidly white but checkered with alternating groups of black and white scales. Further, in *Philotes* there are no silver scales associated with the orange marginal band of the ventral hindwing. In many places these two kinds of Blues fly together, which affords good opportunity to observe differences in behavior, such as the more wary and jerky movements of *Philotes*. The larvae of both feed on *Eriogonum* (wild buckwheat) and may be tended by ants.

Our two species look so much alike, even with regard to parallel variation of their subspecies, that they can be securely separated only by examination of the male genitalia. To further compound the problem, both species may be found in the same area. The genitalial differences are fortunately very pronounced and easy to recognize: in *P. battoides* the valves are bifurcated and possess three prominent spines; in *P. enoptes* the valves are whole, the straight outer margin being serrated and ending in one small spine. Once seen in prepared dissections, these features can usually be detected after merely plucking away the terminal tuft of abdominal scales.

Philotes battoides   *Philotes enoptes*

Having identified the species, the assignment to subspecies can be made by color and markings of the wings and attention to the geographic site of capture.

Philotes battoides is represented in Oregon by three subspecies. The scarcest of these is *P. b. intermedia* Barnes & McDunnough, 1917, the Intermediate Blue. It extends from the northern California mountains across the Oregon border into the Siskiyous, with records from Siskiyou Pass, Mt. Ashland, and the Kalmiopsis Wilderness (June and July). Its distinguishing features include dark wing borders in the male that are usually fairly wide; on the underside of both sexes the black spots are small and the orange band along the hind wing margin is reduced to a row of separate and small lunules. In general appearance this variety of *battoides* resembles *P. enoptes enoptes*, which also occurs in the Siskiyous. Shields reports that the larvae feed on *Eriogonum marifolium*.

In the southern and central Cascades and the Warner Mountains we find *Philotes battoides oregonensis* Barnes & McDunnough, 1917, the Oregon Blue. Its type locality is Crater Lake, and as *Eriogonum umbellatum* comes into bloom in late June and early July this butterfly may be found in abundance along Highway 232 in the neighborhood of Sand Creek (4800 feet elevation). It is of striking appearance, with the male deep purplish blue and having very wide black wing borders; underneath, in both sexes, the black spots are large, squarish on the forewing, and the orange marginal lunules of the hindwing are prominent and often confluent. To the north and east this subspecies merges into *P. b. glaucon*.

Throughout northcentral and eastern Oregon *battoides* is represented by the wide ranging Glaucous Blue, *P. b. glaucon* (Edwards), 1871, whose territory extends into the Great Basin. In the Alvord region off the east face of Steens Mountain the Glaucous Blue appears in late May. On the small alpine meadow at the summit of Steens Mountain (9500 feet) a vigorous colony may be seen during the third and fourth weeks of July; the low flying and fast settling behavior of the butterfly is distinctly advantageous on this storm-swept site where a sudden gust of wind could carry it over the precipice into the inhospitable desert five thousand feet below. The Glaucus Blue differs from the other two subspecies in the narrow black wing border of the male, which on the lower wings is broken into a row of black dots. Underneath, the black spots are nearly as heavy as in *oregonensis*, and the orange lunules are also bold and often confluent. This subspecies has a strong resemblance to *Philotes enoptes columbiae*, whose range it overlaps. *Eriogonum umbellatum* is the larval foodplant.

The females of the Battoides Blues (as also of *P. enoptes*) lay their eggs singly on the buds or the sepals of the newly opened flowers of the wild buckwheat. The larvae, cryptically colored like the *Eriogonum* bloom, feed exclusively on the flower heads. Pupation corresponds to end of the blooming period, with diapause through the winter months and emergence of the adult the following spring or early summer. The flight period of the adult butterflies does not usually extend beyond the flowering time of the *Eriogonum*, worth remembering when looking for *Philotes*.

References:
(1) Langston, Robert L. 1969. *Philotes* of North America: synonymic list and distribution. J. Lepid. Soc. 23: 49-62.
(2) Mattoni, Rudolf H. T. 1977. The Scolitantidini. I. Two new genera and a generic rearrangement (Lycaenidae). J. Res. Lepid. 16: 223-242.
(3) Shields, Oakley. 1973. Studies on North American *Philotes* (Lycaenidae). I. Roosting behavior, tending ants, parasites, and predators. Bull. Allyn Museum, No. 10, 5 pp.
(4) Shields, Oakley. 1975. Studies on North American *Philotes* (Lycaenidae). IV. Taxonomic and biological notes, and a new subspecies. Bull. Allyn Museum, No. 28, 36 pp.
(5) Shields, Oakley. 1977. Studies on North American *Philotes* (Lycaenidae). V. Taxonomic and biological notes, continued. J. Res. Lepid. 16: 1-67.

Philotes (Euphilotes) enoptes (Boisduval), 1852
Enoptes Blue

Plate 42, figs. 4, 5. Maps 155, 156.
The overall geographic distribution of *Philotes enoptes* in western North America resembles that of *P. battoides*, and these two species moreover look so much alike that positive identification, as pointed out in the discussion of *battoides*, requires examination of the genitalia. The outer margin of the valve in *enoptes* is straight, serrated, and ends in a short spine. Also, as in *battoides*, the larvae of *enoptes* feed on *Eriogonum*, and their development up to pupation, as well as the flying time of the adults, corresponds to the flowering period of the host plant.

Two subspecies can be distinguished in Oregon. In the southern portion of the State, coming northward from the coastal mountains and Cascades of California, we find the nominotypic variety, *P. enoptes en-*

optes (Boisduval), the Dotted Blue. It corresponds in appearance to *P. battoides intermedia,* also of southern Oregon, but is much more common. The males may have a wide dark border, though this is not always the case, and the orange band of the female upperside is often poorly developed. On the underside the black spots are small and the orange marginal lunules are much reduced. At lower altitudes in the Siskiyous this butterfly appears in late May, but at higher elevations and eastward it flies through July. Shields reports the larval foodplant to be *Eriogonum nudum.*

Widely scattered over the northern half of Oregon and extending into Washington, a subspecies larger in size and resembling *battoides glaucon* is *P. enoptes columbiae* Mattoni, 1955, the Columbia Blue. Its distribution generally corresponds to the drainage system of the Columbia River and its tributaries, and includes colonies on the east slope of the Coast Range. Like *P. b. glaucon,* the marginal dark band of the male is narrow and breaks into a series of black dots on the hindwings; the black spots of the underside tend to be bolder than in *e. enoptes* and the orange lunules more strongly developed. Specimens from Harney County sometimes show a darker ventral gray ground color and may be transitional to *P. enoptes ancilla* Barnes & McDunnough, the dominant variety of the Rockies and Great Basin. The larvae of *P. e. columbiae* have been found on *Eriogonum compositum* and *heracleides.* A detailed account of the life history of *Philotes enoptes* has been published by Langston & Comstock for the Californian subspecies *bayensis.*

References:

(1) Langston, Robert L. & John Adams Comstock. 1966. Life history of *Philotes enoptes bayensis* (Lepidoptera: Lycaenidae). Pan-Pacific Entomologist 42: 102-108.

(2) See under *Philotes battoides.*

Glaucopsyche piasus (Boisduval), 1852
Arrowhead Blue

Plate 42, fig. 6. Map 157.

Our largest Blue, *Glaucopsyche piasus,* is at once recognizable by its checkered fringes and the row of white markings on the underside of the hindwings which resemble long, inward pointing arrowheads. This is a relatively uncommon butterfly, and though widely distributed from the Cascades eastward across the mountainous country of Oregon, its colonies are very local and restricted. It may occur at altitudes ranging from 2000 to 8000 feet, which accounts for captures from late April to early August. Finding an Arrowhead Blue is always something of a surprise and one seldom sees more than a few specimens, despite the fact that the larvae feed on various species of lupine which grow in profusion everywhere.

Brown has recently pointed out that the structural characteristics of the Arrowhead Blue (genitalia, venation, head features, androconial scales) are almost identical to those of *Glaucopsyche lygdamus,* despite great difference in the wing pattern, and therefore *piasus* is a member of the same genus, not of *Scolitantides* (a *Philotes*-like European group) with which it has for many years been mistakenly associated.

In most Oregon localities the white arrow-marks of the hindwings stand in strong contrast to the brownish-gray ground color, and in this respect our populations resemble those of the Rocky Mountains more than they do the Californian subspecies *G. p. piasus* where the ground color is lighter and the contrast low. According to Brown the Oregon populations of the Arrowhead Blue need some careful taxonomic study and cannot at present be assigned to any named subspecies; they may, in large part, be intergrades.

The slightly flattened eggs of the Arrowhead Blue have a net-like sculptured surface. The larvae, often attended by ants, are either yellow-brown or bluish green and are marked along the back with a grayish brown line and on the sides with slanted white dashes. Overwintering occurs in the pupal stage.

References:

(1) Brown, F. Martin. 1971. The "Arrowhead Blue", *Glaucopsyche piasus* Boisduval (Lycaenidae: Plebejinae). J. Lepid. Soc. 25: 240-246.

(2) Brown, F. Martin. 1975. A new subspecies of *Glaucopsyche (Phaedrotes) piasus* from Nevada (Lepidoptera: Lycaenidae). Proc. Ent. Soc. Wash. 77: 501-504.

Glaucopsyche lygdamus columbia
Skinner, 1917
Columbia Silvery Blue

Plate 42, fig. 7. Map 158.

Unlike *Glaucopsyche piasus* which is strictly western, the species *lygdamus,* the Silvery Blue, ranges clear across the continent in the northern United States and Canada. In the Rockies it extends southward to the mountains of Arizona and in California to the Mexican border. It can be found at elevations ranging from sea level to above timberline.

The subspecies of the Pacific Northwest, widespread throughout Oregon, is *G. l. columbia.* At lower elevations the first specimens appear early in the spring and by May the butterfly is common in most parts of the State; in the higher mountains it may be seen as late as August.

A husky butterfly as Blues go, the male is light silvery blue above, narrowly dark-bordered, and with white fringe scales; the female is brownish gray but commonly has an overlay of blue scales at the wing bases the extent of which is quite variable. Underneath, in both sexes, the pale gray ground color is traversed by a simple row of rounded black spots ringed with white; unlike most other Blues there are no marginal crescents or markings of any kind.

The Columbia Silvery Blue is a single-brooded species. The eggs, flattened and with a raised white network, are laid in the spring or early summer, singly, on the flower buds of various legumes, particularly species of *Astragalus* (locoweed), *Lotus* (trefoils), and lupines. The larvae, which feed on the flower parts, are of various colors (green, brown, purple), marked dorsally with a broad rusty stripe, laterally with oblique white dashes, and are covered with a frosting of white hairs. They may be attended by ants which are attracted to the integumental honey glands that open at the middle of the tenth segment. The overwintering brown pupae, speckled with black dots and having a pale-colored metathorax and wing covers, attach to the host plant by a silken girdle and cremaster (terminal button) and are later found amid debris on the ground.

Studies on Colorado populations of the Silvery Blue in relation to their larval foodplants have shown that certain lupines are exposed to a floral predation which can destroy more than fifty percent of their potential seed production. These particular lupines, interestingly, possess a high content of varied alkaloids which presumably represents an evolutionary response against the larval attack, met, in turn, by larval selection in favor of *lygdamus* mutants capable of detoxifying the alkaloids. One is reminded of the development of pesticide-resistant insects.

References:
(1) Breedlove, D. E. & P. R. Ehrlich. 1972. Coevolution: patterns of legume predation by a lycaenid butterfly. Oecologia 10: 99-104.
(2) Dolinger, Peter M., Paul R. Ehrlich, William L. Fitch, & Dennis E. Breedlove. 1973. Alkaloid and predation patterns in Colorado lupine populations. Oecologia 13: 191-204.
(3) Langston, Robert L. 1969. A review of *Glaucopsyche*, the Silvery Blues, in California (Lycaenidae). J. Lepid. Soc. 23: 149-154.

Celastrina argiolus echo (Edwards), 1864
Echo Blue

Plate 41, fig. 7. Map 159.

A harbinger of spring, the Echo Blue makes its appearance on the first warm days of the year. In the East it is appropriately known as the Spring Azure. Usually producing several broods, its first emergence in the lowlands during March is followed by overlapping generations until mid-summer. A delicate butterfly with a preference for protected habitats and moisture, the Echo Blue is abundant at the edge of the forest, gathers below spring-wetted cliffs, and congregates at puddles by the roadside, often in surprising numbers.

This is a species with an enormous range. Except for the southwestern deserts it is common throughout North America and occurs as well in Europe and western Asia. As may be expected in a non-migratory species, *argiolus* shows a great deal of geographic variability, and in the eastern United States there are also seasonal differences in the successive broods. Our Pacific Coast subspecies, found from British Columbia to Baja California, is, however, relatively stable.

The male of *C. argiolus echo* is delicately lilac blue above and solidly colored except for a thin black marginal line and dark fringe scales at the tips of the veins; in the female the sides of the forewings are broadly darkened, and a row of black dots encased in a band of dark crescents lies along the margin of the hindwings. The grayish white underside is delicately marked with short bars and dots and with faint marginal lunules. Occasional spring specimens from the Cascades and Blue Mountains are peculiarly mottled beneath, the dark spots elongated and expanded into blotches and the margins sometimes broadly darkened; these are known as the form "lucia" and are the consequence of pupal exposure to a cold winter.

The eggs of the Echo Blue, usually laid on the flower buds of the foodplants, are green, turban-shaped, and covered with raised points. The larvae are variably colored, mostly greenish, marked with a dorsal stripe and slanted dashes along the sides, and are covered with a frosting of short white hairs. Association with ants is common. The brown pupae are ovoid and plump.

The foodplants utilized by the larvae are very diverse and include various legumes, dogwood, *Ceanothus*, blueberries, huckleberries, *Spiraea*, and others. Feeding is largely confined to flower buds.

In 1944 Clench, studying a short series of *C. argiolus* from Oregon, believed these butterflies to differ from the Californian *C. a. echo*, and introduced the name *bakeri*. The distinction, however, does not seem to be real, and the observations can be accounted for by the normal variability.

Reference:
(1) Clench, Harry K. 1944. Two new subspecies of *Lycaenopsis pseudargiolus* Bdv. & Lec. (Lepidoptera, Lycaenidae). J. N.Y. Ent. Soc. 52: 273-276.

Family HESPERIIDAE

The Hesperiidae make up the large family of Skippers, so called because of their swift and darting flight. Though of world-wide distribution, their greatest diversity occurs in the American Tropics. Together with the family Megathymidae, the Giant Skippers of Florida and the Southwest, they differ from all other butterflies in many structural characters, some of which remind one of moths.

Skippers are small to medium in size. Their stout, moth-like bodies are furnished with a broad head and a furry thorax. The eyes are set far apart, as are the antennae. The clubs of the antennae have a tapered end, or apiculus, which is usually bent back like a hook. The wings are proportionately short and narrow, and the veins that arise from the forewing discal cell are simple and unbranched. The rapid wing-beats which characterize the flight of Skippers are facilitated by powerful wing muscles. The stiffness of these muscles after death makes setting of the wings difficult, but this can be helped by carefully slitting each side of the thorax below the wing bases with the point of a broken razor blade.

The relatively unornamented and nearly hairless larvae of Skippers have a large head and a tapered body; the prothorax is restricted and neck-like. The pupae are smooth and elongated, suspended by a silken girdle, and generally enclosed in a loosely woven leafy cocoon. The eggs, deposited singly, are hemispherical in shape, broadened at the base.

Our members of the Hesperiidae fall into two subfamilies, the Hesperiinae, or Branded Skippers, whose larvae are grass feeders, and the Pyrginae, or Broad-winged Skippers, whose larvae feed mainly on dicots. The Hesperiinae (*Amblyscirtes, Euphyes, Ochlodes, Atalopedes, Polites, Hesperia,* and *Carterocephalus*) are mostly small and tawny yellow or dark brown; the tibiae of the middle legs are spined; and the forewings of the males usually bear a *stigma* on the disc, a slanted patch of androconial scales. The Pyrginae (*Pholisora, Heliopetes, Pyrgus, Erynnis, Thorybes,* and *Epargyreus*) average larger in size and are dark brown or black-and-white checkered; the middle tibiae are not spined; and the androconial scales of the males are carried in a long costal fold of the forewing.

The identification of some Skippers is difficult, particularly in the genera *Hesperia* and *Erynnis,* and one must resort to examination of the genitalia, the androconial scales, or other anatomical structures.

There is still much to be learned about the Skippers of Oregon. They have not been as extensively collected as other butterflies, as is apparent from evident gaps in the distribution maps. The Idaho border and the arid regions of southeastern Oregon are particularly likely to yield new data, possibly including additional species.

References:

(1) Burns, John M. 1964. Evolution of skipper butterflies of the genus *Erynnis*. Univ. Calif. Publ. Entom. 37: 1-216.

(2) Lindsey, A. W., E. L. Bell & R. C. Williams. 1931. The Hesperioidea of North America. Denison Univ. Bull., J. Sci. Labs. 26: 1-142.

(3) Lindsey, Arthur Ward. 1942. A preliminary revision of *Hesperia*. Denison Univ. Bull., J. Sci. Labs. 37: 1-50.

(4) MacNeill, C. Don. 1964. The skippers of the genus *Hesperia* in western North America with special reference to California (Lepidoptera: Hesperiidae). Univ. Calif. Publ. Entom. 85: 1-130.

(5) MacNeill, C. Don. 1975. Family Hesperiidae. *In* Howe, William H. (ed.), The Butterflies of North America. Doubleday & Co., Garden City, N.Y. Pp. 423-579.

Amblyscirtes vialis (Edwards), 1862
Roadside Skipper

Plate 43, fig. 1. Map 160.

This little Roadside Skipper, *Amblyscirtes vialis*, occurs throughout the United States, and is the only member of its genus to be so widely distributed; some twenty other species inhabit mainly the southwest. In Oregon it may be seen from April to August, and should be looked for in moist woodlands, usually along ditches by the roadside and flying close to the ground, often alighting on the wet soil. It is absent from the dry and semiarid regions of southeastern Oregon, but is probably more widely present in the central and eastern forested mountain areas than present records show.

The Roadside Skipper can be recognized by its solidly dark brown color, relieved only by a tiny group of three white spots near the apex at the upper edge of the forewing; the wing fringes are checkered brown and buff; the underside has a characteristic flush of violet-gray overscaling on the apex of the forewing and over the outer half of the hindwing. The two sexes are similar, except that the male possesses a small, concolorous, and very inconspicuous stigma (sex-patch, androconium) on the forewing. This Skipper should not be confused with *Pholisora catullus* which it superficially resembles; the latter is darker, has more white spotting, wholly brown fringes, and a dark brown underside without gray overscaling.

The finely dotted larvae of *Amblyscirtes vialis* are of pale green color and bear a dull white head ornamented with reddish stripes. They feed on grasses, including *Poa* (bluegrass), *Agrostis* (bent-grass), and *Avena* (wild oats). The green pupae have a yellow to red coloration about the head.

References:

(1) Freeman, Hugh Avery. 1973. A review of the *Amblyscirtes* with the description of a new species from Mexico (Hesperiidae). J. Lepid. Soc. 27: 40-57.

Euphyes vestris vestris (Boisduval), 1852
Dun Skipper

Plate 43, fig. 2. Map 161.

Easily identified by its almost solid chocolate brown color, *Euphyes vestris vestris* is locally common along the West Coast, from Baja California to Washington. East of our region this species is distributed across the United States and southern Canada as the somewhat darker subspecies *E. v. metacomet* (Harris). In Oregon *vestris* occurs from the coastal mountains to the east slope of the Cascades, but has not been reported from the eastern part of the State. Though most usually seen in mid summer, this Skipper has been taken from May to September and is generally attracted to damp spots along roadsides and in waste areas.

Our subspecies owes its chocolate color to an overlay of orange scales on a brown ground; this is especially noticeable in the diffuse orange patch around the prominent black stigma of the male forewing which is made up of two confluent oval-shaped masses. The forewing of the female bears two or three small creamish-white spots and the underside of the hindwing shows a faint crescent of pale spots.

The immature stages of the Dun Skipper have been described for the eastern race *metacomet* by Heitzman. He reports that the eggs are laid singly on the underside of a leaf of grass or near its edge; the eggs are pale green, ornamented with an encircling red band and a red apical blotch. The mature larvae are translucent green, densely overcast with white wavy dashes; the brown head bears two cream colored vertical bands and a velvety black spot on the face. The pupae are formed in a silk-lined tube made up of four leaves; they are whitish green, with a yellow-green thorax and a pale brown head. The larval foodplants are sedges (*Cyperus*) and grasses (*Tridens*).

References:

(1) Heitzman, John Richard. 1964. The early stages of *Euphyes vestris*. J. Res. Lepid. 3: 151-153.

Ochlodes sylvanoides sylvanoides (Boisduval), 1852
Woodland Skipper

Plate 43, figs. 3, 4. Map 162.

In the late summer and early fall no Skipper is more ubiquitous or abundant than *Ochlodes sylvanoides*. Though its name implies a woodland habitat, this species is, in fact, exceedingly common along roadsides, on dry slopes, in rough fields, and in gardened yards. It is as much at home along the coast as in clearings at middle altitudes in the mountains, and known in all parts of the State, in fact along the entire Pacific area and eastward to the central Rockies.

Ruddy orange, the wings of *sylvanoides* have a brown border that is inwardly dentate between the ends of the veins. On the forewings a brown patch connects the apex with the discal cell and is followed in the male by a prominent diagonally slanted black stigma which in the female is replaced by a second patch of brown. On the underside of the hindwings a curved row of large and squarish yellow spots lies weakly contrasted against a yellowish-brown background. In coastal populations, however, the contrast is increased by a darker brown ground color.

The eggs of this Skipper are cream colored. Overwintering may occur in this stage or in first instar larvae. The mature larvae, which are grass feeders, vary in color from buff yellow to pale green, have a tan or black head, and are marked with several longitudinal stripes of dark shade. The pupae, brownish-cream in color and covered with a white frost, are anteriorly darker and have reddish-brown eye cases.

Ochlodes agricola agricola
(Boisduval), 1852
Rural Skipper

Plate 43, fig. 5. Map 163.

Ochlodes agricola is essentially a Californian species with populations scattered the length of the State west of the Sierras. In the northern portion of its range it is found in the coastal mountains and valleys and has been suspected to extend into southwestern Oregon. Its presence in our State has only recently been confirmed with specimens from the Siskiyous, some seven miles southwest of Selma in Josephine County.

Smaller than *Ochlodes sylvanoides*, *agricola* has a relatively blunter and thicker male stigma which is separated from the broader marginal border by a row of small glassy spots readily detected by viewing the wing against a light. The underside of the male hindwing is almost solidly yellow.

Agricola prefers more wooded habitats than *sylvanoides* and appears earlier in the year, commonly May and June. The Oregon specimens were taken June 23 on shrubbery by the side of a forested mountain road.

Atalopedes campestris (Boisduval), 1852
Field Skipper

Plate 43, fig. 6. Map 164.

This Skipper is common across the southern half of the United States and is known farther north (New York to the Dakotas) as a casual wanderer. On the West Coast its northward limit was long thought to be San Francisco and before 1967 this butterfly remained unreported from Oregon. In that year, which had an unusually warm summer, *campestris* appeared in great numbers in the Willamette Valley and has been present and common ever since. Whether this represents a permanent northward shift in its range, a temporary one, or a repeated invasion remains to be seen. The first adults appear in the middle of May and fly through the month of June; a second and much larger generation flies from late July to the end of October. During late summer and early fall the abundance of this butterfly in gardens and fields approaches that of *Ochlodes sylvanoides*.

Atalopedes campestris is a robust Skipper, larger than *O. sylvanoides* but not unlike it in general color and pattern. A distinctive feature of the male is its huge, squarish, and cushion-like stigmal patch; the underside is yellowish brown and on the hindwing bears a discal band and basal patch of rectangular yellow spots. On the forewing of the somewhat larger female there is a postmedian group of light hyaline spots; the yellow bandspots of the hindwing underside are more sharply defined than in the male. Midwestern specimens of *campestris* are dorsally darker than ours, especially in the female.

The larvae feed on a variety of grasses, including *Cynodon* (Bermuda grass) and *Digiteria* (crab grass) and they reside in a tent-like enclosure at the leaf base. When mature, the larvae are olive-green, marked with a darker line along the back, and are covered with tiny, blackish, hair-bearing papillae; they have a black head. The pupae are blackish-brown, darker on the wing cases and anteriorly.

Polites coras (Cramer), 1775
Peck's Skipper

Plate 44, fig. 1. Map 165.

For many years known under the synonym *Polites peckius* (Kirby), hence Peck's Skipper, *P. coras* is a common butterfly in the eastern and midwestern United States. Its range extends westward across southern Canada to British Columbia, eastern Washington, and down to the Wallowa Mountains of Oregon. In our region it is an uncommon find, though further records in northeastern Oregon may be expected. Grassy meadows and roadsides in the mountains should be searched.

The tawny orange upperside of Peck's Skipper is deeply invaded by a broad dark brown margin which leaves only a few spots of light color on the forewing and a central patch on the hindwing which is crossed by dark-lined veins. In the male the narrow black stigma is outwardly bordered by a grayish brown patch. The hindwing underside immediately distinguishes this species, as the central area is filled with greatly enlarged and fused yellow spots, sharply defined at the edges and connected with yellow basal patches; the middle spot of the discal band is distinctly elongated.

The few Oregon records of this Skipper are dated from the month of July, but it probably flies from late spring to end of summer and may include a second brood. The life history is known from Eastern populations. The eggs, at first pale green, later become mottled with red lines. The larvae, which feed on grasses, are deep maroon, bear light brown mottling, and have a black head marked with white streaks and patches. The pupae are dull purple but have white wing pads and covers over the antennae, legs, and tongue.

Polites sabuleti (Boisduval), 1852
Sandhill Skipper

Plate 44, fig. 2. Map 166.

From the Cascades eastward *Polites sabuleti* is a common skipper on grasslands across all of Oregon, along open roadsides, in parks, on lawns, and is adapted to all elevations. Its wider range extends from Washington to Baja California and across the Great Basin to Colorado and Arizona. We see the first adults in May and June, and these are followed by a second and more abundant generation that flies from late July to September.

Relatively small in size and the lightest of our *Polites*, the tawny orange disc of *sabuleti* is rimmed by a dark, inwardly dentate border. The black stigma of the male forewing is short and has at its outer edge a grayish brown patch. In the female the orange area of the hindwing is restricted by dark patches at the base and on the inner portion of the disc. On the underside the ground color is either pale yellowish orange and lightly sanded with dark scales, or darker brownish orange; the lighter ground color is characteristic of the populations in the drier regions of eastern Oregon, the darker in the Cascades. In both cases the bandspots of the hindwing are purely yellow, fused, and connected to the wing margins and bases by thin but conspicuous yellow lines along the veins; at the wing margins the veins are terminated by tiny black dots.

The larvae of the Sandhill Skipper feed on various grasses. Newcomer has given a detailed account of the immature stages. The dome-shaped eggs are bluish green and hatch in seven days. When mature, the larvae are light gray and covered with numerous small brown patches; the head is shiny black and marked in the front with two short, vertical white bars. The larval life extends from 35 to 50 days. The pupae, from which the adults emerge in 10 to 13 days, except in the hibernating second generation, are greenish, with brown coloration on the head, the tips of the legs, and the last two abdominal segments.

Reference:
(1) Newcomer, E. J. 1966. Life histories of three Western species of *Polites*. J. Res. Lepid. 5: 243-247.

Polites mardon (Edwards), 1881
Mardon Skipper

Plate 44, fig. 3. Map 167.

Polites mardon is a Skipper of the Northwest and generally considered rare. It was originally described from specimens taken by H. K. Morrison near Tenino, Washington (not Mt. Hood as erroneously stated by Edwards). Reports of its occurrence in Oregon have been incorrect or questionable. Yet a search for it should continue, as this species is present some fifty miles to the north in Yakima County, Washington (Mt. Adams and Signal Peak) and in Thurston County below Puget Sound (area of Tenino and Grand Mound). In these locations the Mardon Skipper inhabits grassy meadows and slopes to an altitude of 6500 feet.

Mardon roughly resembles *Ochlodes sylvanoides* but is shorter winged and stubbier in appearance, with wider dark margins and dull brown below. The male stigma is very short and the grayish patch beside it is smaller than that of *Polites sabuleti*. Both sexes are otherwise similar in appearance, with the yellow spotband of the hindwing enclosed by the broad dark border and basal area; the rectangular spots have pointed attenuations along the veins but these do not reach the margins as in *sabuleti*. Underneath, these yellow spots have a dull and smoky look.

The early stages have been described by Newcomer. The hemispherical eggs change from cream to yellow-orange in color and hatch in six to seven days. The larval period lasts about three months. Mature larvae are light gray, speckled with dark brown, and have a black median stripe; the head is black and bears two light dorsal bars. The hibernating ashy-gray pupae are of smooth texture and have light brown areas on the abdominal segments, wing-pads, and thorax; their eye-covers are dark brown. The larvae, like those of other *Polites*, are grass feeders.

Reference:
See under *Polites sabuleti*.

Polites themistocles (Latreille), 1824
Tawny-edged Skipper

Plate 44, fig. 4. Map 168.

There are as yet no records of *Polites themistocles* for Oregon, but its occurrence somewhere in the eastern part of our State is probable. It is a very common Skipper in the eastern United States and the Midwest, in the Rockies, and across southern Canada. In the Pacific area it is known in southern British Columbia and northeastern Washington, and has been taken around Bartle in Siskiyou County, California, some sixty-five miles south of Klamath Falls. The Northwest records are dated from May to July, during which time *themistocles* should be looked for, with likely sites being the meadows and forest glades of northeastern Oregon and grassy areas east of Klamath Falls to the Warners.

Polites themistocles is easily identified by the solid brown color of the hindwings, which ventrally has a somewhat olivaceous overcast. The brown border of the forewings extends deeply into the disc, almost to the narrowly S-shaped stigma in the male, along whose outer edge there is a slender gray patch and above which the cell and costa are bright orange. On the forewings of the female there are two or three yellowish discal spots and a triplet of small apical ones.

The eggs of the Tawny-edged Skipper are small and pale green. The larvae feed on grasses of the genus *Panicum* and are yellowish-brown to chocolate in color when mature, except for the head which is black and marked frontally with short white bars. The light brown pupae have dull greenish wing pads and a dark head.

Polites mystic (Edwards), 1863
Long Dash Skipper

Plate 44, fig. 5. Map 169.

Like *coras* and *themistocles*, *mystic* is another Eastern *Polites* that has found its way across southern Canada and into the Pacific Northwest. Though common over the northern half of the Midwest and the East, it is not well known in our area. In Washington *mystic* may be found in the northeastern counties, and it has been taken in the Blue Mountains of Oregon near Anthony Lake (Union County). Though undoubtedly scarce, a search of moist grassy meadows, slopes, and roadsides between June and August may reveal further localities in this general region.

This is a moderately large *Polites*, not unlike *mardon* in color and markings, but bigger and with more elongated wings. The slender stigma gains apparent breadth by an adjacent black (rather than gray) patch and gives the impression of prolongment ("long dash") by its connection with the brown apical patch. Where this brown patch meets the forewing cell its inner margin tends to have a sharp vertical edge. The brown wing border is broad and on the hindwing encircles the curved band of elongated yellow spots; on the underside the spots are separated by thin and more darkly colored veins. In the western prairie populations of *mystic* the underside ground color is yellowish, with the spotband showing low contrast; this is the subspecies *P. m. dacotah* (Edwards), 1871, and Northwest specimens are closer to this than to the Eastern variety whose ground color is brown.

The eggs are hemispherical and pale green. The larvae, which live in tubelike nests of grass (they feed on bluegrass, *Poa*), are dark brown when mature, mottled with dull white, and have a rough-surfaced black head. Hibernation occurs in the larval stage. The pupae, hairy on the head and abdomen, are dark brown to black, and the long tongue-case is terminally free.

Polites sonora siris (Edwards), 1881
Sonora Skipper

Plate 44, fig. 6. Map 170.

Polites sonora is a medium sized Skipper whose range extends from British Columbia to southern California and eastward into the northern and central Rockies. The Northwestern subspecies is *P. s. siris* (Edwards), darker than the nominotypic *P. s. sonora* (Scudder), 1872, of the Great Basin and California Sierras. Ours is mainly a mountain form, common in small meadows and forest clearings of the Cascades, the Ochocos, the Blue Mountains, and the Warners; it also strays into the Willamette Valley.

Dorsally this Skipper has a broad reddish-brown border on both wings, and on the hindwings also a dark central area. The forewing costal region and cell are orange, and orange spots lie along the inner margin of the dark border. The male stigma appears thick due to a black flank and connects apically to a brown patch. The orange on the hindwing is restricted to a basal spot and a narrow curved macular band. Underneath, the hindwing is yellowish-brown to chocolate and distinctively marked with short yellow spots arranged into a narrow discal curve, plus a few spots at the base.

Toward the Great Basin of southeastern Oregon some of our Sonora Skippers get a little lighter but are hardly as yellowish below as the Sierran populations. They are at best transitional to the race *sonora*.

Newcomer has reported that the eggs of *P. sonora siris* are light green and hatch in about eight days. The third instar larvae are grayish green, covered with fine black hairs, and have a punctate black head. He suspects they feed on fescue grasses (*Festuca*). A more complete study of the life history is needed.

Reference:
See under *Polites sabuleti*.

Genus *Hesperia*

The tawny colored Skippers of the genus *Hesperia* can be recognized by the macular pattern of the hindwing underside. The white, silvery, or yellowish spots are arranged in the form of an outwardly pointed chevron on the disc plus a small loop-like patch at the base. The several Oregon species differ with respect to the size, color, and disposition of these spots as well as the surrounding ground color. Also useful is the overall size and the color and border marking of the upperside. Males are easier to identify than females, though the latter resemble their male counterparts in the underside spot pattern. Some species are rare or restricted in distribution, others widespread and abundant.

The stigma on the male forewing of *Hesperia* has a silvery mid-line, and inside the stigma is a felt-like androconial material (easily removed with the point of a needle) that is black in all our species except *H. columbia,* where it is yellow.

Genitalial differences are generally not needed to separate Oregon species, but in this regard the shape of the male uncus (the hood-like dorsal plate at the tip of the abdomen), as seen from above, is the most useful and easily observed character. It can be revealed by carefully plucking and brushing away the hairy vestiture, which then allows one to see whether the tip of the uncus is blunt, pointed, or extended into a beak.

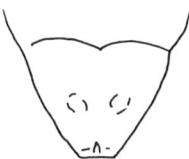

blunt uncus

H. uncas
H. juba
H. comma

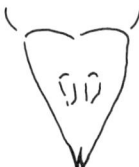

pointed uncus

H. columbia

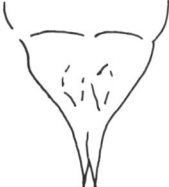

beaked uncus

H. lindseyi
H. nevada

References:
(1) Lindsey, Arthur Ward. 1942. A preliminary revision of *Hesperia.* Denison Univ. Bull., J. Sci. Labs. 37: 1-50.
(2) MacNeill, C. Don. 1964. The skippers of the genus *Hesperia* in western North America with special reference to California (Lepidoptera: Hesperiidae). Univ. Calif. Publ. Entom. 85: 1-130.

Hesperia uncas Edwards, 1863
Uncas Skipper

Plate 45, fig. 1. Map 171.

Hesperia uncas has only recently been found to occur in Oregon, a few specimens having been taken in Harney and Malheur Counties in late May and early June. The species is known to range from Canada southward through the upper Great Plains and the Rockies to Mexico; westward it appears in dry regions of the Californian Sierras and portions of the Great Basin.

Our specimens, few as they are, seem to combine features of the Great Basin subspecies *H. u. lasus* (Edwards), 1884, and the Sierran *H. u. macswaini* MacNeill, 1964. Fairly large in size, the upper side of the male is bright orange and without a dark border; the female has orange patches. The stigma is slender and contains black "felt". The white spots of the hindwing underside form a complete chevron; as in the subspecies *lasus* they are extended along the veins as thin white lines, and between the posterior arm of the macular band and the basal spots there are blackish patches between the veins. As in *macswaini,* however, the ground color of the hindwing is grayish green; this ground color also occurs in *Hesperia nevada* which, however, lacks the white vein lines and has the innermost spot of the lower band-arm displaced toward the base (not displaced in *uncas*). The tip of the uncus is blunt.

The larvae of *uncas* are reported in California to feed on needlegrass (*Stipa*). The hemispherical eggs are large, smooth, and greenish white. Details of the life history remain to be studied.

References:
See under Genus *Hesperia.*

Hesperia juba (Scudder), 1872
Juba Skipper

Plate 45, fig. 2. Map 172.

The boldly marked and robust Juba Skipper, found throughout Oregon, is our largest species of *Hesperia.* Its range extends from British Columbia to Baja California and eastward to the northern and central Rockies. Though primarily a Skipper of open areas and sagebrush country, it readily adapts to a wide variety of ecological environments and can be found from sea level to an altitude of 7000 feet. Though ordinarily not seen in great numbers, *juba* is at times locally abundant. Oregon records indicate two principal flying periods, one extending from late April to end of June, and a second from August to October.

Large and uniformly well marked, *juba* is easy to recognize. Both sexes are pale orange above and have an inwardly toothed dark border. The slender and almost straight stigma of the male contains black "felt". Underneath, the bold white spots are partially or completely connected, the last one of the lower arm slightly offset basally and somewhat angulate; the ground color is grayish to light brownish green. Further characteristics include a blunt and globose antennal club (narrower and more elongate in *H. comma*) and a rather pointed forewing in the male.

The eggs are small, pink-tinged to white, and surfaced with a shallow raised network. The larvae feed on a variety of grasses, and when mature are creamish except for a black head. In the brown pupae the head and thorax are dark and the abdominal segments are marked with dark dashes.

References:
See under Genus *Hesperia*.

Hesperia comma (Linnaeus), 1758
Comma Skipper

Plate 45, figs. 3, 4. Maps 173, 174.

The Comma Skipper is the most widely dispersed, complex, and variable species of the genus *Hesperia*. It occurs throughout most of Europe, extends to northern Africa, temperate Asia, and in North America is present in southeastern Canada, the northeastern United States, and most of the West. The Western area contains some dozen named subspecies, many of which intergrade at their borders. Two are found in Oregon.

H. comma harpalus (Edwards), 1881, the Harpalus Skipper, is found throughout eastern Oregon; its total range, in fact, extends from the east slope of the Cascades and Sierras to the Rockies, and from British Columbia to south-central California, including all of the Great Basin. In much of the older literature it has been recorded under the synonym *H. c. idaho* (Edwards), 1883.

Smaller than *H. juba*, but not unlike it in the pale color of the tawny upperside, the dark border of *H. c. harpalus* is less sharply defined along its inner edge. The stigmal "felt" is black. The ground color of the hindwing underside is generally light, varying from grayish-yellow to yellowish-green, often somewhat darker in the female. The macular band forms the normal chevron shape; the spots are silky white, proportionately smaller than in *juba*, often angulate in appearance by being slightly extended along the veins, connected or partially separated, and sometimes reduced in number and size.

A very common and abundant Skipper, *harpalus* is attracted in great numbers to the rabbitbrush of the central Oregon highlands. It may be found from June to September and at all elevations. The larvae are reported to feed on needlegrass (*Stipa*); their heads are mottled with broad pale areas. The pupae are brown and bear rows of small dashes on the abdominal segments.

H. comma oregonia (Edwards), 1883, the Oregon Skipper, is a Cascadian race, found from British Columbia to northern California. In southwestern Oregon it extends into the Siskiyous. Here it may appear in June, but in the higher altitudes of the Cascades it flies during July and August.

As is so often the case with Cascadian races, *oregonia* is darker than the more eastern *harpalus*. The upperside is reddish orange and the dark borders are better defined. The ground color of the hindwing underside is golden olive. The spots are dull white, approaching yellowish in the male; as in *harpalus*, they may be partially disconnected or reduced in size and number. In some Siskiyou populations I have seen almost immaculate specimens; in these the black stigmal "felt" will distinguish them from the sympatric *H. columbia*. On the east slope of the Cascades *oregonia* merges into *harpalus*.

The life history and habits of the Oregon Skipper are only slightly known. The grasses of the genera *Lolium* (rye-grass) and *Bromus* (brome-grass) constitute the larval foodplants on Vancouver Island.

References:
See under Genus *Hesperia*.

Hesperia columbia (Scudder), 1872
Columbia Skipper

Plate 45, fig. 5. Map 175.

The Columbia Skipper is a *Hesperia* of the Pacific Coast Ranges, found from southwestern Oregon to southern California. In our State it occurs in brushy spaces and forest clearings of the Siskiyous and adjacent Cascades, flying in May and June, and again in late summer.

Not unlike *H. comma oregonia* in the reddish orange color of the upperside, the wing borders are also dark and broad. In the male the stigma has a gray patch at its outer edge and the enclosed "felt" is yellow (not black, as in *comma*). Underneath, the hindwings have an olive gold ground color. The shape and spots of the macular band are distinctive; the lustrous white spots in the lower arm, usually small and of even size in the male, lie close together in straight transverse alignment; in the female the outermost spot is enlarged; the upper arm is reduced to a single spot or may be missing. There is no basal spot above the discal cell. In the male genitalia the tip of the uncus is pointed.

The eggs of the Columbia Skipper are relatively large, white, and smooth surfaced. The pale yellowish larvae have a dark brown head whose face is marked with creamish streaks. The pupae are pale brown, darkly mottled, and have a long tongue case. In Marin County, California, oviposition and presumably larval feeding occurs on the bunchgrass *Koeleria*. No life history observations have been made on Oregon populations.

References:
See under Genus *Hesperia*.

Hesperia lindseyi (Holland), 1930
Lindsey's Skipper

Plate 45, fig. 6. Map 176.

Like *Hesperia columbia,* Lindsey's Skipper is found in the coastal mountains from southwestern Oregon to southern California; there are, however, also populations in the Sierras of northeastern California and adjoining areas. In Oregon it is a common Skipper in the Siskiyous and is found on Bly Mountain east of Klamath Falls. In June and July *lindseyi* may be seen in substantial numbers on the slopes and in the gullies about Siskiyou Pass.

Lindsey's Skipper is moderately large and broad-winged, extensively light orange above, and has a dark border that is inwardly not well defined. The ground color of the hindwing underside is yellowish orange, finely peppered with dark overscaling. The macular band is yellowish in the male, creamish to white in the female, and complete; the spots are bold, angulate, and drawn out as thin lines along the veins; the outer ends of the veins are tipped with dark scales that extend across the yellow fringes. In the male the uncus of the genitalia has a beak-like tip, and the stigmal "felt" is black.

The large, white, flattened eggs are flanged at the base and have a coarsely reticulate surface. They are, rather remarkably, deposited on arboreal lichens and, with their enclosed first-instar larvae, pass the summer and winter in diapause. Upon hatching the following spring, the young larvae must find their foodplants, fescue (*Festuca*) or wild oat-grass (*Danthonia*). When mature they are yellow and have a brown head capsule that is marked on the face with two cream-colored vertical bars and an inverted V. The solidly pale brown pupae are covered with a light waxy "bloom" and possess a long tongue-case.

References:
See under Genus *Hesperia.*

Hesperia nevada (Scudder), 1874
Nevada Skipper

Plate 45, fig. 7. Map 177.

This is essentially a Skipper of the Rocky Mountains which extends westward to British Columbia, eastern Washington, Oregon, and California, and is found at higher elevations in the Great Basin. The Oregon records are very few (Umatilla and Baker Counties), but a search of the dry sagebrush slopes and meadows of our northeastern region should turn up more sites for this species. The specimens at hand were taken in May and June.

The Nevada Skipper is about the size of *H. comma.* It is bright to reddish orange above, the dark border blending inwardly into the orange disc; in the darker female the orange of the hindwing is sharply restricted to the discal spots. On the underside, the ground color of the hindwing is dark greenish-gray, against which the white spots, which are large, quadrate or angular, and clearly defined, stand in strong contrast. The macular band is irregular in shape, but complete; the outermost spot lies close to the wing margin and the anal spot of the lower limb is strongly displaced toward the base. The uncus of the male genitalia has a long, pointed beak; the stigmal "felt" is black.

The hemispherical and dull white egg of the Nevada Skipper is large and smooth surfaced. The larva has a blackish head, the front of which is marked with light brown and whitish patches. The foodplant is needlegrass (*Stipa*). A full account of the life history is still to be furnished.

References:
See under Genus *Hesperia.*

Carterocephalus palaemon mandan (Edwards), 1863
Arctic Skipper

Plate 46, fig. 1. Map 178.

This unique, small, and beautiful Skipper cannot be mistaken for any other. It is a northern species known on both the Eurasian and North American Continents. Our subspecies stretches across Canada and the northern United States, and on the West Coast extends southward to northern California. In Oregon it occurs in the Cascades and westward into the Coast Range; it has also been found in the Wallowas. The Arctic Skipper cannot, however, be said to be common, as it lives in isolated colonies along streams and moist glades of forested areas, usually, but not exclusively, in the mountains. It flies in the spring and early summer and is always a surprising find.

The antennal club of the Arctic Skipper does not have an apiculus and there is no stigma on the male forewing. The wing pattern is so unlike that of any other Skipper that the illustration is sufficient to identify it. The upperside is black and orange; underneath, the ground color of the hindwing is orange brown and the narrowly black-rimmed spots are yellow. The markings may vary with respect to the size of the spots.

The hemispherical eggs are small and greenish white. The mature larvae are yellowish-green to creamish in color; they have a dark stripe along the back and a light one on each side, below which there is a row of blackish spots. The foodplants of the larvae are broad-leafed grasses.

Pholisora catullus (Fabricius), 1793
Common Sooty Wing

Plate 46, fig. 2. Map 179.

This small, dark Skipper of the subfamily Pyrginae superficially resembles *Amblyscirtes vialis* in color and markings but can be quickly separated by the absence of a checkered fringe. It ranges across the entire United States (except Florida) and the adjacent Canadian Provinces; in Oregon it is widely distributed east of the Cascades and flies from April through August.

The sooty black color of *Pholisora catullus* is relieved by small white dots, of which a diagonal row of five, repeated on the underside, crosses the forewing apex; additional tiny dots appear on the disc and a faint row extends along the outer margin, sometimes also of the hindwing. The expression of these white dots is quite variable, though the apical group is fairly constant. The androconial scales of the male are carried in a fold of the forewing costa whose inner lining is yellowish brown.

The Common Sooty Wing is seen along streams and moist roadsides, at the weedy edges of fields and meadows, and gathered at puddles; its flight pattern is erratic and close to the ground. The larvae utilize a variety of foodplants, including pigweed (*Chenopodium*), tumbleweed (*Amaranthus*), snowberry (*Symphoricarpus*), ragweed (*Ambrosia*), and others.

The pale yellowish-brown eggs are small, conical, and strongly ribbed along the side. The pale dull green larvae have a rough black head and are covered with short white hairs borne on tiny tubercles; they feed at night and hide in the foliage during the day; hibernation occurs in the last instar. The pupae are various shades of brown and are covered with a powdery bloom.

Pholisora libya lena (Edwards), 1882
Lena Sooty Wing

Plate 46, fig. 3. Map 180.

A butterfly of the desert, *Pholisora libya* inhabits arid regions of the West, from Montana and the Pacific Northwest to Arizona, southern California, and western Mexico. Our populations belong to the northern subspecies *P. l. lena*, whose center of distribution lies in the Great Basin. It flies from June to August on the alkaline sage flats of Lake, Harney, and Malheur Counties, where one finds *Atriplex canescens* (saltbush), the larval foodplant.

The upperside of this large *Pholisora* is dark brown and somewhat glossy when fresh; three or four closely set white spots cross the forewing apex; in the female a row of spots also passess downward to the inner margin and another lies near the cell (these spots are faint or absent in the male); the fringe tips near the forewing apex are white. Underneath, the forewing is very glossy and dark brown except for a grayish apex and outer margin; the hindwings are strongly overcast with white scales and bear bold white spots, one near the base, a curved group on the middle of the disc, and a faint row along the margin. The male of this species does not have a costal fold.

The eggs of *Pholisora libya* are large, ivory white in color, and ridged. The larvae, much of the time concealed in nests of the saltbush foliage, are pale bluish green, finely white-dotted, and provided with a black head that is stippled with short orange hair. The plump pupae have a downward-bent abdomen and are light brown except for darker thorax and wing cases.

Pholisora alpheus oricus Edwards, 1879
Oricus Sooty Wing

Plate 46, fig. 4. Map 181.

Pholisora alpheus, like *P. libya*, is a desert butterfly that inhabits the arid regions of the Southwest, the Mojave Desert in California, and the Great Basin. *P. a. oricus* is the Californian and Great Basin race. Although at present unrecorded from Oregon, the species does occur in Humboldt and Washoe Counties, Nevada, and therefore may be expected along the southern borders of Lake, Harney, and Malheur Counties. It should be looked for, April to June, in association with the larval foodplant, *Atriplex canescens* (saltbush), which grows in the alkaline soil of this region.

Similar to *Pholisora catullus* in size, *oricus* is vaguely reminiscent of a small *Erynnis* in appearance but with a boldly checkered fringe. The forewing of the male is dark gray above; it is marked on the disc with a row of black, wedgeshaped dashes, outside of which there is light gray scaling; a linear group of small white dots lies near the apex. In the female the amount of white overscaling is greatly increased, giving it a lighter appearance. The hindwings in both sexes are dorsally dark brown, and in the female there is a submarginal row of faint white spots. The underside is brownish black, with much gray overscaling on the outer half of the hindwings; the submarginal white spots of the female are prominent on the under surface.

The immature stages and life history of the Oricus Sooty Wing have not been described.

Reference:

(1) MacNeill, C. Don. 1970. A new *Pholisora* with notes on *P. alpheus* (Edw.) (Lepidoptera: Hesperiidae). Ent. News 81: 177-184.

Heliopetes ericetorum (Boisduval), 1852
Large White Skipper

Plate 46, fig. 5. Map 182.

The Large White Skipper, not likely to be mistaken for any other, is encountered in northeastern Oregon where it inhabits the arid regions of the upper Columbia and Snake River Basins. Though not yet reported from southeastern Oregon, this species does occur in Nevada and is widespread in the desert areas of the Southwest. Look for it in canyon bottoms, by rocky streamsides where there is good growth of malvaceous plants, or in nearby dry, weedy fields. Flight records extend from June to September, implying at least two broods.

The male of *H. ericetorum* is chalky to creamish white on the upperside, with a flush of black scales at the wing bases and a narrow black pattern along the outer wing margins that consists of a thin terminal line and an adjoining row of black crescents. In the female the dark basal area is greatly broadened and the white disc is interrupted by additional black banding; the pattern reminds one of *Pyrgus communis,* a related but decidedly smaller Skipper. Underneath both sexes look much alike, with the inner and outer thirds of the hindwing flushed and marked with shades of pale pinkish brown. In the male the forewing is provided with a costal fold and from the base of the hindleg tibia there protrudes a plume-like tuft of white hairs.

The chalky-white eggs of the Large White Skipper are nearly spherical and are covered with a network of crossribbing. The pale greenish-yellow and down-covered larvae are marked with a green line along the back and yellowish stripes on the sides; the head is black and hairy. The pupae are yellowish brown, posteriorly pinkish, and completely covered with a bluish frost. The larval foodplants include several species and genera of mallows (*Malva, Iliamna, Athaea, Sphaeralcea*) as well as redwood pigweed (*Amaranthus*).

Pyrgus ruralis (Boisduval), 1852
Two-Banded Checkered Skipper

Plate 46, fig. 6. Map 183.

This black-and-white Checkered Skipper is known from British Columbia to southern California and from Alberta to Colorado. It is a common Oregon species that can be seen flying close to the ground in grassy forest openings of the Coast Range, the Cascades and Siskiyous, the Blue Mountains, and the Wallowas. Adapted to all altitudes, from the edges of the Willamette Valley to the 9500-foot summit of the Matterhorn (Wallowas), it appears in western Oregon as early as March and April, flying through June, and at high altitudes is seen through July and August.

The white spots of the forewing are somewhat squarish and cross the disc in two slanted rows; there is also a small apical triplet. The spots of the hindwing, crescentic in shape, form two rows also, of which the inner is sometimes incomplete, especially in specimens from high altitudes, which also tend to be dwarfed. The wing fringes are conspicuously checkered. On the lower surface the dark areas have a reddish brown cast. Males of this Skipper have a forewing costal fold and a tibial tuft on the hindlegs.

The larvae of *Pyrgus ruralis* feed on cinquefoil (*Potentilla*) and probably wild hollyhock (*Sidalcea*). The immature stages, life history, and behavior of this common Skipper remain, surprisingly, to be fully studied and described.

Pyrgus communis communis (Grote), 1872
Common Checkered Skipper

Plate 46, fig. 7. Map 184.

Unlike *Pyrgus ruralis* which is restricted to the Western States, the Common Checkered Skipper ranges from coast to coast and from Canada to Mexico; indeed, there are subspecies that extend to Argentina! It is common throughout Oregon and encountered at all elevations, from sea level to the highest mountain meadows. Producing several broods a year, it is seen from April to September, and favors open areas, vacant lots, weedy fields, and roadsides.

The pattern of white spots resembles that of *Pyrgus ruralis,* but the spots are larger and broader, narrowing the dark areas and giving to the Skipper a lighter and more strongly white-banded appearance. In females the width of the white bands is somewhat reduced. A bluish-gray hairy overscaling suffuses the wing bases. The fringes are checkered. Underneath, the dark areas are grayish olive in color, not red-brown, also smaller and more sharply delimited than in *ruralis*. The males are provided with a costal fold on the forewing, but the tibiae of the hindlegs do not possess a basal tuft.

The eggs of this Skipper are small, rounded, greenish-white to cream colored, and have a reticulated raised surface. The yellowish-white to brownish mature larvae are marked with a middorsal and lateral lines and are covered with fine hairs; the head is black. The pupae are anteriorly greenish-brown but brown and black-dotted on the abdomen. A variety of Malvaceae (mallows) serve as the larval foodplants.

Erynnis icelus (Scudder & Burgess), 1870
Dreamy Duskywing

Plate 47, fig. 1. Map 185.

The dark grayish-brown and rather drab Duskywing Skippers of the genus *Erynnis* look very much alike. Some eighteen species occur in North America and their separation is often difficult, requiring attention to genitalial structures as well as such more obvious characters as overall size, wing pattern, color of the fringe, and presence or absence of tibial tufts. Fortunately the four species known to occur in Oregon can be determined with relative ease.

Erynnis icelus is one of three small species found in our area, the other two being *E. persius* and *E. pacuvius*. It is known in all of the Western States from the Rockies to the Pacific, also in the Great Lakes region, the Appalachians, the Northeast, and across Canada. In Oregon we find this species at low and middle elevations in the Coastal Mountains, the Cascades, and the mountains of northeastern Oregon, generally in or near forested areas. It flies in May, June, and July, but is relatively uncommon.

The forewings of *icelus* are mainly gray and do not have the small, translucent white spots found on our other species of *Erynnis*. The vertical black band across the disc is made up of a series of oval or parentheses-like marks that connect to resemble a link-chain. Males have an androconial fold along the costa, buff in color when open. The deep brown hindwings are marked with a row of marginal and of submarginal light spots; on the underside these spots appear also on the forewing. The hindlegs of the male are provided with a conspicuous tibial tuft.

The male genitalia in the genus *Erynnis* are peculiar in being asymmetrical. They are easily examined by brushing away the overlying scales under a magnifier or dissecting microscope. The shape of the left valve (clasper) is sufficient to distinguish our species. In *icelus* the ventral process (at left in drawings) is short and the middle lobe forms a blunt knob.

The small, pale green eggs of *icelus* are deposited singly on new foliage of poplars, aspen, and willows. The larvae construct shelters in the leaves of these foodplants; they are pale green, densely covered with fine white dots, and have a black head capsule that is ornamented with reddish blotches; they hibernate in the last instar and pupate the following spring.

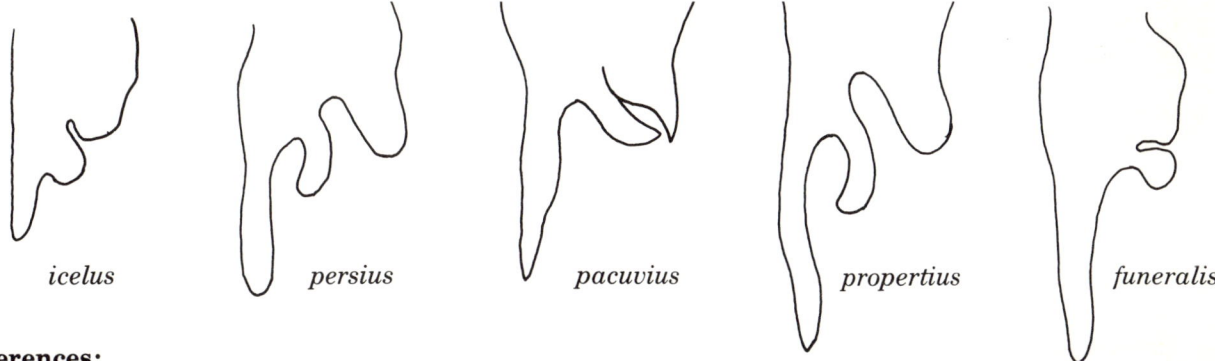

icelus *persius* *pacuvius* *propertius* *funeralis*

References:

(1) Burns, John M. 1964. Evolution of skipper butterflies of the genus *Erynnis*. Univ. Calif. Publ. Entom. 37: 1-216.

(2) Lindsey, A. W., E. L. Bell & R. C. Williams. 1931. The Hesperioidea of North America. Denison Univ. Bull., J. Sci. Labs. 26: 1-142.

Erynnis persius persius (Scudder), 1863
Persius Duskywing

Plate 47, fig. 2. Map 186.

The Persius Duskywing, like *Erynnis icelus*, ranges over most of North America. It is also similar in its Oregon distribution but is a far more abundant species. Depending upon the location it may be seen from April to August and flies in open as well as brushy and forested habitats.

E. persius is close to *icelus* in size and similar in general coloration. The discal band of the forewing, however, encloses a number of small, transparent, white spots, a small cluster near the apex and two or three below. In the male, a furry covering of hair-like scales obscures the wing pattern on the basal half. In the female, patches of gray scales lie on both sides of the discal band (a point of distinction between *persius* and *pacuvius lilius*). In both sexes the deep brown hindwings are mottled with rows of pale spots, as in *icelus*. The male hindlegs bear tibial tufts (not present in *pacuvius lilius*).

In the male genitalia the ventral process of the left valve is longer than that of *icelus*, and the middle lobe is curved and posteriorly extended, away from the dorsal lobe and parallel to the ventral process.

Though this is a common Duskywing, little is specifically known of its life history. The larvae feed on willows or aspen and poplar, possibly also some legumes.

References:

See under *Erynnis icelus*.

Erynnis pacuvius lilius (Dyar), 1904
Dyar's Duskywing

Plate 47, fig. 3. Map 187.

Erynnis pacuvius is a Western species that occurs in the southern and northern Rockies, the Cascades and Sierras, and the Coastal Mountains of California and southern Oregon. *E. p. lilius* is the Northwestern race, which also extends into the Californian Sierras. In Oregon it is found in the Cascades, the Siskiyous, and the Blue Mountains, including the Ochocos, always in association with *Ceanothus,* which is especially abundant in the Ponderosa Pine belt on the eastern Cascadian slope. It flies from May through July and is sympatric at many locations with *Erynnis persius* and *icelus.*

References:
See under *Erynnis icelus.*

E. pacuvius lilius looks very much like the more common *persius* with which it is often confused. It has the same size, coloration, and pattern, though the light mottling on the brown hindwings is often more subdued. In females the gray scaling of the forewings appears only on the outer side of the dark discal band which carries the white hyaline spots. Males can be identified with certainty by noting the absence of a tibial tuft on the hindlegs and by examining the genitalia. The middle lobe of the left valve does not bend posteriorly, as in *persius,* but extends upward, almost meeting the dorsal lobe.

Dyar's Duskywing is single-brooded and the larvae feed on *Ceanothus.* The details of the life history remain to be studied.

Erynnis propertius (Scudder & Burgess), 1870
Propertius Duskywing

Plate 47, fig. 4. Map 188.

A very abundant Skipper throughout western Oregon, *Erynnis propertius* is restricted to the Pacific Coast and is found from British Columbia to southern California. It is a familiar species on hillsides, in clearings, and in forest openings, and is always associated with oaks. On the wing from April to July, it moves with characteristic darting flight from one perch to another and settles with equal speed, resting with outstretched and drooping wings on the end of a twig, atop a tall stalk of grass, or on the ground.

References:
See under *Erynnis icelus.*

Though substantially larger in size, the general pattern and color of this species is not unlike that of *Erynnis persius*. A dense, furry covering of white hairs in the male adds to the grayish appearance of the forewings. The hindwings are brown. Females are lighter and of more contrasting pattern, caused by extensive patches of white scales on the forewing and larger and more conspicuous hyaline spots within the black discal band; the rows of pale spots on the hindwing are also more prominent. The fringe scales in *propertius* are brown.

There is as yet no complete account of the immature stages and life history of this common Skipper.

Erynnis funeralis (Scudder & Burgess), 1870
Funereal Duskywing

Plate 47, fig. 5. Map 189.

The Funereal Duskywing, comparable in size to *Erynnis propertius,* is very dark, the hindwings almost black and formally bordered with a snow-white fringe; its name suits its appearance. This is a Skipper of the Southwest, extending from Texas and Mexico to the Pacific Coast. Though not yet reported from Oregon, the recorded range of *funeralis* in California reaches northward to Alturas (Modoc County), only forty-five miles from the Oregon border. Its presence in southern Klamath and Lake Counties is therefore possible.

Apart from its large size, dark color, and white hindwing fringe, *funeralis* can be recognized by the relatively narrow forewings and the triangular outline of the hindwings. The distinctive genitalia have been pictured and compared with those of other *Erynnis* species in the discussion of *E. icelus.*

The larvae of *funeralis* feed on alfalfa, *Lotus,* and other legumes. They are pale green, laterally striped with a yellow line, and ventrally bluish. This is a very common species in southern California, where it is multibrooded.

References:
See under *Erynnis icelus.*

Thorybes pylades (Scudder), 1870
Northern Cloudy Wing

Plate 48, fig. 1. Map 190.

The Northern Cloudy Wing is the most widespread member of the genus *Thorybes*. This large, chocolate brown Skipper ranges over almost all of the North American Continent. Its occurrence in Oregon is probably broader than present records show, most of which come from the eastern slope and adjacent plateaus of the northern Cascades and from the Siskiyous. The species is undoubtedly also present over more of northeastern Oregon than the single record from Baker County suggests. It flies from May to early July and should be sought in forest clearings, canyons, and on open meadows.

The evenly dark brown upperside is marked on the forewing with groups of small white spots; two of these lie at the costal margin and are arranged in short perpendicular alignment; a third group of small and angulate spots are situated in a triangular disposition on the disc; the white markings reappear on the underside. The brown wing fringes are checkered with alternating light and dark patches. On the underside the hindwings are vertically traversed by two dark, crinkled bands. In the male a costal fold is present on the forewing. The genitalial valves are distinctive and separate this species from *T. mexicana nevada* and *T. diversus*.

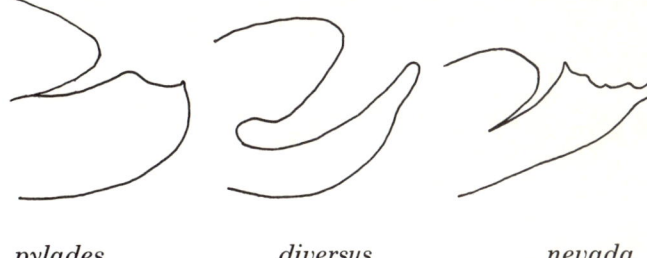

pylades *diversus* *nevada*

The larvae of *Thorybes pylades* build shelters among the leaves of their foodplants, which are various legumes, including clover and alfalfa. When mature, these larvae are dark or maroonish, with a thin line running along the back and two on each side; the head is large and dark. The pupae have a blackish brown head, an olive thorax, a light brown abdomen, and buff colored wing pads.

Thorybes mexicana nevada Scudder, 1872
Nevada Cloudy Wing

Plate 48, fig. 2. Map 191.

A smaller butterfly than *Thorybes pylades,* the Nevada Cloudy Wing is found on the high meadows of the central Oregon Cascades, in subalpine regions of the Californian Sierras and adjacent mountains of Nevada, and in the mountains of eastern Utah and northwestern Colorado. Other subspecies of *T. mexicana* occur in the southern Rockies and in Mexico. A dense population of this Skipper may be seen on Three-Creeks Meadow (6300 ft. alt.) south of the town of Sisters in Deschutes County, where it flies in June and July.

The dark brown ground color of the upperside in *nevada* fades into a paler area on the outer half of the hindwings. The white, hyaline spots on the forewings are relatively larger, more complete, and more elongated than in *T. pylades,* and are rimmed with dark scales. The wing fringes are checkered. On the underside, the outer portions of both fore- and hindwings are covered with fine, dark striations and the hindwings are vertically crossed by two dark bands somewhat as in *pylades*. There is no costal fold in the male, and in the genitalia the distal border of the valve is expanded, coarsely serrated, and pointed at each end.

The life history of the Nevada Cloudy Wing has not been described. Three-Creeks Meadow would afford an excellent site for a field study. The larvae in Sierran populations have been reported to feed on the legumes *Trifolium* and *Lathyrus,* and on the grass *Sitanion*.

Thorybes diversus Bell, 1927
Bell's Cloudy Wing

Plate 48, fig. 3. Map 191.

The presence of Bell's Cloudy Wing in Oregon has been surmised from its occurrence in the mountains of northern California, less than fifty miles from our border. There is at this time only one positively identified Oregon specimen known to me, which was taken July 9, 1925 near Brookings in Curry County. With some effort additional sites should be discovered. Unlike *Thorybes pylades* and *nevada* which fly in open spaces, *diversus* inhabits damp glades and small clearings in coniferous forests. The species is known in western Colorado and Wyoming, and in California from moderate elevations in the northern mountains and the central Sierras.

Thorybes diversus approaches the size of *T. pylades* but has forewing markings more like *nevada,* with the white spot below the cell slender and elongated. Also, as in *nevada,* there is no costal fold in the male. On the under surface the brown hindwings are outwardly pale and are obscurely marked; the bands are poorly defined and there are no *nevada*-like striations. The genitalia differ distinctly from those of *pylades* and *nevada,* the valve being terminally narrowed.

The immature stages of *diversus* have been observed by Burns and MacNeill in Sierran populations. The egg is small and changes in color from turquoise to green and finally translucent gray. The mature larva is olive brown, covered with a yellowish down of minute pale stipples and short hairs; a dark olive line runs along the back and two pale stripes are present on each side; behind the black head the first thoracic segment is reddish brown.

Epargyreus clarus californicus (Smith), 1891
Silver-spotted Skipper

Plate 48, fig. 4. Map 192.

There is no mistaking this largest of our Skippers, distinguished by the great silver spot on the hindwings. This fine species occurs throughout the United States and southern Canada and extends into South America. In Oregon it has been recorded from April to August and is widespread, though local, west of the Cascades and along the Columbia drainage of central and northern Oregon. It flies at low and middle elevations and can be met along roadsides and hedgerows, in weedy fields and small forest clearings, and even in town gardens.

Brown above, the forewings are marked with a band of translucent golden patches and are pointed; the hindwings are elongated and end in a blunt, taillike projection. Males can be recognized by the costal fold on the forewing. The conspicuous underside feature is the large silver patch on the hindwings. In our West Coast subspecies, *californicus*, this patch is abruptly narrowed in its upper half, and the lowest golden spot on the upperside of the forewings is small and almost detached.

In the immature stages of the Silver-spotted Skipper, the egg is heavily ribbed and green in color except for a red spot on its top. The larvae feed on various legumes, including *Lotus, Lathyrus, Robinia* (black locust), and *Wisteria*. When fully grown they are lemon yellow, marked with darker green transverse lines, and provided with a large brownish head decorated with two reddish spots; they make loosely woven nests among the leaves and feed at night. The pupae, enclosed in a loose cocoon, are chestnut brown in color.

Appendices

Color Plates

Legend to Color Plate I

1. *Papilio zelicaon.* Male.
2. *Papilio rutulus.* Male.
3. *Papilio indra.* Male.
4. *Parnassius phoebus xanthus.* Male.
5. *Coenonympha tullia eunomia.* Male.
6. *Danaus plexippus.* Female.
7. *Neophasia menapia tau.* Male.
8. *Pieris sisymbrii.* Male.
9. *Pieris occidentalis.* Male.
10. *Pieris napi marginalis.* Male, underside.
11. *Colias eurytheme.* Female.
12. *Colias occidentalis.* Female.
13. *Colias alexandra edwardsii.* Male.
14. *Colias interior.* Female.
15. *Anthocharis sara flora.* Male.
16. *Anthocharis lanceolata.* Male, underside.
17. *Euchloe ausonides.* Female, underside.
18. *Neominois ridingsii stretchii.* Female.
19. *Cercyonis pegala boopis.* Female.
20. *Cercyonis oetus.* Male.
21. *Erebia epipsodea hopfingeri.* Male.
22. *Oeneis nevadensis.* Male.

Legend to Color Plate II

1. *Limenitis lorquini burrisonii*. Male.
2. *Vanessa atalanta rubria*. Male.
3. *Vanessa anabella*. Female.
4. *Junonia coenia*. Female.
5. *Nymphalis californica*. Male.
6. *Nymphalis milberti furcillata*. Male.
7. *Polygonia oreas silenus*. Female.
8. *Nymphalis antiopa*. Male.
9. *Phyciodes campestris*. Male.
10. *Chlosyne palla whitneyi*. Female.
11. *Euphydryas chalcedona chalcedona*. Male.
12. *Euphydryas editha remingtoni*. Male.
13. *Euphydryas anicia macyi*. Female.
14. *Speyeria cybele pugetensis*. Female.
15. *Chlosyne leanira oregonensis*. Male, underside.
16. *Boloria epithore chermocki*. Female.
17. *Speyeria coronis snyderi*. Female.
18. *Speyeria zerene conchyliatus*. Female, underside.
19. *Speyeria zerene gunderi*. Female, underside.
20. *Speyeria egleis macdunnoughi*. Male, underside.
21. *Speyeria callippe elaine*. Male, underside.
22. *Speyeria callippe semivirida*. Male, underside.
23. *Speyeria atlantis dodgei*. Female, underside.
24. *Speyeria mormonia erinna*. Female, underside.
25. *Speyeria hydaspe purpurascens*. Male, underside.

Legend to Color Plate III

1. *Apodemia mormo mormonia.* Female.
2. *Habrodais grunus herri.* Female.
3. *Satyrium fuliginosum.* Female.
4. *Satyrium behrii.* Male.
5. *Incisalia eryphon.* Female, underside.
6. *Satyrium saepium.* Male.
7. *Mitoura spinetorum.* Female.
8. *Mitoura nelsoni.* Female, underside.
9. *Callophrys dumetorum.* Male, underside.
10. *Strymon melinus setonia.* Female, underside.
11. *Atlides halesus corcorani.* Male.
12. *Thysalea arota arota.* Female, underside.
13. *Lycaena heteronea.* Male.
14. *Lycaena editha editha.* Male, underside.
15. *Lycaena mariposa.* Male, underside.
16. *Lycaena rubidus.* Male.
17. *Lycaena helloides.* Female.
18. *Lycaeides melissa melissa.* Male, underside.
19. *Lycaeides melissa melissa.* Female.
20. *Plebejus saepiolus saepiolus.* Male.
21. *Icaricia acmon acmon.* Male.
22. *Icaricia icarioides icarioides.* Female, underside.
23. *Philotes battoides oregonensis,* Female, underside.
24. *Glaucopysyche lygdamus columbia.* Male, underside.
25. *Celastrina argiolus echo.* Female.
26. *Euphyes vestris vestris.* Male.
27. *Ochlodes sylvanoides.* Female.
28. *Atalopedes campestris.* Male.
29. *Polites sonora siris.* Female.
30. *Hesperia comma harpalus.* Male.
31. *Hesperia juba.* Female, underside.
32. *Carterocephalus palaemon mandan.* Male.
33. *Pholisora catullus.* Female.
34. *Heliopetes ericetorum.* Male.
35. *Pyrgus communis.* Male.
36. *Erynnis persius.* Male.
37. *Erynnis propertius.* Female.
38. *Thorybes mexicana nevada.* Female.
39. *Epargyreus clarus.* Male.

Oregon's State Insect
The Oregon Swallowtail
Papilio oregonius

Plate 4 shows male above, female below.

Black and White Plates

Plate 1

Family Papilionidae

Fig. 1. *Papilio oregonius*. Male, (a) upperside, (b) underside. Cecil, Morrow Co., Ore. Aug. 29, 1961. Female resembles male. Text p. 40. Map 1.

Fig. 2. *Papilio zelicaon*. Male, (a) upperside, (b) underside. Corvallis, Benton Co., Ore. July 11, 1960. Female resembles male. Text p. 41. Map 2.

Fig. 3. *Papilio indra indra*. Male, (a) upperside, (b) underside. Pine Cr., Baker Co., Ore. June 8, 1961. Female resembles male. Text p. 41. Map 3.

Plate 1

Plate 2

Family Papilionidae

Fig. 1. *Papilio rutulus rutulus*. Male. Marks Cr., Crook Co., Ore. June 23, 1959. Yellow, with black bars. Female resembles male. Text p. 41. Map 4.

Fig. 2. *Papilio eurymedon*. Male. Corvallis, Benton Co., Ore. June 4, 1967. White, with black bars. Female resembles male. Text p. 42. Map 6.

Fig. 3. *Papilio multicaudata*. Male. Pine Cr., Baker Co., Ore. June 21, 1959. Yellow, with black bars. Female resembles male. Text p. 42. Map 5.

Fig. 4. *Battus philenor hirsuta*. Male. Lafayette, Contra Costa Co., Calif. May 7, 1966 (reared). Female resembles male. Text p. 42. Map 7.

Plate 2

1

2

3

4

Plate 3

Family Papilionidae

Fig. 1. *Parnassius clodius claudianus.* (a) Male, upperside. Alsea, Benton Co., Ore. July 5, 1946. (b) Female, upperside. McDonald Fst., Benton Co., Ore. July 1, 1956. Text p. 42. Map 8.

Fig. 2. *Parnassius phoebus xanthus.* (a) Male, upperside. Aneroid Lake Trail, Wallowa Co., Ore. July 25, 1967. (b) Female, upperside. Hurricane Cr., Wallowa Co., Ore. July 24, 1965. Text p. 43. Map 9.

Fig. 3. *Parnassius phoebus sternitzkii.* (a) Male, upperside. Mt. Ashland, Jackson Co., Ore. June 22, 1970. (b) Female, upperside. Castle Lake, Siskiyou Co., Calif. July 29, 1959. Text p. 43. Map 9.

Fig. 4. *Parnassius clodius claudianus.* Female, showing side views of sphragis. McDonald Fst., Benton Co., Ore. June 14, 1969.

Fig. 5. *Parnassius phoebus xanthus.* Female, showing side view of sphragis. Hurricane Cr., Wallowa Co., Ore. July 24, 1967.

Plate 3

Plate 4
Family Pieridae

Fig. 1. *Neophasia menapia tau.* (a) Male, upperside. Cascadia, Linn Co., Ore. Aug. 12, 1957. (b,c) Female, upper and underside. McDonald Fst., Benton Co., Ore. Sept. 4, 1965. Text p. 45. Map 10.

Fig. 2. *Pieris beckerii.* (a) Male, upperside. Cecil, Morrow Co., Ore. Sept. 4, 1961. (b,c) Female, upper and underside. Viewpoint Rd., Ochoco Mts., Crook Co., Ore. July 23, 1960. Text p. 45. Map 11.

Fig. 3. *Pieris beckerii,* spring form. (a,c) Male, upper and underside. Rattlesnake Cn., Malheur Co., Ore. May 7, 1967. (b) Female, upperside. Five mi. S of Devil's Garden, Lake Co., Ore. June 1, 1969.

Fig. 4. *Pieris sisymbrii sisymbrii.* (a,c) Male, upper and underside. Burns, Harney Co., Ore. May 6, 1964. (b) Female, upperside. Frenchglen, Harney Co., Ore. May 8, 1967. Females may be white or yellow. Text p. 45. Map 12.

Fig. 5. *Pieris protodice.* (a,c) Male, upper and underside. Frenchglen, Harney Co., Ore. July 26, 1962. (b) Female, upperside. Horse Pr., Warner Mts., Lake Co., Ore. June 29, 1973. Underside of the female resembles *P. occidentalis.* Text p. 46. Map 13.

Plate 4

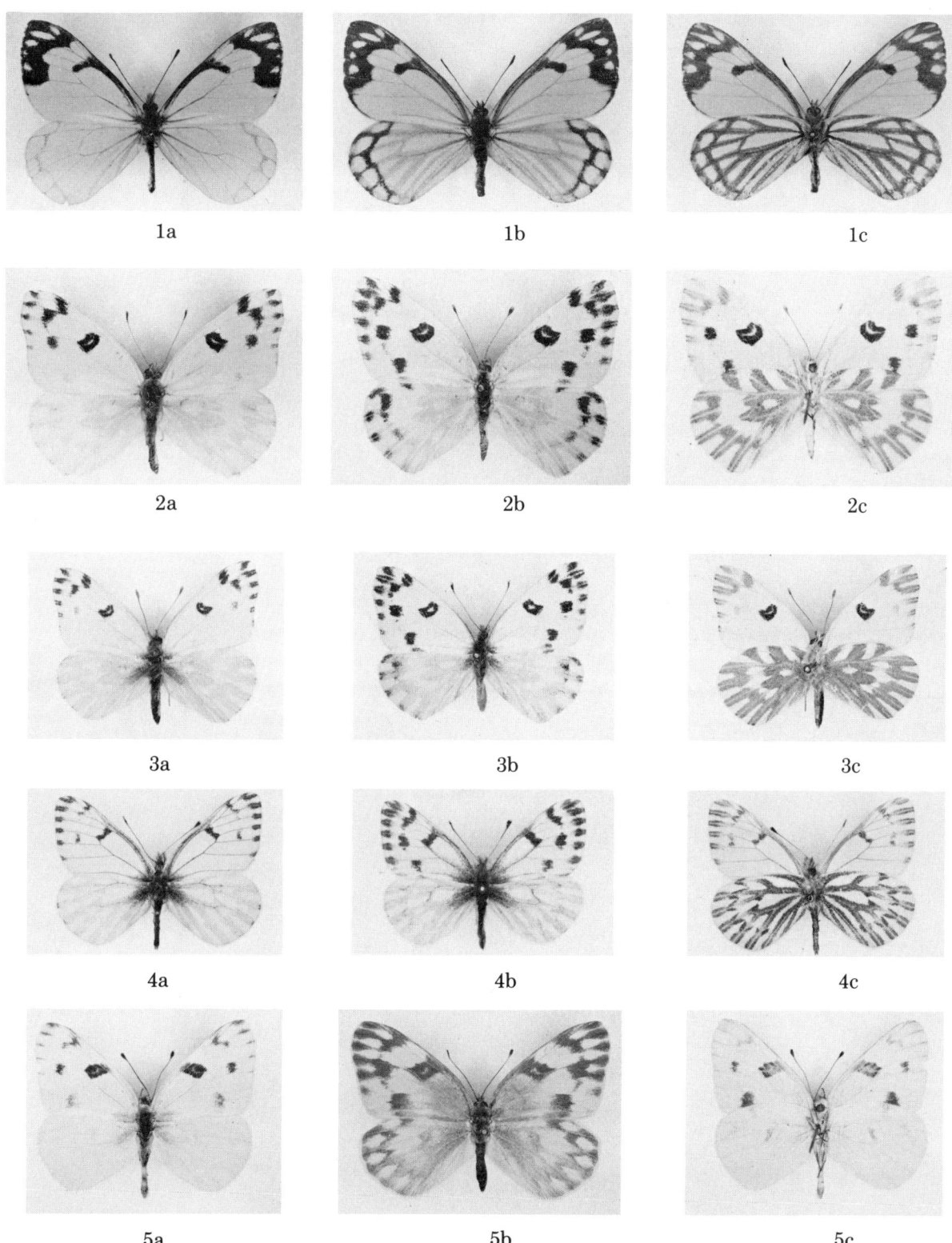

1a 1b 1c
2a 2b 2c
3a 3b 3c
4a 4b 4c
5a 5b 5c

Plate 5

Family Pieridae

Fig. 1. *Pieris occidentalis*. (a,c) Male, upper and underside. Hurricane Cr., Wallowa Co., Ore. July 23, 1965. (b) Female, upperside. Lostine River Rd., Wallowa Co., Ore. July 22, 1965. Text p. 46. Map 14.

Fig. 2. *Pieris occidentalis,* spring form "calyce". (a,c) Male, upper and underside. Wright's Point, Harney Co., Ore. May 8, 1967. (b) Female, upperside. Frenchglen, Harney Co., Ore. May 8, 1967.

Fig. 3. *Pieris napi marginalis*. (a,c) Male, upper and underside. Rose Lodge, Lincoln Co., Ore. May 22, 1955. (b) Female, upperside. McDonald Fst., Benton Co., Ore. April 8, 1959. Text p. 46. Map 15.

Fig. 4. *Pieris napi marginalis,* summer form "pallida". (a,c) Male, upper and underside. McDonald Fst., Benton Co., Ore. May 21, 1962 (reared). (b) Female, upperside. McDonald Fst., Benton Co., Ore. May 21, 1962 (reared).

Fig. 5. *Pieris rapae*. (a) Male, upperside. Corvallis, Benton Co., Ore. April 2, 1953. (b,c) Female, upper and underside. Corvallis, Benton Co., Ore. June 30, 1958. Text p. 47. Map 16.

Plate 5

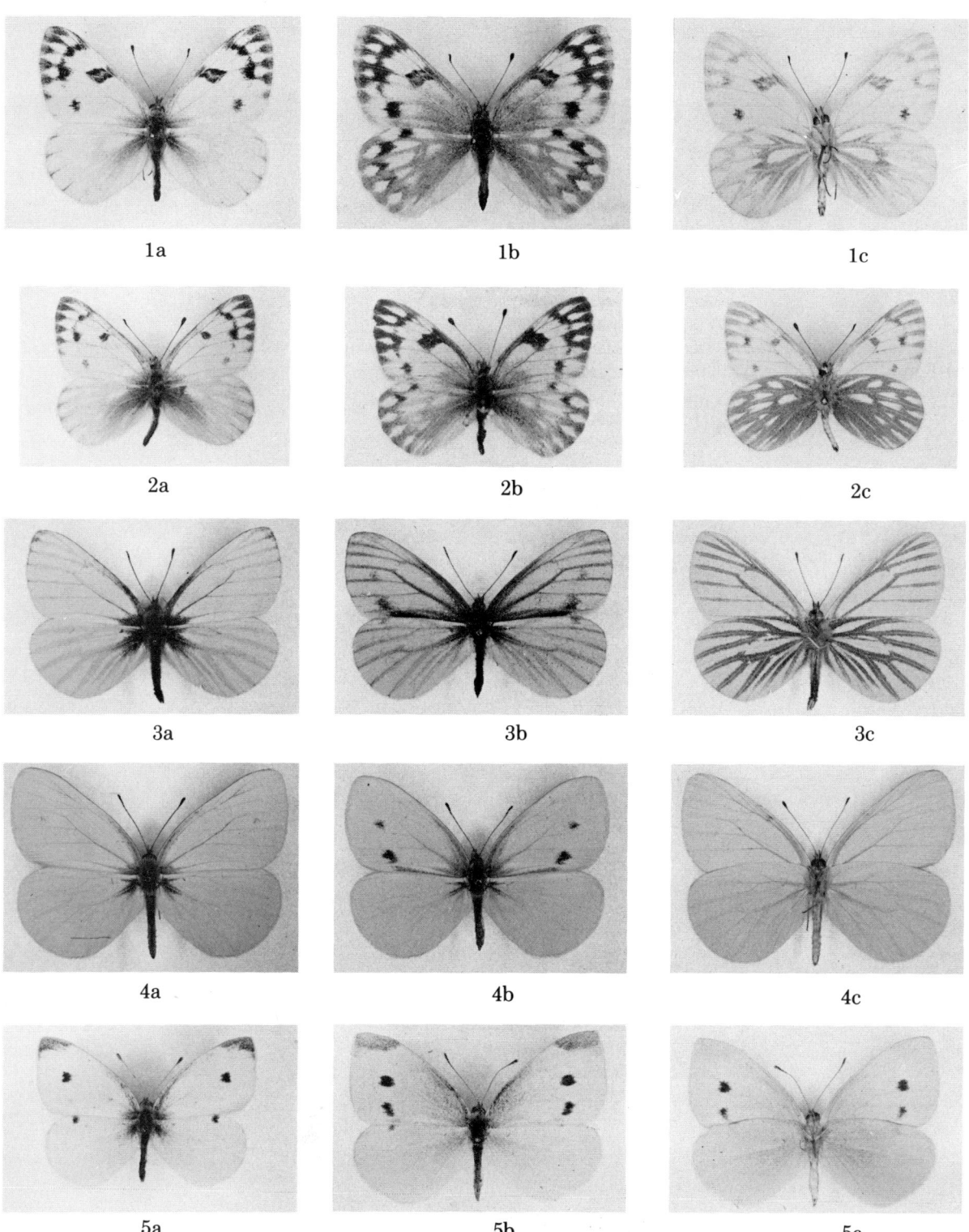

Plate 6

Family Pieridae

Fig. 1. *Colias eurytheme eurytheme*. (a,c) Male, upper and underside. Fish Lake, Steens Mt., Harney Co., Ore. Aug. 2, 1961. (b) Female, upperside. Gilchrist, Klamath Co., Ore. July 28, 1957. Text p. 47. Map 17.

Fig. 2. *Colias eurytheme eurytheme*. (a) Male, upperside, form "ariadne". Gilchrist, Klamath Co., Ore. Oct. 11, 1958. (b) Female, upperside, form "alba" (white). Viewpoint Rd., Ochoco Mts., Crook Co., Ore. July 23, 1960. (c) Female, upperside, form "ariadne". French Gulch Rd. nr. Copper, Jackson Co., Ore. June 15, 1968.

Fig. 3. *Colias philodice eriphyle*. (a) Male, upperside. Viewpoint Rd., Ochoco Mts., Crook Co., Ore. July 23, 1960. (b,c) Female, upper and underside. Viewpoint Rd., Ochoco Mts., Crook Co., Ore. July 23, 1960. Text p. 48. Map 18.

Fig. 4. *Colias occidentalis occidentalis*. (a) Male, upperside. Camp Sherman, Jefferson Co., Ore. July 13, 1971. (b,c) Female (yellow), upper and underside. Viewpoint Rd., Ochoco Mts., Crook Co., Ore. July 23, 1962. Text p. 48. Map 19.

Fig. 5. *Colias occidentalis occidentalis*. (a) Female (white), upperside. Viewpoint Rd., Ochoco Mts., Crook Co., Ore. July 23, 1960. (b) Female (yellow), upperside. Viewpoint Rd., Ochoco Mts., Crook Co., Ore. July 23, 1962. (c) Female (white), upperside. Viewpoint Rd., Ochoco Mts., Crook Co., Ore. July 2, 1961.

Plate 6

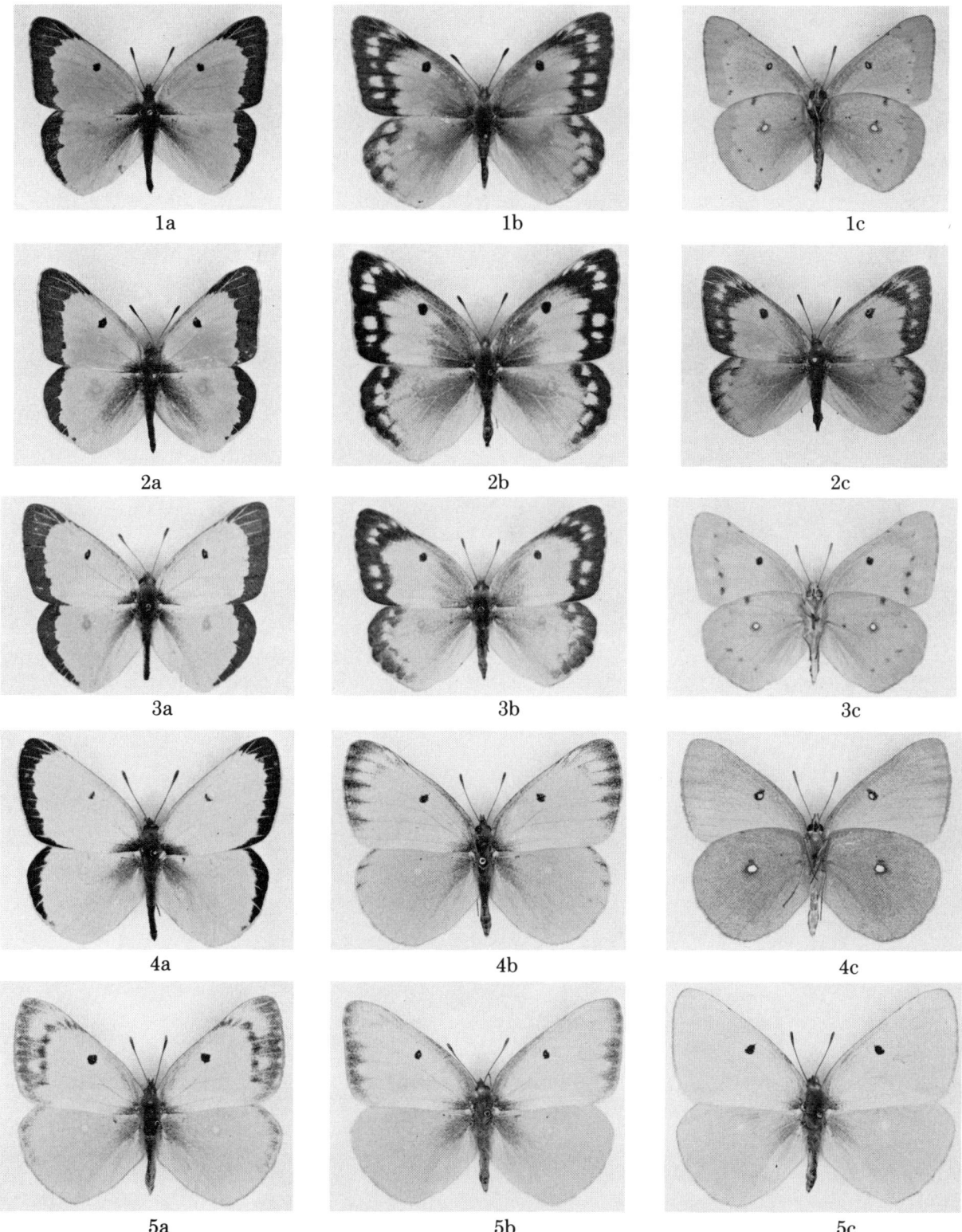

141

Plate 7

Family Pieridae

Fig. 1. *Colias alexandra edwardsii.* (a) Male, upperside. Hurricane Cr., Wallowa Co., Ore. July 24, 1965. (b, c) Female, upper and underside. Frenchglen, Harney Co., Ore. Aug. 1, 1961. Text p. 48. Map 20.

Fig. 2. *Colias alexandra edwardsii.* (a) Female, upperside. Cornez Cr., Ochoco Mts., Crook Co., Ore. July 8, 1960. (b,c) Female, upper and underside. Hurricane Cr., Wallowa Co., Ore. July 24, 1965.

Fig. 3. *Colias interior interior.* (a,c) Male, upper and underside. Camp Sherman, Jefferson Co., Ore. July 13, 1971. (b) Female, upperside. Anthony Lake, Baker Co., Ore. July 23, 1959. Text p. 49. Map 21.

Fig. 4. *Colias pelidne skinneri.* (a,c) Male, upper and underside. Aneroid Lake trail, Wallowa Co., Ore. July 25, 1967. (b) Female, upperside. Aneroid Lake trail, Wallowa Co., Ore. July 22, 1967. Text p. 49. Map 22.

Fig. 5. *Nathalis iole.* (a,b) Male, upper and underside. Paradise Hills Lkt., Jefferson Co., Colo. June 25, 1966. (c,d) Female, upper and underside. Salida, Chaffee Co., Colo. Aug. 15, 1965. Text p. 50. Map 23.

Plate 7

1a　　　　　　　1b　　　　　　　1c

2a　　　　　　　2b　　　　　　　2c

3a　　　　　　　3b　　　　　　　3c

4a　　　　　　　4b　　　　　　　4c

5a　　　5b　　　5c　　　5d

Plate 8

Family Pieridae

Fig. 1. *Anthocharis sara flora.* (a,c) Male, upper and underside. McDonald Fst., Benton Co., Ore. April 27, 1958. (b) Female, upperside. McDonald Fst., Benton Co., Ore. April 27, 1958. Text p. 50. Map 24.

Fig. 2. *Anthocharis sara stella.* (a,c) Male, upper and underside. Devine Cn., Harney Co., Ore. May 31, 1964. (b) Female, upperside. Trout Mts., Malheur Co., Ore. May 14, 1960. Text p. 50. Map 24.

Fig. 3. *Anthocharis lanceolata lanceolata.* (a) Male, upperside. Tubb Springs, Jackson Co., Ore. June 17, 1958. (b,c) Female, upper and underside. Siskiyou Pass, Jackson Co., Ore. June 19, 1970. Text p. 50. Map 25.

Fig. 4. *Euchloe hyantis lotta.* (a,c) Male, upper and underside. Burns, Harney Co., Ore. May 21, 1964. (b) Female, upperside. Rockville, Malheur Co., Ore. May 18, 1961. Text p. 50. Map 26.

Fig. 5. *Euchloe ausonides ausonides.* (a,c) Male, upper and underside. Bly Mt., Klamath Co., Ore. June 16, 1963. (b) Female, upperside. Mt. Ashland, Jackson Co., Ore. June 19, 1970. Text p. 51. Map 27.

Plate 8

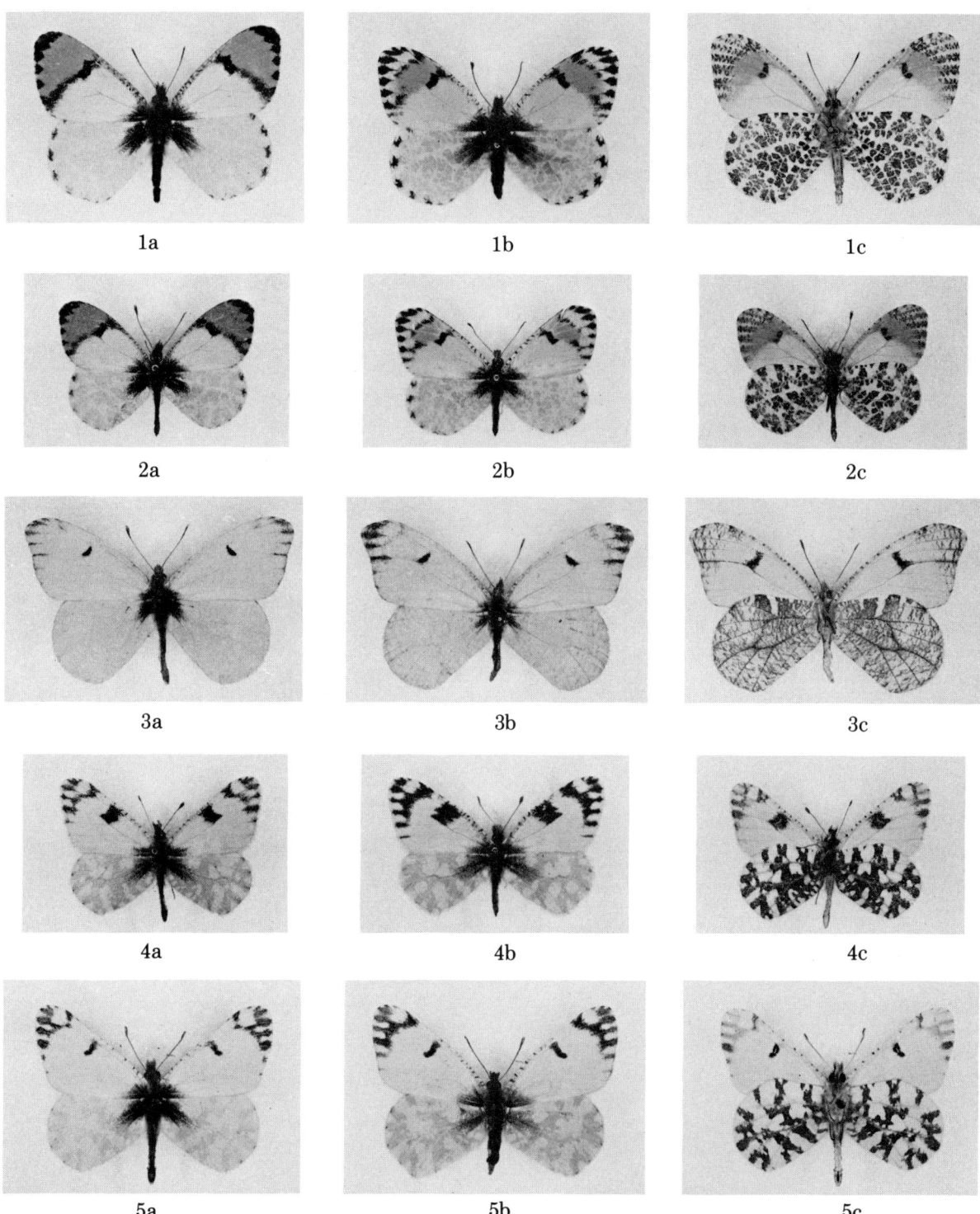

Plate 9

Family Satyridae

Fig. 1. *Coenonympha tullia eunomia*. 1st generation. (a,b) Male, upper and underside. McDonald Fst., Benton Co., Ore. June 3, 1961. (c,d) Female, upper and underside. McDonald Fst., Benton Co., Ore. May 31, 1959. Text p. 53. Map 28.

Fig. 2. *Coenonympha tullia eunomia*. 2nd generation. (a,b) Male, upper and underside. Corvallis, Benton Co., Ore. Sept. 1, 1954. (c,d) Female, upper and underside. Corvallis, Benton Co., Ore. July 4, 1945.

Fig. 3. *Coenonympha tullia ampelos*. 1st generation. (a,b) Male, upper and underside. Viewpoint Rd., Ochoco Mts., Crook Co., Ore. July 2, 1961. (c,d) Female, upper and underside. Devine Cn., Harney Co., Ore. May 20, 1964. Text p. 53. Map 29.

Fig. 4. *Coenonympha tullia ampelos*. 2nd generation. (a,b) Male, upper and underside. Frenchglen, Harney Co., Ore. July 25, 1962. (c,d) Female, upper and underside. Emigrant Cr., Harney Co., Ore. Aug. 20, 1964.

Fig. 5. *Coenonympha tullia eryngii*. 1st generation. (a,b) Male, upper and underside. Pinehurst, Jackson Co., Ore. May 29, 1960. (c,d) Female, upper and underside. Bly Mt., Klamath Co., Ore. June 16, 1960. Text p. 53. Map 30.

Fig. 6. *Coenonympha tullia eryngii*. 2nd generation. (a,b) Male, upper and underside. Tubb Springs, Jackson Co., Ore. Aug. 16, 1960. (c,d) Female, upper and underside. Butte Falls, Jackson Co., Ore. June 20, 1966.

Plate 9

1a 1b 1c 1d
2a 2b 2c 2d
3a 3b 3c 3d
4a 4b 4c 4d
5a 5b 5c 5d
6a 6b 6c 6d

Plate 10
Family Satyridae

Fig. 1. *Neominois ridingsii stretchii.* (a,c) Male, upper and underside. Drake Peak, Lake Co., Ore. Aug. 3, 1963. (b) Female, upperside. Drake Peak, Lake Co., Ore. Aug. 3, 1963. Text p. 53. Map 31.

Fig. 2. *Cercyonis pegala boopis.* (a,b) Male, upper and underside. Corvallis, Benton Co., Ore. July 15, 1956. Text p. 54. Map 32.

Fig. 3. *Cercyonis pegala boopis.* (a,b) Female, upper and underside. Viewpoint Rd., Ochoco Mts., Crook Co., Ore. July 23, 1962.

Fig. 4. *Cercyonis sthenele silvestris.* (a) Male, upperside. Gilchrist, Klamath Co., Ore. July 28, 1962. (b,c) Female, upper and underside. Gilchrist, Klamath Co., Ore. Aug. 19, 1961. Text p. 54. Map 34.

Plate 10

Plate 11

Family Satyridae

Fig. 1. *Cercyonis pegala ariane.* (a,b) Male, upper and underside. Ana Spgs., Lake Co., Ore. July 24, 1964. Text p. 54. Map 33.

Fig. 2. *Cercyonis pegala ariane.* (a) Female, upperside. Ana Spgs., Lake Co., Ore. Aug. 18, 1962. (b) Female, upperside, form "stephensi". Fandango Pass Rd., Modoc Co., Calif. July 22, 1964.

Fig. 3. *Cercyonis sthenele paulus.* (a,b) Male, upper and underside. Glass Buttes, Lake Co., Ore. Aug. 1, 1961. (c) Female, upperside. Baker, Baker Co., Ore. July 30, 1956. Text p. 54. Map 34.

Fig. 4. *Cercyonis oetus oetus.* (a,b) Male, upper and underside. Sand Cr. at Hwy. 232, Klamath Co., Ore. July 10, 1962. (c) Female, upperside. Fish L., Harney Co., Ore. Aug. 5, 1960. Text p. 55. Map 35.

Fig. 5. *Cercyonis sthenele paulus.* Female, underside. Baker, Baker Co., Ore. July 30, 1956.

Fig. 6. *Cercyonis oetus oetus.* Female, underside. Fish L., Harney Co., Ore. Aug. 5, 1960.

Plate 11

Plate 12

Family Satyridae

Fig. 1. *Oeneis nevadensis.* (a,b) Male, upper and underside. Gilchrist, Klamath Co., Ore. July 4, 1956. Text p. 55. Map 36.

Fig. 2. *Oeneis nevadensis.* (a,b) Female, upper and underside. French Gulch Rd., Jackson Co., Ore. June 15, 1968.

Fig. 3. *Erebia epipsodea hopfingeri.* (a,b) Male, upper and underside. Aneroid Lake trail, Wallowa Co., Ore. July 27, 1967. Text p. 56. Map 37.

Fig. 4. *Erebia epipsodea hopfingeri.* (a,b) Female, upper and underside. Aneroid Lake trail, Wallowa Co., Ore. July 22, 1967.

Plate 12

Plate 13

Family Danaidae

Fig. 1. *Danaus plexippus*. Male. Malheur Refuge Hdq., Harney Co., Ore. June 6, 1956. Text p. 58. Map 38.

Fig. 2. *Danaus plexippus*. Female. Gilchrist, Klamath Co., Ore. Oct. 4, 1956.

Family Nymphalidae

Fig. 3. *Limenitis archippus*. Male. Powder R., 26 mi. E of Baker, Baker Co., Ore. Aug. 9, 1937. Text p. 60. Map 39.

Fig. 4. *Limenitis archippus* x *lorquini* hybrid. Male. Hermiston, Umatilla Co., Ore. Spring, 1969.

Plate 13

1

2

3

4

Plate 14
Family Nymphalidae

Fig. 1. *Limenitis weidemeyerii latifascia*. Male, (a) upperside, (b) underside. Millcreek Cn., Salt Lake Co., Utah. June 18, 1960. Text p. 60. Map 40.

Fig. 2. *Limenitis lorquini burrisoni*. Male, (a) upperside, (b) underside. McDonald Fst., Benton Co., Ore. July 17, 1955. Text p. 61. Map 41.

Fig. 3. *Adelpha bredowii californica*. Female, (a) upperside, (b) underside. Tubb Springs, Jackson Co., Ore. Sept. 3, 1959. Text p. 61. Map 42.

Plate 14

1a

1b

2a

2b

3a

3b

Plate 15

Family Nymphalidae

Fig. 1. *Vanessa atalanta rubria*. Female. Corvallis, Benton Co., Ore. Sept. 14, 1956. Text p. 61. Map 43.

Fig. 2. *Junonia coenia coenia*. Female. Bly Mt., Klamath Co., Ore. June 17, 1963. Text p. 63. Map 47.

Fig. 3. *Vanessa virginiensis*. Female, (a) upperside, (b) underside. Diamond Lake, Douglas Co., Ore. Aug. 14, 1957. Text p. 62. Map 44.

Fig. 4. *Vanessa cardui*. Male, (a) upperside, (b) underside. Corvallis, Benton Co., Ore. July 4, 1945. Text p. 62. Map 45.

Fig. 5. *Vanessa annabella*. Female, (a) upperside, (b) underside. Corvallis, Benton Co., Ore. Oct. 19, 1956. Text p. 63. Map 46.

Plate 15

Plate 16

Family Nymphalidae

Fig. 1. *Nymphalis vau-album watsoni.* Female, (a) upperside, (b) underside. Priest River, Bonner Co., Idaho. Aug. 1, 1920. Text p. 64. Map 48.

Fig. 2. *Nymphalis californica.* Female, (a) upperside, (b) underside. Lost Prairie, Linn Co., Ore. June 21, 1959. Text p. 64. Map 49.

Fig. 3. *Nymphalis milberti furcillata.* Male, (a) upperside, (b) underside. Steens Mt., Harney Co., Ore. June 11, 1961. Text p. 65. Map 50.

Fig. 4. *Nymphalis antiopa antiopa.* Female, (a) upperside, (b) underside. Gilchrist, Klamath Co., Ore. June 17, 1957. Text p. 65. Map 51.

Plate 16

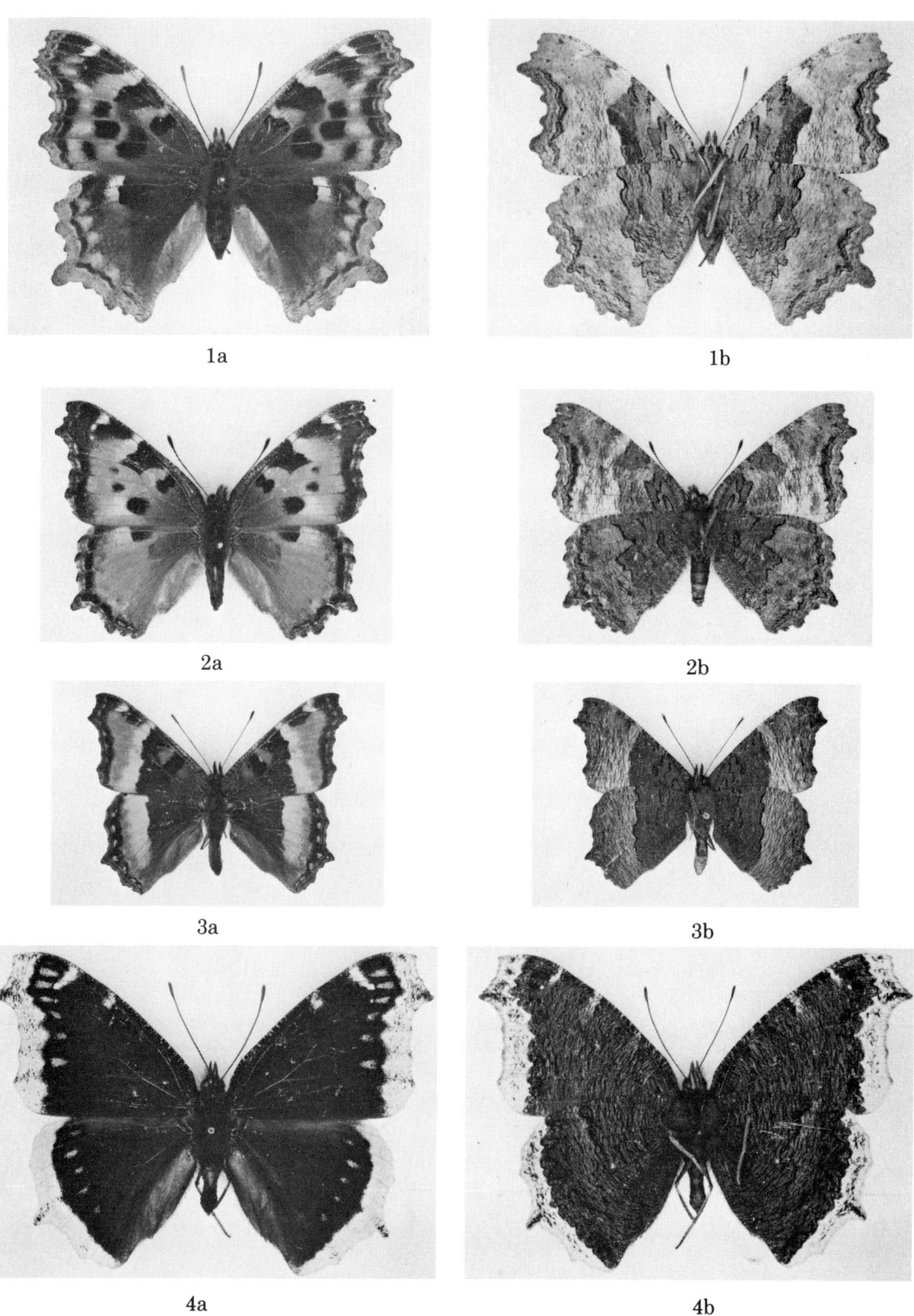

1a 1b

2a 2b

3a 3b

4a 4b

161

Plate 17

Family Nymphalidae

Fig. 1. *Polygonia satyrus neomarsyas.* (a,b) Male, upper and underside. Mary's Peak, Benton Co., Ore. July 5, 1958. (c) Female, underside. Corvallis, Benton Co., Ore. March 18, 1960. Text p. 65. Map 52.

Fig. 2. *Polygonia faunus rusticus.* (a,b) Male, upper and underside. Hurricane Cr., Wallowa Co., Ore. Aug. 24, 1968. (c) Female, underside. Hurricane Cr., Wallowa Co., Ore. Aug. 24, 1968. Text p. 66. Map 53.

Fig. 3. *Polygonia zephyrus.* (a,b) Male, upper and underside. Marks Cr. Lodge, Hwy. 26, Ochoco Mts., Crook Co., Ore. July 20, 1958. (c) Female, underside. Paulina L., Deschutes Co., Ore. Aug. 21, 1961. Text p. 66. Map 54.

Fig. 4. *Polygonia oreas silenus.* (a,b) Male, upper and underside. Mary's Peak, Benton Co., Ore. Aug. 9, 1958. (c) Female, underside. Mary's Peak, Benton Co., Ore. Sept. 9, 1976. Text p. 66. Map 55.

Plate 17

Plate 18

Family Nymphalidae

Fig. 1. *Phyciodes tharos pascoensis.* (a,b) Male, upper and underside. Snake River Rd. near Oxbow, Baker Co., Ore. June 20, 1971. (c,d) Female, upper and underside. Brewster, Okanogan Co., Wash. May 25, 1956. Text p. 67. Map 56.

Fig. 2. *Phyciodes campestris campestris.* (a,b) Male, upper and underside. McDonald Fst., Benton Co., Ore. May 21, 1958. (c,d) Female, upper and underside. Bly Mt., Klamath Co., Ore. June 26, 1965. Text p. 67. Map 57.

Fig. 3. *Phyciodes campestris montana.* (a,b) Male, upper and underside. Fallen Leaf L., Eldorado Co., Calif. June 29, 1961. (c,d) Female, upper and underside. Lost Pr., Linn Co., Ore. June 24, 1962. Text p. 67. Map 58.

Fig. 4. *Phyciodes orseis orseis.* (a,b) Male, upper and underside. Kinney Cr., Jackson Co., Ore. May 8, 1976. (c,d) Female, upper and underside. Kinney Cr., Jackson Co., Ore. May 8, 1976. Text p. 68. Map 59.

Fig. 5. *Phyciodes mylitta mylitta.* (a,b) Male, upper and underside. Corvallis, Benton Co., Ore. April 28, 1957. (c,d) Female, upper and underside. McDonald Fst., Benton Co., Ore. May 5, 1957. Text p. 68. Map 60.

Fig. 6. *Phyciodes pallida barnesi.* (a,b) Male, upper and underside. Kah-Nee-Ta, Wasco Co., Ore. May 22, 1976. (c,d) Female, upper and underside. Sherar Falls, Wasco Co., Ore. May 17, 1953. Text p. 68. **Map 61.**

Plate 18

Plate 19

Family Nymphalidae

Fig. 1. *Chlosyne acastus acastus.* (a,b) Male, upper and underside. Wildhorse Cr., Alvord Basin, Harney Co., Ore. May 28, 1960. (c) Female, upperside. Near Trout Cr. Ranch, Harney Co., Ore. May 29, 1960. Text p. 69. Map 62.

Fig. 2. *Chlosyne palla palla.* (a,b) Male, upper and underside. No. Pine Cr. east of Halfway, Baker Co., Ore. June 20, 1959. (c) Female, upperside. Bly Mt., Klamath Co., Ore. July 7, 1962. Text p. 69. Map 63.

Fig. 3. *Chlosyne palla palla,* form "eremita". (a,b) Female, upper and underside. Bly Mt., Klamath Co., Ore. June 26, 1965. Text p. 69.

Fig. 4. *Chlosyne palla whitneyi.* Female, upperside. Sand Cr. at Hwy. 232, Klamath Co., Ore. July 10, 1962. Text p. 69. Map 64.

Fig. 5. *Chlosyne palla sterope.* (a,b) Male, upper and underside. 20 miles NW of Condon, Gilliam Co., Ore. June 20, 1961. (c) Female, upperside. Kah-Nee-Ta, Wasco Co., Ore. June 20, 1972. Text p. 70. Map 65.

Fig. 6. *Chlosyne hoffmanni segregata.* (a,b) Male, upper and underside. Tombstone Pr., Linn Co., Ore. July 27, 1976. (c) Female, upperside. Hoodoo Ski Bowl, Linn Co., Ore. July 27, 1963. Text p. 70. Map 66.

Fig. 7. *Chlosyne leanira oregonensis.* (a,b) Male, upper and underside. Rogue R., 5 miles SW of Prospect, Jackson Co., Ore. June 22, 1976. (c) Female, upperside. Rogue R., 5 miles SW of Prospect, Jackson Co., Ore. June 22, 1976. Text p. 70. Map 67.

Plate 19

Plate 20

Family Nymphalidae

Fig. 1. *Euphydryas chalcedona chalcedona.* (a,b) Male, upper and underside. Siskiyou Pass, Jackson Co., Ore. June 19, 1970. (c) Female, upperside. Rough & Ready Cr., Josephine Co., Ore. May 23, 1964. Text p. 72. **Map 68.**

Fig. 2. *Euphydryas chalcedona macglashanii.* (a,b) Male, upper and underside. Bly Mt., Klamath Co., Ore. June 22, 1959. (c) Female, upperside. Bly Mt., Klamath Co., Ore. June 21, 1958. Text p. 72. **Map 69.**

Fig. 3. *Euphydryas chalcedona colon.* (a,b) Male, upper and underside. McDonald Fst., Benton Co., Ore. May 21, 1958. (c) Female, upperside. Cascadia State Park, Linn Co., Ore. July 3, 1956. Text p. 72. **Map 70.**

Fig. 4. *Euphydryas chalcedona wallacensis.* (a,b) Male, upper and underside. Devine Cn., Harney Co., Ore. June 29, 1964. (c) Female, upperside. Seneca, Grant Co., Ore. July 5, 1964. Text p. 72. **Map 71.**

Fig. 5. *Euphydryas chalcedona chalcedona.* Female. Underside of fig. 1c.

Fig. 6. *Euphydryas chalcedona macglashanii.* Female. Underside of fig. 2c.

Fig. 7. *Euphydryas chalcedona colon.* Female. Underside of fig. 3c.

Plate 20

Plate 21

Family Nymphalidae

Fig. 1. *Euphydryas anicia bakeri.* (a,b) Male, upper and underside. Cave Cr., near Durkee, Baker Co., Ore. May 25, 1964. (c) Female, upperside. Cave Cr., near Durkee, Baker Co., Ore. May 25, 1964. Text p. 73. Map 73.

Fig. 2. *Euphydryas anicia macyi.* (a,b) Male, upper and underside. Andrews, Alvord Basin, Harney Co., Ore. May 23, 1973. (c) Female, upperside. Trout Cr., Alvord Basin, Harney Co., Ore. May 29, 1960. Text p. 73. Map 74.

Fig. 3. *Euphydryas anicia veazieae.* (a,b) Male, upper and underside. Paratype. Jackass Mts., Harney Co., Ore. May 22, 1950. (c) Female, upperside. Paratype. Jackass Mts., Harney Co., Ore. May 23, 1950. Text p. 73. Map 72.

Fig. 4. *Euphydryas anicia howlandi.* (a,b) Male, upper and underside. Matterhorn (9500′), Wallowa Co., Ore. July 25, 1965. (c) Female, upperside. Matterhorn (9500′), Wallowa Co., Ore. July 25, 1965. Text p. 73. Map 75.

Fig. 5. *Euphydryas anicia bakeri.* Female. Underside of fig. 1c.

Fig. 6. *Euphydryas anicia macyi.* Female. Underside of fig. 2c.

Fig. 7. *Euphydryas anicia veazieae.* Female. Underside of fig. 3c.

Plate 21

Plate 22

Family Nymphalidae

Fig. 1. *Euphydryas editha taylori.* (a,b) Male, upper and underside. McDonald Fst., Benton Co., Ore. April 27, 1958. (c) Female, upperside. McDonald Fst., Benton Co., Ore. April 27, 1958. Text p. 73. Map 76.

Fig. 2. *Euphydryas editha baroni.* (a,b) Male, upper and underside. Rough & Ready Cr., Josephine Co., Ore. April 28, 1953. (c) Female, upperside. Ruch, Jackson Co., Ore. April 2, 1940. Text p. 73. Map 77.

Fig. 3. *Euphydryas editha edithana.* (a,b) Male, upper and underside. Big Summit Pr., Ochoco Mts., Crook Co., Ore. May 27, 1961. (c) Female, upperside. Big Summit Pr., Ochoco Mts., Crook Co., Ore. May 27, 1961. Text p. 73. Map 78.

Fig. 4. *Euphydryas editha colonia.* (a,b) Male, upper and underside. Monument Peak, Linn Co., Ore. July 12, 1972. (c) Female, upperside. Monument Peak, Linn Co., Ore. July 12, 1972. Text p. 73. Map 79.

Fig. 5. *Euphydryas editha remingtoni.* (a,b) Male, upper and underside. Skookum Mdw., Klamath Co., Ore. July 14, 1971. (c) Female, upperside. Gilchrist, Klamath Co., Ore. July 10, 1960. Text p. 74. Map 80.

Fig. 6. *Euphydryas editha lawrencei.* (a,b) Male, upper and underside. Mt. Thielsen, Douglas Co., Ore. Aug. 2, 1955. (c) Female, upperside. Gilchrist, Klamath Co., Ore. July 10, 1960. Text p. 74. Map 81.

Plate 22

Plate 23

Family Nymphalidae

Fig. 1. *Boloria selene tollandensis.* (a,b) Male, upper and underside. Moxee Bog, Yakima Co., Wash. July 5, 1968. (c) Female, underside. Big Summit Pr., Ochoco Mts., Crook Co., Ore. July 1, 1962. **Text p. 74. Map 82.**

Fig. 2. *Boloria epithore chermocki.* (a,b) Male, upper and underside. Cascadia, Linn Co., Ore. May 23, 1959. (c) Female, underside. McDonald Fst., Benton Co., Ore. May 16, 1958. Text p. 74. Map 83.

Fig. 3. *Boloria epithore borealis.* (a,b) Male, upper and underside. Lostine River, Wallowa Co., Ore. July 22, 1965. Text p. 75. Map 84.

Fig. 4. *Speyeria cybele pugetensis.* (a,b) Male, upper and underside. McDonald Fst., Benton Co., Ore. July 12, 1964. Text p. 76. Map 85.

Fig. 5. *Speyeria cybele pugetensis.* Female, upperside. McDonald Fst., Benton Co., Ore. July 15, 1956.

Fig. 6. *Speyeria cybele leto.* Male, upperside. Hurricane Cr., Wallowa Co., Ore. July 24, 1965. Text p. 76. **Map 86.**

Plate 23

Plate 24

Family Nymphalidae

Fig. 1. *Speyeria coronis simaetha*. (a,b) Male, upper and underside. Bear Springs Cmpgd., Wasco Co., Ore. June 25, 1967. Text p. 76. Map 87.

Fig. 2. *Speyeria coronis simaetha*. (a,b) Female, upper and underside. Bear Springs Cmpgd., Wasco Co., Ore. June 25, 1967.

Fig. 3. *Speyeria coronis snyderi*. (a,b) Male, upper and underside. Viewpoint Rd., Ochoco Mts., Crook Co., Ore. July 2, 1961. Text p. 76. **Map** 87.

Fig. 4. *Speyeria coronis snyderi*. (a,b) Female, upper and underside. Maury Mts., Crook Co., Ore. July 31, 1961.

Plate 24

1a 1b
2a 2b
3a 3b
4a 4b

177

Plate 25

Family Nymphalidae

Fig. 1. *Speyeria zerene conchyliatus*. (a,b) Male, upper and underside. Bly Mt., Klamath Co., Ore. June 21, 1958. Text p. 77. Map 88.

Fig. 2. *Speyeria zerene conchyliatus*. (a,b) Female, upper and underside. Crater Lake, Klamath Co., Ore. July 28, 1972.

Fig. 2. *Speyeria zerene conchyliatus* (small form). (a) Male, underside. Gilchrist, Klamath Co., Ore. July 28, 1957. (b) Female, underside. Gilchrist, Klamath Co., Ore. Aug. 9, 1956. Text p. 77.

Fig. 4. *Speyeria zerene gloriosa*. (a,b) Female, upper and underside. McGuire Gulch, Illinois Valley, Josephine Co., Ore. July 4, 1958. Text p. 77. Map 89.

Plate 25

1a 1b

2a 2b

3a 3b

4a 4b

Plate 26

Family Nymphalidae

Fig. 1. *Speyeria zerene behrensii*. (a) Male, underside. Cape Blanco, Curry Co., Ore. Aug. 31, 1973. (b) Female, underside. Cape Blanco, Curry Co., Ore. Aug. 29, 1973. Text p. 77. Map 90.

Fig. 2. *Speyeria zerene hippolyta*. (a,b) Male, upper and underside. Boiler Bay, Lincoln Co., Ore. Aug. 31, 1969. Text p. 77. Map 91.

Fig. 3. *Speyeria zerene hippolyta*. (a,b) Female, upper and underside. Rock Cr., Lane Co., Ore. Sept. 16, 1972.

Fig. 4. *Speyeria zerene bremnerii*. (a) Male, underside. McDonald Fst., Benton Co., Ore. July 1, 1961. (b) Female, underside. McDonald Fst., Benton Co., Ore. July 2, 1960. Text p. 78. Map 92.

Plate 26

Plate 27

Family Nymphalidae

Fig. 1. *Speyeria zerene picta*. (a) Male, underside. Marks Cr. Lodge, Ochoco Mts., Crook Co., Ore. July 20, 1958. (b) Female, underside. Marks Cr. Lodge, Ochoco Mts., Crook Co., Ore. July 20, 1958. Text p. 78. Map 93.

Fig. 2. *Speyeria zerene garretti*. (a) Male, underside. Indian Spgs., Strawberry Mts., Grant Co., Ore. July 20, 1961. (b) Female, underside. Hurricane Cr., Wallowa Co., Ore. July 24, 1965. Text p. 78. Map 93.

Fig. 3. Speyeria zerene gunderi. (a,b) Male, upper and underside. Fish Lake, Steens Mt., Harney Co., Ore. Aug. 5, 1960. Text p. 78. Map 94.

Fig. 4. *Speyeria zerene gunderi*. (a,b) Female, upper and underside. Camas Cr., Warner Mts., Lake Co., Ore. July 31, 1966.

Plate 27

Plate 28

Family Nymphalidae

Fig. 1. *Speyeria callippe semivirida*. (a,b) Male, upper and underside. Sun Pass, Klamath Co., Ore. July 10, 1962. Text p. 78. Map 95.

Fig. 2. *Speyeria callippe semivirida*. (a,b) Female, upper and underside. Sand Cr. at Hwy. 232, Klamath Co., Ore. July 3, 1968.

Fig. 3. *Speyeria callippe semivirida*. (a,b) Male, upper and underside. East Lake, Deschutes Co., Ore. July 9, 1962.

Fig. 4. *Speyeria callippe semivirida*. (a,b) Female, upper and underside. East Lake, Deschutes Co., Ore. July 9, 1962.

Plate 28

1a 1b

2a 2b

3a 3b

4a 4b

185

Plate 29

Family Nymphalidae

Fig. 1. *Speyeria callippe harmonia.* (a,b) Male, upper and underside. Fish Lake, Steens Mt., Harney Co., Ore. July 27, 1962. Text p. 78. Map 96.

Fig. 2. *Speyeria callippe harmonia.* (a,b) Female, upper and underside. Fish Lake, Steens Mt., Harney Co., Ore. July 27, 1962.

Fig. 3. *Speyeria callippe elaine.* (a,b) Male, upper and underside. Siskiyou Pass, Jackson Co., Ore. June 11, 1966. Text p. 79. Map 97.

Fig. 4. *Speyeria callippe elaine.* (a,b) Female, upper and underside. Siskiyou Pass, Jackson Co., Ore. June 19, 1966.

Plate 29

Plate 30

Family Nymphalidae

Fig. 1. *Speyeria egleis oweni.* (a,b) Male, upper and underside. Camas Cr., Warner Mts., Lake Co., Ore. July 31, 1966. Text p. 79. Map 98.

Fig. 2. *Speyeria egleis oweni.* (a,b) Female, upper and underside. Camas Cr., Warner Mts., Lake Co., Ore. July 31, 1966.

Fig. 3. *Speyeria egleis* ssp. ("Sand Creek" form). (a,b) Male, upper and underside. Crescent, Klamath Co., Ore. July 10, 1954. Text p. 79. Map 99.

Fig. 4. *Speyeria egleis* ssp. ("Sand Creek" form). (a,b) Female, upper and underside. Skookum Mdw., Walker Rim, Klamath Co., Ore. Aug. 13, 1964.

Fig. 5. *Speyeria egleis linda.* (a,b) Male, upper and underside. Hurricane Cr., Wallowa Mts., Wallowa Co., Ore. Aug. 24, 1968. Text p. 79. Map 101.

Plate 30

Plate 31

Family Nymphalidae

Fig. 1. *Speyeria egleis macdunnoughi.* (a,b) Male, upper and underside. Pole Spg., Skyline Rd., Umatilla Co., Ore. July 2, 1967. Text p. 79. Map 100.

Fig. 2. *Speyeria egleis macdunnoughi.* (a,b) Female, upper and underside. Viewpoint Rd., Ochoco Mts., Crook Co., Ore. July 14, 1965.

Fig. 3. *Speyeria atlantis dodgei.* (a,b) Male, upper and underside. Marks Cr. Gd. Sta., Ochoco Mts., Crook Co., Ore. July 23, 1962. Text p. 80. Map 102.

Fig. 4. *Speyeria atlantis dodgei.* (a,b) Female, upper and underside. Marks Cr. Lodge, Ochoco Mts., Crook Co., Ore. July 20, 1958.

Plate 31

1a 1b
2a 2b
3a 3b
4a 4b

191

Plate 32

Family Nymphalidae

Fig. 1. *Speyeria hydaspe purpurascens.* (a,b) Male, upper and underside. Tupper Rd., Morrow Co., Ore. July 13, 1961. Text p. 80. Map 103.

Fig. 2. *Speyeria hydaspe purpurascens.* (a,b) Female, upper and underside. Tubb Springs, Jackson Co., Ore. July 8, 1962.

Fig. 3. *Speyeria hydaspe rhodope.* (a,b) Male, upper and underside. McDonald Fst., Benton Co., Ore. July 7, 1961. Text p. 81. Map 104.

Fig. 4. *Speyeria hydaspe rhodope.* (a,b) Female, upper and underside. Mary's Peak, Benton Co., Ore. July 30, 1961.

Plate 32

Plate 33

Family Nymphalidae

Fig. 1. *Speyeria mormonia erinna*. (a,b) Male, upper and underside. Skookum Mdw., Walker Rim, Klamath Co., Ore. July 23, 1961. Text p. 80. Map 105.

Fig. 2. *Speyeria mormonia erinna*. (a,b) Female, upper and underside. Crescent Cr., Klamath Co., Ore. Aug. 17, 1963.

Fig. 3. *Speyeria mormonia artonis*. (a,b) Male, upper and underside. Fish Lake, Steens Mt., Harney Co., Ore. Aug. 5, 1960. Text p. 80. Map 106.

Fig. 4. *Speyeria mormonia artonis*. (a,b) Female, upper and underside. Steens Mt., Harney Co., Ore. July 11, 1961.

Plate 33

Plate 34

Family Riodinidae

Fig. 1. *Apodemia mormo mormonia*. (a,b) Male, upper and underside. Tygh Valley Rd. near Sherar Bridge, Wasco Co., Ore. Sept. 7, 1969. (c,d) Female, upper and underside. Four miles S of Sherar Bridge, Wasco Co., Ore. Sept. 19, 1976. Text p. 84. Map 107.

Family Lycaenidae

Fig. 2. *Habrodais grunus herri*. (a,b) Male, upper and underside. Clear Lake, Wasco Co., Ore. Sept. 19, 1976. (c,d) Female, upper and underside. Clear Lake, Wasco Co., Ore. Aug. 31, 1972. Text p. 86. Map 108.

Fig. 3. *Harkenclenus titus immaculosus*. (a,b) Male, upper and underside. Hurricane Cr., Wallowa Co., Ore. July 24, 1965. (c,d) Female, upper and underside. Devine Cn., Harney Co., Ore. July 18, 1968. Text p. 86. Map 109.

Fig. 4. *Satyrium fuliginosum*. (a,b) Male, upper and underside. Fish Lake, Steens Mt., Harney Co., Ore. Aug. 2, 1961. (c,d) Female, upper and underside. Three Creek Mdw., Deschutes Co., Ore. July 28, 1972. Text p. 86. Map 110.

Fig. 5. *Satyrium behrii behrii*. (a,b) Male, upper and underside. Sand Cr. at Hwy. 232, Klamath Co., Ore. July 25, 1962. (c,d) Female, upper and underside. Gilchrist, Klamath Co., Ore. July 28, 1962. Text p. 87. Map 111.

Fig. 6. *Satyrium tetra*. (a,b) Male, upper and underside. Summer Lake, Lake Co., Ore. Aug. 18, 1962. (c,d) Female, upper and underside. W end of Warner Cn., Lake Co., Ore. Aug. 9, 1970. Text p. 87. Map 112.

Fig. 7. *Satyrium saepium saepium*. (a,b) Male, upper and underside. Sams Valley, Jackson Co., Ore. Reared; larva leg. May 16, 1962. (c,d) Female, upper and underside. Century Drive near Bend, Deschutes Co., Ore. Aug. 7, 1961. Text p. 87. Map 113.

Plate 34

Plate 35

Family Lycaenidae

Fig. 1. *Satyrium sylvinus sylvinus*. (a,b) Male, upper and underside. Catlow Valley, Harney Co., Ore. July 20, 1935. (c,d) Female, upper and underside. Siskiyou Pass, Jackson Co., Ore. July 9, 1969. Text p. 88. Map 114.

Fig. 2. *Satyrium californica*. (a,b) Male, upper and underside. Illinois River Rd. near Store Gulch, Josephine Co., Ore. June 21, 1976. (c,d) Female, upper and underside. Gilchrist, Klamath Co., Ore. July 10, 1960. Text p. 88. Map 115.

Fig. 3. *Strymon melinus setonia*. (a,b) Male, upper and underside. McDonald Fst., Benton Co., Ore. March 25, 1969. (c,d) Female, upper and underside. Kah-Nee-Ta Hot Spgs., Wasco Co., Ore. June 20, 1968. Text p. 88. Map 116.

Fig. 4. *Mitoura spinetorum*. (a,b) Male, upper and underside. Bly Mt., Klamath Co., Ore. July 7, 1962. (c,d) Female, upper and underside. Sand Cr. at Hwy. 232, Klamath Co., Ore. July 10, 1962. Text p. 89. Map 117.

Fig. 5. *Mitoura johnsoni*. (a,b) Male, upper and underside. Lost Pr., Linn Co., Ore. May 23, 1959. (c,d) Female, upper and underside. Lost Pr., Linn Co., Ore. May 23, 1959. Text p. 89. Map 118.

Fig. 6. *Mitoura nelsoni*. (a,b) Male, upper and underside. Lower Metolius Bridge, Jefferson Co., Ore. June 17, 1971. (c,d) Female, upper and underside. Lost Pr., Linn Co., Ore. June 21, 1959. Text p. 89. Map 119.

Plate 35

Plate 36

Family Lycaenidae

Fig. 1. *Incisalia polios obscurus.* (a,b) Male, upper and underside. Shelton, Mason Co., Wash. Apr. 6, 1960. (c,d) Female, upper and underside. Tenino, Thurston Co., Wash. May 11, 1972. Text p. 90. Map 120.

Fig. 2. *Incisalia fotis mossii.* (a,b) Male, upper and underside. Cape Foulweather, Lincoln Co., Ore. Reared; larva leg. Apr. 20, 1969. (c,d) Female, upper and underside. Rickreall Cr. W. of Dallas, Polk Co., Ore. Reared; larva leg. May, 1974. Text p. 90. Map 121.

Fig. 3. *Incisalia augustinus iroides.* (a,b) Male, upper and underside. Barton, Clackamas Co., Ore. Apr. 22, 1962. (c,d) Female, upper and underside. Corvallis, Benton Co., Ore. March 31, 1968. Text p. 91. Map 122.

Fig. 4. *Incisalia eryphon eryphon.* (a,b) Male, upper and underside. Metolius Spgs., Jefferson Co., Ore. May 23, 1959. (c,d) Female, upper and underside. Devine Cn., Harney Co., Ore. June 13, 1964. Text p. 91. Map 123.

Fig. 5. *Callophrys dumetorum dumetorum.* (a,b) Male, upper and underside. Near Alsea, Benton Co., Ore. May 4, 1967. (c,d) Female, upper and underside. McKee Bridge (Ruch-Copper Rd.), Jackson Co., Ore. Reared; female parent leg. May 22, 1971. Text p. 92. Map 124.

Fig. 6. *Callophrys sheridanii lemberti.* (a,b) Male, upper and underside. Mt. Ashland, Jackson Co., Ore. June 19, 1970 (c,d) Female, upper and underside. Mt. Ashland, Jackson Co., Ore. July 3, 1971. Text p. 92. Map 125.

Fig. 7. *Callophrys sherdanii newcomeri.* (a,b) Male, upper and underside. Ten miles N of Yakima, Yakima Co., Wash. March 25, 1960. (c,d) Female, upper and underside. Burns, Harney Co., Ore. Apr. 20, 1964. Text p. 92. Map 126.

Fig. 8. *Callophrys affinis washingtonia.* (a,b) Male, upper and underside. Willow Creek Rd. (Blue Mts.), Union Co., Ore. May 2, 1970. (c,d) Female, upper and underside. Willow Creek Rd. (Blue Mts.), Union Co., Ore. May 10, 1969. Text p. 93. Map 127.

Plate 36

Plate 37

Family Lycaenidae

Fig. 1. *Atlides halesus corcorani*. (a,b) Male, upper and underside. Coffin Butte, Benton Co., Ore. Oct. 3, 1977. (c,d) Female, upper and underside. Butte Falls, Jackson Co., Ore. July 10, 1970. Text p. 93. Map 128.

Fig. 2. *Tharsalea arota arota*. (a,b) Male, upper and underside. W end of Warner Cn., Lake Co., Ore. July 31, 1966. (c,d) Female, upper and underside. Warner Cn., Lake Co., Ore. July 28, 1961. Text p. 93. Map 129.

Fig. 3. *Lycaena rubidus rubidus*. (a,b) Male, upper and underside. Camas Cr., Warner Mts., Lake Co., Ore. July 31, 1966. (c,d) Female, upper and underside. Frenchglen, Harney Co., Ore. Aug. 1, 1961. Text p. 94. Map 130.

Fig. 4. *Lycaena rubidus duofacies*. (a,b) Female, upper and underside. Devine Cn., Harney Co., Ore. Aug. 14, 1971. Text p. 94. Map 130.

Fig. 5. *Lycaena rubidus perkinsorum*. (a,b) Female, upper and underside. The Dalles Dam, Wasco Co., Ore. June 11, 1963. Text p. 94. Map 130.

Fig. 6. *Lycaena heteronea heteronea*. (a,b) Male, upper and underside. Ice Lake, Wallowa Co., Ore. July 24, 1965. (c,d) Female, upper and underside. Fish Lake, Steens Mt., Harney Co., Ore. Aug. 5, 1960. Text p. 94. Map 131.

Fig. 7. *Lycaena heteronea "gravenotata"*. (a,b) Male, upper and underside. Sand Cr. at Hwy. 232, Klamath Co., Ore. July 25, 1962. (c,d) Female, upper and underside. Juniper Flat, Wasco Co., Ore. June 28, 1963. Text p. 95. Map 131.

Plate 37

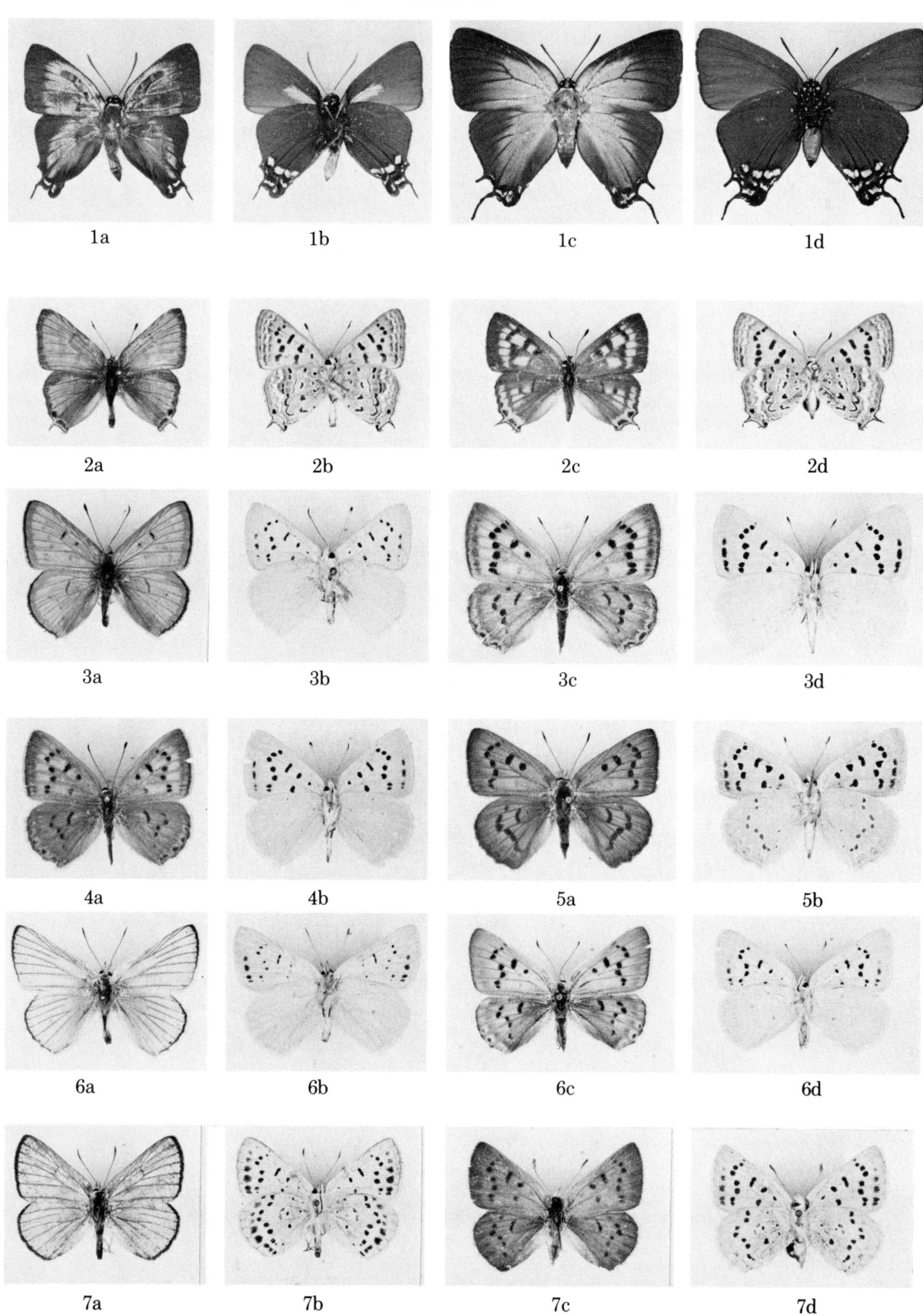

Plate 38

Family Lycaenidae

Fig. 1. *Lycaena xanthoides xanthoides.* (a,b) Male, upper and underside. Siskiyou Pass, Jackson Co., Ore. June 16, 1968. (c,d) Female, upper and underside. Decanso, San Diego Co., Calif. July 5, 1960. Text p. 95. Map 132.

Fig. 2. *Lycaena editha editha.* (a,b) Male, upper and underside. Lostine R., Wallowa Co., Ore. July 22, 1965. (c,d) Female, upper and underside. Gilchrist, Klamath Co., Ore. July 28, 1957. Text p. 95. Map 133.

Fig. 3. *Lycaena gorgon.* (a,b) Male, upper and underside. Illinois River Rd. near Store Gulch, Josephine Co., Ore. June 21, 1976. (c,d) Female, upper and underside. Fst. Rd. 3836 west of $8-Mt. Rd., Josephine Co., Ore. June 23, 1979. Text p. 96. Map 134.

Fig. 4. *Lycaena mariposa mariposa.* (a,b) Male, upper and underside. Camp Sherman, Jefferson Co., Ore. Aug. 16, 1964. (c,d) Female, upper and underside. Monument Peak, Linn Co., Ore. July 16, 1960. Text p. 96. Map 135.

Plate 38

1a 1b 1c 1d

2a 2b 2c 2d

3a 3b 3c 3d

4a 4b 4c 4d

Plate 39

Family Lycaenidae

Fig. 1. *Lycaena helloides.* (a,b) Male, upper and underside. Corvallis, Benton Co., Ore. May 30, 1962. (c,d) Female, upper and underside. Eight-dollar Mt. Rd., 5 mi. SW of Selma, Josephine Co., Ore. May 29, 1978. Text p. 96. Map 136.

Fig. 2. *Lycaena nivalis,* "Form 1". (a,b) Male, upper and underside. Tombstone Pr., Linn Co., Ore. Aug. 11, 1976. (c,d) Female, upper and underside. Tombstone Pr., Linn Co., Ore. Aug. 11, 1976. Text p. 97. Map 137.

Fig. 3. *Lycaena nivalis,* "Form 2". (a,b) Male, upper and underside. Viewpoint Rd., Ochoco Mts., Crook Co., Ore. July 23, 1962. (c,d) Female, upper and underside. Cutsforth Mdw., Morrow Co., Ore. July 9, 1961. Text p. 97. Map 138.

Fig. 4. *Lycaena phlaeas arctodon.* (a,b) Male, upper and underside. Beartooth Pass, Carbon Co., Mont. Aug. 1, 1973. (c,d) Female, upper and underside. Beartooth Pass, Carbon Co., Mont. Aug. 1, 1973. Text p. 97. Map 139.

Fig. 5. *Lycaena phlaeas arctodon.* (a,b) Male, upper and underside. Matterhorn (9500 ft.), Wallowa Mts., Wallowa Co., Ore. Aug. 16, 1964.

Fig. 6. *Lycaena phlaeas hypophlaeas.* (a,b) Female, upper and underside. Mt. Dana, Mono Co., Calif. Aug. 6, 1960. Text p. 97.

Fig. 7. *Lycaena cupreus cupreus.* (a,b) Male, upper and underside. Gilchrist, Klamath Co., Ore. May 24, 1959. (c,d) Female, upper and underside. Gilchrist, Klamath Co., Ore. May 24, 1959. Text p. 98. Map 140.

Plate 39

207

Plate 40
Family Lycaenidae

Fig. 1. *Brephidium exilis.* (a,b) Male, upper and underside. Valley Falls, Lake Co., Ore. Aug. 16, 1967. (c,d) Female, upper and underside. White Horse Ranch, Harney Co., Ore. Aug. 13, 1967. Text p. 98. **Map 141.**

Fig. 2. *Lycaeides argyrognomon ricei.* (a,b) Male, upper and underside. Mt. Hood, Hood River Co., Ore. Aug. 10, 1968. (c,d) Female, upper and underside. Hoodoo Bowl, Santiam Pass, Linn Co., Ore. Aug. 16, 1964. Text p. 98. Map 142.

Fig. 3. *Lycaeides melissa melissa.* (a,b) Male, upper and underside. Marks Creek Lodge, Ochoco Mts., Crook Co., Ore. July 20, 1958. (c,d) Female, upper and underside. Aneroid Lake trail, Wallowa Co., Ore. July 22, 1967. Text p. 99. Map 143.

Fig. 4. *Plebejus saepiolus saepiolus.* (a,b) Male, upper and underside. Aneroid Lake trail, Wallowa Co., Ore. July 25, 1967. (c,d) Female, upper and underside. Fish Lake, Steens Mt., Harney Co., Ore. July 17, 1968. Text p. 99. Map 144.

Fig. 5. *Icaricia icarioides icarioides.* (a,b) Male, upper and underside. Gilchrist, Klamath Co., Ore. June 18, 1960. (c,d) Female, upper and underside. Three-Creek Mdw., Deschutes Co., Ore. Aug. 2, 1974. Text p. 100. Map 145.

Fig. 6. *Icaricia icarioides ardea.* (a,b) Male, upper and underside. Rockville, Malheur Co., Ore. May 18, 1961. Text p. 100. Map 145.

Fig. 7. *Icaricia icarioides pembina.* (a,b) Female, upper and underside. Eagle Cr., near Richland, Baker Co., Ore. July 11, 1960. Text p. 100. Map 145.

Fig. 8. *Icaricia icarioides fenderi.* (a,b) Male, upper and underside. Wren, Benton Co., Ore. May 23, 1937. (c,d) Female, upper and underside. Wren, Benton Co., Ore. May 23, 1937. Text p. 100. Map 145.

Plate 40

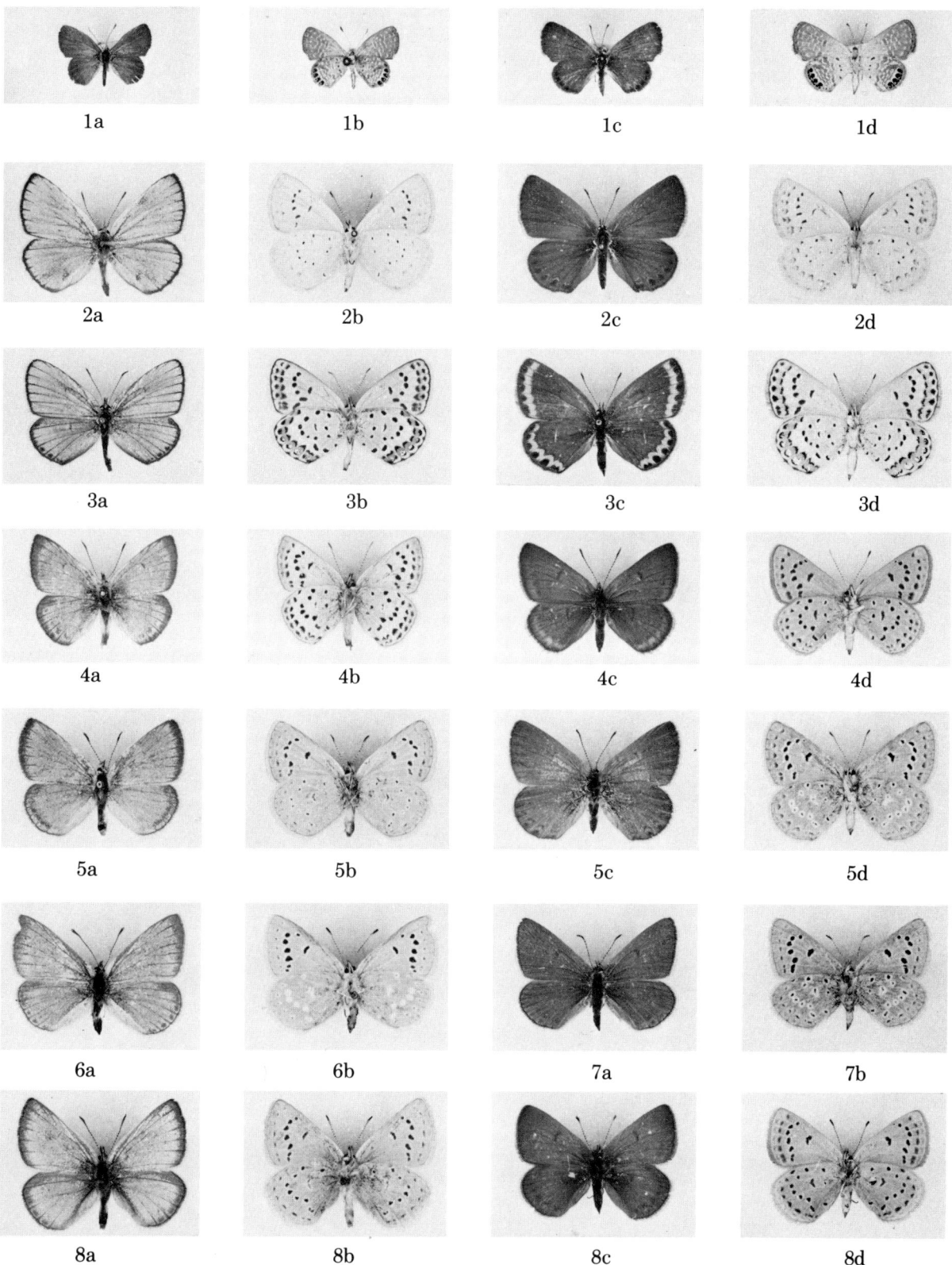

1a 1b 1c 1d
2a 2b 2c 2d
3a 3b 3c 3d
4a 4b 4c 4d
5a 5b 5c 5d
6a 6b 7a 7b
8a 8b 8c 8d

Plate 41

Family Lycaenidae

Fig. 1. *Icaricia shasta shasta.* (a,b) Male, upper and underside. Camp Sherman, Jefferson Co., Ore. July 6, 1972. (c,d) Female, upper and underside. Davis Lake, Deschutes Co., Ore. July 23, 1934. Text p.101. Map 146.

Fig. 2. *Icaricia acmon acmon.* (a,b) Male, upper and underside. Lolo Pass, Mt. Hood, Hood River Co., Ore. July 16, 1958. (c,d) Female, upper and underside. Burns, Harney Co., Ore. June 13, 1964. Text p. 101. Map 147.

Fig. 3. *Icaricia lupini lupini.* (a,b) Male, upper and underside. Sand Cr. at Hwy. 232, Klamath Co., Ore. July 14, 1971. (c,d) Female, upper and underside. Sand Cr. at Hwy. 232, Klamath Co., Ore. June 27, 1965. Text p. 102. Map 148.

Fig. 4. *Agriades aquilo podarce.* (a,b) Male, upper and underside. Mt. Ashland, Jackson Co., Ore. July 11, 1970. (c,d) Female, upper and underside. Mt. Ashland, Jackson Co., Ore. July 11, 1970. Text p. 102. Map 149.

Fig. 5. *Everes comyntas comyntas.* (a,b) Male, upper and underside. McDonald Fst., Benton Co., Ore. May 2, 1958. (c,d) Female, upper and underside. McDonald Fst., Benton Co., Ore. July 15, 1957. Text p. 102. Map 150.

Fig. 6. *Everes amyntula amyntula.* (a,b) Male, upper and underside. Camp Sherman, Jefferson Co., Ore. June 14, 1964. (c,d) Female, upper and underside. Tombstone Pr., Linn Co., Ore. June 15, 1961. Text p. 103. Map 151.

Fig. 7. *Celastrina argiolus echo.* (a,b) Male, upper and underside. McDonald Fst., Benton Co., Ore. Apr. 14, 1964. (c) Female, upperside. Drew, Douglas Co., Ore. June 20, 1966. (d) Spring form "lucia". Male, underside. Willow Creek Rd., Blue Mts., Union Co., Ore. May 16, 1970. Text p. 106. Map 159.

Plate 41

211

Plate 42

Family Lycaenidae

Fig. 1. *Philotes battoides intermedia.* (a,b) Male, upper and underside. Mt. Ashland, Jackson Co., Ore. June 29, 1977. (c,d) Female, upper and underside. Mt. Ashland, Jackson Co., Ore. June 22, 1973. Text p. 104 Map 152.

Fig. 2. *Philotes battoides oregonensis.* (a,b) Male, upper and underside. Sand Cr. at Hwy. 232, Klamath Co., Ore. July 3, 1968. (c,d) Female, upper and underside. Sand Cr. at Hwy. 232, Klamath Co., Ore. July 10, 1962. Text p. 104. Map 153.

Fig. 3. *Philotes battoides glaucon.* (a,b) Male, upper and underside. Devine Cn., Harney Co., Ore. June 29, 1964. (c,d) Female, upper and underside. Steens Mt. summit, Harney Co., Ore. July 17, 1968. Text p. 104. Map 154.

Fig. 4. *Philotes enoptes enoptes.* (a,b) Male, upper and underside. Siskiyou Pass, Jackson Co., Ore. June 16, 1968. (c,d) Female, upper and underside. Eight-Dollar Mt. Rd. near Selma, Josephine Co., Ore. May 31, 1978. Text p. 104. Map 155.

Fig. 5. *Philotes enoptes columbiae.* (a,b) Male, upper and underside. Sherar Falls, Wasco Co., Ore. May 17, 1953. (c,d) Female, upper and underside. 16 miles E of Prineville, Crook Co., Ore. June 9, 1958. Text p. 105. Map 156.

Fig. 6. *Glaucopsyche piasus.* (a,b) Male, upper and underside. Lonerock, Gilliam Co., Ore. June 12, 1965. (c,d) Female, upper and underside. Biggs, Sherman Co., Ore. May 15, 1964. Text p. 105. Map 157.

Fig. 7. *Glaucopsyche lygdamus columbia.* (a,b) Male, upper and underside. Corvallis, Benton Co., Ore. Apr. 28, 1957. (c,d) Female, upper and underside. McDonald Fst., Benton Co., Ore. May 14, 1967. Text p. 105. Map 158.

Plate 42

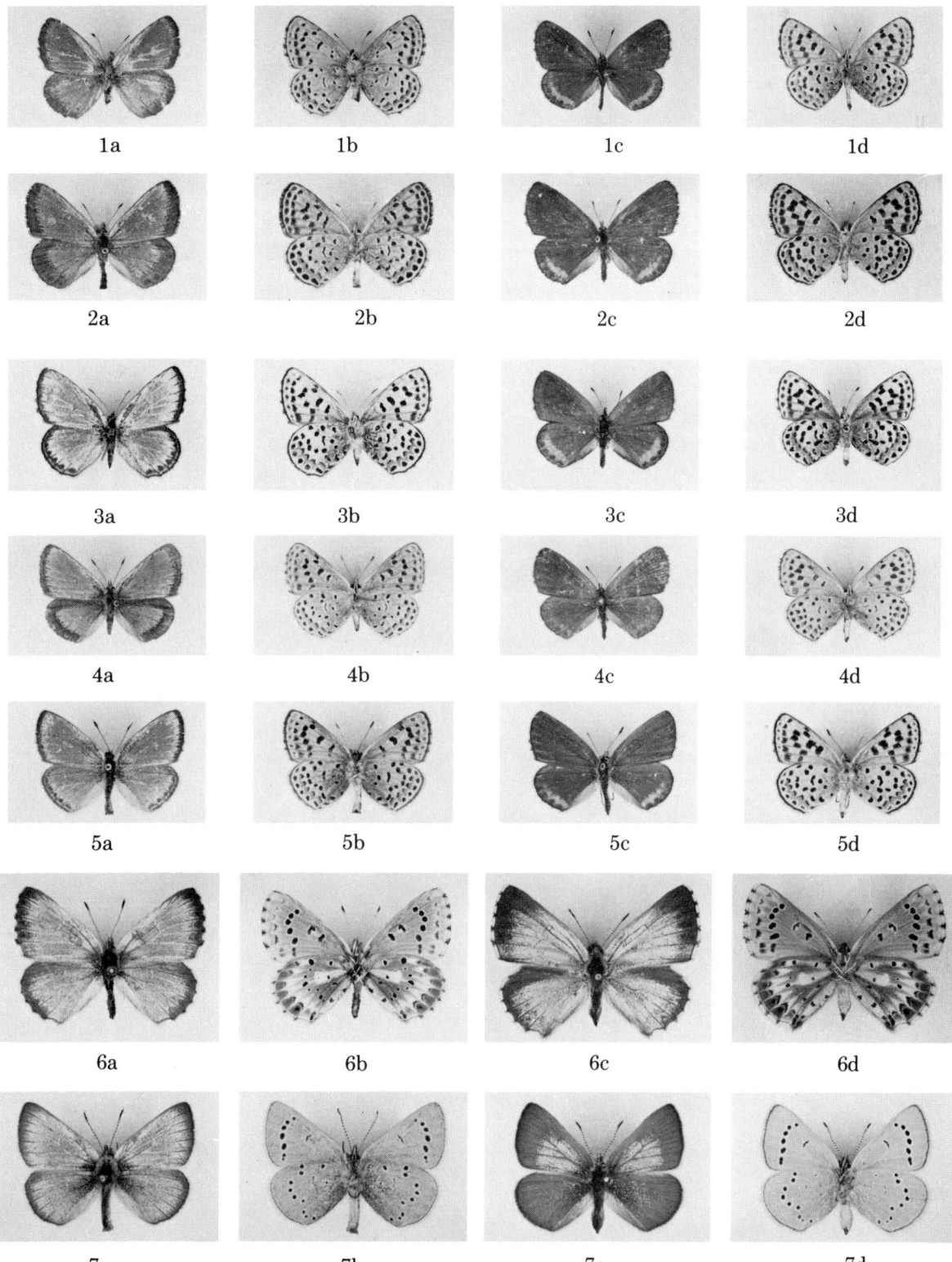

1a 1b 1c 1d
2a 2b 2c 2d
3a 3b 3c 3d
4a 4b 4c 4d
5a 5b 5c 5d
6a 6b 6c 6d
7a 7b 7c 7d

Plate 43

Family Hesperiidae

Fig. 1. *Amblyscirtes vialis*. (a,b) Male, upper and underside. Camp Sherman, Jefferson Co., Ore. June 10, 1962. (c,d) Female, upper and underside. Camp Sherman, Jefferson Co., Ore. June 10, 1962. Text p.108. Map 160.

Fig. 2. *Euphyes vestris vestris*. (a,b) Male, upper and underside. Metolius River, Jefferson Co., Ore. July 9, 1952. (c,d) Female, upper and underside. Camp Sherman, Jefferson Co., Ore. July 28, 1963. Text p. 108. Map 161.

Fig. 3. *Ochlodes sylvanoides sylvanoides*. (a,b) Male, upper and underside. Wallowa Lake, Wallowa Co., Ore. July 26, 1967. (c,d) Female, upper and underside. Corvallis, Benton Co., Ore. Sept. 3, 1961. Text p.108. Map 162.

Fig. 4. *Ochlodes sylvanoides* (dark coastal form). (a,b) Male, upper and underside. Cullaby Lake, Clatsop Co., Ore. Sept. 3, 1957. (c,d) Female, upper and underside. Cape Perpetua Fst. Camp, Lane Co., Ore. Sept. 4, 1963.

Fig. 5. *Ochlodes agricola agricola*. (a,b) Male, upper and underside. Alum Rock Park, Santa Clara Co., Calif. June 7, 1959. (c,d) Female, upper and underside. Big Basin, Santa Cruz Co., Calif. July 6, 1947. Text p. 109. Map 163.

Fig. 6. *Atalopedes campestris*. (a,b) Male, upper and underside. Corvallis, Benton Co., Ore. Sept. 24, 1967. (c,d) Female, upper and underside. Corvallis, Benton Co., Ore. Sept. 24, 1967. Text p. 109. Map 164.

Plate 43

Plate 44

Family Hesperiidae

Fig. 1. *Polites coras*. (a,b) Male, upper and underside. Big Sheep Cr., Wallowa Co., Ore. July 7, 1966. (c,d) Female, upper and underside. Big Sheep Cr., Wallowa Co., Ore. July 7, 1966. Text p. 109. Map 165.

Fig. 2. *Polites sabuleti*. (a,b) Male, upper and underside. Sand Cr. at Hwy. 232, Klamath Co., Ore. Aug. 12, 1964. (c,d) Female, upper and underside. Chemult, Klamath Co., Ore. Aug. 24, 1972. Text p. 110. Map 166.

Fig. 3. *Polites mardon*. (a,b) Male, upper and underside. Gotchen Guard Sta., Pinchot Nat. Fst., Yakima Co., Wash. June 30, 1978. (c,d) Female, upper and underside. Gotchen Guard Sta., Pinchot Nat. Fst., Yakima Co., Wash. June 30, 1978. Text p. 110. Map 167.

Fig. 4. *Polites themistocles*. (a,b) Male, upper and underside. 7 mi. ESE of Oroville, Okanogan Co., Wash. June 26, 1977. (c,d) Female, upper and underside. 7 mi. ESE of Oroville, Okanogan Co., Wash. June 26, 1977. Text p. 110. Map 168.

Fig. 5. *Polites mystic*. (a,b) Male, upper and underside. Tiger Mdws., Pend Oreille Co., Wash. June 29, 1977. (c,d) Female, upper and underside. Tiger Mdws., Pend Oreille Co., Wash. June 29, 1977. Text p. 111. Map 169.

Fig. 6. *Polites sonora siris*. (a,b) Male, upper and underside. Viewpoint Rd. off Hwy. 26, Ochoco Mts., Crook Co., Ore. July 2, 1968. (c,d) Female, upper and underside. Camp Sherman, Jefferson Co., Ore. July 29, 1971. Text p. 111. Map 170.

Plate 44

217

Plate 45

Family Hesperiidae

Fig. 1. *Hesperia uncas*. (a,b) Male, upper and underside. Owyhee River Cn., Malheur Co., Ore. May 24, 1978. (c,d) Female, upper and underside. Frenchglen, Harney Co., Ore. June 1, 1973. Text p. 112. Map 171.

Fig. 2. *Hesperia juba*. (a,b) Male, upper and underside. Paulina Lake, Deschutes Co., Ore. Aug. 21, 1961. (c,d) Female, upper and underside. Lost Prairie, Linn Co., Ore. June 15, 1961. Text p. 112. Map 172.

Fig. 3. *Hesperia comma harpalus*. (a,b) Male, upper and underside. Frenchglen, Harney Co., Ore. Aug. 1, 1961. (c,d) Female, upper and underside. Paulina Cr., Deschutes Co., Ore. Aug. 21, 1961. Text p. 113. Map 173.

Fig. 4. *Hesperia comma oregonia*. (a,b) Male, upper and underside. Mule Prairie, Hwy. 58, Lane Co., Ore. Aug. 10, 1970. (c,d) Female, upper and underside. Diamond L., Douglas Co., Ore. Aug. 17, 1956. Text p. 113. Map 174.

Fig. 5. *Hesperia columbia*. (a,b) Male, upper and underside. Eight-dollar Mt. Rd., Josephine Co., Ore. May 31, 1978. (c,d) Female, upper and underside. Eight-dollar Mt. Rd., Josephine Co., Ore. May 31, 1978. Text p. 113. Map 175.

Fig. 6. *Hesperia lindseyi*. (a,b) Male, upper and underside. Siskiyou Pass, Jackson Co., Ore. June 16, 1968. (c,d) Female, upper and underside. Siskiyou Pass, Jackson Co., Ore. June 16, 1968. Text p. 114. Map 176.

Fig. 7. *Hesperia nevada*. (a,b) Male, upper and underside. Signal Peak, Yakima Co., Wash. July 6, 1964. (c,d) Female, upper and underside. Signal Peak, Yakima Co., Wash. July 6, 1964. Text p. 114. Map 177.

Plate 45

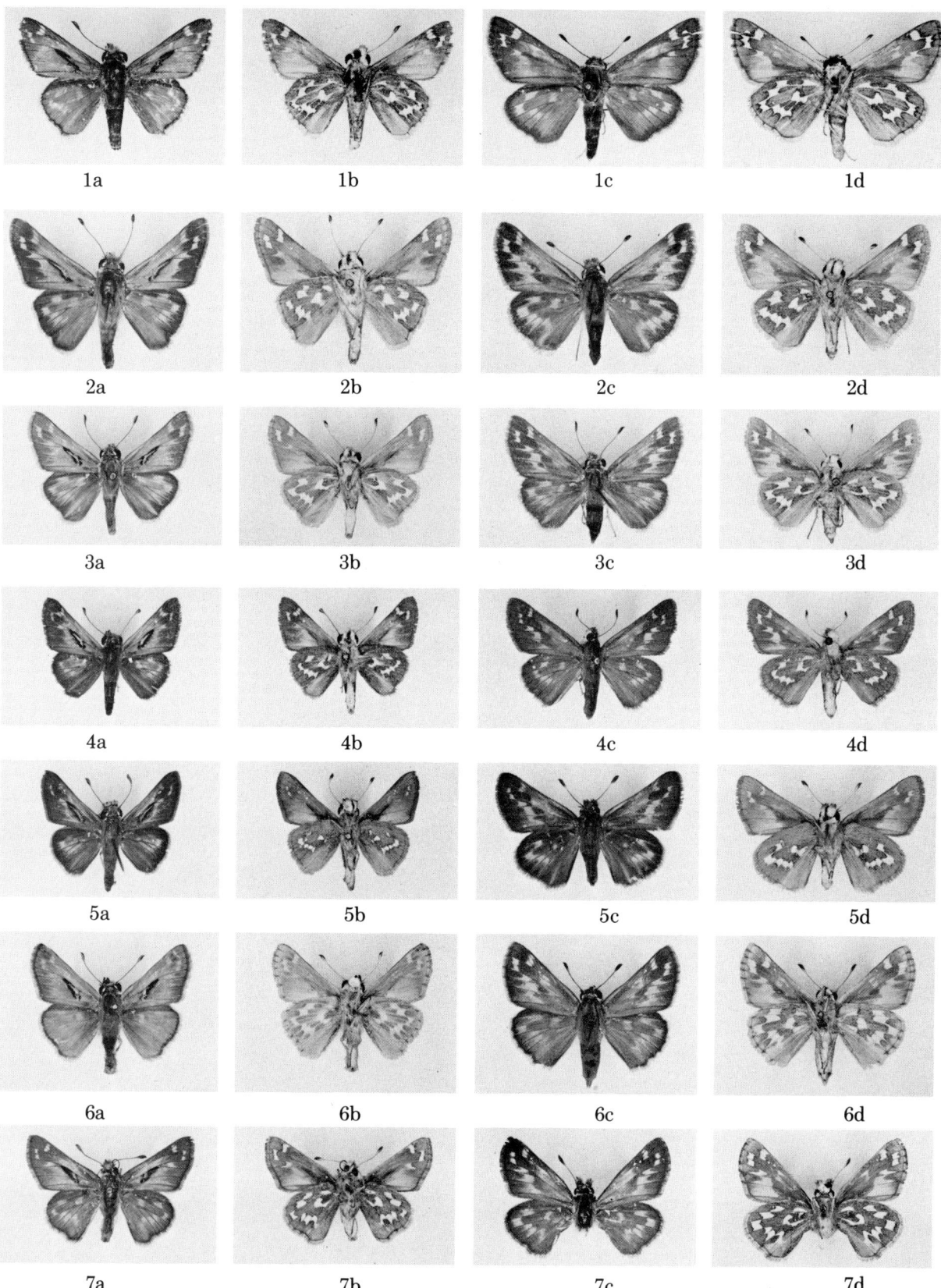

Plate 46

Family Hesperiidae

Fig. 1. *Carterocephalus palaemon mandan*. (a,b) Male, upper and underside. Gilchrist, Klamath Co., Ore. June 18, 1960. (c,d) Female, upper and underside. Marion Forks, Linn Co., Ore. June 14, 1964. Text p. 114. Map 178.

Fig. 2. *Pholisora catullus*. (a,b) Male, upper and underside. The Dalles, Wasco Co., Ore. June 23, 1963. (c,d) Female, upper and underside. Juntura, Malheur Co., Ore. July 15, 1965. Text p. 115. Map 179.

Fig. 3. *Pholisora libya lena*. (a,b) Male, upper and underside. 4 mi. N of Denio, Harney Co., Ore. July 2, 1978. (c,d) Female, upper and underside. Alvord Desert, Harney Co., Ore. July 12, 1979. Text p.115. Map 180.

Fig. 4. *Pholisora alpheus oricus*. (a,b) Male, upper and underside. 6 mi. SE of Lucerne Valley, San Bernardino Co., Calif. Apr. 15, 1964. (c,d) Female, upper and underside. Lee Cn., Spring Mts., Clark Co., Nev. May 4, 1967. Text p. 115. Map 181.

Fig. 5. *Heliopetes ericetorum*. (a,b) Male, upper and underside. Hermiston, Umatilla Co., Ore. Sept. 14, 1967. (c,d) Female, upper and underside. Oak Cr. off White Pass Hwy., Yakima Co., Wash. June 13, 1960. Text Text p. 116. Map 182.

Fig. 6. *Pyrgus ruralis*. (a,b) Male, upper and underside. McDonald Fst., Benton Co., Ore. May 5, 1957. (c,d) Female, upper and underside. Alsea Fish Hatchery, Benton Co., Ore. Apr. 11, 1965. Text p.116. Map 183.

Fig. 7. *Pyrgus communis communis*. (a,b) Male, upper and underside. Dayville, Grant Co., Ore. July 14, 1978. (c,d) Female, upper and underside. Gilchrist, Klamath Co., Ore. June 17, 1957. Text p. 116. Map 184.

Plate 46

Plate 47

Family Hesperiidae

Fig. 1. *Erynnis icelus*. (a,b) Male, upper and underside. North Pine Cr., Baker Co., Ore. June 20, 1959. (c) Female, upperside. Satus Pass, Klickitat Co., Wash. June 12, 1959. Text p. 117. Map 185.

Fig. 2. *Erynnis persius persius*. (a,b) Male, upper and underside. Camp Sherman, Jefferson Co., Ore. May 31, 1970. (c) Female, upperside. Camp Sherman, Jefferson Co., Ore. May 31, 1970. Text p. 117. Map 186.

Fig. 3. *Erynnis pacuvius lilius*. (a,b) Male, upper and underside. Gilchrist, Klamath Co., Ore. June 15, 1958. (c) Female, upperside. Gilchrist, Klamath Co., Ore. June 15, 1959. Text p. 118. Map 187.

Fig. 4. *Erynnis propertius*. (a,b) Male, upper and underside. Long Prairie, 10 mi. E of Pinehurst, Klamath Co., Ore. June 17, 1958. (c) Female, upperside. McDonald Fst., Benton Co., Ore. May 20, 1959. Text p. 118. Map 188.

Fig. 5. *Erynnis funeralis*. (a,b) Male, upper and underside. Palms-Cheviot Hills, W. Los Angeles, Los Angeles Co., Calif. Aug. 24, 1955. (c) Female, upperside. 6 mi. E of Banner, San Diego Co., Calif. June 26, 1963. Text p. 118. Map 189.

Plate 47

1a 1b 1c
2a 2b 2c
3a 3b 3c
4a 4b 4c
5a 5b 5c

Plate 48

Family Hesperiidae

Fig. 1. *Thorybes pylades.* (a,b) Male, upper and underside. Simnasho Rd., Warm Springs Res., Wasco Co., Ore. May 11, 1968. (c) Female, upperside. Siskiyou Pass, Jackson Co., Ore. July 3, 1971. Text p. 119. Map 190.

Fig. 2. *Thorybes mexicana nevada.* (a,b) Male, upper and underside. Three-Creeks Mdw., Deschutes Co., Ore. July 6, 1973. (c) Female, upperside. Elk Lake, Deschutes Co., Ore. June 30, 1963. Text p. 119. Map 191.

Fig. 3. *Thorybes diversus.* (a,b) Male, upper and underside. Ackerson Mdws., Tuolumne Co., Calif. June 12, 1961. (c) Female, upperside. Scott Mt., Trinity Co., Calif. July 5, 1963. Text p. 119. Map 191.

Fig. 4. *Epargyreus clarus californicus.* (a,b) Male, upper and underside. Hoskins, Benton Co., Ore. June 1, 1958. (c) Female, upperside. Spanish Hollow, Sherman Co., Ore. April 27, 1968. Text p. 120. Map 192.

Addendum, Family Nymphalidae

Fig. 5. *Chlosyne leanira alma.* (a,b) Male, upper and underside. Alvord Desert, Harney Co., Ore. May 26, 1979. (c,d) Female, upper and underside. Alvord Desert, Harney Co., Ore. May 26, 1979. Text p. 70. **Map** 67.

Plate 48

Distribution Maps

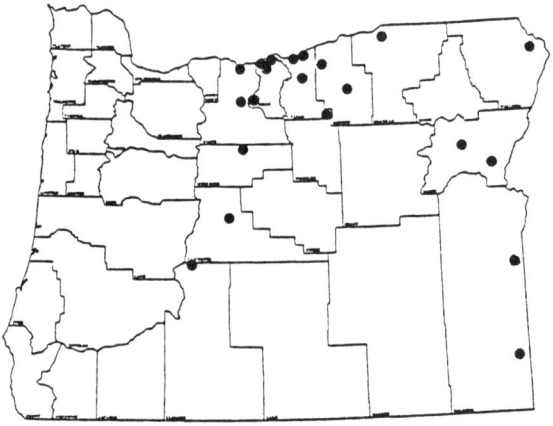
1. Papilio oregonius

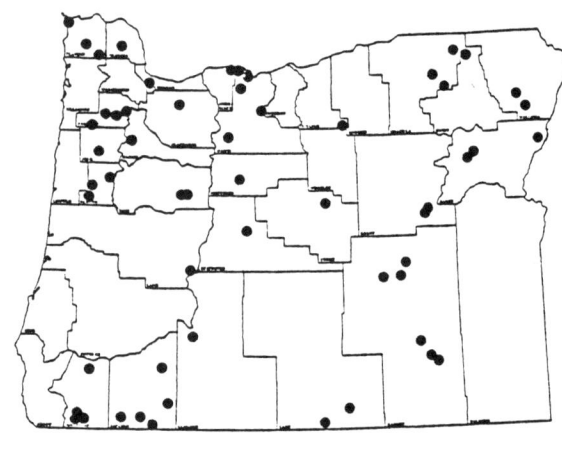
2. Papilio zelicaon

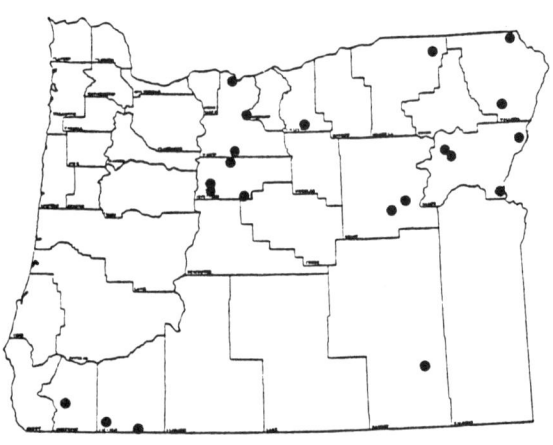
3. Papilio indra indra

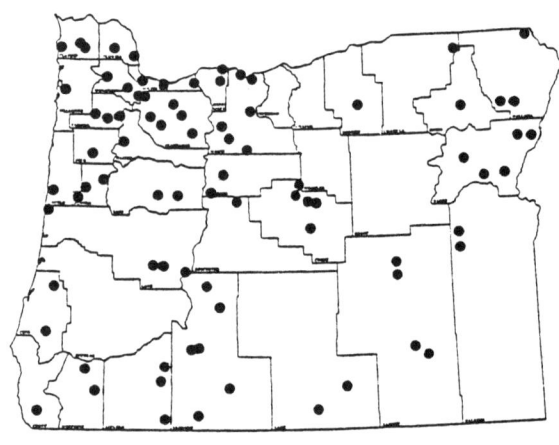
4. Papilio rutulus rutulus

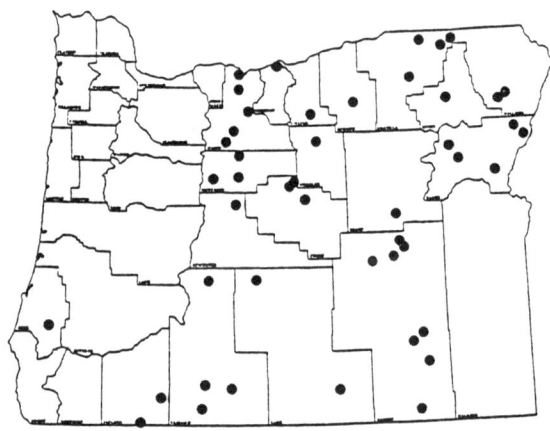
5. Papilio multicaudata

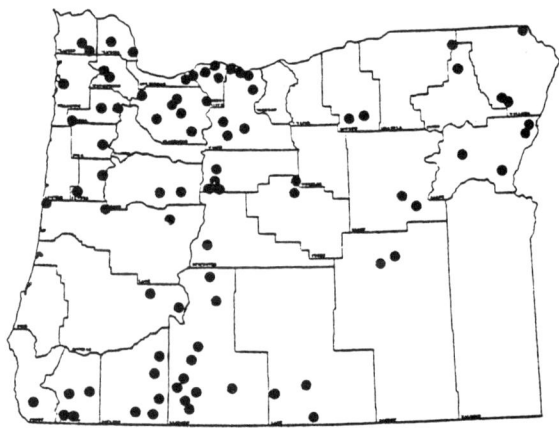
6. Papilio eurymedon

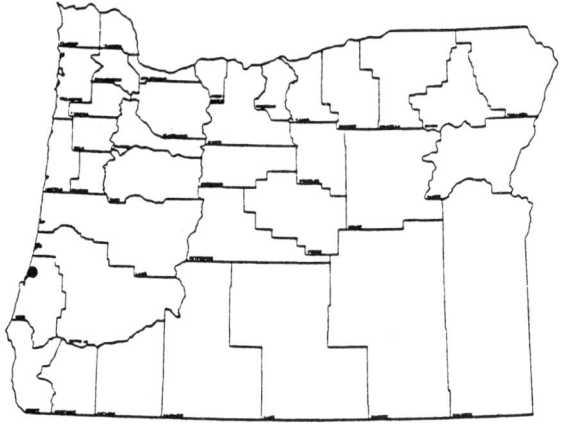
7. Battus philenor hirsuta

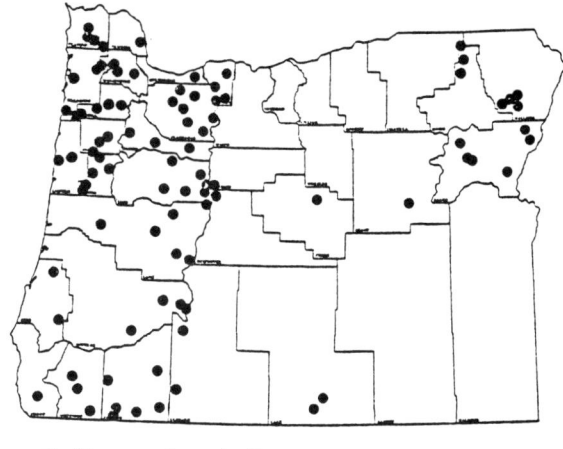
8. Parnassius clodius

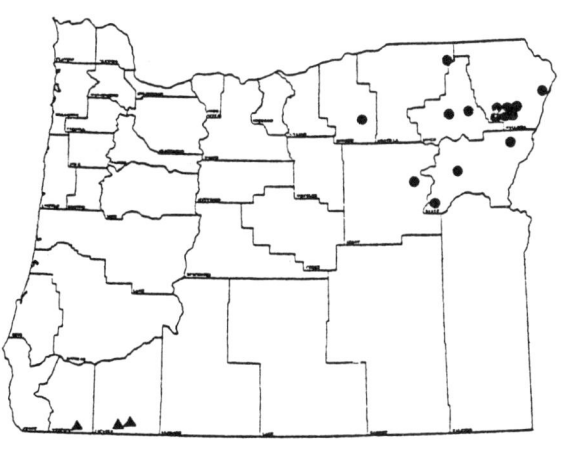
9. Parnassius phoebus xanthus   ●
     "   "   sternitzkii ▲

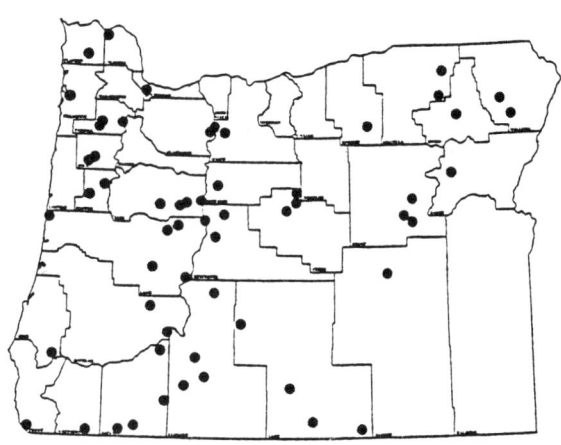
10. Neophasia menapia tau

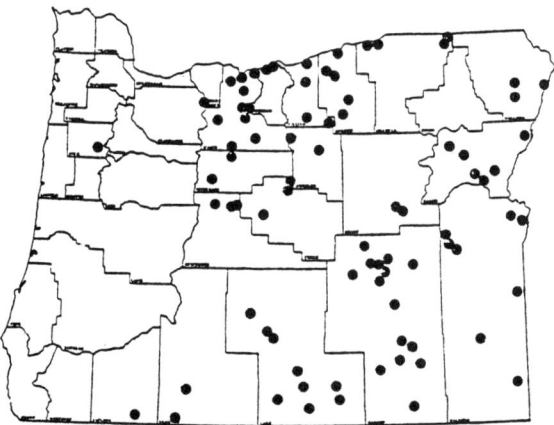
11. Pieris beckerii

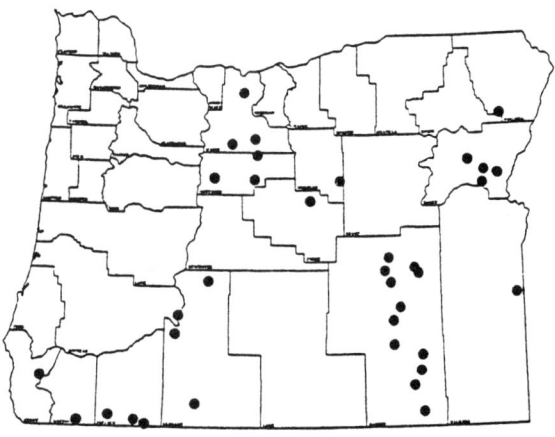
12. Pieris sisymbrii

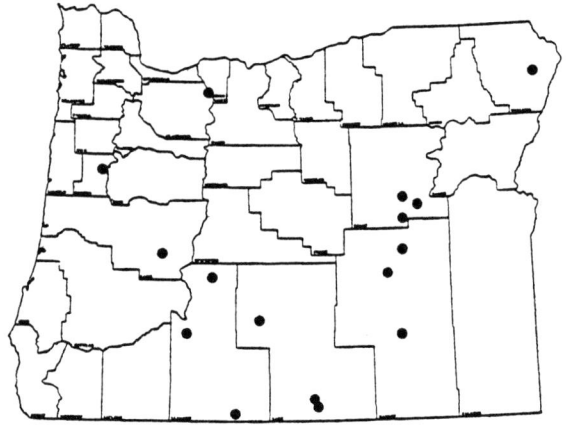

13. Pieris protodice

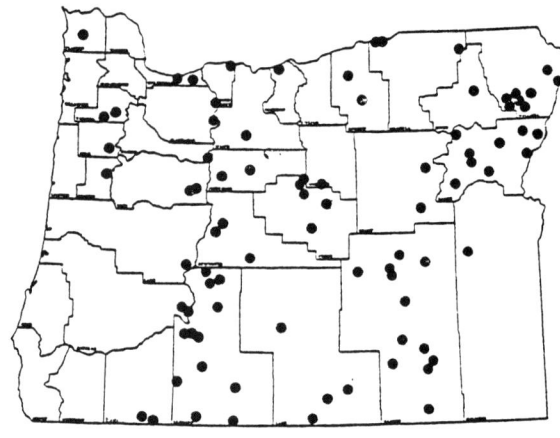

14. Pieris occidentalis

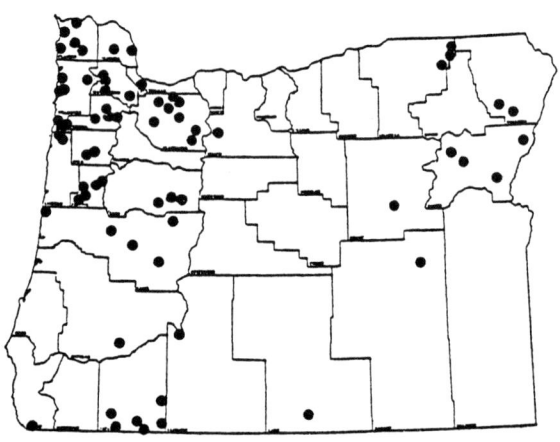

15. Pieris napi

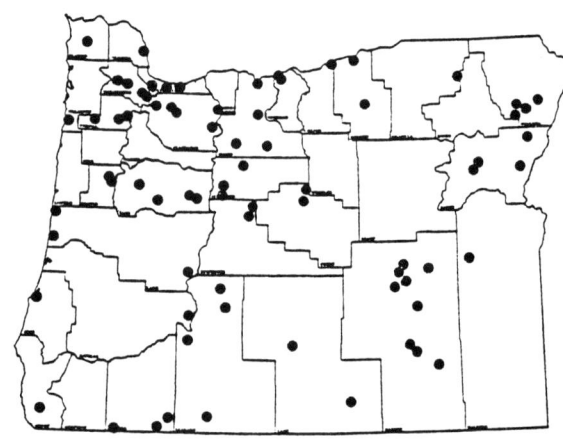

16. Pieris rapae

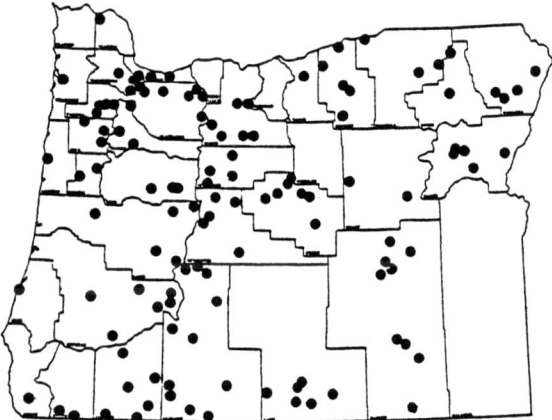

17. Colias eurytheme eurytheme

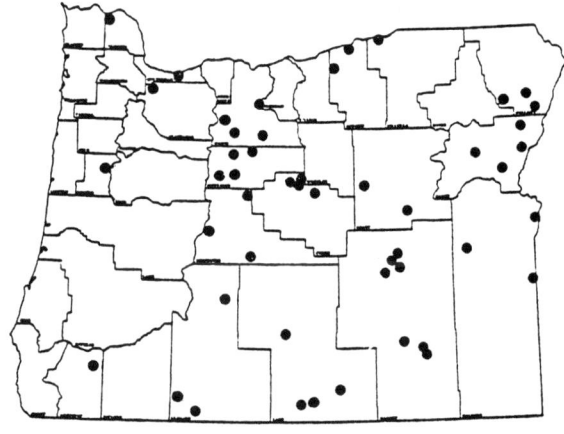

18. Colias philodice eriphyle

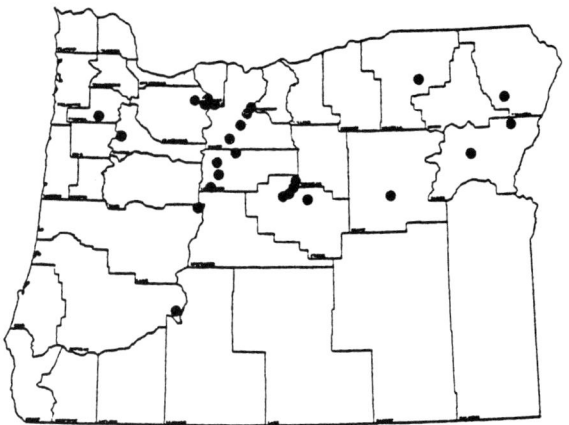

19. Colias occidentalis occidentalis

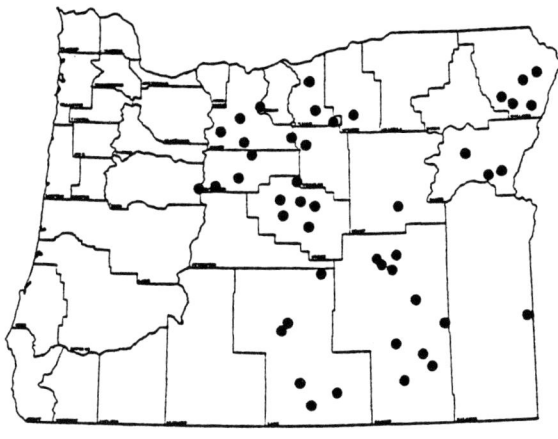

20. Colias alexandra edwardsii

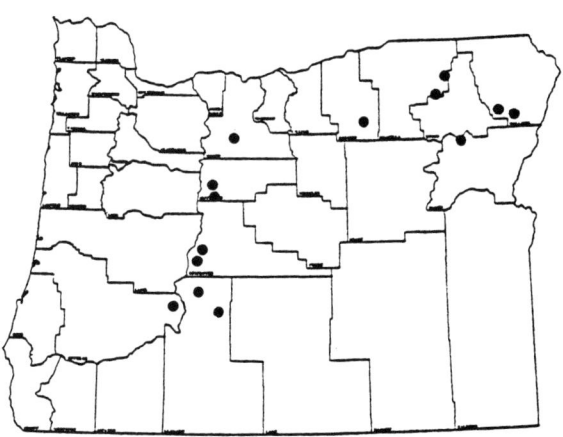

21. Colias interior interior

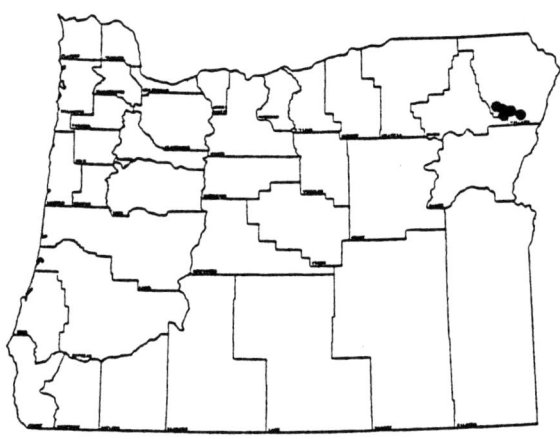

22. Colias pelidne skinneri

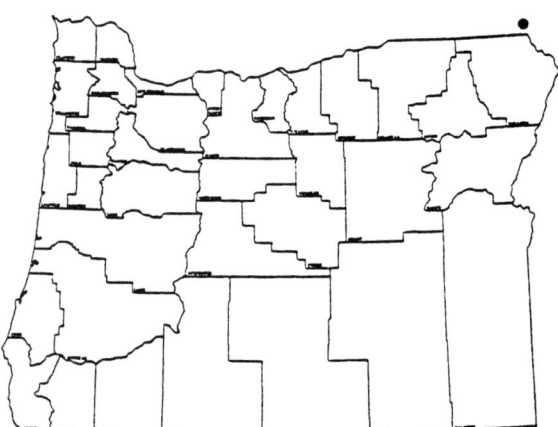

23. Nathalis iole

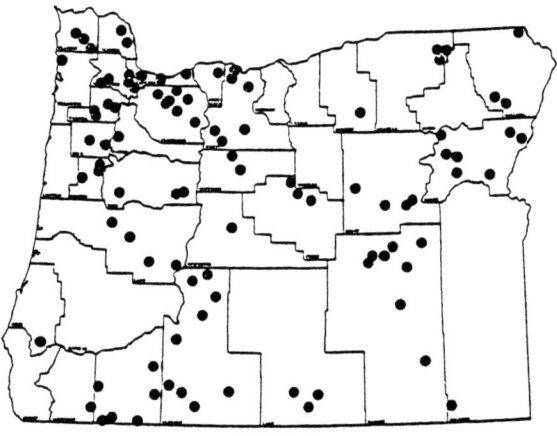

24. Anthocharis sara

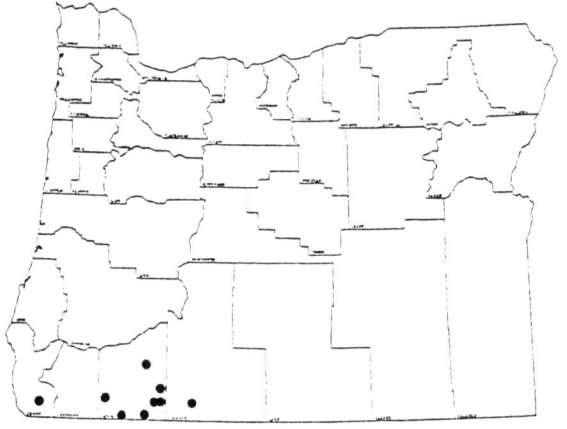
25. Anthocharis lanceolata lanceolata

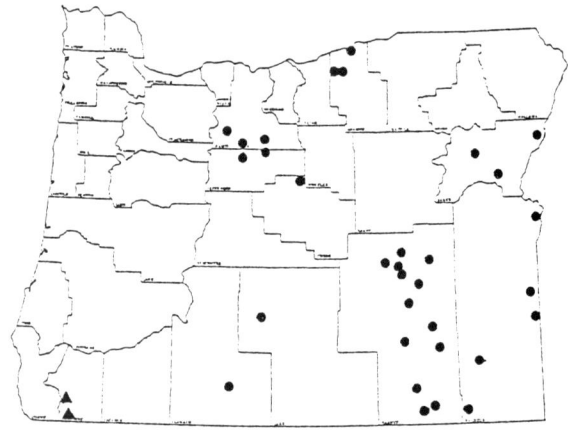
26. Euchloe hyantis lotta

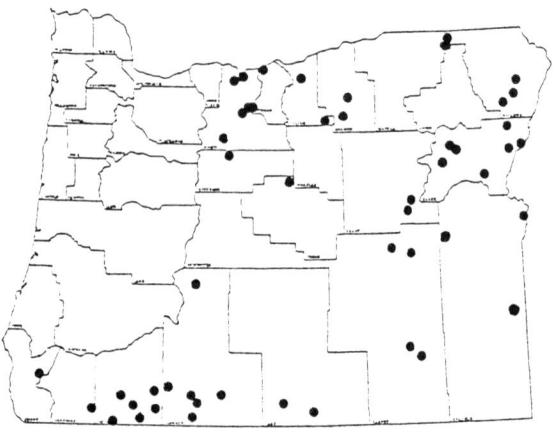
27. Euchloe ausonides ausonides

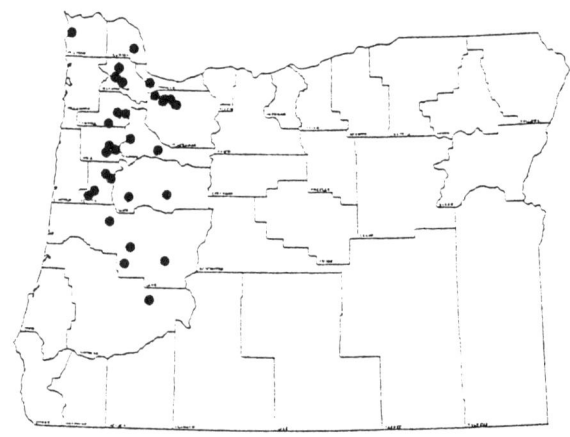
28. Coenonympha tullia eunomia

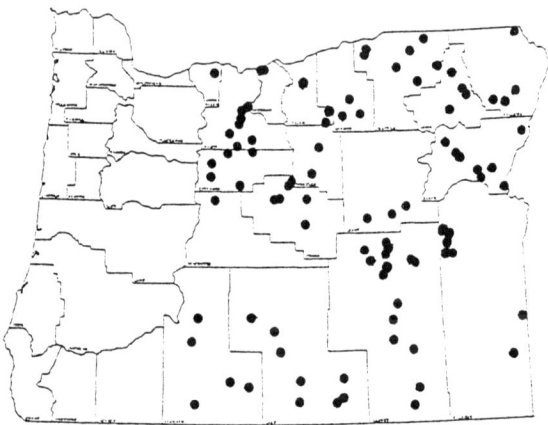
29. Coenonympha tullia ampelos

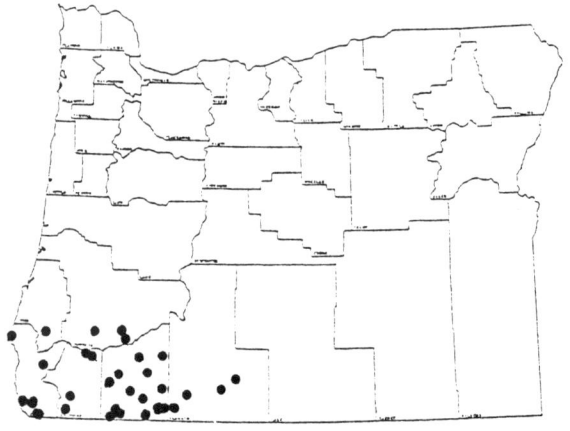
30. Coenonympha tullia eryngii

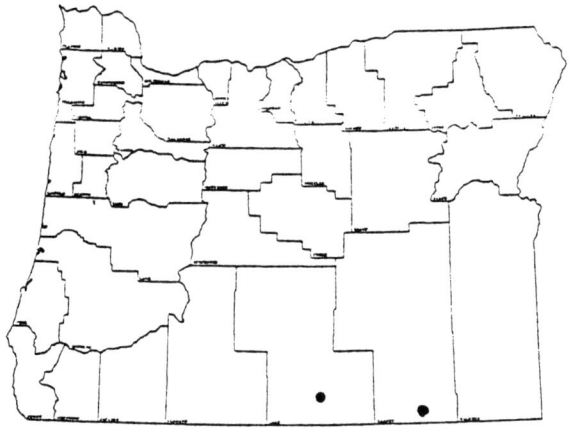

31. Neominois ridingsii stretchii

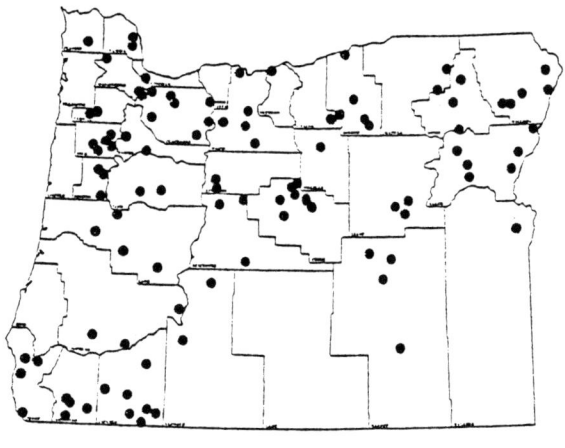

32. Cercyonis pegala boopis

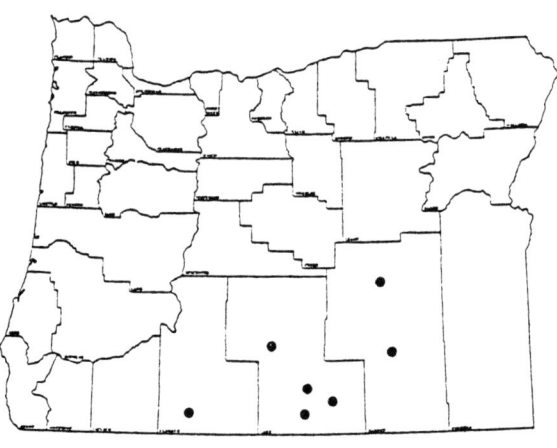

33. Cercyonis pegala ariane

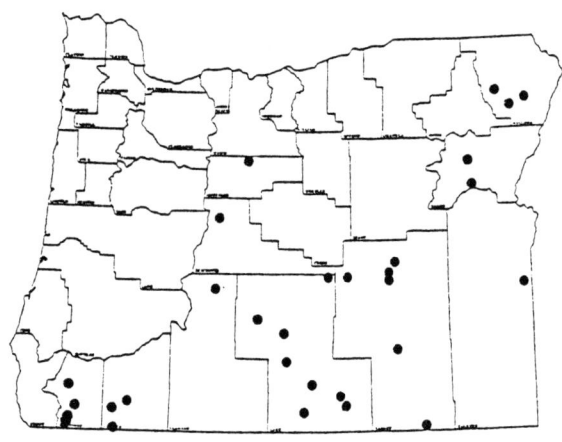

34. Cercyonis sthenele

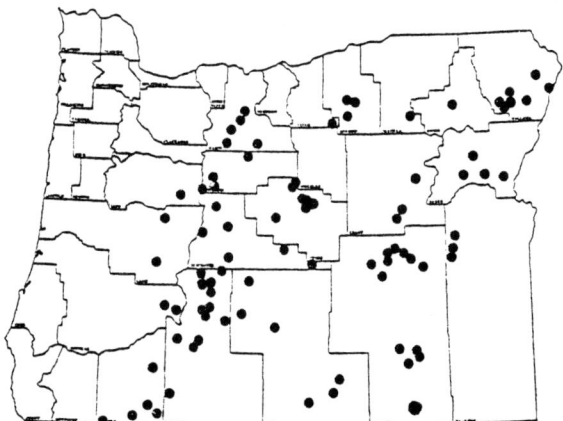

35. Cercyonis oetus oetus

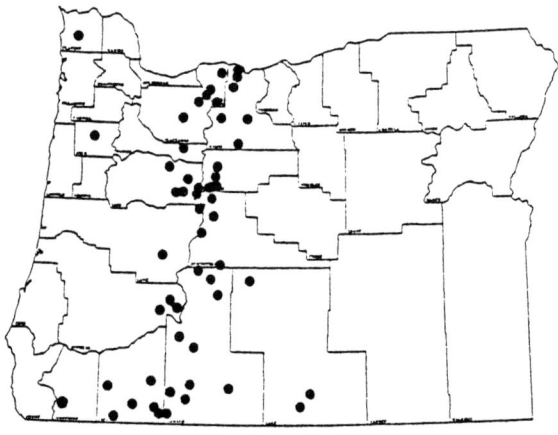

36. Oeneis nevadensis

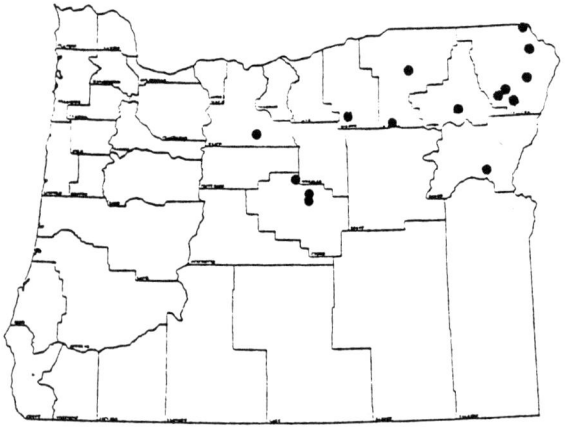
37. Erebia epipsodea hopfingeri

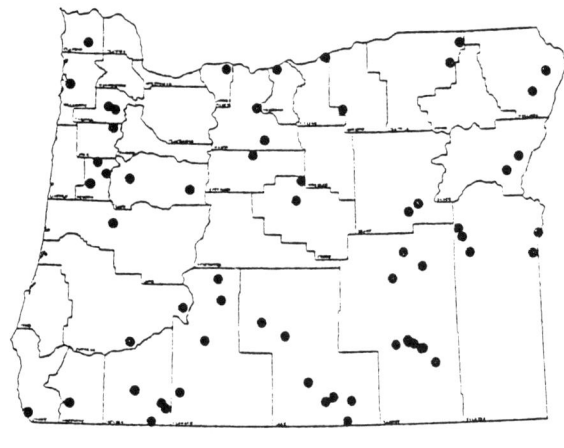
38. Danaus plexippus

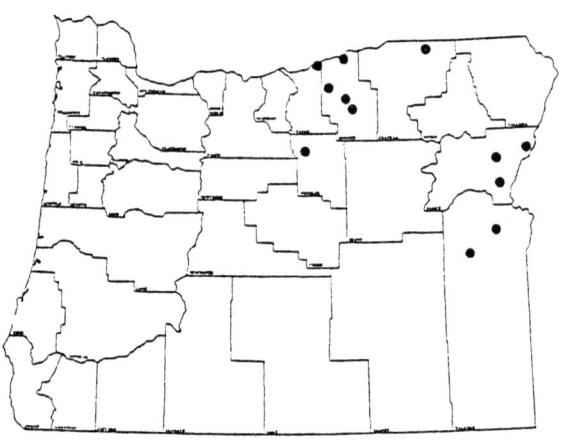
39. Limenitis archippus

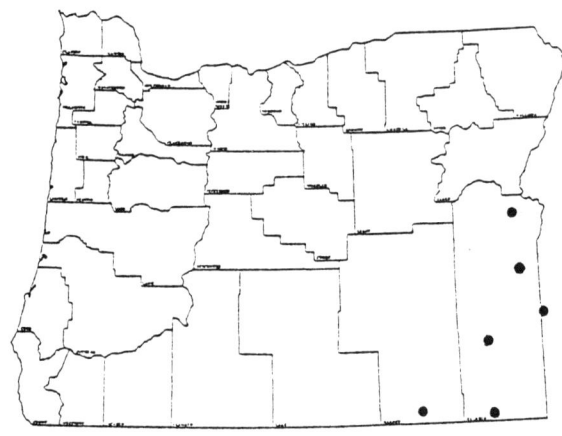
40. Limenitis weidemeyerii

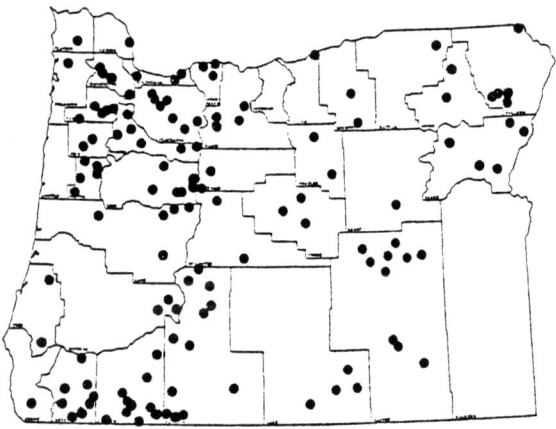
41. Limenitis lorquini

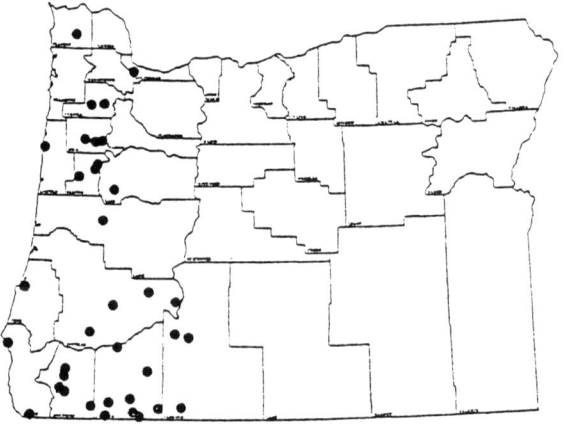
42. Adelpha bredowii californica

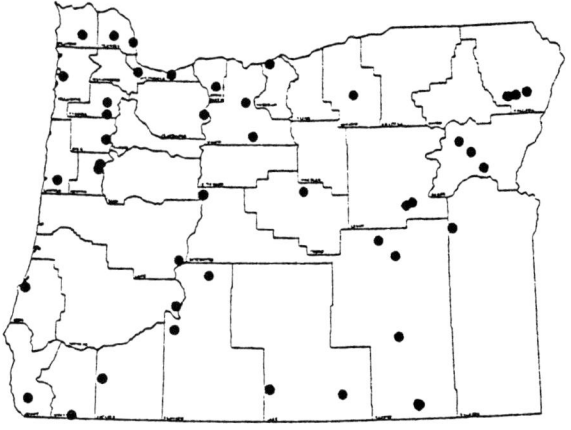
43. Vanessa atalanta rubria

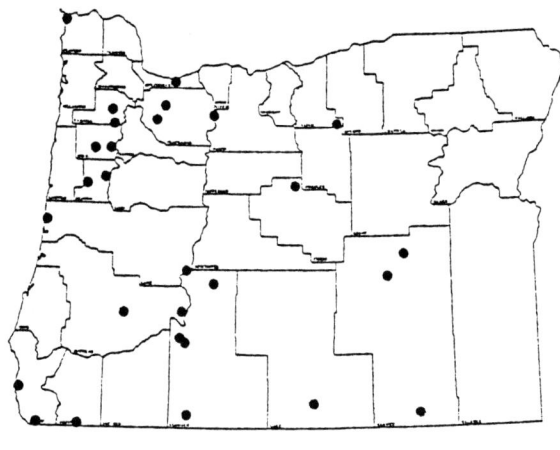
44. Vanessa virginiensis

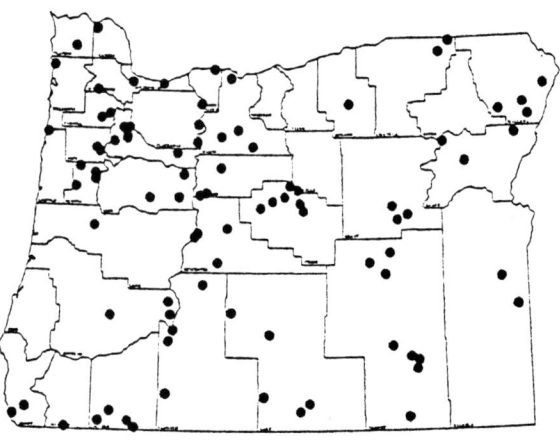
45. Vanessa cardui

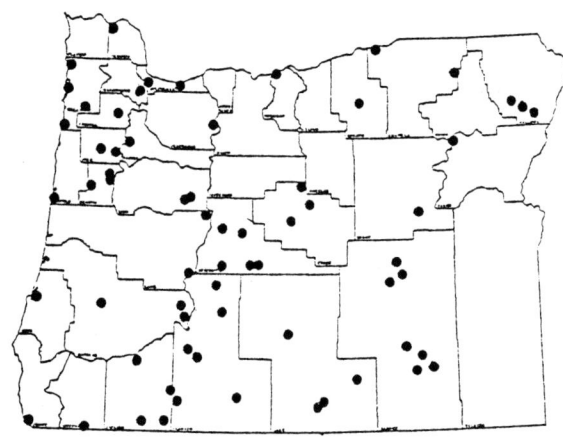
46. Vanessa annabella

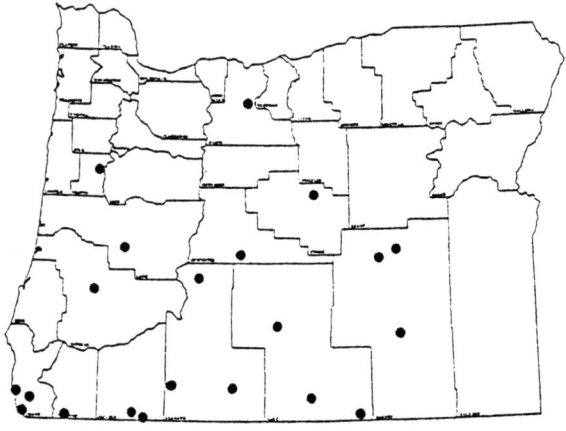
47. Junonia coenia coenia

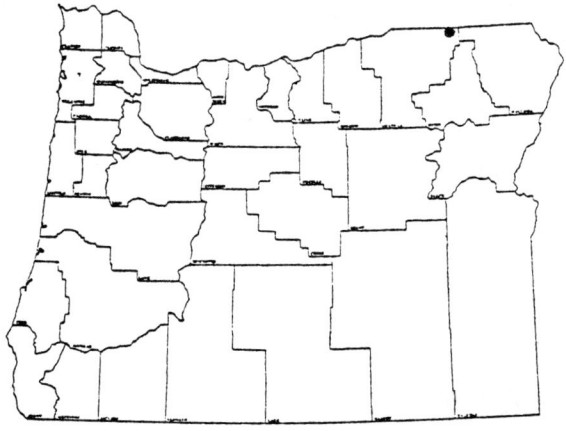
48. Nymphalis vau-album watsoni

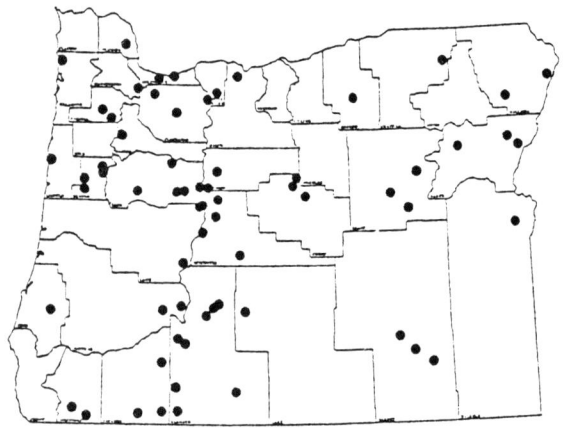
49. Nymphalis californica

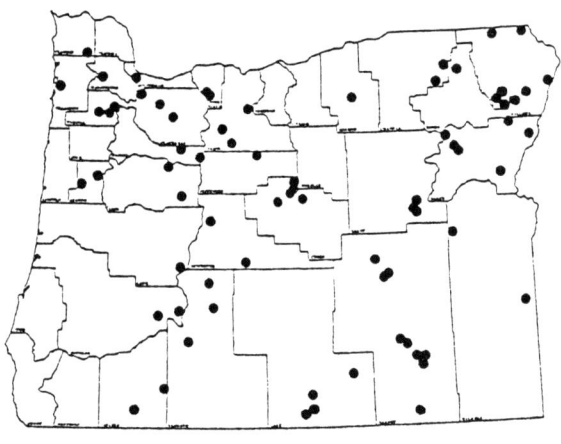
50. Nymphalis milberti furcillata

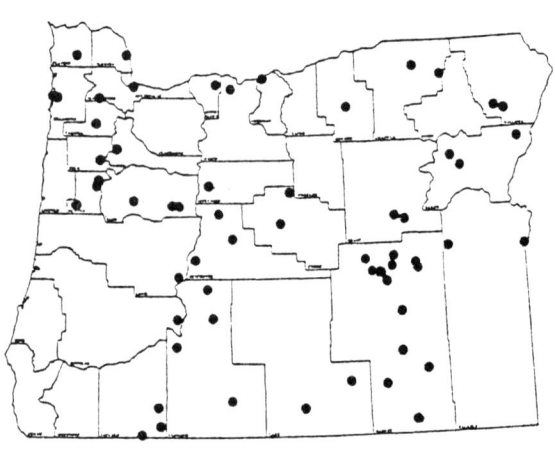
51. Nymphalis antiopa

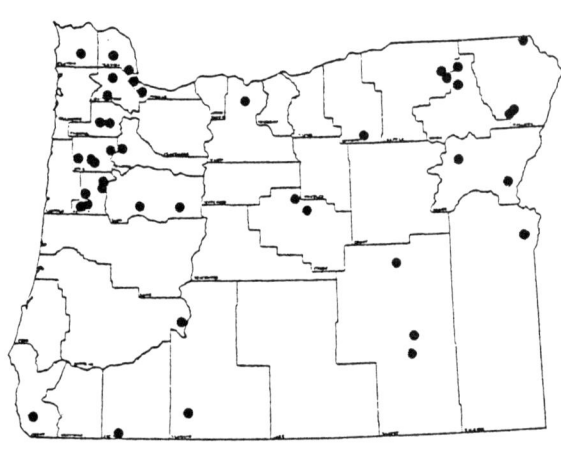
52. Polygonia satyrus neomarsyas

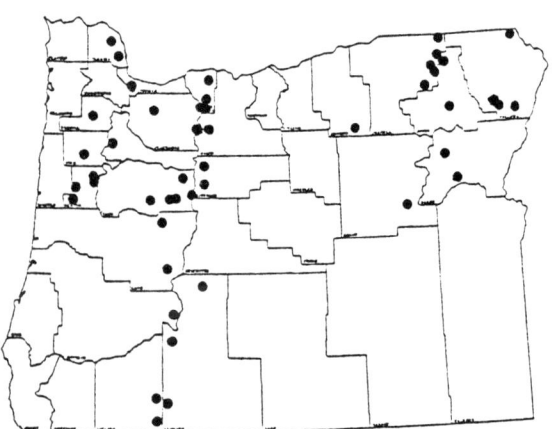
53. Polygonia faunus rusticus

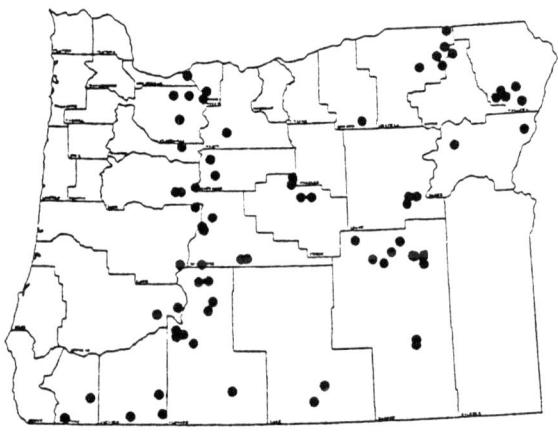
54. Polygonia zephyrus

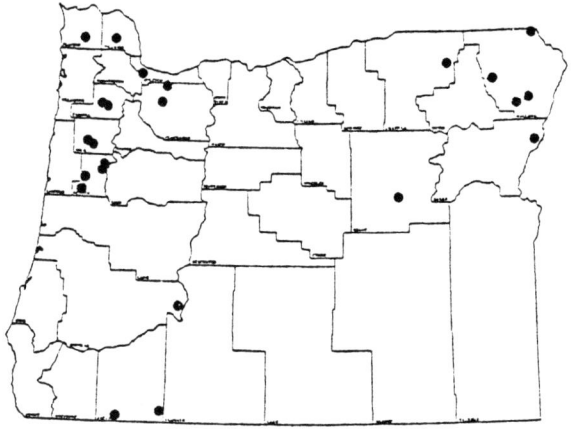
55. Polygonia oreas silenus

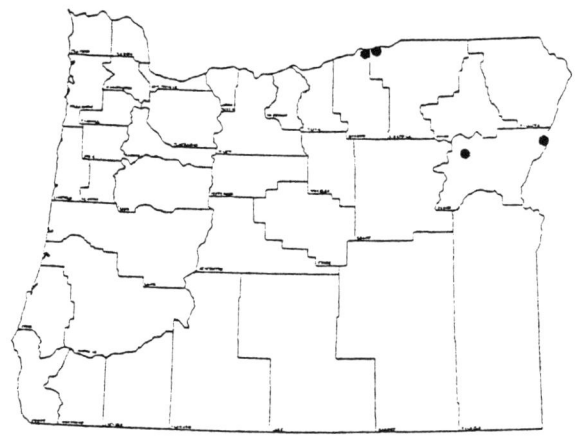
56. Phyciodes tharos pascoensis

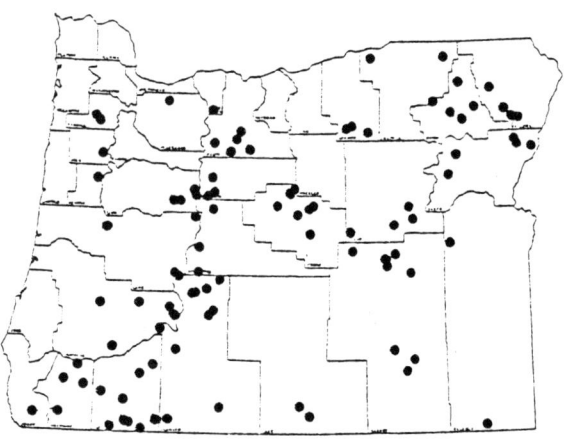
57. Phyciodes campestris campestris

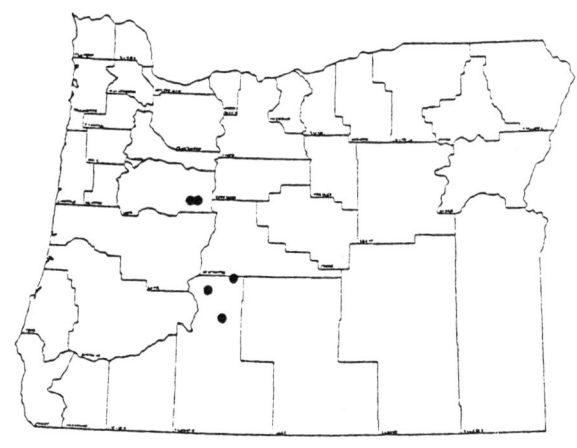
58. Phyciodes campestris montana

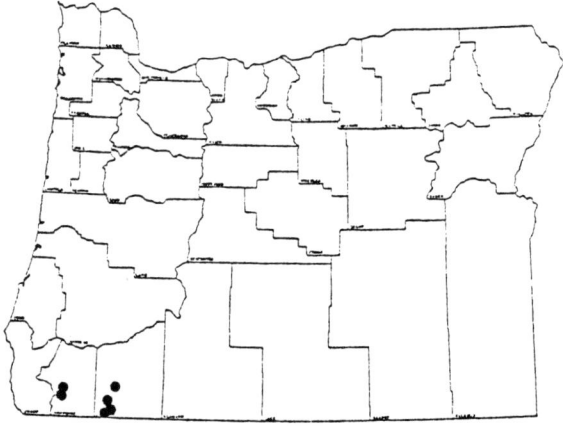
59. Phyciodes orseis orseis

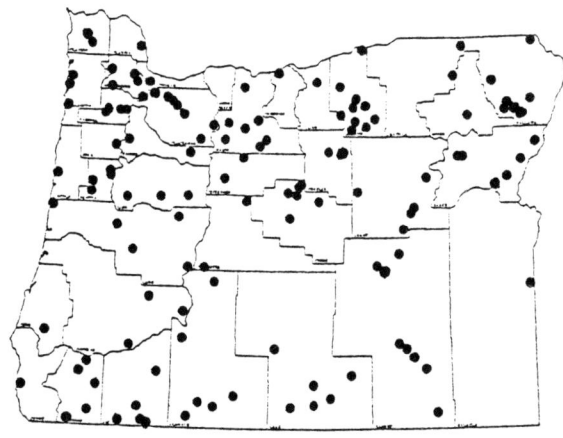
60. Phyciodes mylitta mylitta

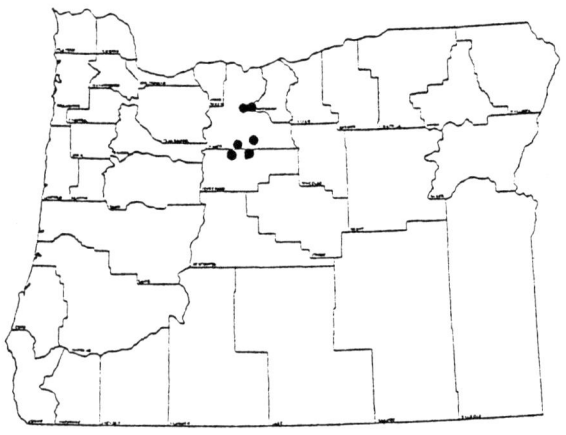

61. Phyciodes pallida barnesi

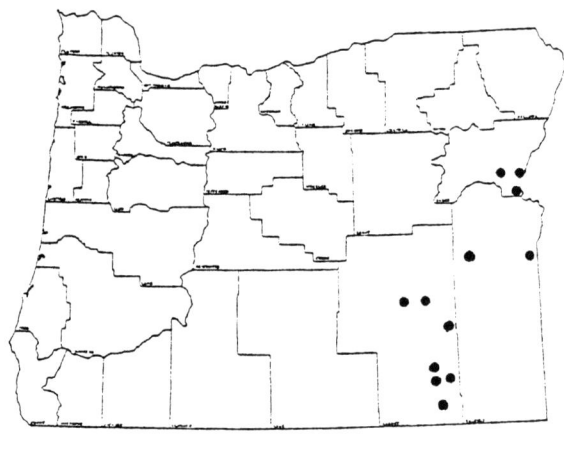

62. Chlosyne acastus

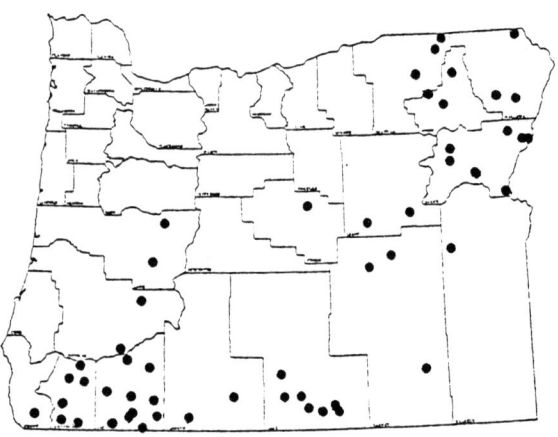

63. Chlosyne palla palla

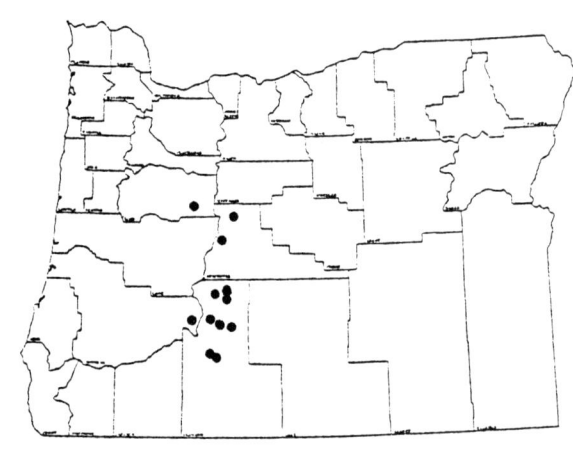

64. Chlosdyne palla whitneyi

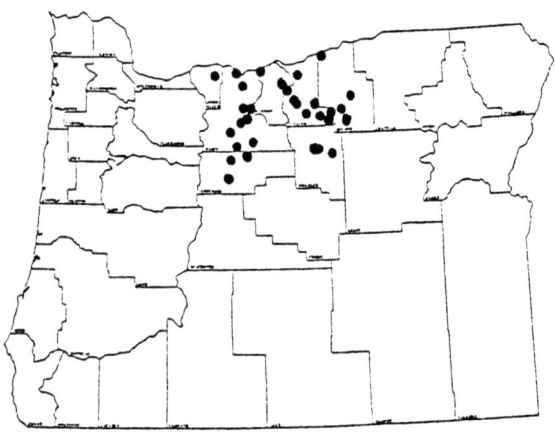

65. Chlosyne palla sterope

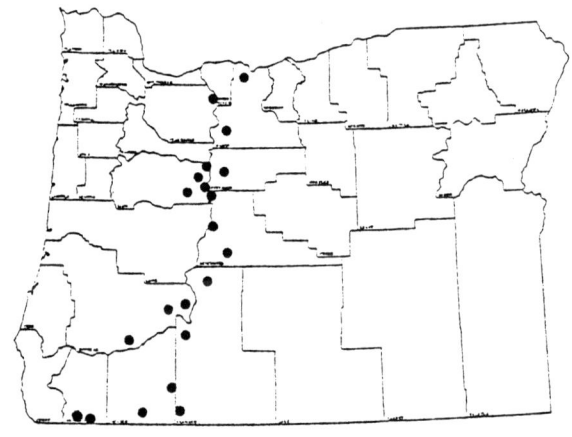

66. Chlosyne hoffmanni segregata

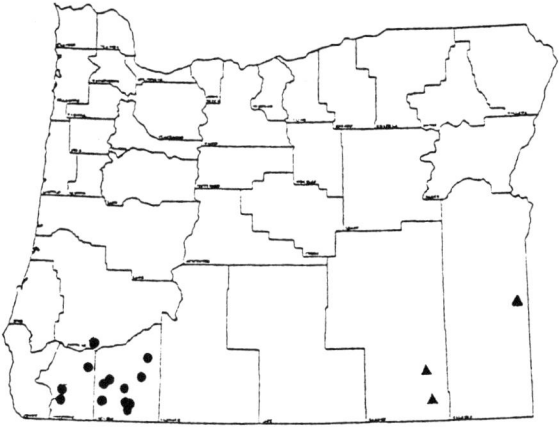

67. Chlosyne leanira oregonensis ●
    "   "   cerrita ▲

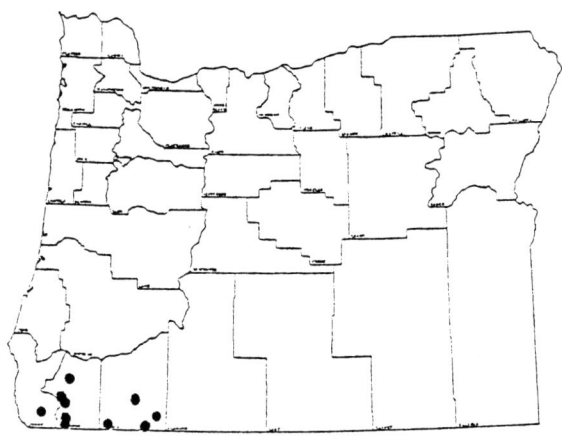

68. Euphydryas chalcedona chalcedona

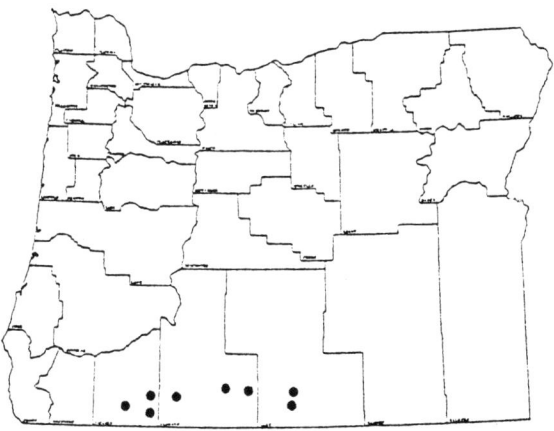

69. Euphydryas chalcedona macglashanii

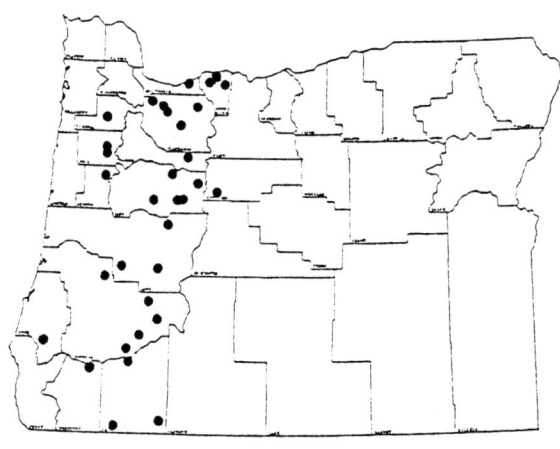

70. Euphydryas chalcedona colon

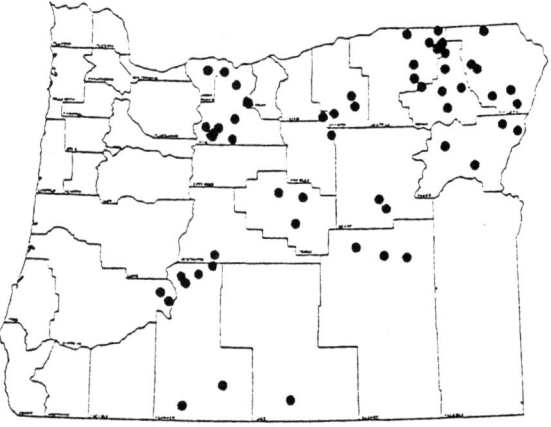

71. Euphydryas chalcedona wallacensis

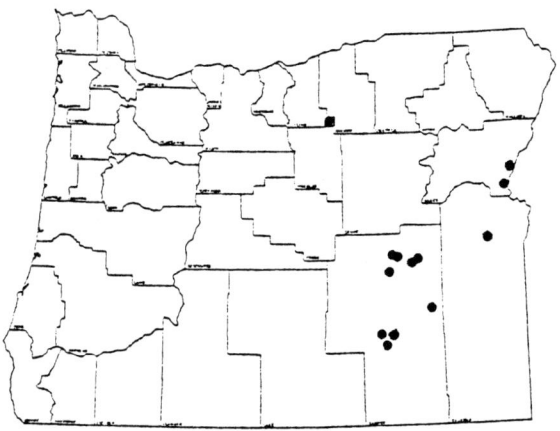

72. Euphydryas anicia veazieae

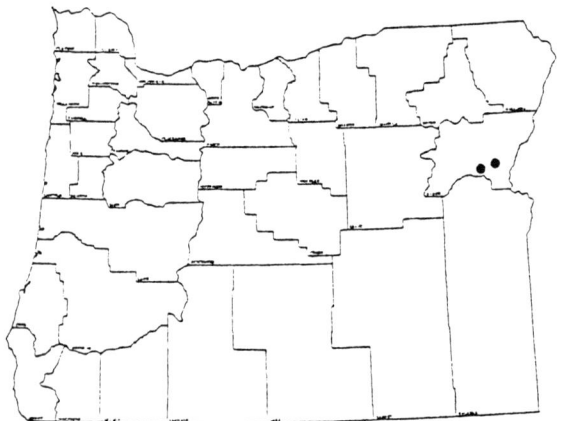
73. Euphydryas anicia bakeri

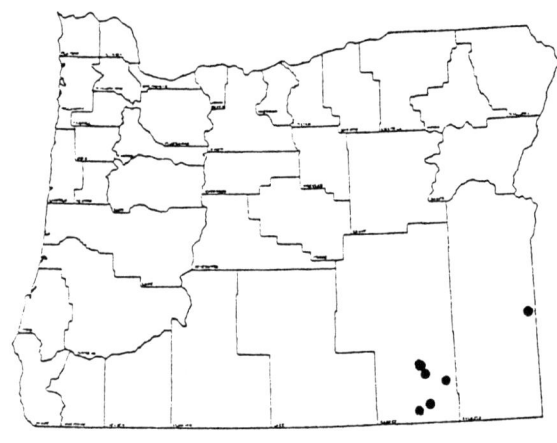
74. Euphydryas anicia macyi

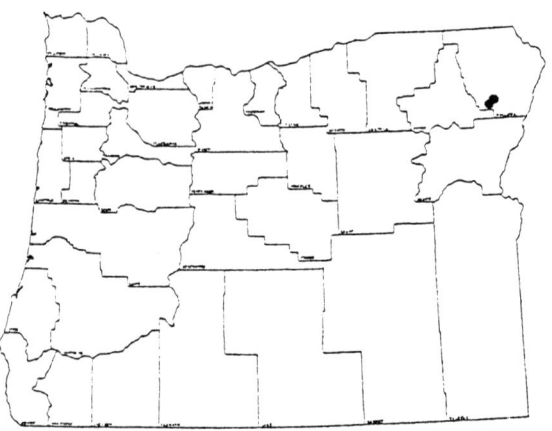
75. Euphydryas anicia howlandi

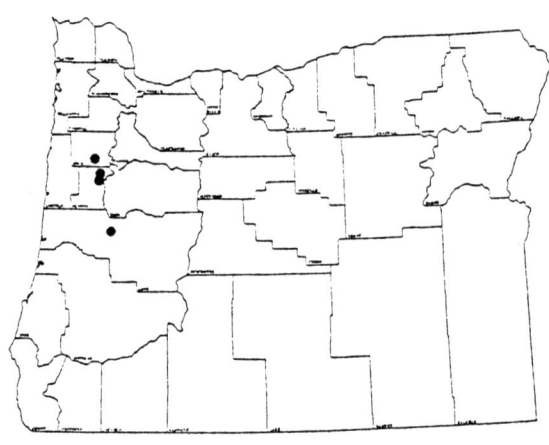
76. Euphydryas editha taylori

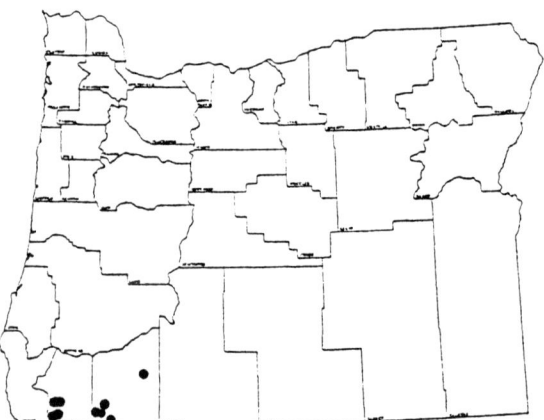
77. Euphydryas editha baroni

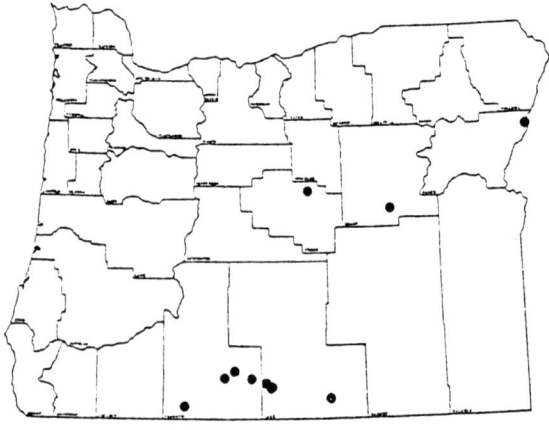
78. Euphydryas editha edithana

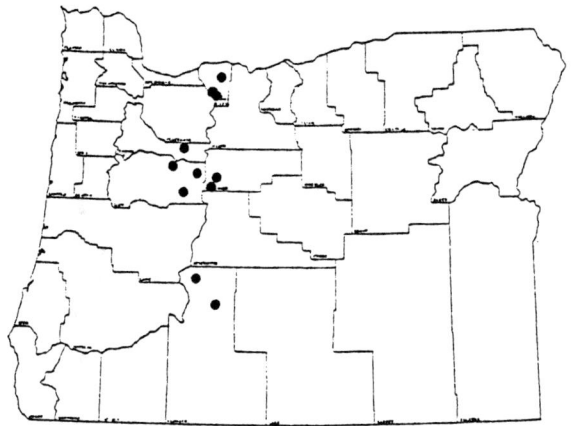
79. Euphydryas editha colonia

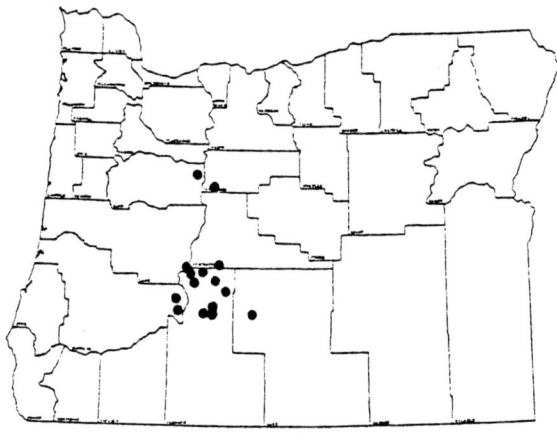
80. Euphydryas editha remingtoni

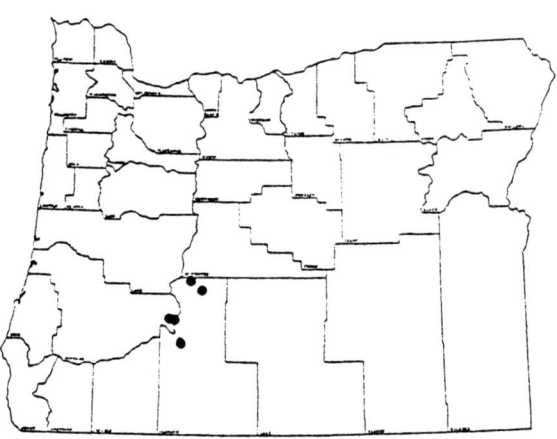
81. Euphydryas editha lawrencei

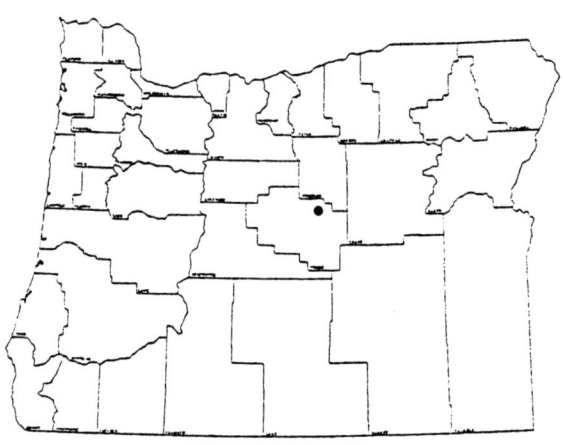
82. Boloria selene tollandensis

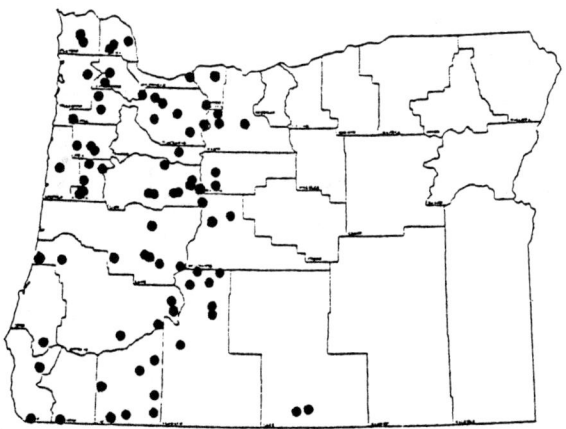
83. Boloria epithore chermocki

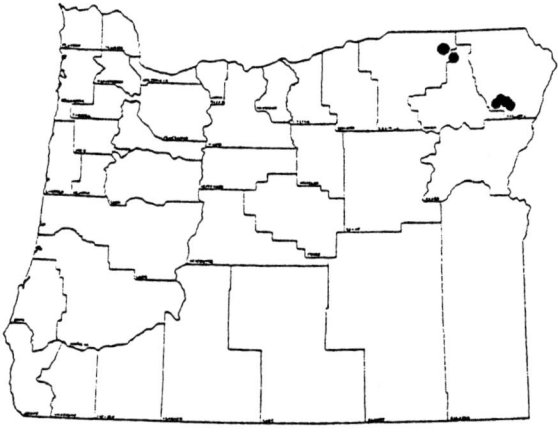
84. Boloria epithore borealis

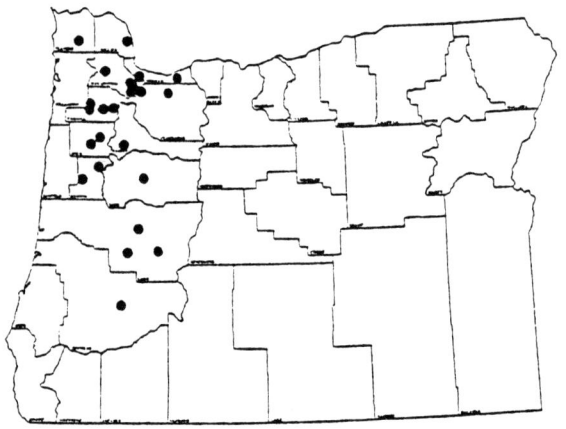
85. Speyeria cybele pugetensis

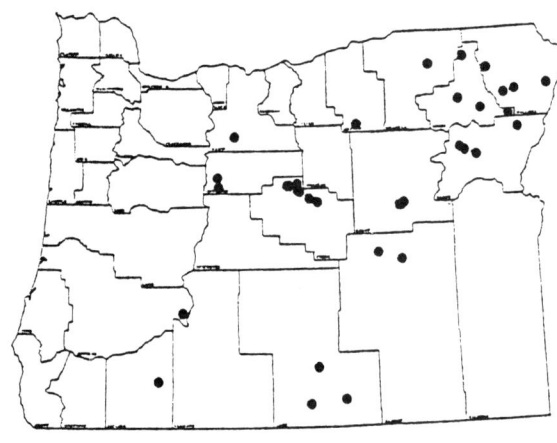
86. Speyeria cybele leto

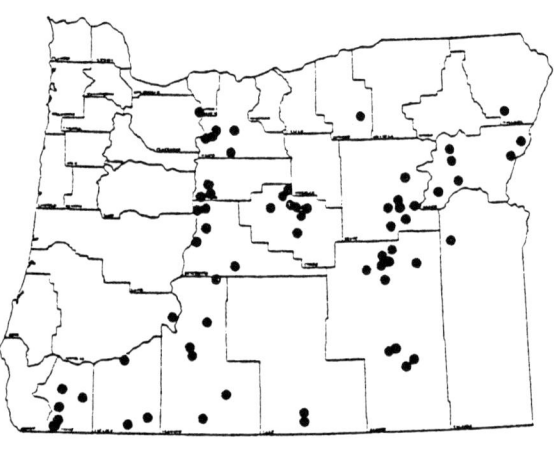
87. Speyeria coronis

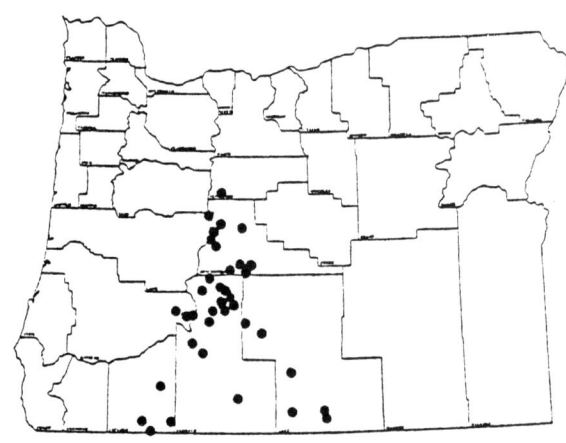
88. Speyeria zerene conchyliatus

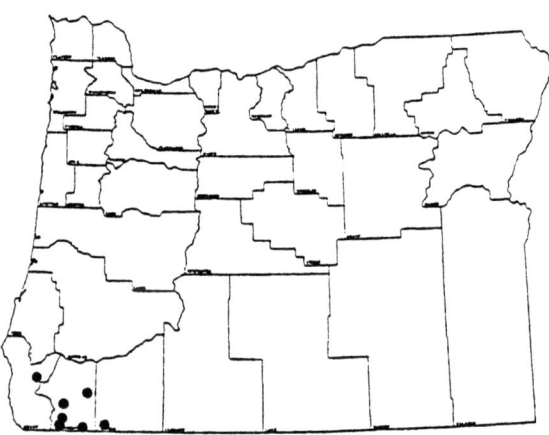
89. Speyeria zerene gloriosa

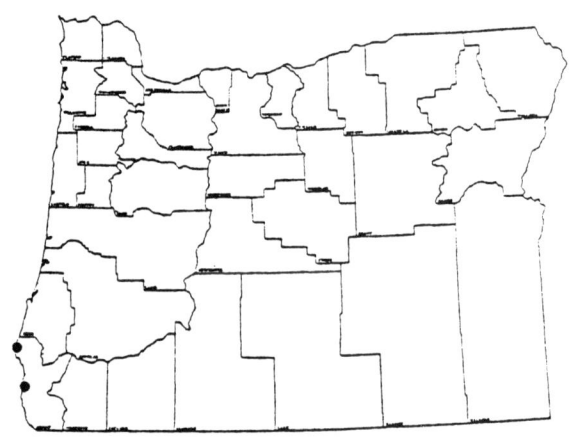
90. Speyeria zerene behrensii

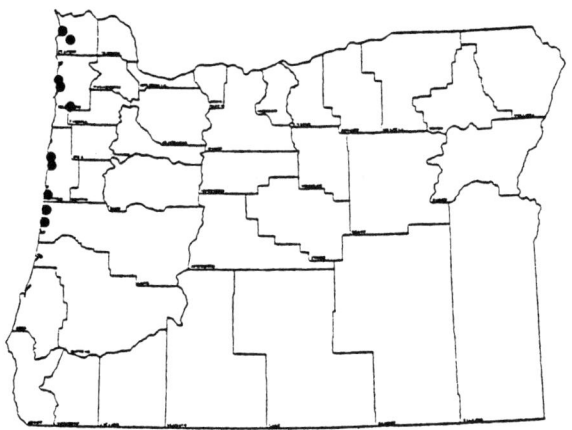
91. Speyeria zerene hippolyta

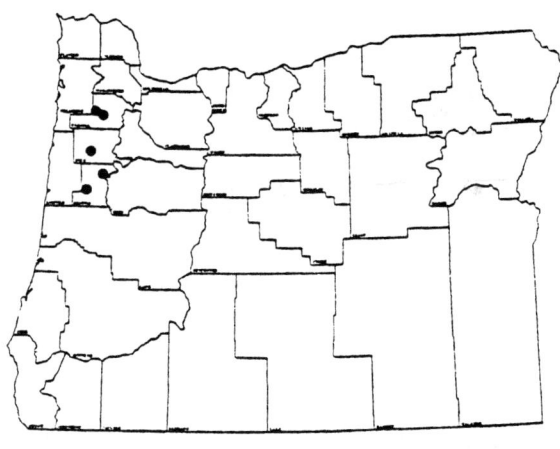
92. Speyeria zerene bremnerii

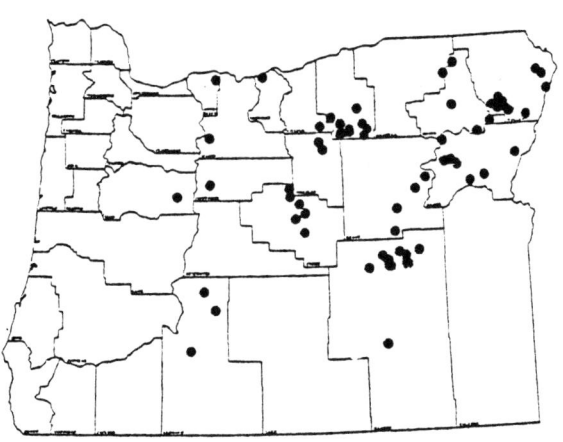
93. Speyeria zerene picta-garretti

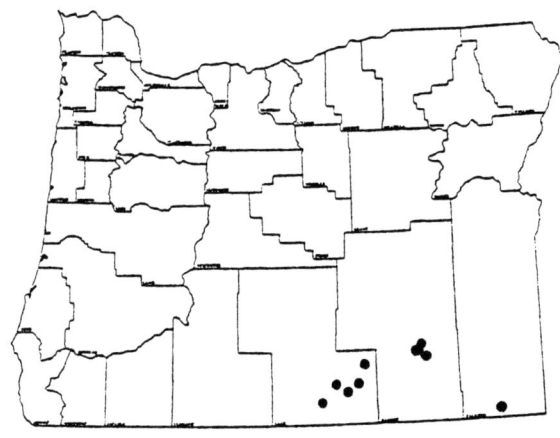
94. Speyeria zerene gunderi

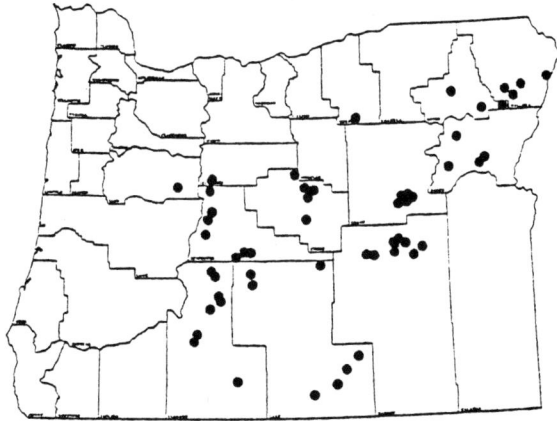
95. Speyeria callippe semivirida

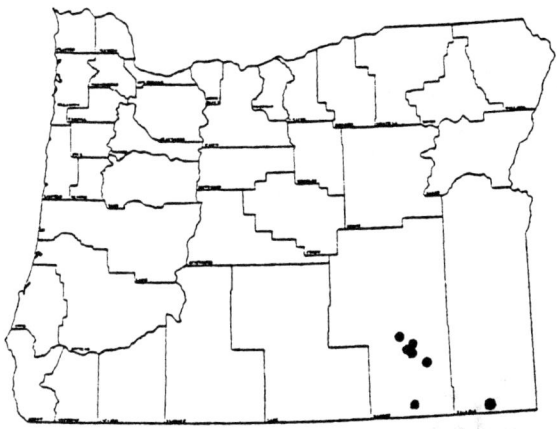
96. Speyeria callippe harmonia

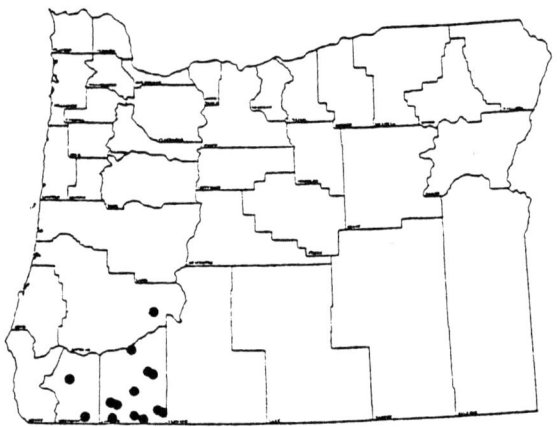

97. Speyeria callippe elaine

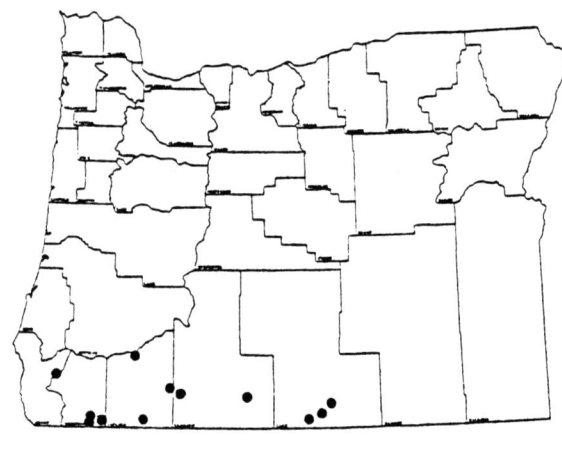

98. Speyeria egleis oweni

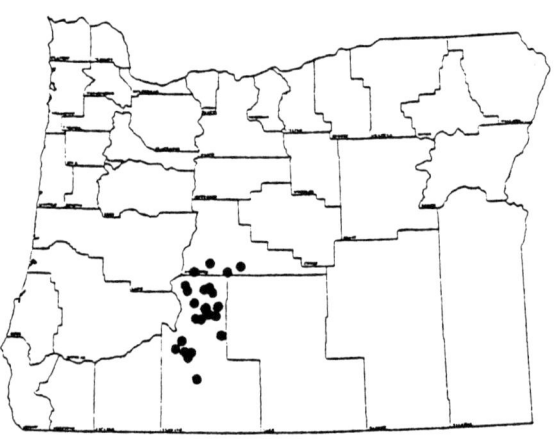

99. Speyeria egleis (Sand Cr.)

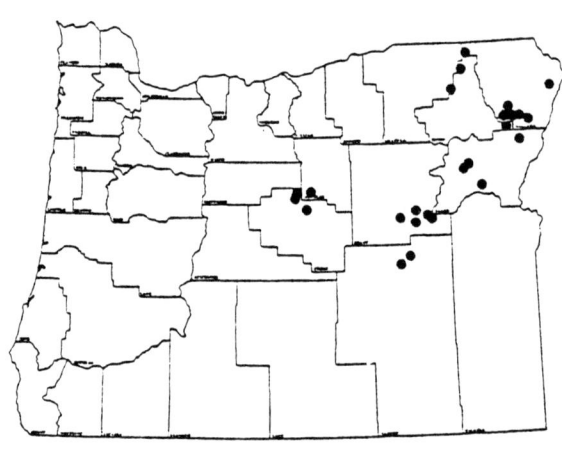

100. Speyeria egleis macdunnoughi

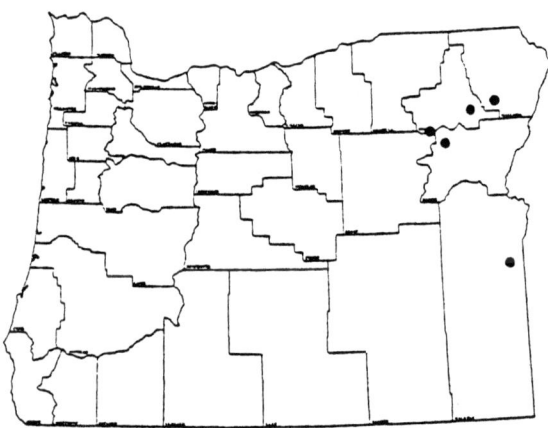

101. Speyeria egleis linda

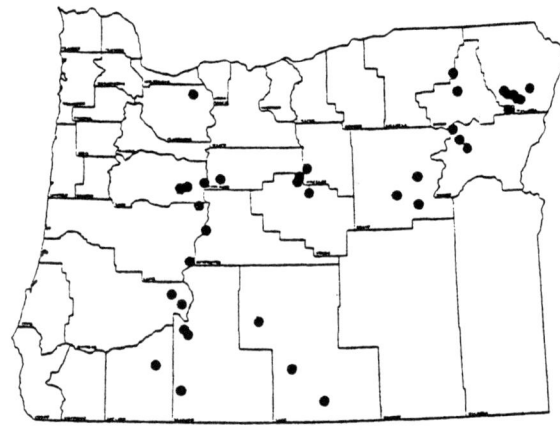

102. Speyeria atlantis dodgei

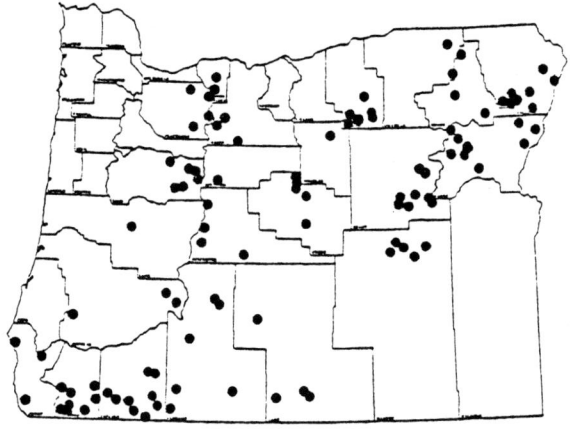
103. Speyeria hydaspe purpurascens

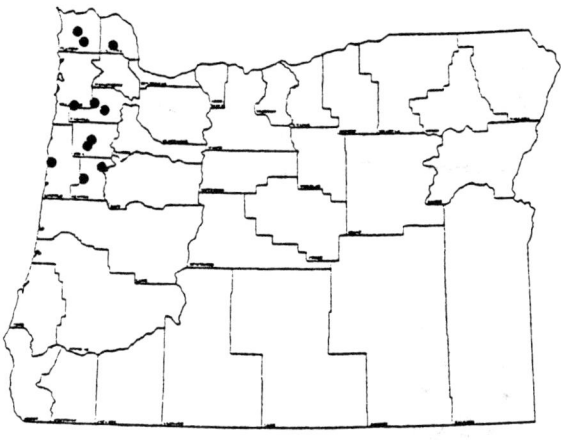
104. Speyeria hydaspe rhodope

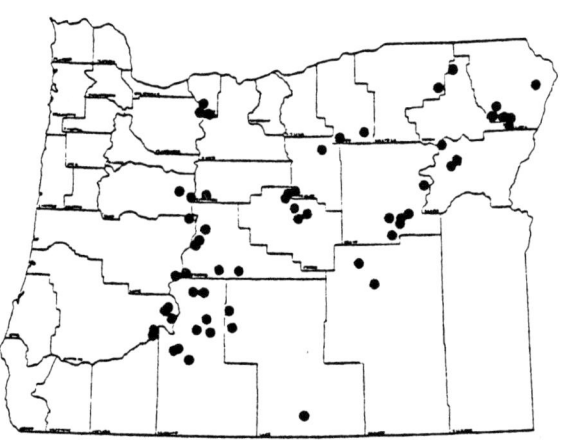
105. Speyeria mormonia erinna

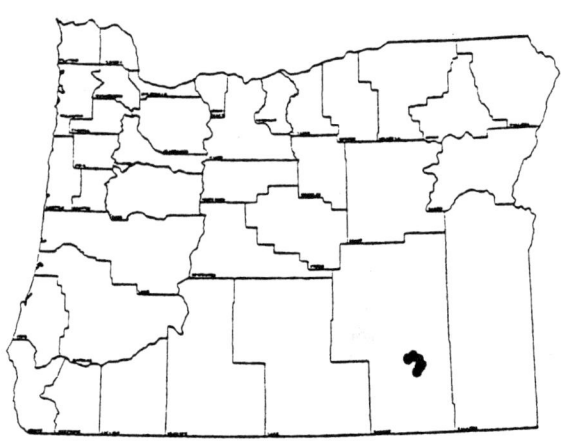
106. Speyeria mormonia artonis

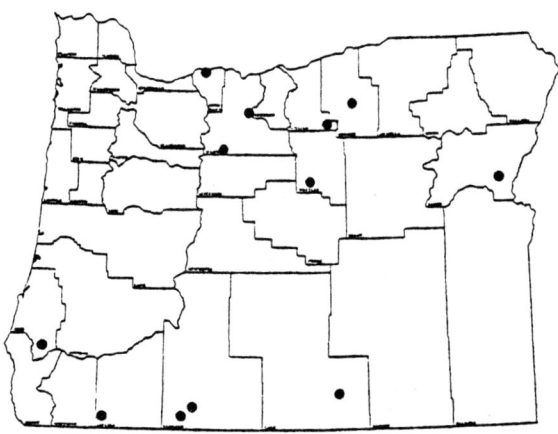
107. Apodemia mormo mormonia

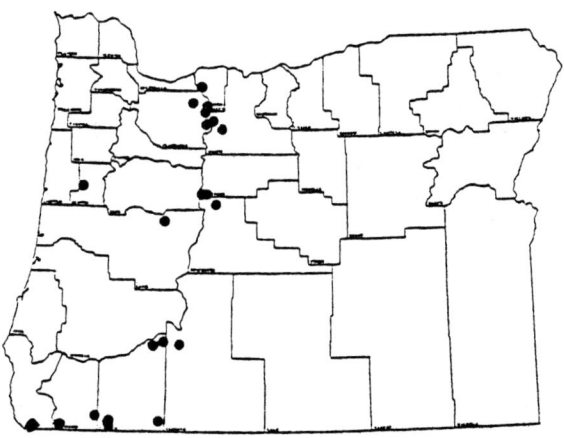
108. Habrodais grunus

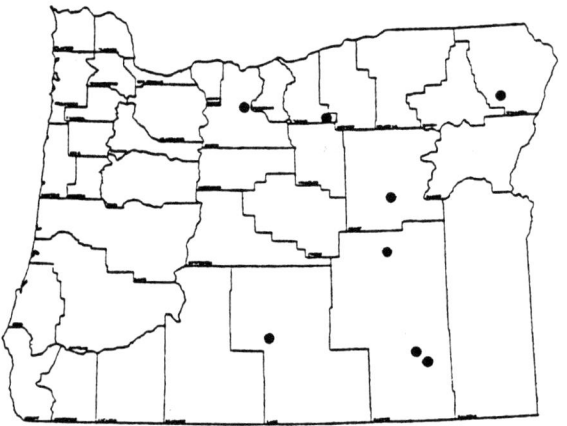

109. Harkenclenus titus immaculosus

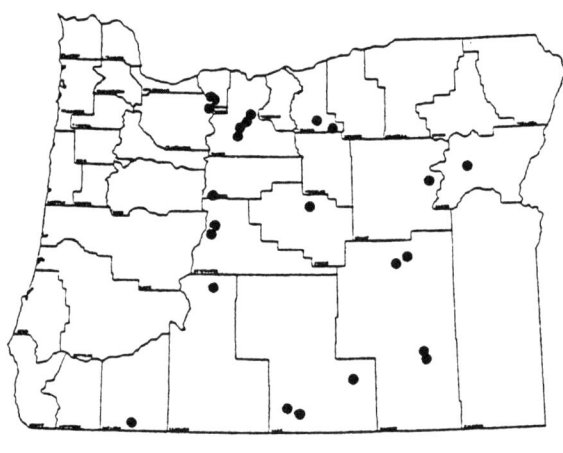

110. Satyrium fuliginosum

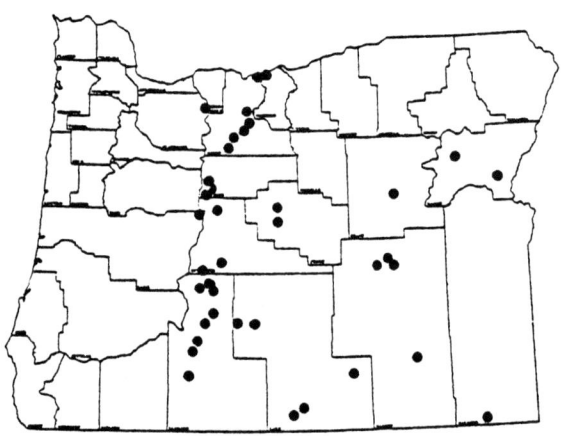

111. Satyrium behrii behrii

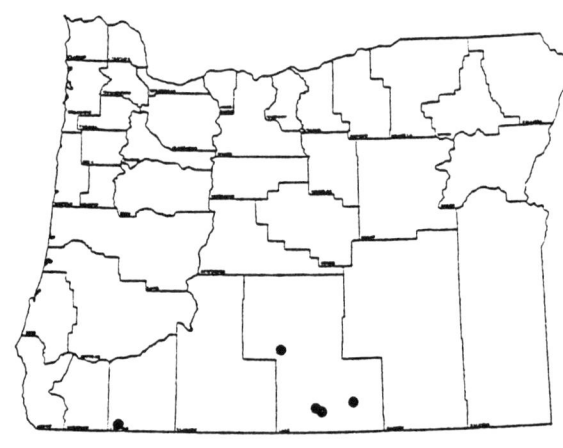

112. Satyrium tetra

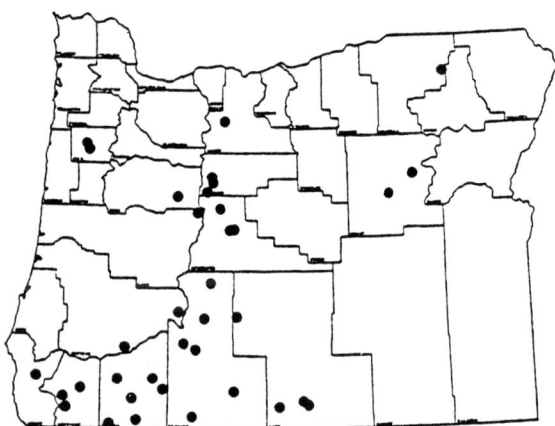

113. Satyrium saepium saepium

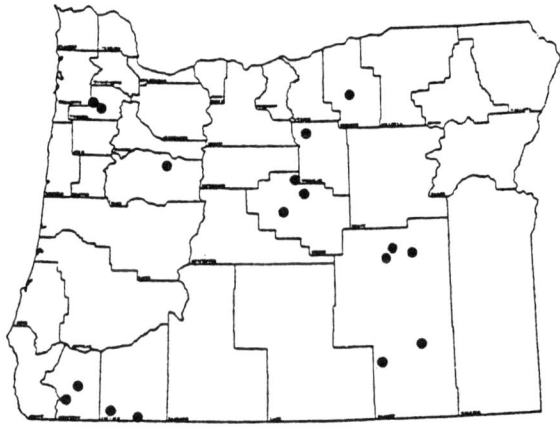

114. Satyrium sylvinus sylvinus

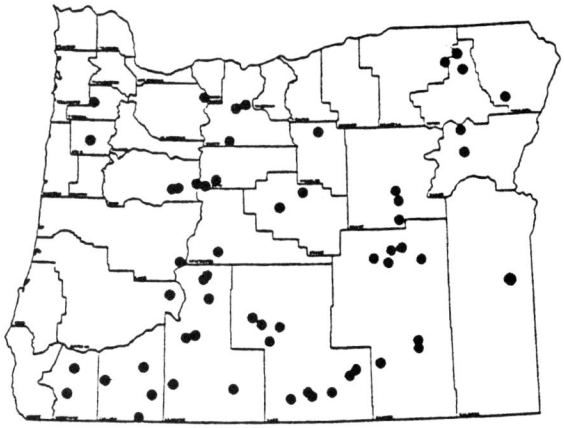
115. Satyrium californica

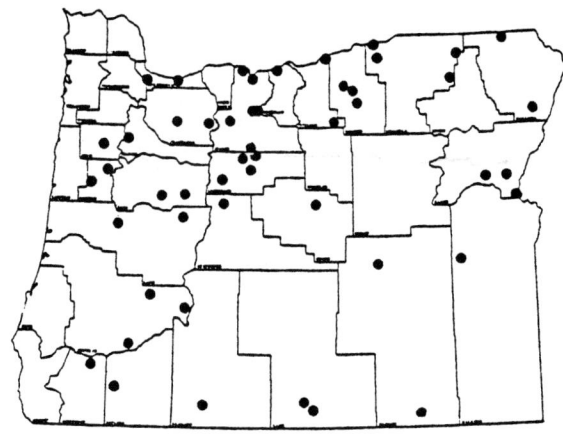
116. Strymon melinus

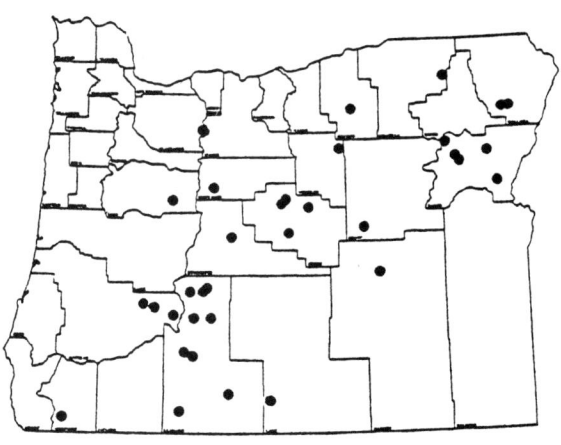
117. Mitoura spinetorum

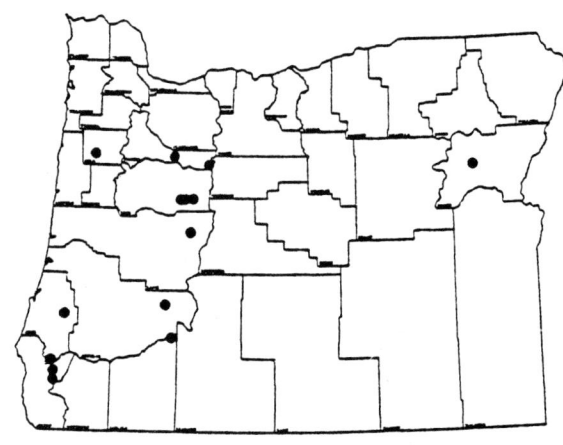
118. Mitoura johnsoni

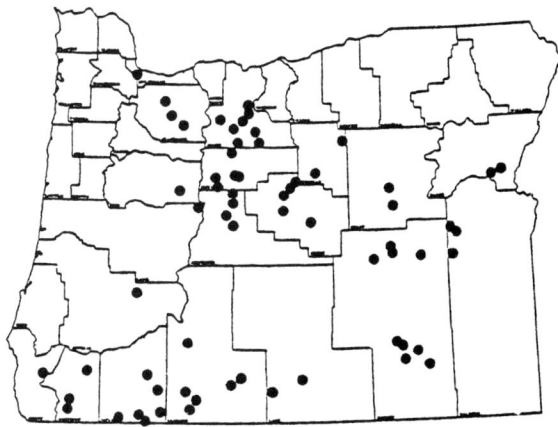
119. Mitoura nelsoni

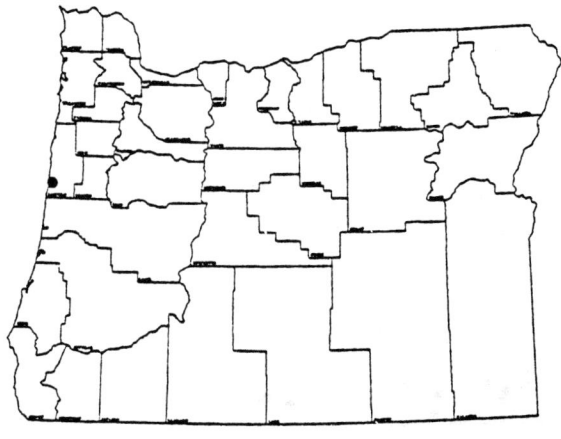
120. Incisalia polios obscurus

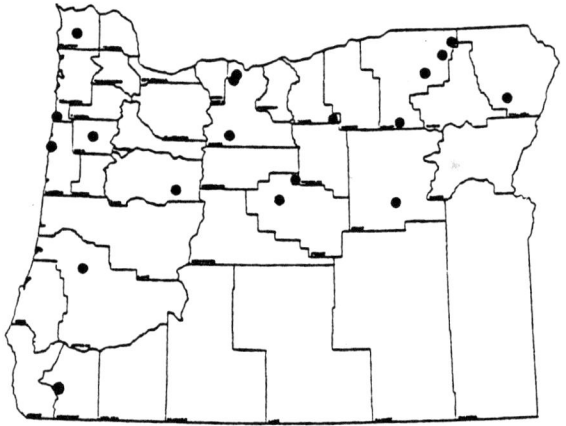

121. Incisalia fotis mossii

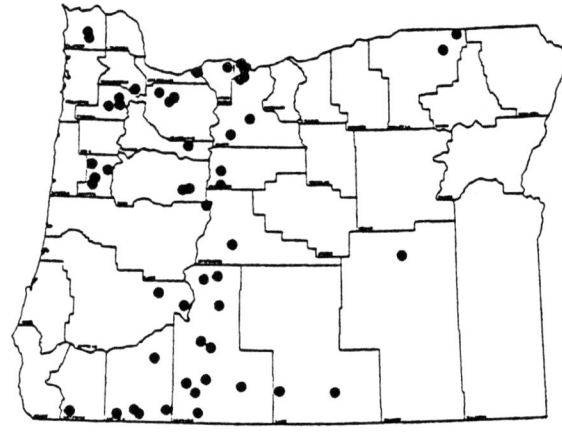

122. Incisalia augustinus iroides

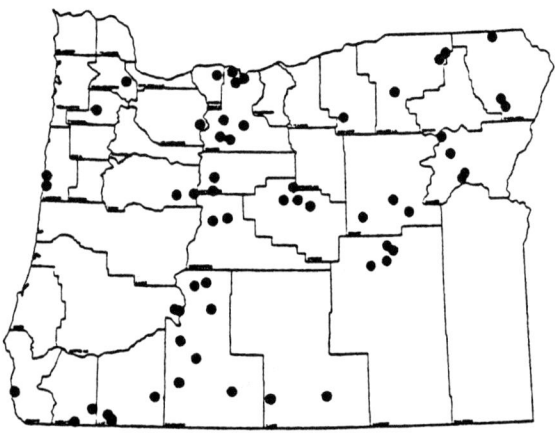

123. Incisalia eryphon eryphon

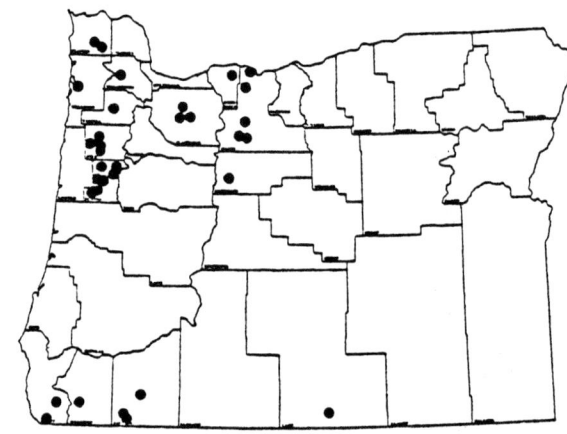

124. Callophrys dumetorum

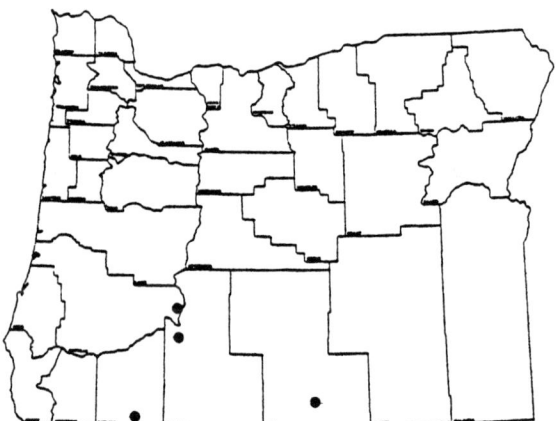

125. Callophrys sheridanii lemberti

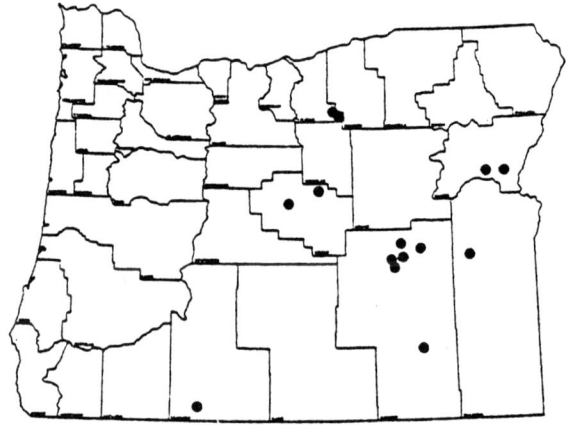

126. Callophrys sheridanii newcomeri

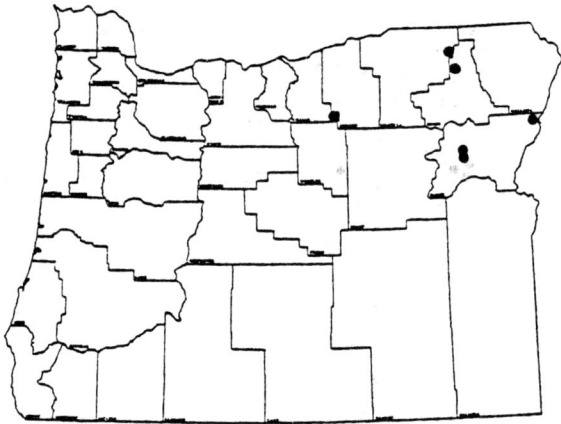
127. Callophrys affinis washingtonia

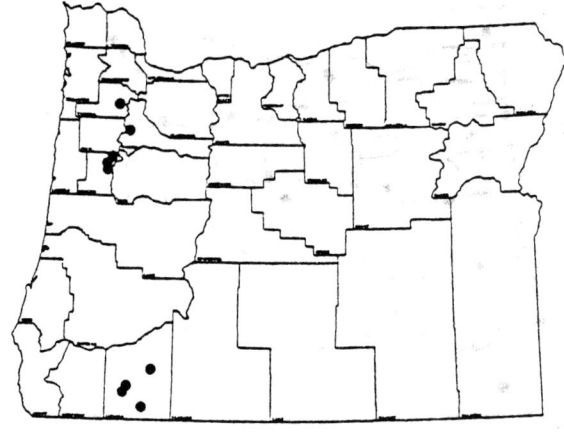
128. Atlides halesus corcorani

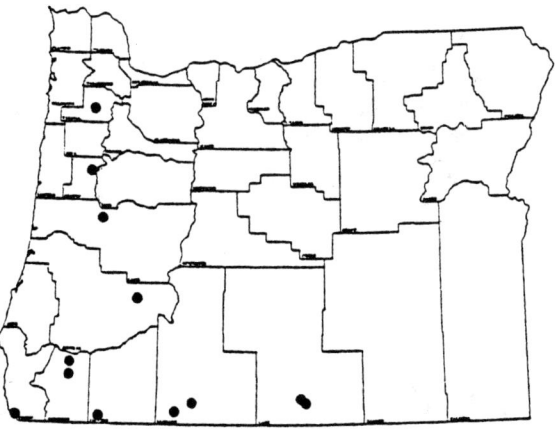
129. Tharsalea arota arota

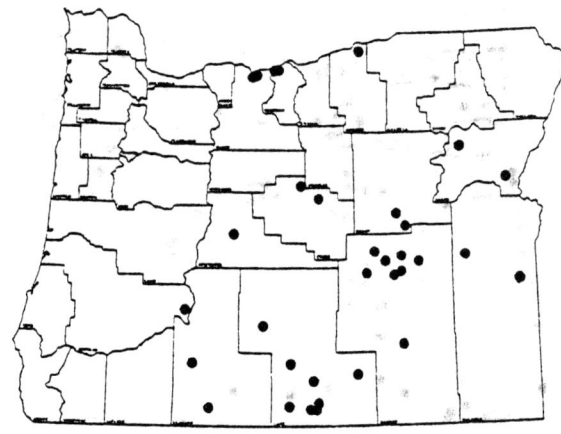
130. Lycaena rubidus

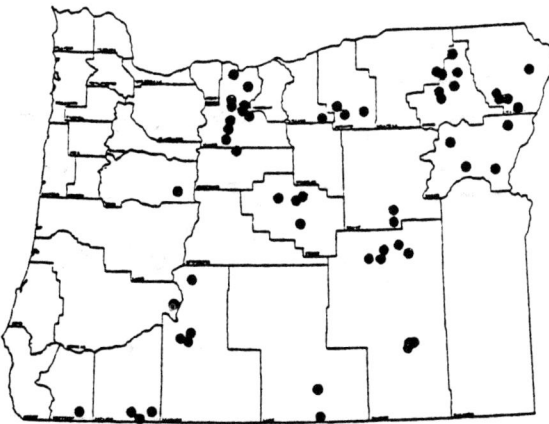
131. Lycaena heteronea

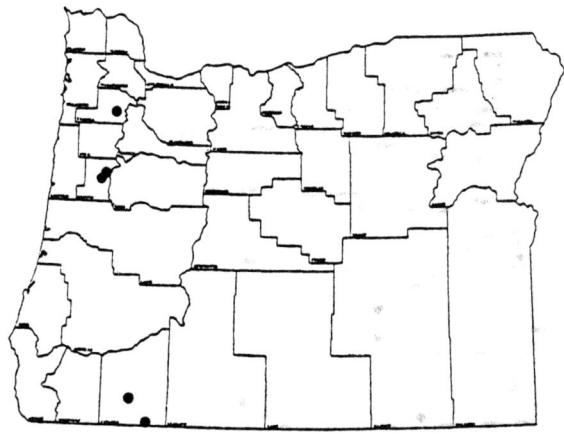
132. Lycaena xanthoides xanthoides

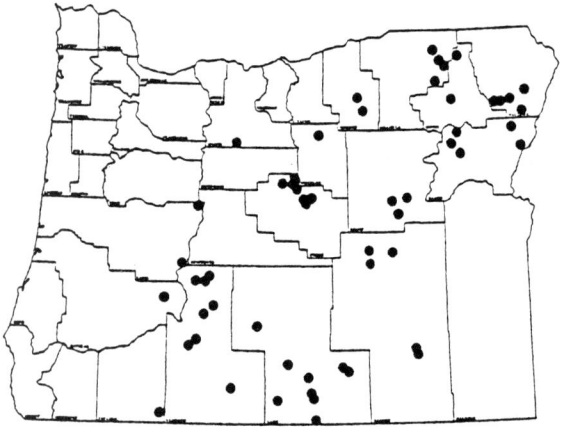

133. Lycaena editha editha

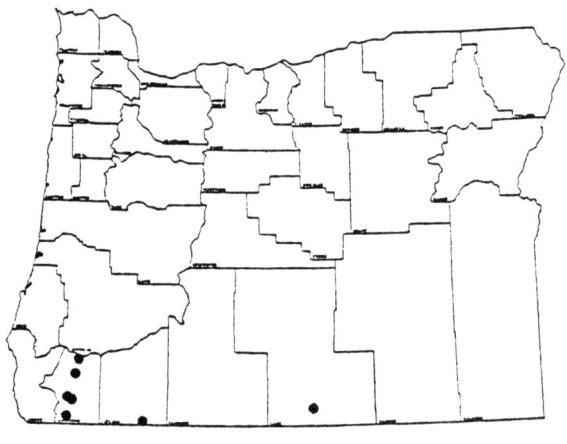

134. Lycaena gorgon

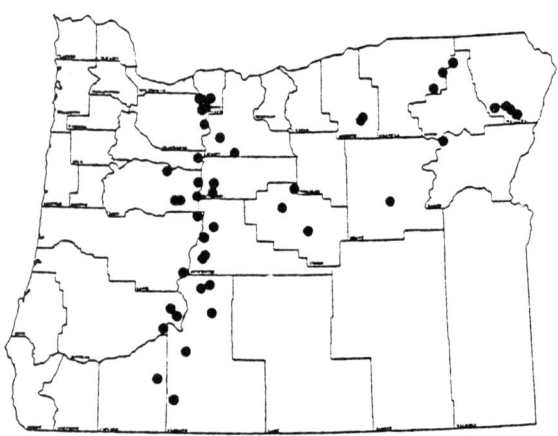

135. Lycaena mariposa mariposa

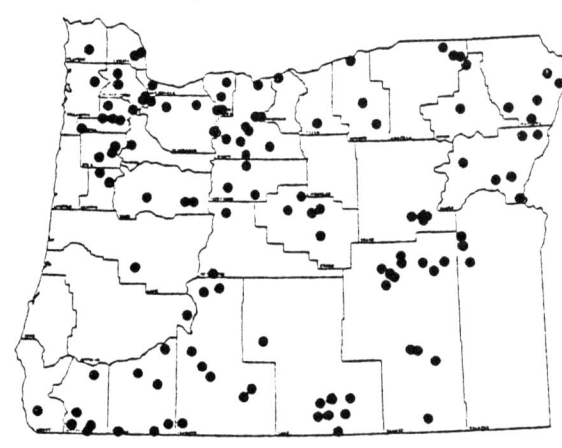

136. Lycaena helloides

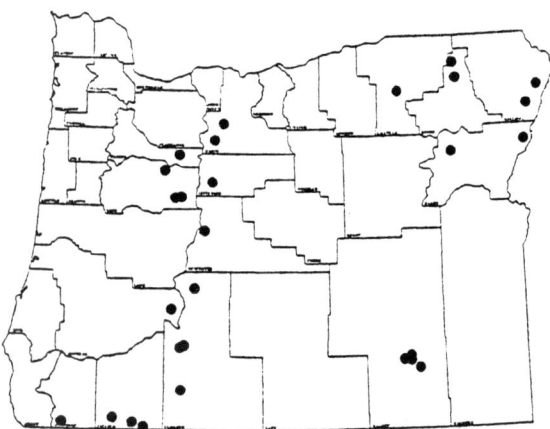

137. Lycaena nivalis "form 1"

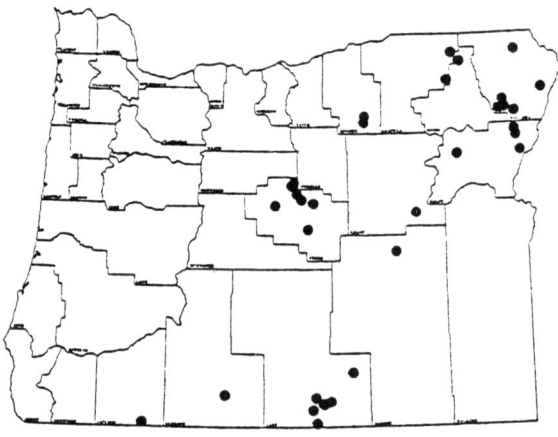

138. Lycaena nivalis "form 2"

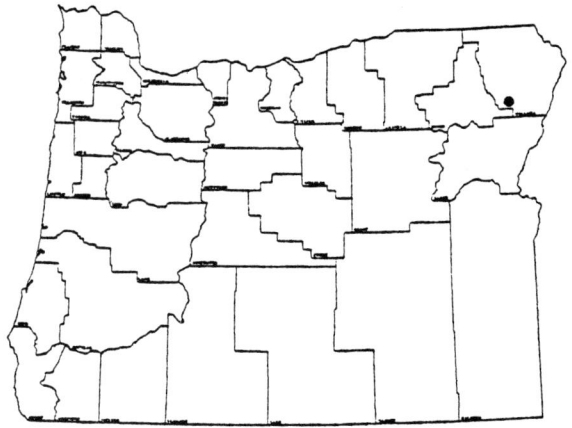
139. Lycaena phlaeas arctodon

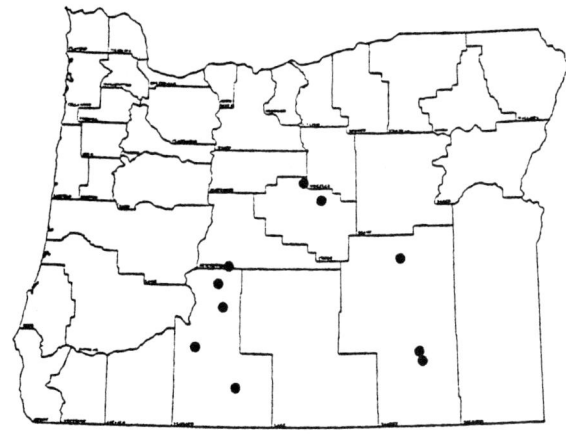
140. Lycaena cupreus cupreus

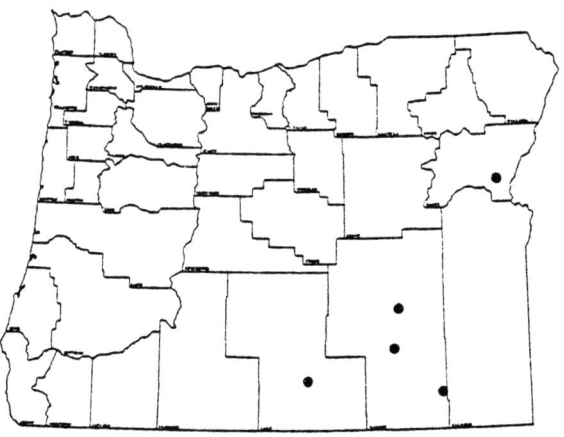
141. Brephidium exilis

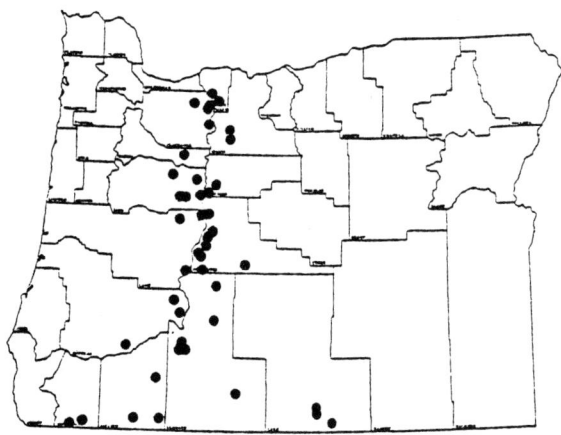
142. Lycaeides argyrognomon ricei

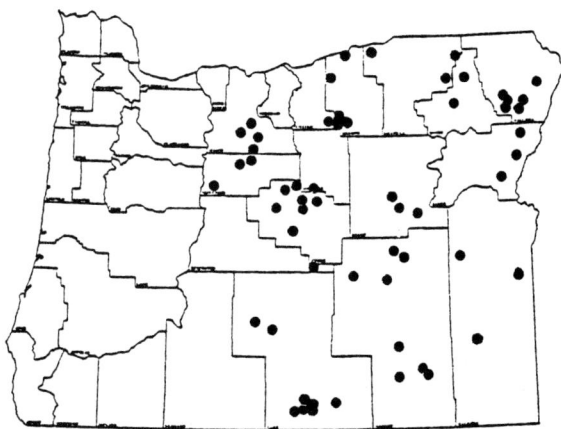
143. Lycaeides melissa melissa

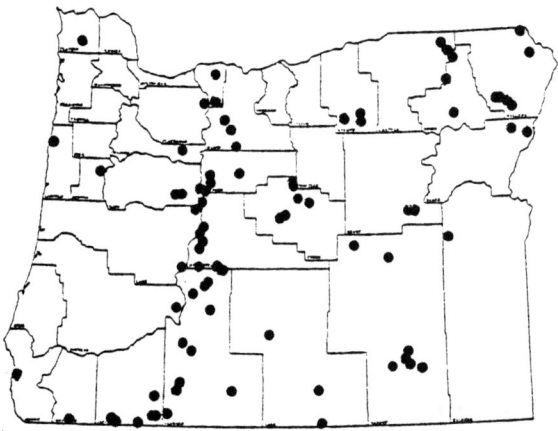
144. Plebejus saepiolus saepiolus

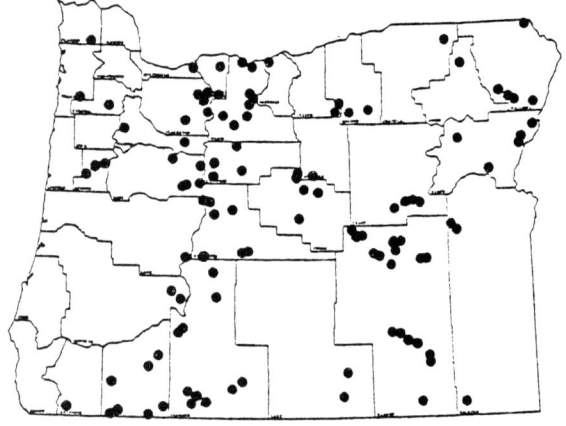
145. Icaricia icarioides

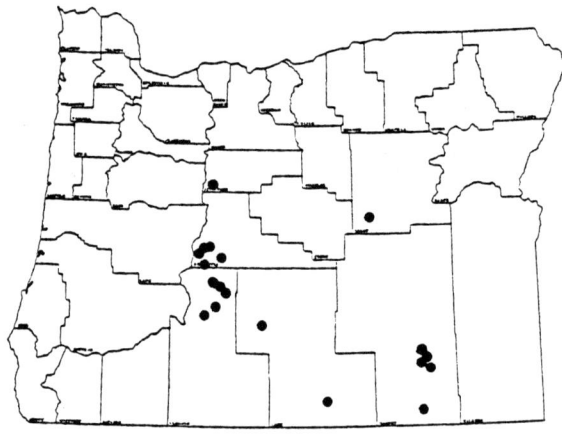
146. Icaricia shasta shasta

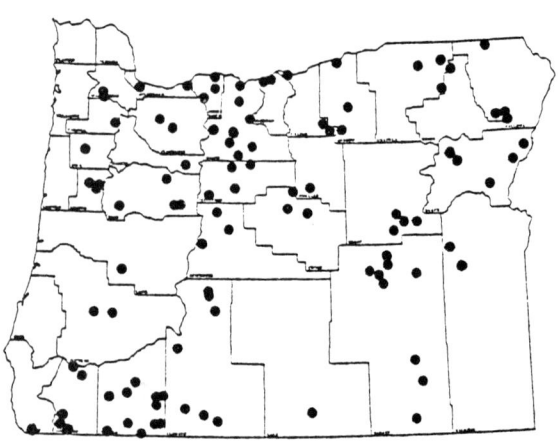
147. Icaricia acmon

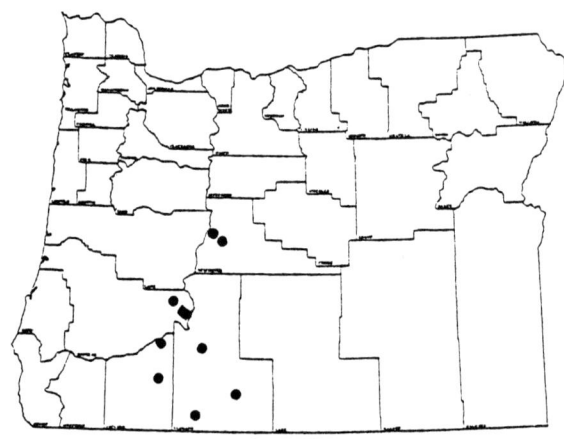
148. Icaricia lupini lupini

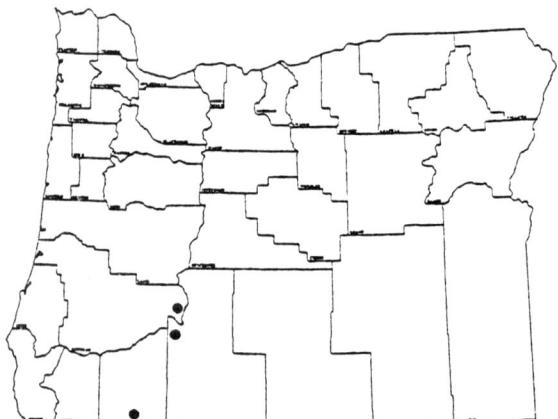
149. Agriades aquilo podarce

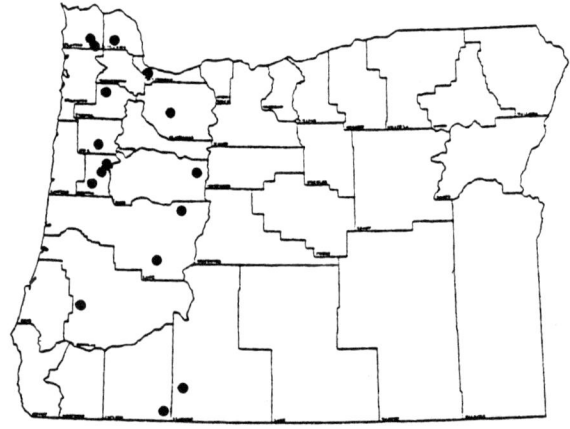
150. Everes comyntas comyntas

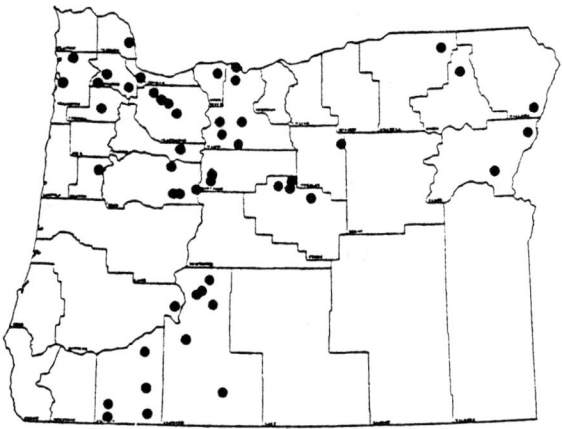
151. Everes amyntula amyntula

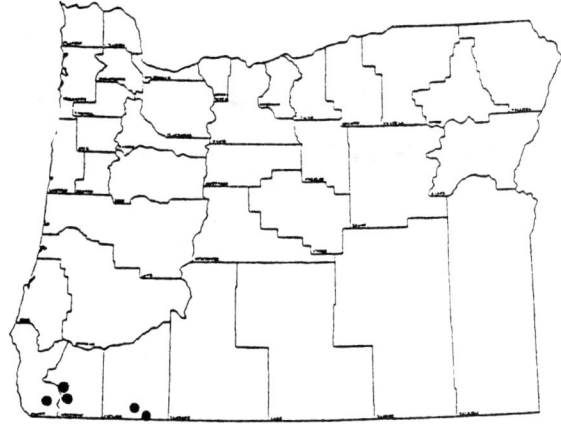
152. Philotes battoides intermedia

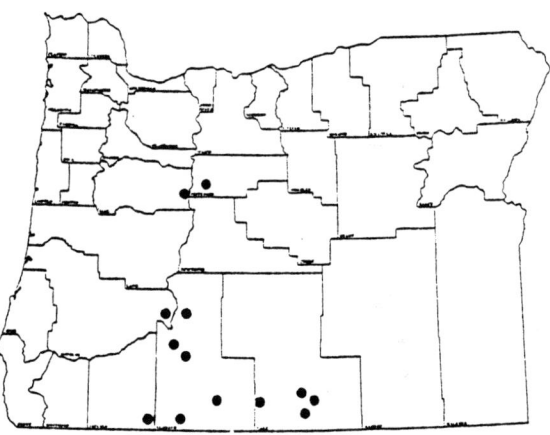
153. Philotes battoides oregonensis

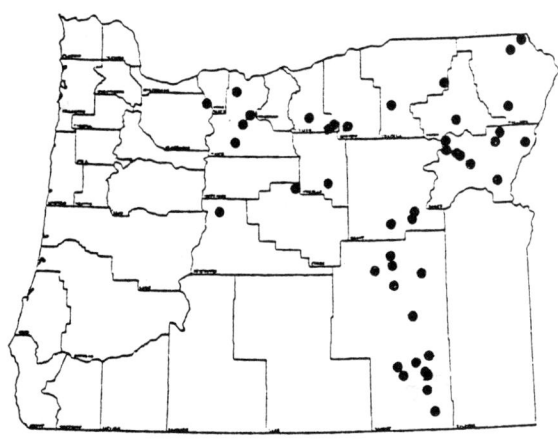
154. Philotes battoides glaucon

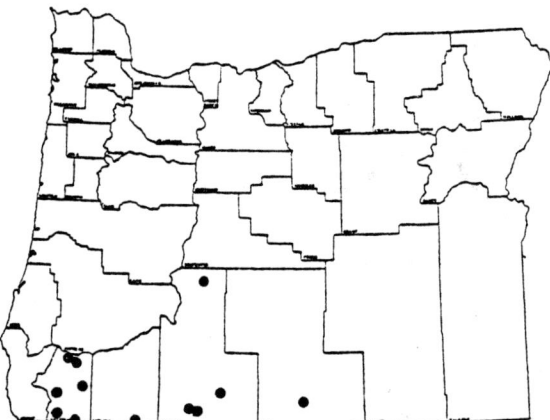
155. Philotes enoptes enoptes

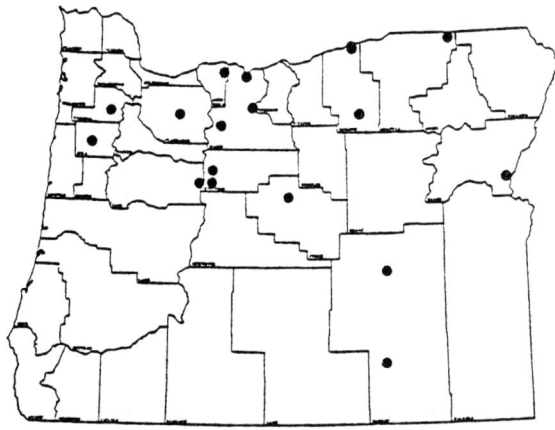
156. Philotes enoptes columbiae

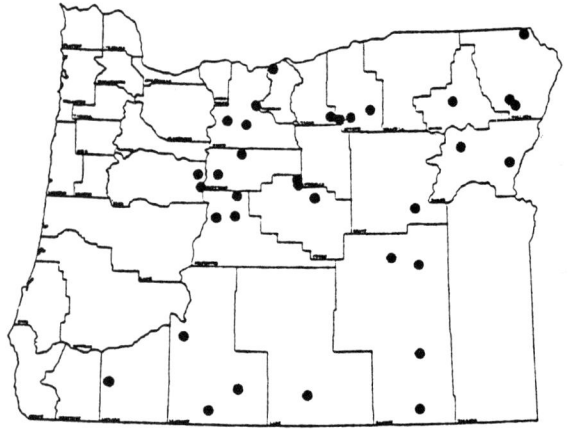

157. Glaucopsyche piasus

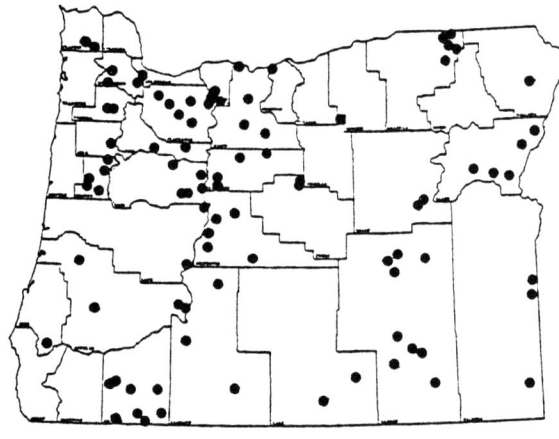

158. Glaucopsyche lygdamus columbia

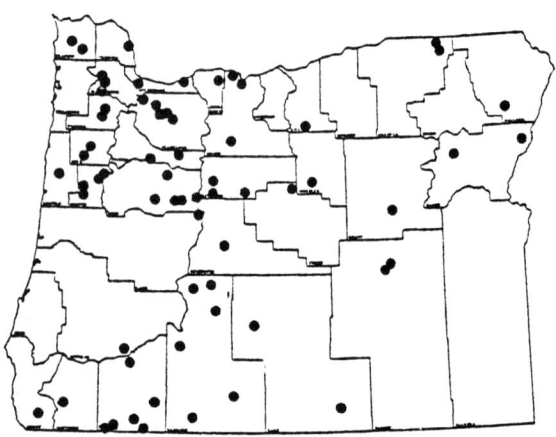

159. Celastrina argiolus echo

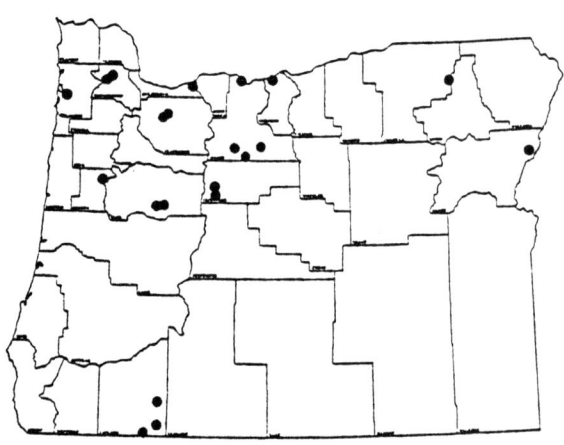

160. Amblyscirtes vialis

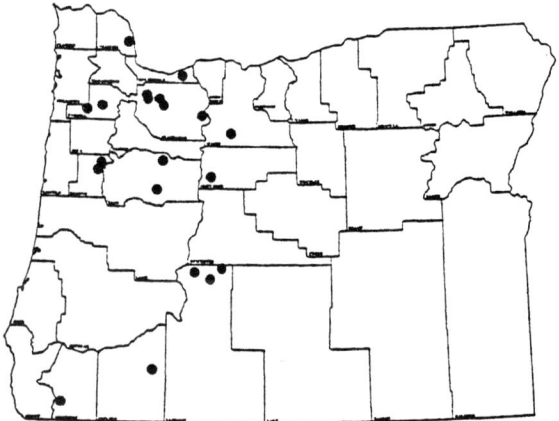

161. Euphyes vestris vestris

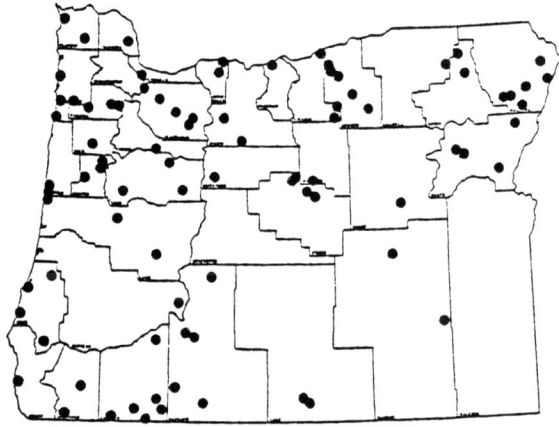

162. Ochlodes sylvanoides sylvanoides

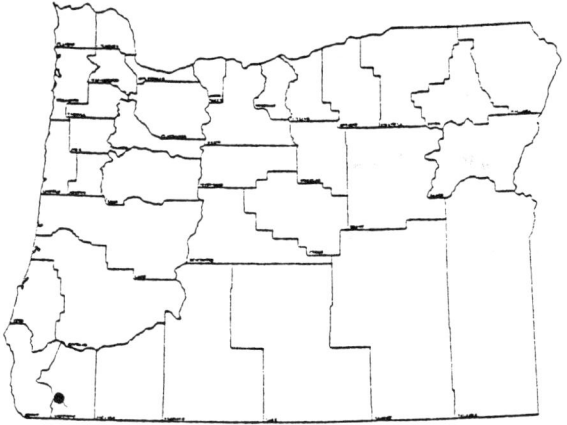

163. Ochlodes agricola agricola

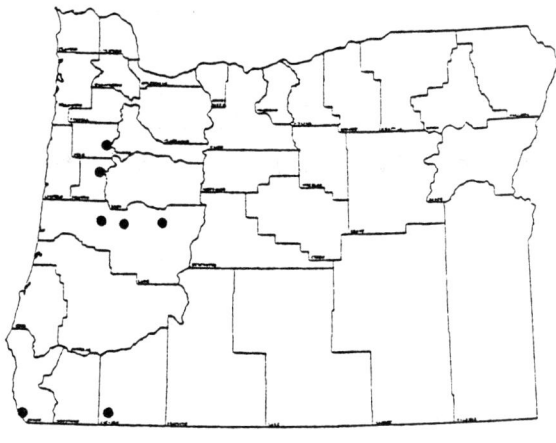

164. Atalopedes campestris

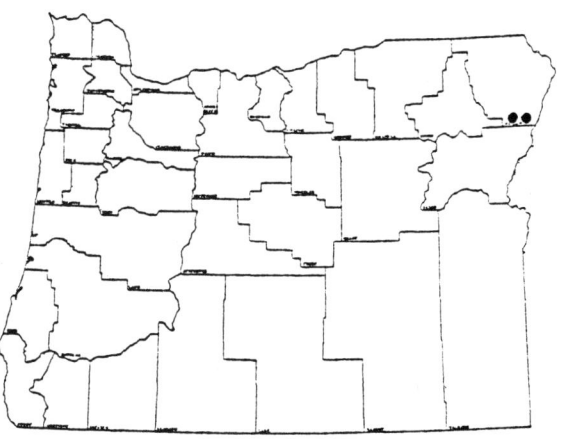

165. Polites coras

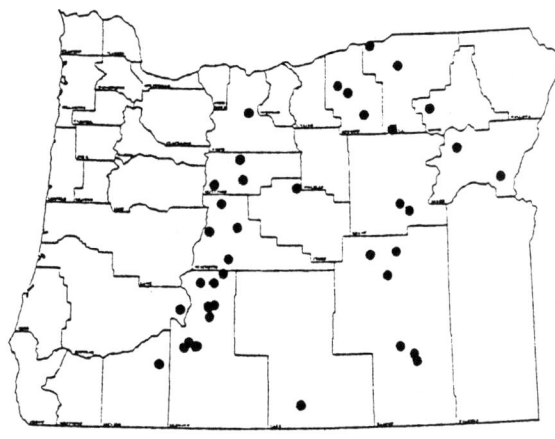

166. Polites sabuleti

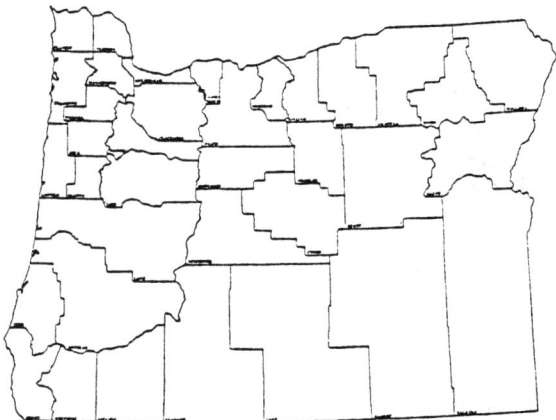

167. Polites mardon

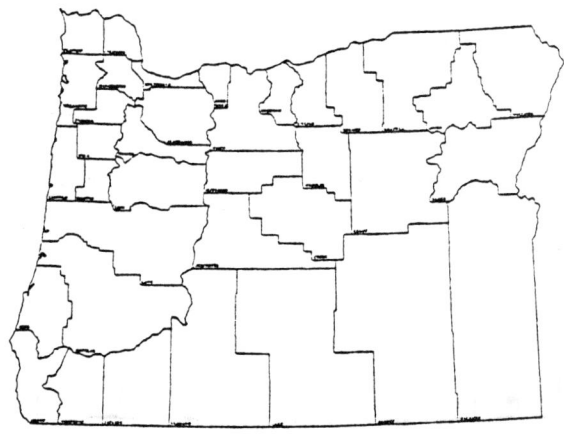

168. Polites themistocles

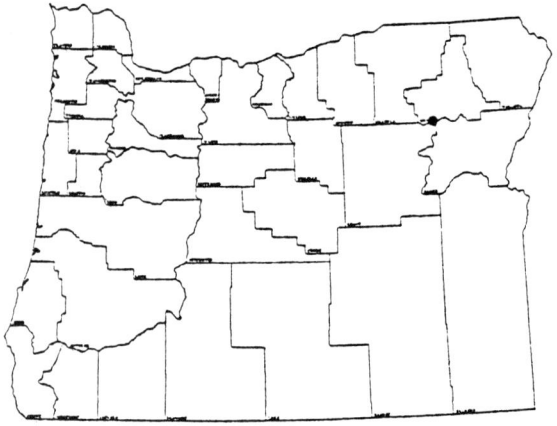
169. Polites mystic

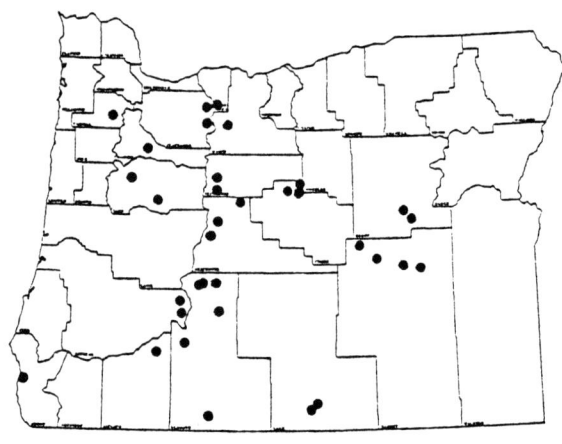
170. Polites sonora siris

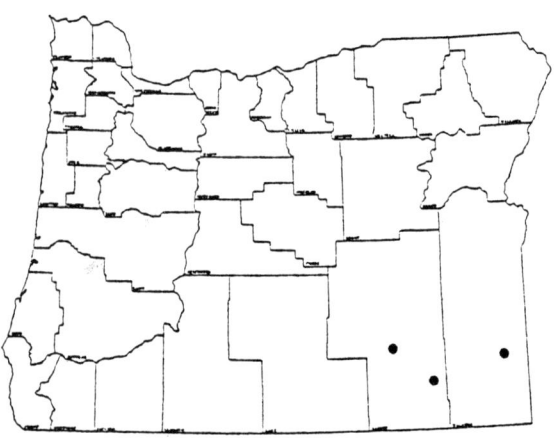
171. Hesperia uncas

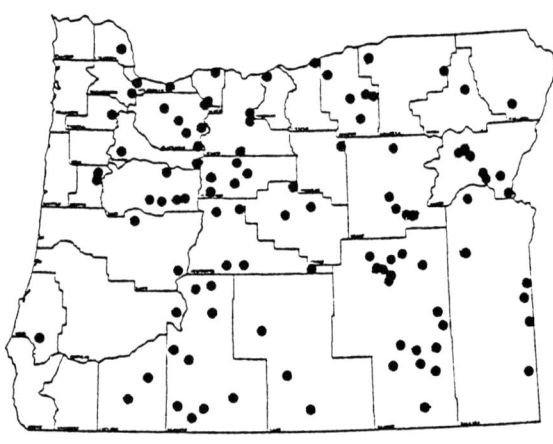
172. Hesperia juba

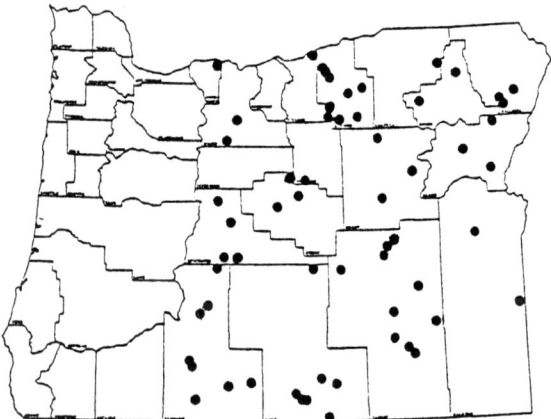
173. Hesperia comma harpalus

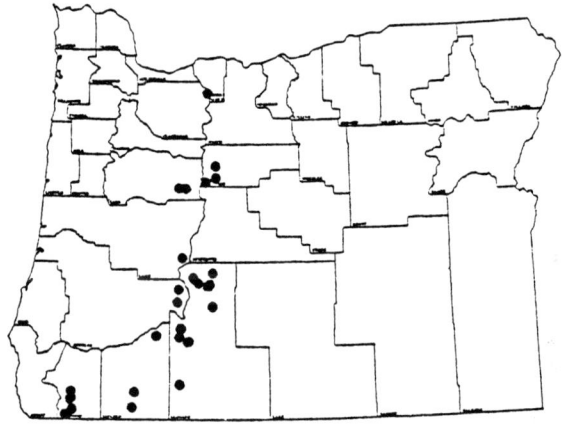
174. Hesperia comma oregonia

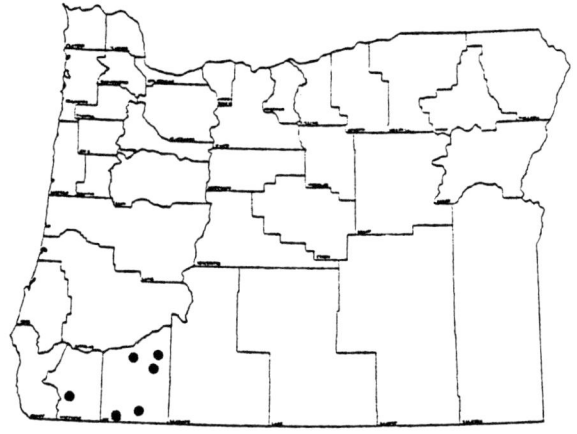
175. Hesperia columbia

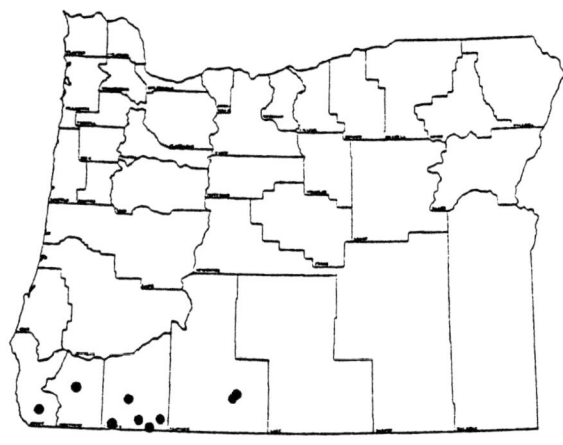
176. Hesperia lindseyi

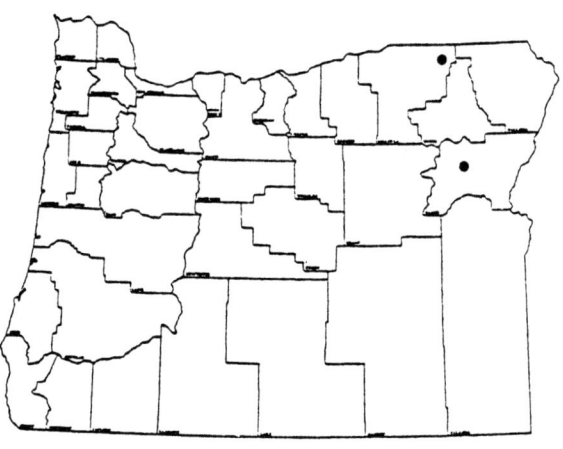
177. Hesperia nevada

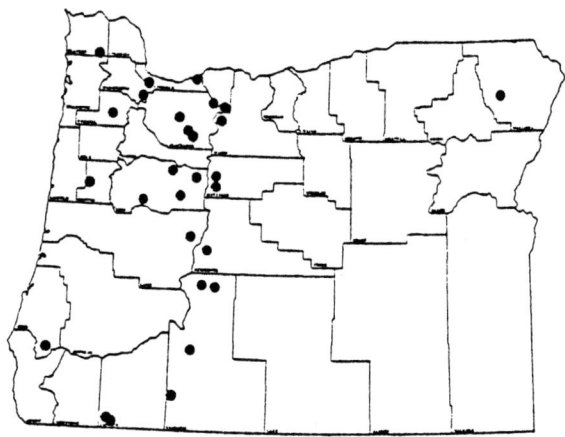
178. Carterocephalus palaemon mandan

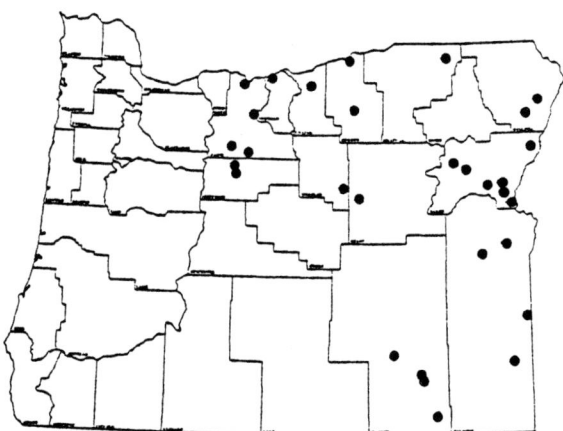
179. Pholisora catullus

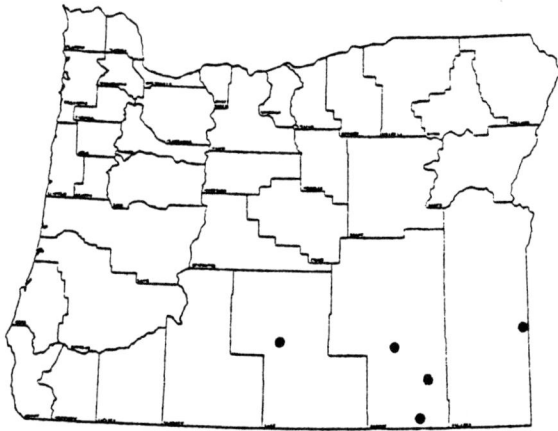
180. Pholisora libya lena

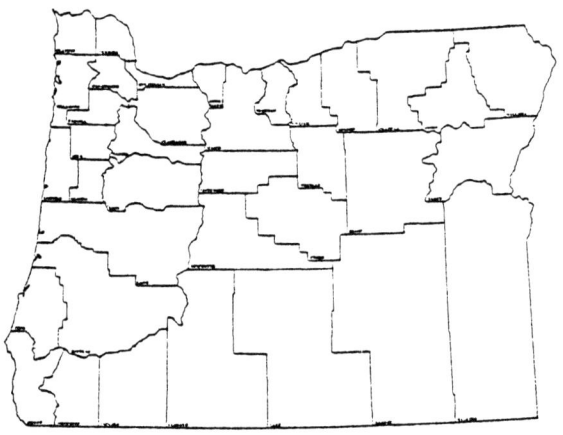
181. Pholisora alpheus oricus

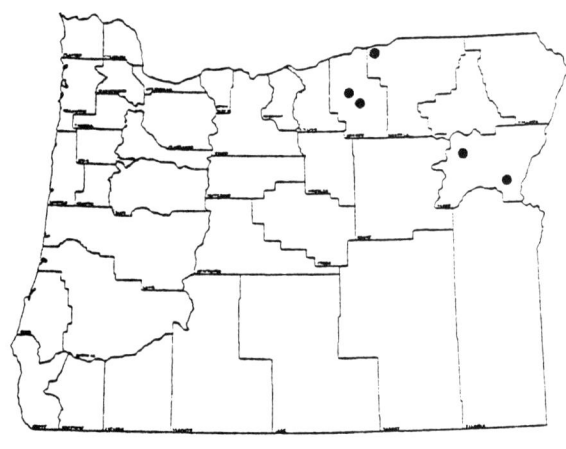
182. Heliopetes ericetorum

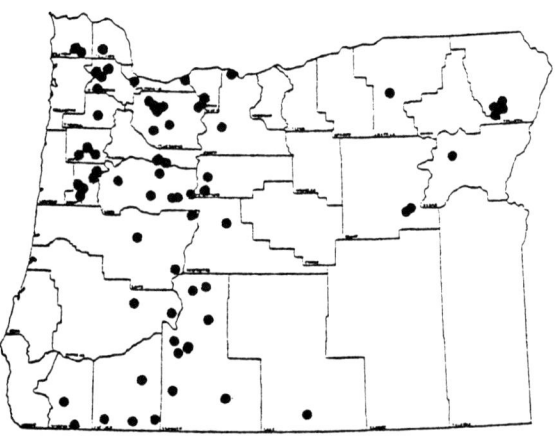
183. Pyrgus ruralis

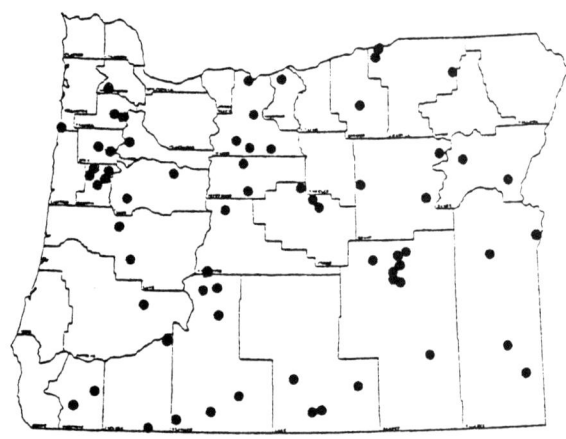
184. Pyrgus communis communis

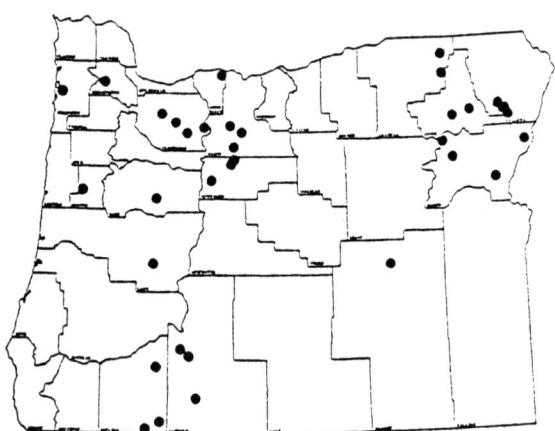
185. Erynnis icelus

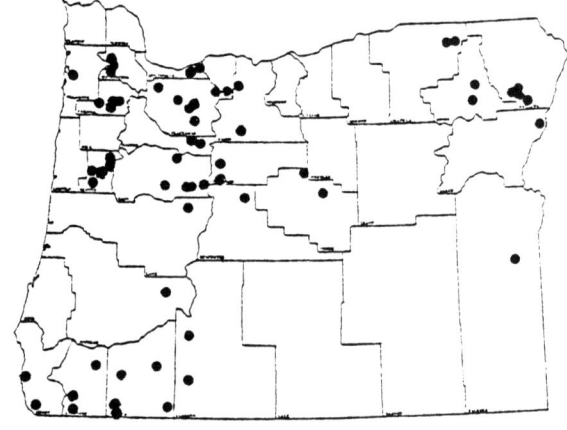
186. Erynnis persius persius

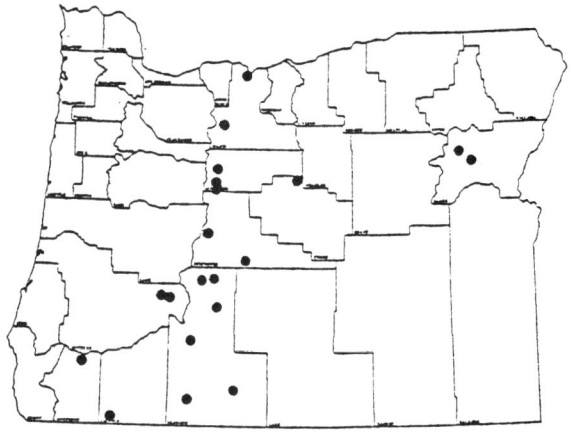

187. Erynnis pacuvius lilius

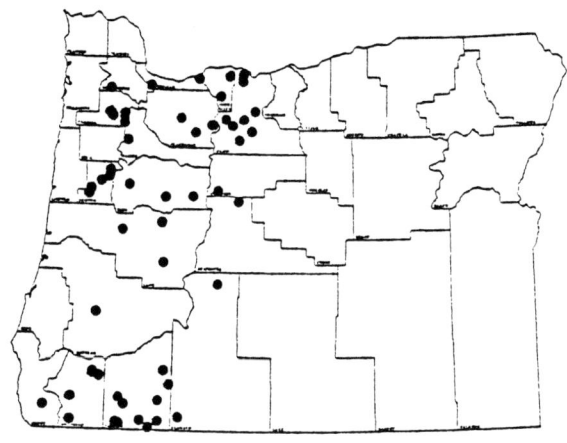

188. Erynnis propertius

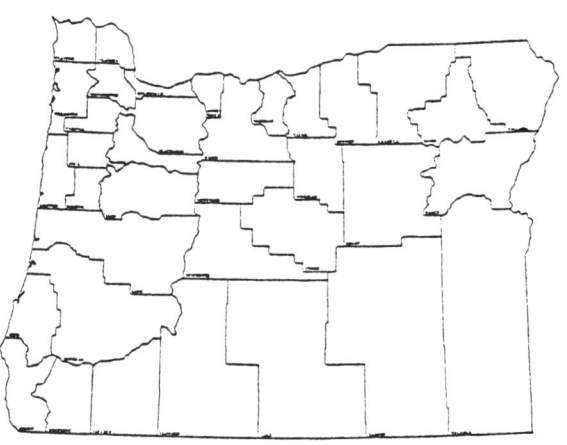

189. Erynnis funeralis

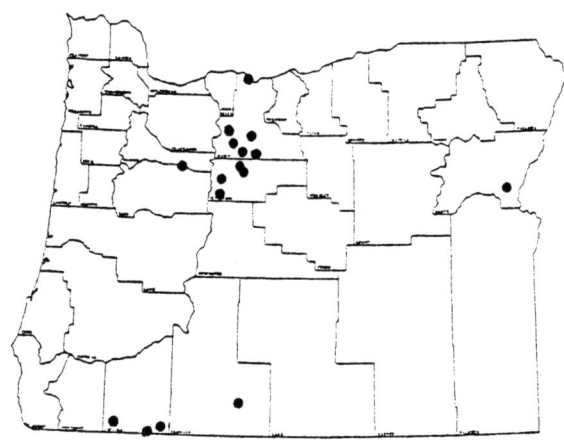

190. Thorybes pylades

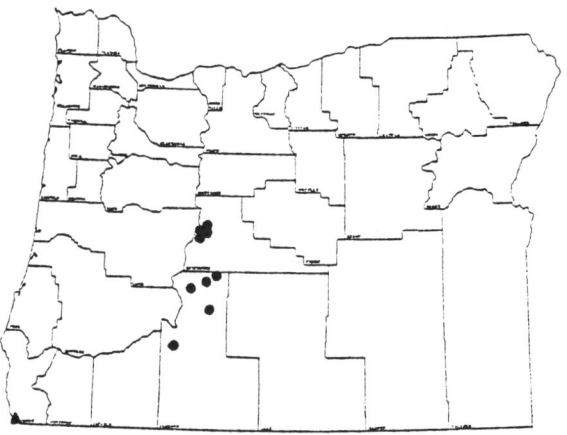

191. Thorybes mexicana nevada ●
    " diversus ▲

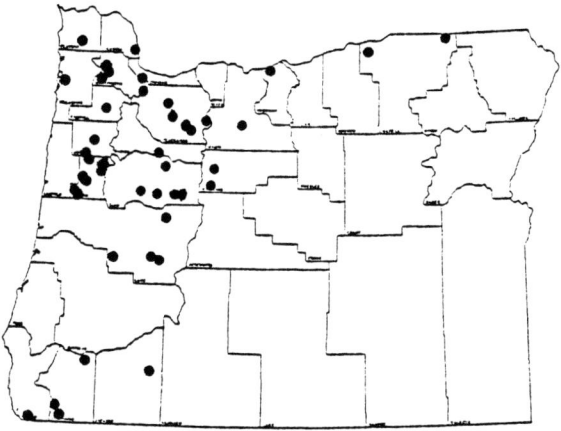

192. Epargyreus clarus californicus

CHECKLIST OF OREGON BUTTERFLIES

Note: An asterisk (*) indicates probable but unconfirmed presence within the borders of the State.

PAPILIONIDAE
 1. *Papilio oregonius* Edwards
 2. *Papilio zelicaon* Lucas
 3. *Papilio indra indra* Reakirt
 4. *Papilio rutulus rutulus* Lucas
 5. *Papilio multicaudata* Kirby
 6. *Papilio eurymedon* Lucas
 7. *Battus philenor hirsuta* (Skinner)
 8. *Parnassius clodius* Menetries
   a. *P. c. claudianus* Stichel
   b. *P. c. altaurus* Dyar
 9. *Parnassius phoebus* Fabricius
   a. *P. p. xanthus* Ehrmann
   b. *P. p. sternitzkyi* McDunnough

PIERIDAE
 10. *Neophasia menapia tau* (Scudder)
 11. *Pieris beckerii* Edwards
 12. *Pieris sisymbrii sisymbrii* Boisduval
 13. *Pieris protodice* Boisduval & LeConte
 14. *Pieris occidentalis* Reakirt
 15. *Pieris napi* (Linnaeus)
   a. *P. n. marginalis* Scudder
   b. *P. n. macdunnoughi* Remington (*)
 16. *Pieris rapae* (Linnaeus)
 17. *Colias eurytheme eurytheme* Boisduval
 18. *Colias philodice eriphyle* Edwards
 19. *Colias occidentalis occidentalis* Scudder
 20. *Colias alexandra edwardsii* Edwards
 21. *Colias interior interior* Scudder
 22. *Colias pelidne skinneri* Barnes
 23. *Nathalis iole* Boisduval (*)
 24. *Anthocharis sara* Lucas
   a. *A. s. flora* Wright
   b. *A. s. stella* Edwards
 25. *Anthocharis lanceolata lanceolata* Lucas
 26. *Euchloe hyantis* (Edwards)
   a. *E. h. hyantis* (Edwards)
   b. *E. h. lotta* (Beutenmüller)
 27. *Euchloe ausonides ausonides* (Lucas)

SATYRIDAE
 28. *Coenonympha tullia* (Mueller)
   a. *C. t. eunomia* Dornfeld
   b. *C. t. ampelos* Edwards
   c. *C. t. eryngii* Hy. Edwards
 29. *Neominois ridingsii stretchii* (Edwards)
 30. *Cercyonis pegala* (Fabricius)
   a. *C. p. boopis* (Behr)
   b. *C. p. ariane* (Boisduval)
   c. *C. p. blanca* Emmel & Mattoon (*)
 31. *Cercyonis sthenele* (Boisduval)
   a. *C. s. silvestris* (Edwards)
   b. *C. s. paulus* (Edwards)
 32. *Cercyonis oetus oetus* (Boisduval)
 33. *Oeneis nevadensis* (Felder & Felder)
 34. *Erebia epipsodea hopfingeri* Ehrlich

DANAIDAE
 31. *Danaus plexippus* (Linnaeus)

NYMPHALIDAE
 36. *Limenitis archippus* (Cramer)
   a. *L. a. archippus* (Cramer)
   b. *L. a. lahontani* Herlan (*)
 37. *Limenitis weidemeyerii latifascia* Perkins & Perkins
 38. *Limenitis lorquini* (Boisduval)
   a. *L. l. lorquini* (Boisduval)
   b. *L. l. burrisonii* Maynard
 39. *Adelpha bredowii californica* (Butler)
 40. *Vanessa atalanta rubria* (Fruhstorfer)
 41. *Vanessa virginiensis* (Drury)
 42. *Vanessa cardui* (Linnaeus)
 43. *Vanessa annabella* (Field)
 44. *Junonia coenia coenia* (Hübner)
 45. *Nymphalis vau-album watsoni* (Hall)
 46. *Nymphalis californica* (Boisduval)
 47. *Nymphalis milberti furcillata* (Say)
 48. *Nymphalis antiopa antiopa* (Linnaeus)
 49. *Polygonia satyrus neomarsyas* dos Passos
 50. *Polygonia faunus rusticus* (Edwards)
 51. *Polygonia zephyrus* (Edwards)
 52. *Polygonia oreas silenus* (Edwards)
 53. *Phyciodes tharos pascoensis* Wright
 54. *Phyciodes campestris campestris* (Behr)
 55. *Phyciodes orseis orseis* Edwards
 56. *Phyciodes mylitta mylitta* (Edwards)
 57. *Phyciodes pallida barnesi* Skinner
 58. *Chlosyne acastus* (Edwards)
   a. *C. a. acastus* (Edwards)

    b. *C. a. dorothyi* Bauer
59. *Chlosyne palla* (Boisduval)
    a. *C. p. palla* (Boisduval)
    b. *C. p. whitneyi* (Behr)
    c. *C. p. sterope* (Edwards)
60. *Chlosyne hoffmanni segregata* (Barnes & McDunnough)
61. *Chlosyne leanira* (Felder & Felder)
    a. *C. l. oregonensis* Bauer
    b. *C. l. alma* (Strecker)
62. *Euphydryas chalcedona* (Doubleday)
    a. *E. c. chalcedona* (Doubleday)
    b. *E. c. macglashanii* (Rivers)
    c. *E. c. colon* (Edwards)
    d. *E. c. wallacensis* Gunder
63. *Euphydryas anicia* (Doubleday)
    a. *E. a. veazieae* Fender & Jewett
    b. *E. a. bakeri* Stallings & Turner
    c. *E. a. macyi* Fender & Jewett
    d. *E. a. howlandi* Stallings & Turner
64. *Euphydryas editha* (Boisduval)
    a. *E. e. taylori* (Edwards)
    b. *E. e. baroni* (Edwards)
    c. *E. e edithana* (Strand)
    d. *E. e. colonia* (Wright)
    e. *E. e. remingtoni* Burdick
    f. *E. e. lawrencei* Gunder
65. *Boloria selene tollandensis* (Barnes & Benjamin)
66. *Boloria epithore* (Edwards)
    a. *B. e. chermocki* Perkins & Perkins
    b. *B. e. borealis* Perkins
67. *Speyeria cybele* (Fabricius)
    a. *S. c. pugetensis* Chermock & Frechin
    b. *S. c. leto* (Behr)
68. *Speyeria coronis* (Behr)
    a. *S. c. simaetha* dos Passos & Grey
    b. *S. c. snyderi* (Skinner)
69. *Speyeria zerene* (Boisduval)
    a. *S. z. conchyliatus* (Comstock)
    b. *S. z. gloriosa* Moeck
    c. *S. z. behrensii* (Edwards)
    d. *S. z. hippolyta* (Edwards)
    e. *S. z. bremnerii* (Edwards)
    f. *S. z. picta* (McDunnough)
    g. *S. z. garretti* (Gunder)
    h. *S. z. gunderi* (Comstock)
70. *Speyeria callippe* (Boisduval)
    a. *S. c. semivirida* (McDunnough)
    b. *S. c. harmonia* dos Passos & Grey
    c. *S. c. elaine* dos Passos & Grey
71. *Speyeria egleis* (Behr)
    a. *S. e. oweni* (Edwards)
    b. *S. e.* "Sand Creek type"
    c. *S. e. linda* (dos Passos & Grey)
    d. *S. e. macdunnoughi* (Gunder)
72. *Speyeria atlantis dodgei* (Gunder)
73. *Speyeria hydaspe* (Boisduval)
    a. *S. h. purpurascens* (Hy. Edwards)
    b. *S. h. rhodope* (Edwards)
74. *Speyeria mormonia* (Boisduval)
    a. *S. m. erinna* (Edwards)
    b. *S. m. artonis* (Edwards)

RIODINIDAE
74. *Apodemia mormo mormonia* (Boisduval)

LYCAENIDAE
76. *Habrodais grunus* (Boisduval)
    a. *H. g. lorquini* Field
    b. *H. g. herri* Field
77. *Harkenclenus titus immaculosus* (Comstock)
78. *Satyrium fuliginosum* (Edwards)
    a. *S. f. fuliginosum* (Edwards)
    b. *S. f. semiluna* Klots
79. *Satyrium behrii behrii* (Edwards)
80. *Satyrium tetra* (Edwards)
81. *Satyrium saepium saepium* (Boisduval)
82. *Satyrium sylvinus sylvinus* (Boisduval)
83. *Satyrium californica* (Edwards)
84. *Strymon melinus setonia* McDunnough
85. *Mitoura spinetorum* (Hewitson)
86. *Mitoura johnsoni* (Skinner)
87. *Mitoura nelsoni* (Boisduval)
88. *Incisalia polios obscurus* Ferris & Fisher
89. *Incisalia fotis mossii* (Hy. Edwards)
90. *Incisalia augustinus iroides* (Boisduval)
91. *Incisalia eryphon* (Boisduval)
    a. *I. e. eryphon* (Boisduval)
    b. *I. e. sheltonensis* Chermock & Frechin
92. *Callophrys dumetorum dumetorum* (Boisduval)
93. *Callophrys sheridanii* (Carpenter)
    a. *C. s. newcomeri* Clench
    b. *C. s. lemberti* Tilden
94. *Callophrys affinis washingtonia* Clench
95. *Atlides halesus corcorani* Clench
96. *Tharsalea arota arota* (Boisduval)
97. *Lycaena rubidus* (Behr)
    a. *L. r. rubidus* (Behr)
    b. *L. r. duofacies* Johnson & Balogh
    c. *L. r. perkinsorum* Johnson & Balogh
98. *Lycaena heteronea* (Boisduval)
    a. *L. h. heteronea* (Boisduval)
    b. *L. h. gravenotata* Klots
    c. *L. h. klotsi* Field
99. *Lycaena xanthoides xanthoides* (Boisduval)
100. *Lycaena editha editha* (Mead)
101. *Lycaena gorgon* (Boisduval)
102. *Lycaena mariposa mariposa* Reakirt
103. *Lycaena helloides* (Boisduval)
104. *Lycaena nivalis* (Boisduval)
    a. *L. n.* "Cascadian form"
    b. *L. n.* "Ochoco form"
105. *Lycaena phlaeas arctodon* Ferris
106. *Lycaena cupreus cupreus* (Edwards)
107. *Brephidium exilis* (Boisduval)
108. *Lycaeides argyrognomon ricei* (Cross)
109. *Lycaeides melissa melissa* (Edwards)
110. *Plebejus saepiolus saepiolus* (Boisduval)
111. *Icaricia icarioides* (Boisduval)
    a. *I. i. icarioides* (Boisduval)
    b. *I. i. ardea* (Edwards)
    c. *I. i. pembina* (Edwards)
    d. *I. i. fenderi* (Macy)
112. *Icaricia shasta shasta* (Edwards)
113. *Icaricia acmon* (Westwood & Hewitson)
    a. *I. a. acmon* (Westwood & Hewitson)

    b. *I. a. lutzi* (dos Passos)
114. *Icaricia lupini lupini* (Boisduval)
115. *Agriades aquilo podarce* (Felder & Felder)
116. *Everes comyntas comyntas* (Godart)
117. *Everes amyntula amyntula* (Boisduval)
118. *Philotes battoides* (Behr)
    a. *P. b. intermedia* Barnes & McDunnough
    b. *P. b. oregonensis* Barnes & McDunnough
    c. *P. b. glaucon* (Edwards)
119. *Philotes enoptes* (Boisduval)
    a. *P. e. enoptes* (Boisduval)
    b. *P. e. columbiae* Mattoni
120. *Glaucopsyche piasus* (Boisduval)
121. *Glaucopsyche lygdamus columbia* Skinner
122. *Celastrina argiolus echo* (Edwards)

HESPERIIDAE
123. *Amblyscirtes vialis* (Edwards)
124. *Euphyes vestris vestris* (Boisduval)
125. *Ochlodes sylvanoides sylvanoides* (Boisduval)
126. *Ochlodes agricola agricola* (Boisduval)
127. *Atalopedes campestris* (Boisduval)
128. *Polites coras* (Cramer)
129. *Polites sabuleti* (Boisduval)
130. *Polites mardon* (Edwards) (*)
131. *Polites themistocles* (Latreille) (*)
132. *Polites mystic* (Edwards)
133. *Polites sonora siris* (Edwards)
134. *Hesperia uncas lasus* (Edwards)
135. *Hesperia juba* (Scudder)
136. *Hesperia comma* (Linnaeus)
    a. *H. c. harpalus* (Edwards)
    b. *H. c. oregonia* (Edwards)
137. *Hesperia columbia* (Scudder)
138. *Hesperia lindseyi* (Holland)
139. *Hesperia nevada* (Scudder)
140. *Carterocephalus palaemon mandan* (Edwards)
141. *Pholisora catullus* (Fabricius)
142. *Pholisora libya lena* (Edwards)
143. *Pholisora alpheus oricus* (Edwards) (*)
144. *Heliopetes ericetorum* (Boisduval)
145. *Pyrgus ruralis* (Boisduval)
146. *Pyrgus communis communis* (Grote)
147. *Erynnis icelus* (Scudder & Burgess)
148. *Erynnis persius persius* (Scudder)
149. *Erynnis pacuvius lilius* (Dyar)
150. *Erynnis propertius* (Scudder & Burgess)
151. *Erynnis funeralis* (Scudder & Burgess) (*)
152. *Thorybes pylades* (Scudder)
153. *Thorybes mexicana nevada* Scudder
154. *Thorybes diversus* Bell
155. *Epargyreus clarus californicus* (Smith)

GLOSSARY

Abdomen. The most posterior body division, which follows the thorax.

Aberration. An abnormal individual; a "freak". *Aberrant,* adj.

Aedeagus. Male intromittent organ. See fig. 26.

Albino. An individual deficient in pigment; a whitish aberration. *Albinic, Albinistic,* adj. *Albinism,* n.

Allochronic. Appearing or flying at a different time.

Allopatric. Occupying a different geographic region.

Allotype. A type specimen of opposite sex to the holotype.

Anal (angle, margin, vein). In the direction of the last segment of the abdomen. See fig. 24.

Androconia. Scent scales on the male wing, usually grouped in patches.

Annular. Ring-shaped. *Annulate.* Composed of ring-like segments.

Antennae. Rod-like paired sensory (olfactory) organs of the head; "feelers".

Anterior. Toward the front; in the direction of the head.

Apex (pl. *Apices*). Tip; region furtherest removed from the base. See fig. 24. *Apical,* adj.

Apiculus. Short, pointed prolongation of the antenna beyond the terminal swelling, as in Skippers.

Aureolae. Groups or patches of orange and metallic scales along the margin of the hindwing underside in Blues (Plebejinae).

Autosomal. Referring to chromosomes other than the sex chromosomes.

Basal. Pertaining to the region nearest the body or point of attachment.

Basalt. Dark-gray to black rock, dense to fine-grained, of volcanic origin.

Bilateral. Having both sides equal or symmetrical.

Binomial. Consisting of two names, e.g., *Papilio rutulus* (genus and species).

Bursa copulatrix. Sperm-storing chamber of the female genital system.

Cell. (1) The microscopic unit of biological structure and function, consisting of cytoplasm and nucleus. (2) An area of the wing enclosed by veins, e.g., discal cell. See fig. 24.

Chaparral. A dense thicket of evergreen shrubs or low trees, e.g., Ceanothus, manzanita, or oak.

Chitin. The hard substance of the insect exoskeleton or cuticle, also known as *sclerotin.*

Chromosome. A filament in the cell nucleus bearing the genic material, composed of DNA and protein.

Chrysalis (pl. Chrysalids). The pupal stage of a butterfly.

Clasper. A paired organ of the male genitalia (the *valves*) by which the female abdomen is grasped during copulation. See fig. 26.

Cline. A series of geographic races (subspecies) connected by intergrades.

Cocoon. The silken covering or envelope of a pupa.

Co-evolution. The parallel or reciprocal evolution of insects and their host-plants.

Compound Eye. The large, paired lateral eye of insects composed of several thousand individual units, or ommatidia.

Conspecific. Belonging to the same species.

Costa. The thickened forward edge of the wing. See fig. 24.

Coxa. The basal segment of the insect leg. See fig. 23.

Cremaster. A set of minute hooks at the tip of the pupal abdomen, used for suspension.

Cretaceous. The last geological Period of the Mesozoic Era, 63 to 135 million years before the present.

Crochet. A circular set of terminal hooks on the prolegs (abdominal legs) of lepidopterous larvae.

Cryptic. Hidden or concealed, or imparting concealment.

Cubital Vein. A two-branched vein of the wings arising from the discal cell. See fig. 24.

Diapause. A condition of suspended animation during which development is arrested.

Dimorphic. Occurring in two forms with respect to shape, color, or pattern, e.g., sexual dimorphism.

Disc. The central area of the wing. *Discal,* adj. See fig. 24.

Dorsal. Pertaining to the upper side (opposite of ventral). *Dorsum,* the back.

Ecdysis. Molting. *Ecdysone,* the molt-producing hormone.

Eocene. The geological Epoch of the Tertiary Period preceding the Oligocene, 36 to 58 million years before the present.

Erythropterin. A red pigment derived from uric acid metabolism.

Facet. The hexagonal lens or cornea of an ommatidium, the unit of a compound eye.

Falx (pl. *Falces*). A slender, curved projection arising from the base of the uncus in the male genitalia. See fig. 26.

Family. A taxonomic category that includes a number of related genera; a division of an order.

Femur. The long middle segment of an insect leg, between the trochanter and the tibia. See fig. 23.

Flavones. A class of pigments derived directly from larval foodplants.

Form. One of two or more uniformly differing groups of individuals within a single population, e.g., seasonal forms, sexual dimorphs, genetic polymorphs.

Fringe Scales. Elongated scales that project beyond the membranous wing margin.

Genitalia. The structures associated with the reproductive system; usually applied to the chitinous framework. See fig. 26.

Genus. A taxonomic category that includes a number of related species; a division of a family.

Gynandromorph. An abnormal individual in which both male and female characteristics are present.

Haploid. Referring to a single set of chromosomes, as in an egg or a sperm.

Hemimetabolous. Having an incomplete metamorphosis in which the pupal stage is absent.

Hibernaculum. A shelter of leaves and silk in which a larva hides or hibernates.

Holometabolous. Having a complete metamorphosis that includes larval and pupal stages.

Holotype. A single individual selected as the type specimen by the author of a newly described species or subspecies.

Humeral Vein. A short spur of the costal vein at the base of the hindwing.

Hybrid. A cross between two species or genetically unlike individuals.

Imago. The adult stage of an insect. *Imaginal,* adj.

Immaculate. Devoid of spots or marks.

Instar. A larval stage between molts.

Integument. The outer coat, or cuticle, of the body.

Inter-. Prefix meaning between, e.g., *interspecific* = between species.

Intra-. Prefix meaning within, e.g., *intraspecific* = within a species.

Juvenile Hormone. A hormone that maintains the larval stage.

Labium. The lower lip. *Labial,* adj.

Larva. The second stage in the life cycle; a caterpillar.

Lateral. Relating to the side.

Leucopterin. A white pigment derived from uric acid metabolism.

Limbal Area. The outer portion of the discal area of the wing.

Lunule. A crescent shaped spot.

Maculation. Pattern of spots or blotches. *Macular, maculate,* adj.

Mandible. Jaw.

Margin. The edge, as of the wing. See fig. 24.

Maxillae. A lower pair of palpi-bearing jaws, modified in the adult to form the proboscis.

Median (area, veins). Situated in or at the middle. See fig. 24.

Melanin. A black or dark brown pigment resulting from the oxidation of tyrosin. *Melanic,* adj., dark or blackish, due to melanin deposit. *Melanism,* n.

Mesial. At or toward the middle.

Meso-. Prefix, referring to the middle, e.g. mesothorax.

Meta-. Prefix, designating a posterior region; after, behind; e.g., metathorax.

Mesozoic. The geological Era between the Cenozoic and Paleozoic, 63 to 230 million years before the present.

Metamorphosis. Abrupt change of form in the life cycle, viz., egg/larva/pupa/imago.

Micropyle. A pore or set of pores in the egg for entry of sperm.

Mimic. An individual that closely resembles another of an unrelated kind, known as the model. *Mimicry,* the phenomenon of mimic formation.

Miocene. The Tertiary geological Epoch following the Oligocene, 12 to 25 million years before the present.

Model. The noxious species of insect imitated in appearance by the mimic.

Molt. The shedding of the outgrown skin, or cuticle, between larval instars.

Monotypic. Not divided into geographic races or subspecies.

Mosaic. (1) In insect vision, the type of image produced by the compound eye, a combination of light points from the component ommatidia. (2) A mottled pattern resulting from tissue patches of different genetic composition, e.g., a sex-mosaic.

Myrmecophily. A symbiotic relationship with ants, as in some Lycaenidae.

Neotype. An individual selected to replace a lost or destroyed type specimen.

Nomenclature. The system of names used in classification.

Nominotypic (also, *nominate* or *nymotypic*). The first-named in a series of subspecies, e.g., *Philotes enoptes enoptes.*

Nymph. The middle stage of the life cycle in incomplete metamorphosis.

Ocellus (pl. *Ocelli*). (1) The simple eye of a larva. (2) An eye-like spot. *Ocellated,* marked with eye-like spots.

Oligocene. The geological middle Epoch of the Tertiary Period, 25 to 36 million years before the present.

Ommatidium. A visual unit of the compound eye.

Order. A taxonomic category below a Class, itself divided into Families.

Osmeterium. A pungent-smelling and eversible Y-shaped gland back of the head in papilionid larvae.

Paleozoic. The geological Era before the Mesozoic, 230 to 570 million years before the present.

Palpus (pl. *Palpi*). A paired, feeler-like projection of a mouthpart. See figs. 17 and 22.

Paratype. Any specimen other than the holotype from which an original description has been written.

Pheromone. A volatile chemical substance that functions as a sexual stimulant.

Photoperiod. The amount of daylight per day or of daily exposure to illumination.

Pleistocene. A geological Epoch of the Quaternary Period, 15 thousand to 3 million years before the present.

Polymorphic. Occurring in several forms that differ genetically or with respect to sex. *Polymorphism,* n.

Polyphenic. Occurring in several forms that are environmentally caused, e.g., seasonal forms. *Polyphenism,* n.

Polytypic. Composed of several geographic races, or subspecies.

Posterior. Toward the rear; behind.

Pro-. Prefix meaning anterior, forward, in front; in place of.

Proboscis. The tubular, sucking mouthpart of a butterfly ("tongue").

Proleg. The abdominal "false" leg of a caterpillar. See fig. 18.

Pterins. A class of pigments derived from the metabolism of uric acid.

Pumice. Rock or soil of volcanic origin, very light in weight and porous.

Pupa. The intermediate quiescent stage between larva and adult; the chrysalis.

Quaternary. The last geological period, which includes the Pleistocene and Recent Epochs and extends back about 3 million years.

Radial Veins. Branched veins of the wings posterior to the subcostal and anterior to the median veins. See fig. 24.

Scales. Minute, shingle-like, color-bearing plates (highly modified hairs) that cover the wings of Lepidoptera. See fig. 25.

Scent-pad. A patch of androconial scales.

Sclerite. A chitinous unit of the insect body-wall; an exoskeletal plate.

Sedimentary. Formed from deposits of water-transported rock fragments or salts.

Serpentine. Magnesium-rich rock, usually greenish and mottled; soil of such composition.

Segment. A subdivision of the body or of an appendage.

Seta (pl. *Setae*). A hair or bristle.

Sex Brand. A diagonal line on the forewing of certain male Skippers which demarcates a pocket of androconial scales.

Shale. Cleavable rock formed from compacted layers of silt or clay.

Silt. Sedimentary material of particles smaller than sand but larger than clay.

Silurian. A geological Period of the Paleozoic Era, 400 to 430 million years before the present.

Speciation. The evolutionary process by which species and subspecies are formed.

Species. The primary unit of classification, biologically defined as a population or group of populations the individuals of which are actually or potentially capable of interbreeding and producing fertile offspring and are reproductively isolated from other such groups.

Sphragis. A pouch-like structure at the tip of the abdomen in female Parnassians, secreted by the male during copulation.

Spinneret. The silk extruding organ of the larva. See fig. 17.

Spiracle. An opening on the body-wall through which air enters the tracheae.

Stigma (pl. *Stigmata*). (1) The diagonal mark of an androconial pocket on the forewings of certain Skippers. (2) A spiracle.

Stridulating Organ. A file-and-rasp-like structure for making sound.

Sub-. Prefix meaning under, or slightly less than.

Subspecies. A geographic race.

Super-. Prefix meaning above, beyond.

Symbiosis. A close association or living together of two dissimilar species which is usually of mutual advantage. *Symbiotic,* adj.

Sympatric. Occupying the same geographic region.

Synchronic. Appearing or flying at the same time.

Tarsus. The terminal jointed segment of an insect leg. See fig. 23.

Taxonomy. Classification according to natural relationships.

Tegumen. (1) The upper surface of a body segment. (2) A roof-like plate of the male genitalia. See fig. 26.

Tertiary. The geological Period of the Cenozoic Era before the Quaternary, 3 to 63 million years before the present.

Thermoregulation. The mechanism for producing and maintaining body heat.

Thorax. The middle division of the insect body, from which the legs and wings arise.

Tibia. The segment of the insect leg between the femur and the tarsus. See fig. 23.

Topotype. A specimen from the same locality as the type.

Trachea. An internal air-tube of the insect respiratory system.

Trinomial. Pertaining to a name with three components: genus, species, and subspecies, e.g., *Philotes enoptes columbiae.*

Trochanter. The small segment of an insect leg between the coxa and the femur. See fig. 23.

Tubercle. A small elevation of the larval or pupal cuticle, sometimes bearing setae. *Tuberculate,* covered with tubercles.

Type. A specimen (holotype) or one of series of speciments (paratypes) from which the description of a new species or subspecies is written.

Uncus. In the male genitalia, the terminal dorsal plate whose base articulates with the tegumen. See fig. 26.

Valve. In the male genitalia, one of the pair of claspers that extend posteriorly from the lower sides of the vinculum. See fig. 26.

Veins. The rod-like or tubular structures that traverse and support the wing; the "nerves" of the wing.

Venation. The system of wing veins; the "neuration" of the wings. See fig. 24.

Ventral. Beneath, pertaining to the underside.

Verruca (pl. *Verrucae*). A tubercle or wart-like prominence of the skin bearing a tuft of setae.

Vinculum. In the male genitalia, a U-shaped sclerite whose arms articulate with the tegumen to form a ring. See fig. 26.

Xanthopterin A yellow pigment derived from the metabolism of uric acid.

INDEX

References are to the principal entries in the Systematic Account and to the relevant Plates and Maps. For general topics and technical terms the Table of Contents and the Glossary should be consulted.

acastus, Chlosyne, 69, P-19, M-62
acmon, Icaricia, 101, P-41, M-147
Adelpha
  bredowii californica, 61, P-14, M-42
  bredowii eulalia, 61
adenostomatis, Strymon, 87
Admiral
  Lorquin's, 61, P-14, M-41
  Red, 61, P-15, M-43
  Weidemeyer's, 60, P-14, M-40
affinis, Callophrys, 93, P-36, M-127
Agriades
  aquilo podarce, 102, P-41, M-149
  aquilo rustica, 102
agricola, Ochlodes, 109, P-43, M-163
alba (form), *Colias eurytheme,* 47, P-6
alexandra, Colias, 48, P-7, M-20
Alfalfa Butterfly, 47, P-6, M-17
alma, Chlosyne leanira, 70, P-48, M-67
alpheus, Pholisora, 115, P-46, M-181
Alpine, Common, 56, P-12, M-37
altaurus, Parnassius clodius, 43
Amblyscirtes
  vialis, 108, P-43, M-160
ampelos, Coenonympha tullia, 53, P-9, M-29
amphidusa (form), *Colias eurytheme,* 47, P-6
amyntula, Everes, 103, P-41, M-151
ancilla, Philotes enoptes, 105
Anglewing
  Faun, 66, P-17, M-53
  Satyr, 65, P-17, M-52
  Silenus, 66, P-17, M-55
  Zephyr, 66, P-17, M-54
anicia, Euphydryas, 72, P-21, M-72-75
anna, Lycaeides argyrognomon, 98
annabella, Vanessa, 63, P-15, M-46
Anthocharis
  lanceolata lanceolata, 50, P-8, M-25
  sara flora, 50, P-8, M-24
  sara julia, 50
  sara stella, 50, P-8, M-24
Apodemia
  mormo mormonia, 84, P-34, M-107
aquilo, Agriades, 102, P-41, M-149
archippus, Limenitis, 60, P-13, M-39
Arctic, Great, 55, P-12, M-36

arctodon, Lycaena phlaeas, 97, P-39, M-139
ardea, Icaricia icarioides, 100, P-40, M-145
argiolus, Celastrina, 106, P-41, M-159
Argynninae, 59

Argynnis, 75
argyrognomon, Lycaeides, 98, P-40, M-142
ariadne (form), *Colias eurytheme,* 47, P-6
ariane, Cercyonis pegala, 54, P-11, M-33
arion, Maculinea, 85
arota, Tharsalea, 93, P-37, M-129
arthemis, Limenitis, 60

Artogeia
  napi, 46, P-5, M-15
  rapae, 47, P-5, M-16
artonis, Speyeria mormonia, 80, P-33, M-106
Ascia, 44
atalanta, Vanessa, 61, P-15, M-43
Atalopedes
  campestris, 109, P-43, M-164
atlantis, Speyeria, 80, P-31, M-102
Atlides
  halesus corcorani, 93, P-37, M-128
atrapraetextus, Lycaeides argyrognomon, 99
atrofasciata, Strymon melinus, 88
augustinus, Incisalia, 91, P-36, M-122
ausonides, Euchloe, 51, P-8, M-27
bakeri, Celastrina argiolus, 106
bakeri, Euphydryas anicia, 73, P-21, M-73
Banded Purple, 60
barnesi, Phyciodes pallida, 68, P-18, M-61
baroni, Euphydryas editha, 73, P-22, M-77
Baronia
  brevicornis, 39
barryi, Mitoura, 90
Basilarchia, 60
battoides, Philotes, 103, P-42, M-152-154
Battus
  philenor hirsuta, 42, P-2, M-7
bayensis, Incisalia fotis, 90
bayensis, Philotes enoptes, 105
beckerii, Pieris, 45, P-4, M-11
behrensii, Speyeria zerene, 77, P-26, M-90
behrii, Satyrium, 87, P-34, M-111
Bird-wings, 39
blanca, Cercyonis pegala, 54

Blue
  Acmon, 101, P-41, M-147
  Arctic, 102, P-41, M-149
  Arrowhead, 105, P-42, M-157
  Battoides, 103, P-42, M-152-154
  Boisduval's, 100, P-40, M-145
  Columbia, 105, P-42, M-156
  Columbia Silvery, 105, P-42, M-158
  Dotted, 105, P-42, M-155
  Eastern Tailed, 102, P-41, M-150
  Echo, 106, P-41, M-159
  Enoptes, 104, P-42, M-155-156
  European Large, 85
  Glaucous, 104, P-42, M-154
  Glossy, 99, P-40, M-144
  Intermediate, 104, P-42, M-152
  Karner, 99
  Lupine, 102, P-41, M-148
  Melissa, 99, P-40, M-143
  Oregon, 104, P-42, M-153
  Pigmy, 98, P-40, M-141
  Rice's, 98, P-40, M-142
  Shasta, 101, P-41, M-146
  Western Tailed, 103, P-41, M-151
Boloria
  epithore borealis, 75, P-23, M-84
  epithore chermocki, 74, P-23, M-83
  selene tollandensis, 74, P-23, M-82
boopis, Cercyonis pegala, 54, P-10, M-32
borealis, Boloria epithore, 75, P-23, M-84
bredowii, Adelpha, 61, P-14, M-42
bremnerii, Speyeria zerene, 78, P-26, M-92
Brephidium
  exilis, 98, P-40, M-141
brevicornis, Baronia, 39
Buckeye, 63, P-15, M-47
burrisonii, Limenitis lorquini, 61, P-14, M-41
Cabbage Butterfly, 47, P-5, M-16
c-album, Polygonia, 65
California Sister, 61, P-14, M-42
californica, Adelpha bredowii, 61, P-14, M-42
californica, Nymphalis, 64, P-16, M-49
californica, Satyrium, 88, P-35, M-115
californicus, Epargyreus clarus, 120, P-48, M-192
callippe, Speyeria, 78, P-28,29, M-95-97
Callipsyche
  behrii, 87, P-34, M-111
Callophrys
  affinis washingtonia, 93, P-36, M-127
  dumetorum dumetorum, 92, P-36, M-124
  dumetorum oregonensis, 92
  sheridanii lemberti, 92, P-36, M-125
  sheridanii newcomeri, 92, P-36, M-126
calyce (form), *Pieris occidentalis*, 46, P-5
Camberwell Beauty, 65, P-16, M-51
campestris, Atalopedes, 109, P-43, M-164
campestris, Phyciodes, 67, P-18, M-57,58
cardui, Vanessa, 62, P-15, M-45
Carterocephalus
  palaemon mandan, 114, P-46, M-178
catullus, Pholisora, 115, P-46, M-179
Celastrina
  argiolus bakeri, 106

  argiolus echo, 106, P-41, M-159
Cercyonis
  oetus oetus, 55, P-11, M-35
  pegala ariane, 54, P-11, M-33
  pegala blanca, 54
  pegala boopis, 54, P-10, M-32
  sthenele paulus, 54, P-11, M-34
  sthenele silvestris, 54, P-4, M-34
chalcedona, Euphydryas, 72, P-20, M-68-71
Chalceria
  rubidus, 94, P-37, M-130
  heteronea, 94, P-37, M-131
Charidryas
  acastus, 69, P-19, M-62
  hoffmanni, 70, P-19, M-66
  palla, 69, P-19, M-63-65
Checkerspot
  Acastus, 69, P-19, M-62
  Anicia, 72, P-21, M-72-75
  Baker's, 73, P-21, M-73
  Baron's, 73, P-22, M-77
  Chalcedon, 72, P-20, M-68-71
  Colon, 72, P-20, M-70
  Colonia, 73, P-22, M-79
  Editha, 73, P-22, M-76-81
  Edithana, 73, P-22, M-78
  Gunder's, 72, P-20, M-71
  Hoffmann's, 70, P-19, M-66
  Howland's, 73, P-21, M-75
  Lawrence's, 74, P-22, M-81
  Leanira, 70, P-19,48, M-67
  Macglashan's, 72, P-20, M-69
  Macy's, 73, P-21, M-74
  Northern, 69, P-19, M-63-65
  Palouse, 70, P-19, M-65
  Remington's, 74, P-22, M-80
  Taylor's, 73, P-22, M-76
  Veazie's, 73, P-21, M-72
  Whitney's, 69, P-19, M-64
chermocki, Boloria epithore, 74, P-23, M-83
Chlosyne
  acastus acastus, 69, P-19, M-62
  acastus dorothyi, 69
  hoffmanni manchada, 70
  hoffmanni segregata, 70, P-19, M-66
  leanira alma, 70, P-48, M-67
  leanira oregonensis, 70, P-19, M-67
  palla palla, 69, P-19, M-63
  palla sterope, 70, P-19, M-65
  palla whitneyi, 69, P-19, M-64
chryxus, Oeneis, 56
clarus, Epargyreus, 120, P-48, M-192
claudianus, Parnassius clodius, 43, P-3, M-8
clodius, Parnassius, 42, P-3, M-8
Cloudy Wing
  Bell's, 119, P-48, M-191
  Nevada, 119, P-48, M-191
  Northern, 119, P-48, M-190
coenia, Junonia, 63, P-15, M-47
Coenonympha
  haydenii, 53
  tullia ampelos, 53, P-9, M-29
  tullia eryngii, 53, P-9, M-30

tullia eunomia, 53, P-9, M-28
Colias
  alexandra edwardsii, 48, P-7, M-20
  alexandra emilia, 48
  eurytheme eurytheme, 47, P-6, M-17
  interior interior, 49, P-7, M-21
  occidentalis occidentalis, 48, P-6, M-19
  pelidne skinneri, 49, P-7, M-22
  philodice eriphyle, 48, P-6, M-18
colon, Euphydryas chalcedona, 72, P-20, M-70
colonia, Euphydryas editha, 73, P-22, M-79
columbia, Glaucopsyche lygdamus, 105, P-42, M-158
columbia, Hesperia, 113, P-45, M-175
columbiae, Philotes enoptes, 105, P-42, M-156
Comma Butterflies, 65
comma, Hesperia, 113, P-45, M-173,174
comyntas, Everes, 102, P-41, M-150
conchyliatus, Speyeria zerene, 77, P-25, M-88
Copper
  Arota, 93, P-37, M-129
  Beartooth, 97, P-39, M-139
  Blue, 94, P-37, M-131
  Edith's, 95, P-38, M-133
  Gorgon, 96, P-38, M-134
  Great, 95, P-38, M-132
  Lustrous, 98, P-39, M-140
  Mariposa, 96, P-38, M-135
  Nivalis, 97, P-39, M-137,138
  Purplish, 96, P-39, M-136
  Puddy, 94, P-37, M-130
coras, Polites, 109, P-44, M-165
corcorani, Atlides halesus, 93, P-37, M-128
coronis, Speyeria, 76, P-24, M-87
cottlei (form), *Icaricia acmon,* 101
Crescent
  Barnes', 68, P-18, M-61
  Field, 67, P-18, M-57,58
  Mylitta, 68, P-18, M-60
  Orseis, 68, P-18, M-59
  Pasco, 67, P-18, M-56
creusa, Euchloe, 50
cupreus, Lycaena, 98, P-39, M-140
cybele, Speyeria, 76, P-23, M-85,86
cynna, Speyeria zerene, 78
Cynthia
  annabella, 63, P-15, M-46
  cardui, 62, P-15, M-45
  virginiensis, 62, P-15, M-44
dacotah, Polites mystic, 111, P-44, M-169
Danaidae, family, 57
Danaus
  plexippus, 58, P-13, M-38
diversus, Thorybes, 119, P-48, M-191
dodgei, Speyeria atlantis, 80, P-31, M-102
dorothyi, Chlosyne acastus, 69
dumetorum, Callophrys, 92, P-36, M-124
duofacies, Lycaena rubidus, 94, P-37, M-130
Duskywing
  Dreamy, 117, P-47, M-185
  Dyar's, 118, P-47, M-187
  Funereal, 118, P-47, M-189
  Persius, 117, P-47, M-186
  Propertius, 118, P-47, M-188

Dwarf Yellow, 50, P-7, M-23
echo, Celastrina argiolus, 106, P-41, M-159
editha, Euphydryas, 73, P-22, M-76-81
editha, Lycaena, 95, P-38, M-133
edithana, Euphydryas editha, 73, P-22, M-78
edwardsii, Colias alexandra, 48, P-7, M-20
egleis, Speyeria, 79, P-30, M-98-101
elaine, Speyeria callippe, 79, P-29, M-97
Elfin
  Brown, 91, P-36, M-122
  Hoary, 90, P-36, M-120
  Moss's, 90, P-36, M-121
  Western Pine, 91, P-36, M-123
emilia, Colias alexandra, 48
enoptes, Philotes, 104, P-42, M-155,156
Epargyreus
  clarus californicus, 120, P-48, M-192
Epidemia
  helloides, 96, P-39, M-136
  mariposa, 96, P-38, M-135
  nivalis, 97, P-39, M-137,138
epipsodea, Erebia, 56, P-12, M-37
epithore, Boloria, 74, P-23, M-83,84
Erebia
  epipsodea hopfingeri, 56, P-12, M-37
eremita (form), *Chlosyne palla,* 69, P-19
ericetorum, Heliopetes, 116, P-46, M-182
erinna, Speyeria mormonia, 80, P-33, M-105
eriphyle, Colias philodice, 48, P-6, M-18
eryngii, Coenonympha tullia, 53, P-9, M-30
Erynnis
  funeralis, 118, P-47, M-189
  icelus, 117, P-47, M-185
  pacuvius lilius, 118, P-47, M-187
  persius persius, 117, P-47, M-186
  propertius, 118, P-47, M-188
eryphon, Incisalia, 91, P-36, M-123
Euchloe
  ausonides ausonides, 51, P-8, M-27
  creusa, 50
  hyantis hyantis, 51, M-26
  hyantis lotta, 51, P-8, M-26
eulalia, Adelpha bredowii, 61
eunomia, Coenonympha tullia, 53, P-9, M-28
Euphilotes
  battoides, 103, P-42, M-152-154
  enoptes, 104, P-42, M-155,156
Euphydryas, 71
  anicia bakeri, 73, P-21, M-73
  anicia howlandi, 73, P-21, M-75
  anicia macyi, 73, P-21, M-47
  anicia veazieae, 73, P-21, M-72
  chalcedona chalcedona, 72, P-20, M-68
  chalcedona colon, 72, P-20, M-70
  chalcedona macglashanii, 72, P-20, M-69
  chalcedona wallacensis, 72, P-20, M-71
  editha baroni, 73, P-22, M-77
  editha colonia, 73, P-22, M-79
  editha edithana, 73, P-22, M-78
  editha lawrencei, 74, P-22, M-81
  editha remingtoni, 74, P-22, M-80
  editha taylori, 73, P-22, M-76

Euphyes
  vestris metacomet, 108
  vestris vestris, 108, P-43, M-161
eurymedon, Papilio, 42, P-2, M-6
eurynome, Speyeria mormonia, 80
eurytheme, Colias, 47, P-6, M-17
Everes
  amyntula amyntula, 103, P-41, M-151
  comyntas comyntas, 102, P-41, M-150
exilis, Brephidium, 98, P-40, M-141
Falcapica
  lanceolata, 50, P-8, M-25
faunus, Polygonia, 66, P-17, M-53
fenderi, Icaricia icarioides, 100, P-40, M-145
flava (form), *Pieris sisymbrii,* 45
flora, Anthocharis sara, 50, P-8, M-24
fotis, Incisalia, 90, P-36, M-121
Fritillary
  Artonis, 80, P-33, M-106
  Atlantis, 80, P-31, M-102
  Behrens', 77, P-26, M-90
  Bremner's, 78, P-26, M-92
  Callippe, 78, P-28,29, M-95-97
  Coronis, 76, P-24, M-87
  Dodge's, 80, P-31, M-102
  Egleis, 79, P-30,31, M-98-101
  Elaine's, 79, P-29, M-97
  Erinna, 80, P-33, M-105
  Garrett's, 78, P-27, M-93
  Great Spangled, 76
  Gunder's, 78, P-27, M-94
  Hippolyta, 77, P-26, M-91
  Hydaspe, 80, P-32, M-103,104
  Leto, 76, P-23, M-86
  Linda's, 79, P-30, M-101
  McDunnough's, 79, P-31, M-100
  Mormon, 80, P-33, M-105,106
  Owen's, 79, P-30, M-98
  Painted, 78, P-27, M-93
  Puget Sound, 76, P-23, M-85
  Royal, 77, P-25, M-88
  Sand Creek, 79, P-30, M-99
  Zerene, 77, P-25-27, M-88-94
fuliginosum, Satyrium, 86, P-34, M-110
funeralis, Erynnis, 118, P-47, M-189
furcillata, Nymphalis milberti, 65, P-16, M-50
Gaeides
  editha, 95, P-38, M-133
  gorgon, 96, P-38, M-134
  xanthoides, 95, P-38, M-132
garretti, Speyeria zerene, 78, P-27, M-93
glaucon, Philotes battoides, 104, P-42, M-154
Glaucopsyche
  lygdamus columbia, 105, P-42, M-158
  piasus, 105, P-42, M-157
glaucus, Papilio, 39,41
gloriosa, Speyeria zerene, 77, P-25, M-89
gorgon, Lycaena, 96, P-38, M-134
gravenotata, Lycaena heteronea, 95, P-37
grunus, Habrodais, 86, P-34, M-108
gunderi, Speyeria zerene, 78, P-27, M-94
Habrodais
  grunus herri, 86, P-34, M-108

  grunus lorquini, 86
Hairstreak
  Behr's, 87, P-34, M-111
  Bramble Green, 92, P-36, M-124
  California, 88, P-35, M-115
  Chinquapin, 86, P-34, M-108
  Common, 88, P-35, M-116
  Coral, 86, P-34, M-109
  Gray, 87, P-34, M-112
  Great Blue, 93, P-37, M-128
  Johnson's, 89, P-35, M-118
  Lembert's Green, 92, P-36, M-125
  Nelson's, 89, P-35, M-119
  Newcomer's Green, 92, P-36, M-126
  Russet, 87, P-34, M-113
  Sheridan's Green, 92, P-36, M-125,126
  Sooty, 86, P-34, M-110
  Sylvan, 88, P-35, M-114
  Thicket, 89, P-35, M-117
  Washington Green, 93, P-36, M-127
halesus, Atlides, 93, P-37, M-128
Harkenclenus
  titus immaculosus, 86, P-34, M-109
harmonia, Speyeria callippe, 78, P-29, M-96
harpalus, Hesperia comma, 113, P-45, M-173
haydenii, Coenonympha, 53
Heliopetes
  ericetorum, 116, P-46, M-182
helloides, Lycaena, 96, P-39, M-136
henryae, Lycaena cupreus, 98
herri, Habrodais grunus, 87, P-34, M-108
Hesperia, 111
  columbia, 113, P-45, M-175
  comma harpalus, 113, P-45, M-173
  comma idaho, 113
  comma oregnoia, 113, P-45, M-174
  juba, 112, P-45, M-172
  lindseyi, 114, P-45, M-176
  nevada, 114, P-45, M-177
  uncas lasus, 112, P-45, M-171
  uncas macswaini, 112
Hesperiidae, family, 107
Hesperiinae, 107
Heterochroa, 61
heteronea, Lycaena, 94, P-37, M-131
hippolyta, Speyeria zerene, 77, P-26, M-91
hirsuta, Battus philenor, 42, P-2, M-7
hoffmanni, Chlosyne, 70, P-19, M-66
hopfingeri, Erebia epipsodea, 56, P-12, M-37
howlandi, Euphydryas anicia, 73, P-21, M-75
hunteri, Vanessa, 62
hyantis, Euchloe, 51, P-8, M-26
hydaspe, Speyeria, 80, P-32, M-103,104
hypophlaeas, Lycaena phlaeas, 97, P-39
Icaricia
  acmon acmon, 101, P-41, M-147
  acmon lutzi, 101
  acmon texanus, 102
  icarioides ardea, 100, P-40, M-145
  icarioides fenderi, 100, P-40, M-145
  icarioides icarioides, 100, P-40, M-145
  icarioides pardalis, 100
  icarioides pembina, 100, P-40, M-145

lupini lupini, 102, P-41, M-148
shasta shasta, 101, P-41, M-146
icarioides, Icaricia, 100, P-40, M-145
icelus, Erynnis, 117, P-47, M-185
idaho, Hesperia comma, 113
immaculosus, Harkenclenus titus, 86, P-34, M-109
Incisalia
augustinus iroides, 91, P-36, M-122
eryphon eryphon, 91, P-36, M-123
eryphon sheltonensis, 91
fotis bayensis, 90
fotis mossii, 90, P-36, M-121
polios obscurus, 90, P-36, M-120
indra, Papilio, 41, P-1, M-3
interior, Colias, 49, P-7, M-21
intermedia, Philotes battoides, 104, P-42, M-152
iole, Nathalis, 50, P-7, M-23
iroides, Incisalia augustinus, 91, P-36, M-122
j-album, Nymphalis vau-album, 64
johnsoni, Mitoura, 89, P-35, M-118
juba, Hesperia, 112, P-45, M-172
julia, Anthocharis sara, 50
Junonia
coenia coenia, 63, P-15, M-47
klotsi, Lycaena heteronea, 95
Lady
Painted, 62, P-15, M-45
Virginia, 62, P15, M-44
Western, 63, P-15, M-46
lahontani, Limenitis archippus, 60
lanceolata, Anthocharis, 50, P-8, M-25
lasus, Hesperia uncas, 112, P-45, M-171
latifascia, Limenitis weidemeyerii, 60, P-14, M-40
lawrencei, Euphydryas editha, 74, P-22, M-81
leanira, Chlosyne, 70, P-19,48, M-67
lemberti, Callophrys sheridanii, 92, P-36, M-125
lena, Pholisora libya, 115, P-46, M-180
Lethe, 52
leto, Speyeria cybele, 76, P-23, M-86
libya, Pholisora, 115, P-46, M-180
lilius, Erynnis pacuvius, 118, P-47, M-187
Limenitinae, 59
Limenitis
archippus archippus, 60, P-13, M-39
archippus lahontani, 60
arthemis, 60
lorquini burrisonii, 61, P-14, M-41
lorquini lorquini, 61
weidemeyerii latifascia, 60, P-14, M-40
linda, Speyeria egleis, 79, P-30, M-101
lindseyi, Hesperia, 114, P-45, M-176
lorquini, Habrodais grunus, 86
lorquini, Limenitis, 61, P-14, M-41
lotta, Euchloe hyantis, 51, P-8, M-26
lucia (form), *Celastrina argiolus,* 106, P-41
lupini, Icaricia, 102, P-41, M-148
lutzi, Icaricia acmon, 101
Lycaeides
argyrognomon anna, 98
argyrognomon atrapraetextus, 99
argyrognomon ricei, 98, P-40, M-142
melissa melissa, 99, P-40, M-143
melissa samuelis, 99

Lycaena
cupreus cupreus, 98, P-39, M-140
cupreus henryae, 98
cupreus snowi, 98
editha editha, 95, P-38, M-133
gorgon, 96, P-38, M-134
helloides, 96, P-39, M-136
heteronea gravenotata, 95, P-37, M-131
heteronea heteronea, 95, P-37, M-131
heteronea klotsi, 95
mariposa mariposa, 96, P-38, M-135
nivalis, 97, P-39, M-137,138
phlaeas arctodon, 97, P-39, M-139
phlaeas hypophlaeas, 97, P-39
rubidus duofacies, 94, P-37, M-130
rubidus perkinsorum, 94, P-37, M-130
rubidus rubidus, 94, P-37, M-130
xanthoides xanthoides, 95, P-38, M-132
Lycaenidae, family, 85
Lycaeninae, 85
lygdamus, Glaucopsyche, 105, P-42, M-158
macdunnoughi, Pieris napi, 46
macdunnoughi, Speyeria egleis, 79, P-31, M-100
macglashanii, Euphydryas chalcedona, 72, P-20, M-69
machaon, Papilio, 39,40,41
macswaini, Hesperia uncas, 112
Maculinea
arion, 85
macyi, Euphydryas anicia, 73, P-21, M-74
manchada, Chlosyne hoffmanni, 70
mandan, Carterocephalus palaemon, 114, P-46, M-178
Marble
Creamy, 51, P-8, M-27
Lanceolate, 50, P-8, M-25
Pearly, 50, P-8, M-26
mardon, Polites, 110, P-44, M-167
marginalis, Pieris napi, 46, P-5, M-15
mariposa, Lycaena, 96, P-38, M-135
marsyas, Polygonia satyrus, 65
Meadow Fritillary
Chermock's 74, P-23, M-83
Silver-bordered, 74, P-23, M-82
Western, 74, P-23, M-83,84
Megathymidae, 107
melinus, Strymon, 88, P-35, M-116
melissa, Lycaeides, 99
Melitaeinae, 59
menapia, Neophasia, 45, P-4, M-10
metacomet, Euphyes vestris, 108
Metalmark
Mormon, 84, P-34, M-107
mexicana, Thorybes, 119, P-48, M-191
milberti, Nymphalis, 65, P-16, M-50
Minois, 54
Mitoura
barryi, 90
johnsoni, 89, P-35, M-118
nelsoni nelsoni, 89, P-35, M-119
siva, 90
spinetorum, 89, P-35, M-117
Monarch, 58, P-13, M-38
montana, Phyciodes campestris, 67, P-18, M-58
mormo, Apodemia, 84, P-34, M-107

273

mormonia, Apodemia mormo, 84, P-34, M-107
mormonia, Speyeria, 80, P-33, M-105,106
mossii, Incisalia fotis, 90, P-36, M-121
Mourning Cloak, 65, P16, M-51
multicaudata, Papilio, 42, P-2, M-5
mylitta, Phyciodes, 68, P-18, M-60
mystic, Polites, 111, P-44, M-169
napi, Pieris, 46, P-5, M-15
Nathalis
   iole, 50, P-7, M-23
nelsoni, Mitoura, 89, P-35, M-119
neomarsyas, Polygonia satyrus, 65, P-17, M-52
Neominois
   ridingsii ridingsii, 53
   ridingsii stretchii, 53, P-10, M-31
Neophasia
   menapia menapia, 45
   menapia tau, 45, P-4, M-10
nevada, Thorybes mexicana, 119, P-48, M-191
nevadensis, Oeneis, 55, P-12, M-36
newcomeri, Callophrys sheridianii, 92, P-36, M-126
nivalis, Lycaena, 97, P-39, M-137,138
Nymphalidae, family, 59
Nymphalinae, 59
Nymphalis
   antiopa antiopa, 65, P-16, M-51
   californica, 64, P-16, M-49
   milberti furcillata, 65, P-16, M-50
   vau-album j-album, 64
   vau-album watsoni, 64, P-16, M-48
obscurus, Incisalia polios, 90, P-36, M-120
occidentalis, Colias, 48, P-6, M-19
occidentalis, Pieris, 46, P-5, M-14
Occidryas
   anicia, 72, P-21, M-72-75
   chalcedona, 72, P-20, M-68-71
   editha, 73, P-22, M-76-81
Ochlodes
   agricola agricola, 109, P-43, M-163
   sylvanoides sylvanoides, 108, P-43, M-162
Oenis
   chryxus, 56
   nevadensis, 55, P-12, M-36
oetus, Cercyonis, 55, P-11, M-35
Orange Tip, 50, P-8, M-24
oreas, Polygonia, 66, P-17, M-55
oregonensis, Callophrys dumetorum, 92
oregonensis, Chlosyne leanira, 70, P-19, M-67
oregonensis, Philotes battoides, 104, P-42, M-153
oregonia, Hesperia comma, 113, P-45, M-174
oregonius, Papilio, 40, P-1, M-1
oricus, Pholisora alpheus, 115, P-46, M-181
orseis, Phyciodes, 68, P-18, M-59
oweni, Speyeria egleis, 79, P-30, M-98
pacuvius, Erynnis, 118, P-47, M-187
palaemon, Carterocephalus, 114, P-46, M-178
palla, Chlosyne, 69, P-19, M-63-65
pallida, Phyciodes, 68, P-18, M-61
   pallida (form), *Pieris napi marginalis,* 46, P-5
Papilio
   eurymedon, 42, P-2, M-6
   glaucus, 39,41
   indra indra, 41, P-1, M-3

machaon, 39,40,41
multicaudata, 42, P-2, M-5
oregonius, 40, P-1, M-1
rutulus rutulus, 41, P-2, M-4
zelicaon, 41, P-1, M-2
Papilionidae, family, 39
pardalis, Icaricia icarioides, 100
Parnassian
   Clodius, 42, P-3, M-8
   Creamish, 43, P-3, M-9
   Phoebus, 43, P-3, M-9
   Sternitzky's, 43, P-3, M-9
Parnassius
   clodius altaurus, 43, P-3, M-8
   clodius claudianus, 43, P-3, M-8
   phoebus sternitzkyi, 43, P-3, M-9
   phoebus xanthus, 43, P-3, M-9
pascoensis, Phyciodes tharos, 67, P-18, M-56
paulus, Cercyonis sthenele, 54, P-11, M-34
peckius, Polites, 109
pegala, Cercyonis, 54, P-10,11, M-32-33
pelidne, Colias, 49, P-7, M-22
pembina, Icaricia icarioides, 100, P-40, M-145
perkinsorum, Lycaena rubidus, 94, P-37, M-130
persius, Erynnis, 117, P-47, M-186
philenor, Battus, 42, P-2, M-7
philodice, Colias, 48, P-6, M-18
Philotes
   battoides glaucon, 104, P-42, M-154
   battoides intermedia, 104, P-42, M-152
   battoides oregonensis, 104, P-42, M-153
   enoptes ancilla, 105
   enoptes bayensis, 105
   enoptes columbiae, 105, P-42, M-156
   enoptes enoptes, 104, P-42, M-155
phlaeas, Lycaena, 97, P-39, M-139
Phoebus, 44
phoebus, Parnassius, 43, P-13, M-9
Pholisora
   alpheus oricus, 115, P-46, M-181
   catullus, 115, P-46, M-179
   libya lena, 115, P-46, M-180
Phyciodes
   campestris campestris, 67, P-18, M-57
   campestris montana, 67, P-18, M-58
   mylitta mylitta, 68, P-18, M-60
   orseis orseis, 68, P-18, M-59
   pallida barnesi, 68, P-18, M-61
   tharos pascoensis, 67, M-56
   tharos tharos, 67
piasus, Glaucopsyche, 105, P-42, M-157
picta, Speyeria zerene, 78, P-27, M-93
Pieridae, family, 44
Pieris
   beckerii, 45, P-4, M-11
   napi macdunnoughi, 46
   napi marginalis, 46, P-5, M-15
   occidentalis, 46, P-5, M-14
   protodice, 46, P-4, M-13
   rapae, 47, P-5, M-16
   sisymbrii sisymbrii, 45, P-4, M-12
Plebejinae, 85

Plebejus
  saepiolus saepiolus, 99, P-40, M-144
plexippus, Danaus, 58, P-13, M-38
podarce, Agriades aquilo, 102, P-41, M-149
Polites
  coras, 109, P-44, M-165
  mardon, 110, P-44, M-167
  mystic dacotah, 111, P-44, M-169
  peckius, 109
  sabuleti, 110, P-44, M-166
  sonora siris, 111, P-44, M-170
  sonora sonora, 111
  themistocles, 110, P-44, M-168
polios, Incisalia, 90, P-36, M-120
Polygonia
  c-album, 65
  faunus rusticus, 66, P-17, M-53
  oreas silenus, 66, P-17, M-55
  satyrus neomarsyas, 65, P-17, M-52
  zephyrus, 66, P-17, M-54
Pontia
  beckerii, 45, P-4, M-11
  occidentalis, 46, P-5, M-14
  protodice, 46, P-4, M-13
  sisymbrii, 45, P-4, M-12
Precis, 63
propertius, Erynnis, 118, P-47, M-188
protodice, Pieris, 46, P-4, M-13
pseudochloridice (form), *Pieris beckerii,* 45, P-4
pugetensis, Speyeria cybele, 76, P-23, M-85
purpurascens, Speyeria hydaspe, 80, P-32, M-103
pylades, Thorybes, 119, P-48, M-190
Pyrginae, 107
Pyrgus
  communis communis, 116, P-46, M-184
  ruralis, 116, P-46, M-183
rapae, Pieris, 47, P-5, M-16
remingtoni, Euphydryas editha, 74, P-22, M-80
rhodope, Speyeria hydaspe, 81, P-32, M-104
ricei, Lycaeides argyrognomon, 98, P-40, M-142
ridingsii, Neominois, 53, P-10, M-31
Ringlet
  Tullia, 53, P-9, M-28-30
Riodinidae, family, 83
rubidus, Lycaena, 94, P-37, M-130
rubria, Vanessa, atalanta, 61, P-15, M-43
rupestris, Speyeria callippe, 79
ruralis, Pyrgus, 116, P-46, M-183
rustica, Agriades aquilo, 102
rusticus, Polygonia faunus, 66, P-17, M-53
rutulus, Papilio, 41, P-2, M-4
sabuleti, Polites, 110, P-44, M-166
saepiolus, Plebejus, 99, P-40, M-144
saepium, Satyrium, 87, P-34, M-113
samuelis, Lycaeides melissa, 99
Sand Creek type, *Speyeria egleis,* 79, P-30, M-99
sara, Anthocharis, 50, P-8, M-24
Satyr
  Stretch's, 53, P-10, M-31
Satyridae, family, 52
Satyrium
  behrii behrii, 87, P-34, M-111
  californica, 88, P-35, M-115
  fuliginosum, 86, P-34, M-110
  saepium saepium, 87, P-34, M-113
  sylvinus sylvinus, 88, P-35, M-114
  tetra, 87, P-34, M-112
satyrus, Polygonia, 65, P-17, M-52
Scolitantides, 105
segregata, Chlosyne hoffmanni, 70, P-19, M-66
selene, Boloria, 74, P-23, M-82
semiluna, Satyrium fuliginosum, 86
semivirida, Speyeria callippe, 78, P-28, M-95
setonia, Strymon melinus, 88, P-35, M-116
shasta, Icaricia, 101, P-41, M-146
sheltonensis, Incisalia eryphon, 91
sheridanii, Callophrys, 92, P-36, M-125,126
Shijimiaeoides, 103
silenus, Polygonia oreas, 66, P-17, M-55
simaetha, Speyeria coronis, 76, P-24, M-87
siris, Polites sonora, 111, P-44, M-170
sisymbrii, Pieris, 45, P-4, M-12
siva, Mitoura, 90
skinneri, Colias pelidne, 49, P-7, M-22
Skipper
  Arctic, 114, P-46, M-178
  Checkered (Common), 116, P-46, M-184
  Checkered (Two-banded), 116, P-46, M-183
  Columbia, 113, P-45, M-175
  Comma, 113, P-45, M-173,174
  Dun, 108, P-43, M-161
  Field, 109, P-43, M-164
  Harpalus, 113, P-45, M-173
  Juba, 112, P-45, M-172
  Large White, 116, P-46, M-182
  Lindsey's, 114, P-45, M-176
  Long Dash, 111, P-44, M-169
  Mardon, 110, P-44, M-167
  Nevada, 114, P-45, M-177
  Oregon, 113, P-45, M-174
  Peck's, 109, P-44, M-165
  Roadside, 108, P-43, M-160
  Rural, 109, P-43, M-163
  Sandhill, 110, P-44, M-166
  Silver-spotted, 120, P-48, M-192
  Sonora, 111, P-44, M-170
  Tawny-edged, 110, P-44, M-168
  Uncas, 112, P-45, M-171
  Woodland, 108, P-43, M-162
snowi, Lycaena cupreus, 98
snyderi, Speyeria coronis, 76, P-24, M-87
sonora, Polites, 111, P-44, M-170
Sooty Wing
  Common, 115, P-46, M-179
  Lena, 115, P-46, M-180
  Oricus, 115, P-46, M-181
Speyeria, 75
  atlantis dodgei, 80, P-31, M-102
  callippe elaine, 79, P-29, M-97
  callippe harmonia, 78, P-29, M-96
  callippe rupestris, 79
  callippe semivirida, 78, P-28, M-95
  coronis simaetha, 76, P-24, M-87
  coronis snyderi, 76, P-24, M-87
  cybele cybele, 76
  cybele leto, 76, P-23, M-86

cybele pugetensis, 76, P-23, M-85
egleis linda, 79, P-30, M-101
egleis macdunnoughi, 79, P-31, M-100
egleis oweni, 79, P-30, M-98
egleis, Sand Creek type, 79, P-30, M-99
hydaspe purpurascens, 80, P-32, M-103
hydaspe rhodope, 81, P-32, M-104
mormonia artonis, 80, P-33, M-106
mormonia erinna, 80, P-33, M-105
mormonia eurynome, 80
mormonia washingtonia, 80
zerene behrensii, 77, P-26, M-90
zerene bremnerii, 78, P-26, M-92
zerene conchyliatus, 77, P-25, M-88
zerene cynna, 78
zerene garretti, 78, P-27, M-93
zerene gloriosa, 77, P-25, M-89
zerene gunderi, 78, P-27, M-94
zerene hippolyta, 77, P-26, M-91
zerene picta, 78, P-27, M-93
spinetorum, Mitoura, 89, P-35, M-117
stella, Anthocharis sara, 50, P-8, M-24
stephensi (form), *Cercyonis pegala ariane,* 54, P-11
sternitzkyi, Parnassius phoebus, 43, P-3, M-9
sterope, Chlosyne palla, 70, P-19, M-65
sthenele, Cercyonis, 54, P-10,11, M-34
stretchii, Neominois rindingsii, 53, P-10, M-31
Strymon
    adenostomatis, 87
    melinus atrofasciata, 88
    melinus setonia, 88, P-35, M-116
    titus, 86, P-34, M-109
Sulfur
    Common Yellow, 48, P-6, M-18
    Edward's, 48, P-7, M-20
    Orange, 47, P-6, M-17
    Pink-edged, 49, P-7, M-21
    Skinner's, 49, P-7, M-22
    Western, 48, P-6, M-19
Swallowtail
    Eastern Tiger, 41
    Indra, 41, P-1, M-3
    Oregon, 40, P-1, M-1
    Pipevine, 42, P-2, M-7
    Two-tailed Tiger, 42, P-2, M-5
    Western Tiger, 41, P-2, M-4
    White Tiger, 42, P-2, M-6
    Zelicaon, 41, P-1, M-2
sylvanoides, Ochlodes, 108, P-43, M-162
sylvestris, Cercyonis sthenele, 54, P-10, M-34
sylvinus, Satyrium, 88, P-35, M-114
tau, Neophasia menapia, 45, P-4, M-10
taylori, Euphydryas editha, 73, P-22, M-76
tetra, Satyrium, 87, P-34, M-112
texanus, Icaricia acmon, 102
tharos, Phyciodes, 67, P-18, M-56

Tharsalea
    arota arota, 93, P-37, M-129
Theclinae, 85
themistocles, Polites, 110, P-44, M-168
Thessalia
    leanira, 70, P-19,48, M-67
Thorybes
    diversus, 119, P-48, M-191
    mexicana nevada, 119, P-48, M-191
    pylades, 119, P-48, M-190
titus, Harkenclenus, 86, P-34, M-109
tollandensis, Boloria selene, 74, P-23, M-82
Tortoise-Shell
    California, 64, P-16, M-49
    Compton's, 64
    Milbert's, 65, P-16, M-50
    Watson's, 64, P-16, M-48
tullia, Coenonympha, 53, P-9, M-28-30
uncas, Hesperia, 112, P-45, M-171
Vanessa
    annabella, 63, P-15, M-46
    atalanta rubria, 61, P-15, M-43
    cardui, 62, P-15, M-45
    carye, 63
    virginiensis, 62, P-15, M-44
Vanessinae, 59
vau-album, Nymphalis, 64, P-16, M-48
veazieae, Euphydryas anicia, 73, P-21, M-72
vestris, Euphyes, 108, P-43, M-161
vialis, Amblyscirtes, 108, P-43, M-160
Viceroy, 60, P-13, M-39
virginiensis, Vanessa, 62, P-15, M-44
wallacensis, Euphydryas chalcedona, 72, P-20, M-71
washingtonia, Callophrys affinis, 93, P-36, M-127
washingtonia, Speyeria mormonia, 80
watsoni, Nymphalis vau-album, 64, P-16, M-48
weidemeyerii, Limenitis, 60, P-14, M-40
White
    Becker's, 45, P-4, M-11
    Cabbage, 47, P-5, M-16
    California, 45, P-4, M-12
    Checkered, 46, P-4, M-13
    Margined, 46, P-5, M-15
    Pine, 45, P-4, M-10
    Western, 46, P-5, M-14
whitneyi, Chlosyne palla, 69, P-19, M-64
Woodnymph
    Large, 54, P-10,11, M-32,33
    Least, 55, P-11, M-35
    Small, 54, P-10,11, M-34
xanthoides, Lycaena, 95, P-38, M-132
xanthus, Parnassius phoebus, 43, P-3, M-9
zelicaon, Papilio, 44, P-1, M-2
zephyrus, Polygonia, 66, P-17, M-54
zerene, Speyeria, 77, P-25-27, M-88-94